London
Aug. 19,

Dear Rainey —

This book is ded[icated to those] of us, like you, whose [love] for cinema makes it all worth[whi]le!

I'm glad that after all these years, we have the chance to renew an old friendship —

Your friend and admirer,

Mark

From Cowboy to Mogul to Monster

The Neverending Story of Film Pioneer Mark Damon

by
Linda Schreyer
with
Mark Damon

authorHOUSE®

AuthorHouse™
1663 Liberty Drive, Suite 200
Bloomington, IN 47403
www.authorhouse.com
Phone: 1-800-839-8640

© 2008 Mark Damon and Linda Schreyer. All rights reserved.

No part of this book may be reproduced, stored in a retrieval system, or transmitted by any means without the written permission of the author.

First published by AuthorHouse 5/2/2008

ISBN: 978-1-4343-7736-4 (hc)
ISBN: 978-1-4343-7737-1 (sc)

Library of Congress Control Number: 2008903480

Printed in the United States of America
Bloomington, Indiana

This book is printed on acid-free paper.

TIMES

There's quicktime and slow time

There's sometime and no time

Some time… to gain

No time… to lose

Long time… no see

Overtime (OT)

Seems I've dedicated my life to OT

- Mark Damon

TABLE OF CONTENTS

Co-Author's Notes..xi

PART ONE

PSO
Chapter 1. 1983. Hollywood 1

Alan Harris
Chapter 2. 1942. Chicago 9

PSO
Chapter 3. 1983. Hollywood 19
Chapter 4. 1977. La Costa 23

Alan Harris
Chapter 5. 1946. Los Angeles...29
Chapter 6. 1949. Beverly Hills 37

PSO
Chapter 7. 1978. Hollywood 45
Chapter 8. 1978. Hollywood 51
Chapter 9. 1979. Cannes 59
Chapter 10. 1980. Los Angeles.......................................67

Al Harris
Chapter 11. 1951. Beverly Hills 75
Chapter 12. 1954. Westwood..83

PSO
Chapter 13. 1981. Century City 89

Chapter 14. 1983. Beverly Hills 95

Al Harris/Mark Damon
Chapter 15. 1954. Hollywood 101

PSO
Chapter 16. 1983. Century City 109
Chapter 17. 1983. Cannes 117
Chapter 18. 1983. Century City 125
Chapter 19. 1983. Moscow 137
Chapter 20. 1983. Beverly Hills 147

Mark Damon
Chapter 21. 1955. Burbank 157

PSO
Chapter 22. 1984. Beverly Hills 169

Mark Damon
Chapter 23. 1956. New York 179

PART TWO
Chapter 24. 1984. New York 209

Hollywood
Chapter 25. 1957. Hollywood 221
Chapter 26. 1958. Hollywood 233
Chapter 27. 1960. Hollywood 245
Chapter 28. 1961. Hollywood 251

PSO
Chapter 29. 1984. Munich 257

Italy

Chapter 30. 1961. Los Angeles/Rome 269
Chapter 31. 1961. Elba/Rome 303

PSO

Chapter 32. 1985. Century City 313
Chapter 33. 1985. Beverly Hills 325

Italy

Chapter 34. 1962. Rome 337
Chapter 35. 1965. Rome 349
Chapter 36. 1966. Rome 355

PSO

Chapter 37. 1985. Century City 365

Italy

Chapter 38. 1967. Naples 377
Chapter 39. 1973. Rome 387
Chapter 40. 1973. Rome 397
Chapter 41. 1974. Rome 403
Chapter 42. 1976. Los Angeles 413

PSO

Chapter 43. 1986. Century City 419
Chapter 44. 1986. Century City 427
Chapter 45. 1986. Beverly Hills 433
Chapter 46. 1987. Bel Air 439
Chapter 47. 1987. Cannes 447

PART THREE

Chapter 48. 2001. Santa Monica 457
Chapter 49. 2004. Hollywood 465
EPILOGUE. 2005. Beverly Hills 477

DAMON'S ADDENDUMS 487
    Addendum 1: Buyers, Sellers, and Remembrances of
        Things Past 487
    Addendum 2: Damon's Epilogue to his Epilogue 493

TODAY 499

PSOers 501

Mark Damon Filmography 503

Index..513

Co-Author's Notes

Once there was a seeker named Milarepa who searched far and wide until he came to a renowned yogi named Marpa. "Please tell me, Babaji," Milarepa asked the holy man, "how can I become enlightened?" Marpa pointed to a rocky ridge in the distance. "Build me a stone house over there." And with a wave of his hand he dismissed the seeker.

Milarepa left, stunned. How was he going to build a stone house? It would be hard enough to clear the selected hillside, let alone move all the boulders to the designated spot. Then would come building the house, a daunting task indeed. He decided to embark upon it, certain that when he was done enlightenment would be his.

One year later, after he had laid the last stone Milarepa returned expectantly to Marpa. But the guru frowned as he gazed at the house on the ridge. "I wanted you to build it over there," he intoned as he pointed to a different hill.

Milarepa was ready to quit. Yet he knew he had found his spiritual master. So he took another year to tear down the first house and build another. But when he showed it to Marpa, once again he pointed to another boulder-filled ridge.

In the end, Milarepa built, tore down and re-built nine different houses nine different times over nine long years. In the end, he finally became enlightened, so they say when he realized that Marpa wasn't looking for a finished product. He was teaching Milarepa that it was the *process* of learning humility and patience that led to enlightenment.

For the past five years I was 'Milarepa' to Mark's 'Marpa.' Although Mark doesn't claim to be enlightened, nor can I say that I became so, I definitely grew and changed as I wrote, rewrote and tossed out drafts of this book, only to write and rewrite all over again.

Mark never questioned the process, criticized my pace or hurried me. He waited steadily as I built and tore down nine stone houses of our book, one draft after another. And somewhere along the way I surrendered to the idea that writing this book was about the process. Not the product. Because somewhere along the line I discovered that my process of writing about Mark's life mirrored the way in which he lives it.

"You're leaving no stone unturned," he exclaimed with a laugh in 2005. It was true. In doing this book I had somehow begun to resemble my 'subject' in a quest for perfection I had rarely known before.

Our collaboration began in January, 2001. Mark took a chance on me as he has with so many others. Although I was an experienced television writer and editor, screenwriter, composer, writing coach and teacher I had not yet written a biography. After a dozen years of teaching students to tell *their* stories I had decided I wanted to tell someone else's. Enter Maggie, Mark's wife, who wanted his story told.

For the first six months I interviewed Mark on Sundays in the small building that serves as his home office. A fabulous storyteller, he relished in telling tales he'd told before and others he hadn't. That led to the first draft of the book, the 'what-happened-next' version of his life, which left out something very important.

Every time we got to PSO, the groundbreaking film sales and independent production company he had founded in 1977, Mark would say, "let's talk about that when we can meet with my former partner, John Hyde." Month after month, I waited to hear about PSO. I waited for Mark to return from Milan or Cannes, Toronto, Utah, Berlin, Spain or London. I waited when he came back and John was not available. I waited until July 2001, after I had spent 100 hours interviewing Mark, when we finally met with Hyde, then COO of Film Roman.

In an interview that was supposed to last an hour and went on for four, I finally learned about the company that was founded in the late '70's and imbued with Mark's dreams, hopes and savvy. The company that went belly-up in the late '80's, bringing rancor and enmity along with its demise. I learned that PSO, which lasted less than a decade, had been responsible for production of such timeless classics as *Das Boot, 9 ½ Weeks, Short*

Circuit, The NeverEnding Story, Lost Boys, Flight of the Navigator and sold several hundred Hollywood movies all over the world.

It was the first time Mark and John had talked about the end of PSO. As each man told me what they hadn't been able to tell each other I saw their excitement over the success of the company and their pain and sorrow over its demise. They touched on their enmity. Lightly. Treading carefully. They went over facts and figures and dates and movies made. Stories poured out like rushing water. Each remembered something the other had forgotten. Both were reluctant for our meeting to end.

I left, stunned. This was a book in itself. The rise and fall of PSO, a fabulous experiment whose success and failure mirrored that of the independent film world of the 1980's. I needed to know more. I ventured up to Kate and John Hyde's ranch in Visalia where we unearthed box after box of clippings in the 'trades' about PSO. Bracing against 104-degree heat I Xeroxed 100's of those articles in that barn. Back in LA, starting with the data I gathered, I began to trace the chronology of PSO.

When I interviewed ex-PSOers they all spoke of their years there as the most exciting period of their professional life. Each recalled the company's demise with the sadness of remembering someone who died in the prime of his life. It was uncanny. It was moving. There was something deeply felt and deeply unfinished about it all. Then came the painstaking process of reconstructing the day-to day business of PSO through these clippings and interviews, then matching that with what I already knew of Mark's eventful life.

I began to re-structure the book the way a documentary filmmaker might. Not chronologically but 'cutting' back and forth. I feared it might be confusing but it seemed the best way to tell the story of a man whose life is a never-ending story. That resulted in the second draft of the book.

When a noted editor read it she advised me that I needed more people to talk about Mark. That it wasn't enough to tell his story through his own recollections and those of a few others. Next came "the 'Interview Rewrite." Draft Number Two. Which involved scheduling interviews with dozens in the entertainment industry. On their time I learned how to interview them (although at times I was tongue-tied and awkward.) Luckily, everyone overlooked my stumbling, was generous with their time, well spoken and insightful.

Some of those interviews began to highlight parts of Mark's life I knew little about: his years as a Hollywood actor in the '50's and '60's leading to winning a Golden Globe Award and his 'Dolce Vita' years in Italy in the '60's and '70's before becoming a famed Spaghetti Western cowboy. I realized I also needed to learn about the independent film business and its flamboyant characters in the 1980's, about independent film financing and international distribution. In writing about a man who lived so many lives I needed to know something about all of them. So began my undertaking of copious (and fascinating) research. Which led to "the Research Rewrite"AKA Draft Number Three.

Upon reading it, my daughter, a smart young editor, hinted that the book was, perhaps, a bit glib and superficial. Not that she said that in so many words. But as I started to re-read other fine biographies I came to a grim conclusion: I had a penchant for writing a 'hagiography' (the biography of a saint.) I started to listen again to tapes of my interviews with Mark, years-old by then, and began to hear sections I had never even transcribed. Darker sections. With more painful truths.

I faced the fact that I had fictionalized (white-washed would be a better description) many things including Mark's childhood, depicting his father as having left because he couldn't earn enough to support the family. The truth, something Mark always preferred, was a lot less pretty. "My father was a gambler," he had said to me. "That was his fatal flaw. But it never made me love him less."

I began to incorporate these truths into the next draft. To ask Mark ever more searching questions. All of which he answered thoughtfully. So began "The More Truthful Rewrite." Draft Number Four. And so it went.

Like Milarepa I built, tore down, rebuilt and built again. Like Marpa, Mark was steady in his guidance. Every time I thought I was in the right place, I found another place I hadn't seen before. A different view through the kaleidoscope of Mark's continually changing life. Or, every time I was sure I was done with the manuscript he would do something new, which changed the perspective of the story and made for a better ending - like producing *Monster* or starting yet another company or co-producing the first Russian-American feature in Moscow. There were many, many changes in Mark's life in the years it took to finish this book. But throughout the years there was one constant – he was always busy.

There was never a time when I opened the door to his home office that I didn't see piles of scripts on his antique table. He always had pages to read. DVD's to watch. Calls to return. Breakfasts and lunches and meetings to go to. Deals to complete. Lawyers to call. Festivals to travel to. Over the years we worked together, he journeyed to Cannes, Berlin,

Milan, Utah, Toronto, Deauville, Turkey, Greece, Italy, England, France, Spain, Germany, Japan and other countries. He sandwiched meetings with me in-between MIFED, the AFM, the Cannes Film Festival, the making of *Monster, 11:14, the Upside of Anger* and *Captivity*.

Along the way, he answered every tough question I asked. He told me stories of mistakes he had made and people who bore grudges against him for reasons he understood. He set me up with interviews with 'Damon detractors' and listened thoughtfully when I told him what they said.

I watched him change from a man who recalled PSO as the highlight of his career to become the producer of the Academy Award-winning *Monster*. I witnessed his company morph from MDP Worldwide to Media 8 to Foresight Unlimited. I saw him transform from a father who regretted missing his children's childhood, so focused was he on his work, to one who left productions in Greece and Russia and flew 1000's of miles to be the keynote speaker at his daughter's college graduation.

He let me into his private world. I saw the tears he shed as he grieved for the loss of PSO. He invited me into his public one. I sat in the audience at numerous functions where he spoke and watched producers watch Mark with respect and admiration. I was allowed into private negotiations with distributors where I witnessed his famous pitches firsthand. I learned that to Mark, every movie was "the best script" with "the finest actors" and that he believed every word he said.

I saw him 'think three jumps ahead,' as his son, Jon described. I saw him laugh and I saw him cry. I saw how much he loved his family. I saw how little free time he had. I observed how his mind was always going, even when his hooded eyes seemed to indicate otherwise. In all the years we worked together I rarely saw him relax.

Along the way I saw him change. Or was it that I changed? Did we both change? And throughout the years I wondered how you take the measure of such a man. By his accomplishments? The many milestones he has marked? The mistakes he has made and learned from? All of the decades he's passed through, the various careers he's succeeded in, the way in which he's reinvented himself time and time again?

I wondered what it was about Mark Damon's life that continued to interest, no, to fascinate me over five years, 1000's of pages and countless manuscript drafts. Was it, as others reasoned, that he has lived so many lives? To be sure, that was part of it.

Ultimately, when I faced Mark on his driveway one afternoon my heart spoke the truth. He was leaving again. As usual. This time he was

xv

going to Greece where *Oh, Jerusalem* was shooting; onto Moscow where *Captivity* was starting up; to Cannes, to sell; to Oakland, California, to attend Alexis' college graduation; then back to Moscow. I wouldn't see him for many months.

"My subject's leaving," I wailed. "I'm feeling abandonment anxiety."

We both laughed as we gave each other a goodbye hug. Suddenly, as I looked into the face I had seen so many times I saw the boy he once had been. Emotional. Sweet. Vulnerable. Words tumbled out.

"If I had known when I started this book how much I would come to love you, I would have been amazed," I found myself saying.

"I feel the same," Mark replied.

We said goodbye quickly and Mark strode to his office.

I drove down the Damon's long winding driveway to Benedict Canyon as I had countless times before. When I rounded a turn I noticed a white azalea bush in bloom. Its flowers glowed in the fading light. Had I never noticed that bush before? Or was it new, ever changing, like the man whose story was in my heart?

A sense of well being filled me as I headed for home.

Linda Schreyer
November 17, 2006

PART ONE

PSO

1983

Chapter One

March 29, 1983

Dorothy Chandler Pavilion

Hollywood, California

Mark and Maggie Damon, John Hyde and Kate Morris at the 1983 Academy Awards.

Chapter 1. 1983. Hollywood

If you saw Mark Damon in a tux at the 55th Annual Academy Awards you probably wouldn't picture him in a toga. If he flashed his dazzling smile at his wife, Maggie, your first thought wouldn't be "Oooh, vampire fangs." And if you gazed at his handsome face it would be hard to imagine it covered with beastly hair.

But Mark Damon played a beast and a vampire, rode across the desert in a toga as the son of Cleopatra, walked the streets of Toledo as a Spanish king named Peter the Cruel and cleaned up the West as two Spaghetti Western cowboys named Johnny. He jumped on his horse without putting his feet in the stirrups, raced a Formula 1 Lotus at one hundred and ninety miles per hour and almost rescued his beloved from a cursed haunted house in flames.

As an actor he played a hero, a rebel and a fool in over fifty teenflicks, Spaghetti Westerns and swashbucklers. As a professional puzzle contestant he won a jackpot of money at the age of seventeen. Teen idol, singer, film director, writer and producer, astute businessman, inventor of the foreign film sales business – by 1983, Damon had pursued almost as many careers as a tomcat has lives.

He was happiest when he was working tirelessly. Happier than he was right now, sitting in the Dorothy Chandler Pavilion and waiting to see how close he would get to a 13 ½ inch gold-plated statuette. Mark liked suspense, as long as it was in a movie. There were only two things he hated - waiting helplessly and losing. And when Johnny Carson introduced Jane Fonda to present the award for Best Directing he was doing one and dreading the other.

As CEO of PSO, his small independent film company, Mark had brought *Das Boot* to the attention of the world. When the film was nominated for six Academy Awards, including Wolfgang Petersen for Best Directing, it was stunning. Now the final and most important award was about to be presented.

Das Boot's journey to America began when Mark heard from various studios about an interesting German mini-series that had no distribution. He and his partner, John Hyde, went to Munich to see it and what they saw was astonishing.

The year was 1941, the height of World War II. In German-occupied France a youthful submarine crew gathered for a last night of drunken

3

revelry before they hit the sea. The scene took place in a bar where the crew feasted, made love and lived it up like there was no tomorrow, which there might not be for thirty of the forty thousand Germans who served on U-boats and never returned home.

"There were about 100 extras in that bar scene," Mark recalled, "and from the 75 movies I had acted in, directed and produced I knew that you bought extras by the pound. But here were 100 of them, all real characters, each with his or her own life." And Wolfgang Petersen's camera found each of them, illuminating them as individuals, in clusters or large groups. The scene lasted over ten minutes. "By the time it was over, it was one of the most intense motion picture experiences I'd ever had," Mark remembered.

"We want in," he told the director, Wolfgang Petersen and Gunther Rohrbach, head of Bavaria Studios.

"Excellent," the Germans enthused.

There was just one problem. No German language picture had ever had any success. Anywhere. Undaunted, Mark started calling some of the top distributors around the world. "I've just seen some extraordinary footage and I'd like to show it to you." He invited them to Munich to see it before they came to the Cannes Film Festival. "This is something <u>very</u> special."

Word began to spread and calls started coming in to PSO. If he'd invited one company in a territory, another company would call and ask why they weren't invited. Pretty soon Mark had lined up the top two competitors in each of the top countries in the world to go to Munich, each jockeying to get there first. He screened what he'd seen and pitched the rest. The combination sold one distributor after another. Some wanted to buy it then and there but Mark stalled them off. "Let's wait for Cannes," he suggested, knowing that when 'market hysteria' set in at the Festival the pressure to buy and sell would drive prices up. By the end of the Cannes Festival he had licensed *Das Boot* in every country in the world.

When the picture was released he oversaw its marketing in France, Italy, England and Japan. He went to the theatres and watched audiences as they set out to sea in the German U-boat that prowled the North Atlantic, challenging the British Navy at every turn. He studied audience reactions as they were gripped to their seats by the scared, exhausted and courageous crew that fought an endless series of life-and-death challenges below the sea; as they were moved by the humanity of the young men, by their struggle to return home to their families and loved ones. By the time the end credits rolled, from the looks on the faces of the European audiences he knew he had a hit on his hands. But when it came to selling it to the U.S., studio heads laughed in his face.

"You actually think American audiences are going to go see a sympathetic *sub-titled* German war film about their former enemy?"

"Believe me, this movie is completely unique."

Every studio turned him down. Until his persistence persuaded Columbia Studios, which had never handled a foreign language picture before, to release it. They even set up a new division, which they called *Triumph*, to handle it. Once again, Mark was in theatres when the film opened in the U.S. He saw how the deeply felt anti-war message had audiences gripped to their seats. How, for the first time, as Americans watched young Germans suffer in the claustrophobic setting of the submarine, they came to understand the terrible toll the war had taken on them.

Das Boot's international theatrical release broke box-office records. It earned over $100 million dollars overseas (in today's dollars it would be twice that amount.) It became the most successful German language film of all time. Then the film garnered more Academy Award Nominations than any foreign language film in history.

When another PSO film, *La Traviata* (directed by Franco Zeffirelli) was nominated for three more Academy Awards it was a personal triumph for Mark. Zeffirelli, who had known him since he was an actor in Italy, had initially entrusted PSO to distribute the film in the U.S. (unless a major studio picked it up.) Mark had rented theatres to show it to the public and after critics proclaimed *La Traviata*, starring Placido Domingo "the best opera film ever made," Universal had decided to distribute it.

Now, all Mark could do was wait as Jane Fonda, statuesque in a gown of gold, announced the five nominees for Best Directing: Steven Spielberg for *E.T.*; Sydney Pollack for *Tootsie;* Sir Richard Attenborough for *Gandhi*; Sidney Lumet for *The Verdict;* Wolfgang Petersen for *Das Boot*.

When a clip of *Das Boot* came on the screen Maggie beamed at him proudly. Then the clip ended and two thousand five hundred people, the crème de le crème of Hollywood, applauded the extraordinary film. It was the crowning moment of Mark's career.

Across the world in ninety countries, a billion viewers heard the roar of applause. In Italy, where he had starred in dozens of Spaghetti Westerns. In Spain, where he walked the streets of Toledo as Pedro El Cruel. In Cannes, where he was known as one of the greatest foreign salesmen in the world.

From Cowboy to Mogul to Monster

And on the Northwest side of Chicago, where he grew up as Alan Harris, television viewers heard the massive applause.

But Mark was hearing another sound. The long ago sound of make-believe applause. The way a nine-year-old boy once imagined it in a tenement in Chicago...

Alan Harris

1942

Nothing affects a child like the unlived lives of his parents.
-C.G. Jung

Chapter Two

January 19, 1942

Chicago, Illinois

Future Spaghetti Western star Alan Harris (later to become Mark Damon) at age 5 in Chicago.

Chapter 2. 1942. Chicago

NINE-YEAR OLD ALAN HARRIS SNEERED AT himself in the mirror of the small bathroom. He was George Raft in *Scarface*. A tough-guy who could do anything. He sneered a little more at the imaginary applause from his fans as he pretended he was stepping out of his Cadillac Fleetwood Limousine at the 15th Annual Academy Awards.

If he tried hard enough, the imaginary applause could drown out the other sounds coming from the living room of the tenement. Not the strains of "White Christmas" playing on the radio. He didn't mind that song. It was the angry words his mother, Lillian, was shouting at his father, Irv, that he wanted to block out.

"Don't lie to me. What did you do with the eighteen dollars you earned last week?!"

"I told you I've got it," Irv answered sullenly.

"Show me," she insisted.

Alan peered into the living room. His father was standing near the front door, wearing a trench coat belted at the waist. He looked a little like Tyrone Power. He also looked ready to run. Except that Alan's mother held onto his arm.

"Show me. Before you go and spend it all."

Alan went back to the bathroom and closed the door. He didn't want to hear any more. His parents had the same fight every week. No, lately it was more like every day.

It was 1942, "a year of blood and strength," according to Time Magazine, citing the War that was raging in Europe which the U.S. had just entered. At home the Depression's long shadow was still darkening millions of families' lives, turning the American dream into a nightmare. Alan's family was one of its casualties.

His father, Irving Herskovitz, who changed his name to 'Harris' shortly after Alan was born, was a bright, handsome and affable man who had borne the brunt of the Depression since he quit high school and went to work clerking at his father's grocery store to help support his kid brothers. His middle brother, Jack, subsequently graduated from Northwestern with a PhD in anthropology; his youngest brother, Al, went on to medical school after college and became a doctor; Irv never became more than a clerk in a grocery store, even though his brothers agreed he was the smartest of them all. Despite his expertise at adding up numbers on a brown paper bag faster than an adding machine, Irv's pay didn't add up to enough to take care of his wife and two young sons, Alan and Bobby. Not after he lost most of it on the horses.

"My father was a gambler," Mark admitted. "That was his fatal flaw. But it didn't take away my love for him."

His mother, Lillian, felt differently. "My ex-husband was not doing things right," she would grumble, decades later. "And what's the use of staying with a man if you can't trust him? When he's just giving money away." To Lillian, it was that simple - Irv was not fit to be her husband.

Lillian (Lil) Elfman was a strong, upstanding, good-looking woman who was raised by her strict Polish parents, Rose and Louis in Kenosha, Wisconsin, where Louis had a furniture store. According to Lil, it was Rose who ran the show. "She couldn't read much English but she would come into the store and see things that were wrong. My father would sit back and she would take charge. She was the brains behind everything."

Lillian was raised to believe in right and wrong, black and white, cut and dry. She was strong-willed and determined, had a solid faith in God, was committed to Judaism and fond of telling stories with good, strong morals: "We lived on the second floor along with another family and one time I found toys in the house. Turned out Bobby and his friend, who were about three, had taken them from a candy shop. 'Listen,' I said to the boys, 'just tell the truth because God always sees and knows what we're doing. So let's go give the toys back.' We went to the store and took them back. And that was a lesson for the boys. That they didn't get away with it."

Now she wasn't going to let her husband 'get away with it' either. Not when her mantra was "a man's character is in his bankbook," a phrase she repeated constantly to her two sons. A pretty woman who wore a constantly worried expression, Lillian was given to obsessing, especially over money. It was unfortunate that she'd chosen a dashing gambler like Irv Herskovitz for a husband. Oh, she loved the handsome man she had married. "She was crazy in terms of him," Mark's brother, Bob, would declare decades later. "Even many, many years later you could not mention his name without her going into a tirade." Lil and Irv had vastly different standards and he couldn't live up to hers.

By the age of nine, Alan knew firsthand how high his mother's standards were. When he was seven he had been coached by her to be a "Quiz Kid" on the popular radio show that starred six child prodigies who answered intellectual questions. "I remember how my mother would incessantly push me when I was trying out. Forcing me to read books at night, in a car, walking to school. Just to make certain that I'd covered every aspect. She demanded that I be number one. She required that. I

Chapter 2. 1942. Chicago

think it came from her tremendous need to be recognized. To be someone important."

Lillian pushed Alan to become what she was not. In her elder son, she had discovered a pupil with a curious mind, a near-photographic memory and a highly competitive spirit. As she drilled him to win, she boasted about him to anyone who'd listen: "Alan went to the museum and explained to everyone how the planets revolved around the sun." "One day, the teacher figured out a math problem and he figured it out differently. He corrected the answer and told the teacher and class they were wrong." "I took Alan to a TV show when he was about five. When the orchestra began to play he told them to stop because they were not playing it right. They started laughing."

Now, as he listened to her call his father a disgrace, he felt terrible. He was pretending he was George Raft when he heard the front door slam. He rushed out to find his mother in the living room, her face flushed.

"Where's Dad?"

"He left.."

Alan looked at the door, devastated.

"What are you doing up at this hour? Please go to bed."

He went but Alan laid there, his heart aching, wishing he could have held onto his father's knees and kept him from going. Decades later he would recall, "I remember him leaving us because he had lost a lot of money and couldn't face it. At least that's what my mother told me."

Four months later his parents got divorced. "I was in a courtroom in downtown Chicago when the gavel went down. Boom. 'You're divorced,' the judge said. Boy, it was tough," he revealed many years later. "If I let myself dwell on the day they were divorced I would start to cry, today, more than sixty years later. That's how much of an effect it had on me."

There was no time to cry when he was nine and his brother, Bobby was only four. Alan had to become the man of the family. Fast. "You're my bluebird of happiness," Lillian always told him. But Alan had never seen a bluebird. And as he faced life without his father he didn't see a lot of happiness ahead.

Pretty soon it became clear that the money they received from Social Services and his grandparents wasn't enough for the three of them. So one evening Alan slipped out and walked to the newspaperman on the corner.

"I need a job."

The man eyed him suspiciously. "What time do you go to school in the morning, kid?"

"Eight o'clock."

"Forget it. I need these papers delivered at six AM." He turned away dismissively.

"When do I start?" Alan persisted.

From then on he delivered papers every morning before walking to fourth grade from Humboldt Park to Lowell Grammar School with his neighborhood buddies, Zave Gussin and Al Schwartz.

At first he only made ten cents a day. Pretty soon that became a buck and a half a week. Enough to buy milk at fourteen cents a quart, bread at nine cents a loaf, sometimes even round steak at forty-two cents a pound.

"I could always depend on him," Lillian asserted decades later. "He was wonderful and so very smart."

Alan was sure his life wouldn't always be like this. "I constantly told my mother that someday I would be someone important," he recalled. "I was always thinking about the day when I'd see my name in the papers. When I would be number one. I didn't care what it took to get there. I was going to make it happen."

Without knowing, he had taken on Lillian's need to be important. For the rest of his life, no matter what he did, Alan Harris (later Mark Damon) would always have to win. Have to be number one. No matter what it cost him.

Alan's family lived in Humboldt Park, a small, mostly Jewish neighborhood on the West side of Chicago. It was a tight community with many families from "the old country." There were two drugstores - Zoub's and Klein's; two grocery stores and two kosher butcher shops. Everyone knew which one you went to and if you went to one you didn't go to the other. But all the guys went to Itzkowitz Delicatessen to hang out after school. Alan and his buddies followed along, standing around on the corner, pretending they had something to do while the older guys smoked and whistled at pretty girls.

From a young age, Alan's feelings about girls were very strong. As the family breadwinner he'd grown up fast. So fast that sometimes he dreamed about beautiful women.

Chapter 2. 1942. Chicago

At first he loved those dreams. After awhile they began to worry him. What if he never met the woman of his dreams? What if he never fell in love? One night he dreamed an answer to his questions. "I was walking in a forest when a beautiful blond woman appeared," he recalled decades later. "'Don't worry,' she smiled at me. 'We'll find each other.' A month later, I dreamed the same dream. And again, a few months later. I was always in that forest where the beautiful blond woman told me not to worry."

But he did worry. About the rent money, bill collectors, getting straight A's in school, running out of coal, taking care of Bobby, making sure that they all had enough to eat. It was a tough time. But there were other times, too. When he and his buddies headed for the Crystal or the Rex Theatre to see "Gung Ho" or "Iwo Jima." And there were the times when Alan would slink on his belly through the underbrush of Humboldt Park, playing soldiers. "I was no ordinary soldier. I was a movie star who was acting that he was a soldier. I was Errol Flynn as "The Sea Hawk." I was "The Count of Monte Cristo." When huge Z's were chalked on buildings in Chicago, 'Z for Zorro', I was Zorro. And Z, the Mark of Zorro, was my mark."

When he play-acted he could be anyone he wanted. It was a terrific choice for a bright boy with a great imagination and a workday that started at 6:00 AM.

Alan, like his father, had a passion for numbers. Every night he fell asleep figuring out the Chicago Cubs' batting averages in his head, dividing numbers like 125 by 339 – Bill Nicholson's new average after getting two hits that day. He was running those numbers in his head as he waited for his friend, Zave in front of his apartment building at 1220 Kedzie, across the street from Humboldt Park. That afternoon his father would be picking the boys up at school and taking them to Wrigley Field to see the Cub's playoff game.

Irv always made a big impression on Alan's friends. "I was envious of Alan. His father was tall and handsome; very friendly and a lot younger than my parents," said Al Schwartz. Most importantly, Irv was American in a community where most other parents were from 'the old country.' Alan's friends also found his mother, Lillian, "a very attractive and friendly woman in a modern way." Zave Gussin recalled coming into Alan's apartment and finding her up on a chair changing a light bulb on the ceiling. "I kind-of held the chair for her. She was laughing that I was so

15

From Cowboy to Mogul to Monster

conservative that I was afraid that she would fall. I guess she thought it was cute. I thought she was beautiful." "When I had dinner there she would see me struggling with my knife," Al Schwartz recalled, "and she would say, 'maybe I should cut that up for you.' She left an indelible impression on me for teaching me to use a knife without putting so much pressure on it that I cut through the plate."

Both Al and Zave remembered Alan as "a popular, handsome kid who was almost always smiling. He wasn't the best athlete and he was in love with pretty Marlene Goldzband who didn't love him back. But kids liked him." Looking back, Mark saw himself differently. "I was very smart but a little dorky. Kind of a round kid who was not particularly popular and not much of an athlete." "But he was my hero," his brother Bob stated unequivocally. "Always was. Always will be."

After graduation, all the kids except Alan, headed to Roosevelt High School in Chicago. Lillian had decided her elder son would be better off going to school in California, where her parents and siblings had moved. The plan was for Alan to live with them until she and Bobby joined in a year or so.

At the bus station Alan suffered through his mother's tearful goodbye and gave Bobby a hug. Then he boarded the bus and took a seat by the window. Lillian was waving when the Greyhound pulled out of the terminal but Alan was too busy studying the bus schedule to see. Several stops later, when they pulled into De Kalb, Illinois, the bus was two minutes and forty-three seconds behind schedule. Three people noted it - the bus driver, the dispatcher and Alan. He'd been clocking the bus since he'd gotten on, checking to see if it pulled into a city on time, a couple of minutes ahead or behind.

It was a game he'd made up. Kind of a contest. He'd made a bet with himself that they would arrive late in Los Angeles and was keeping a running scorecard in his head. As with all other games, he was determined to win.

PSO

1983

Chapter Three

March 29, 1983

Dorothy Chandler Pavilion

Hollywood, California

© *Layout and Design Columbia TriStar Home Video*

Chapter 3. 1983. Hollywood

"And the winner is…" Jane Fonda ripped open the envelope for Best Director and gazed into the camera. "Sir Richard Attenborough for *Gandhi*."

Applause broke out, even though many of the 2,500 luminaries in the Dorothy Chandler Pavilion felt that Attenborough's three-hour long epic on the life of Mahatma *Gandhi* was tedious and overlong.

Mark reacted with equanimity as Sir Richard mounted the podium. Yes, Wolfgang Petersen had lost the Oscar. But Mark didn't have to celebrate the director winning an Academy Award to feel he had been triumphant. Nor did he have to be part of making the most wonderful picture in the world so he could go down in posterity. "It's not the end that's important," he believed. "It's the getting there." And getting nine Academy Award nominations for films that PSO, his small, independent company had discovered was an absolute triumph for him.

Mark smiled graciously as Sir Richard began a fatuous speech thanking the Academy for supporting his pacifist vision of *Gandhi*. Then John leaned over and whispered, "Too bad we lost to a guy in a diaper." Mark tried not to laugh out loud as Sir Richard droned on. But even in his mirth he noticed something familiar about Attenborough. Not about him, exactly. About his manner. No, not that either.

It was the glasses and the white hair. They reminded Mark of someone. When he realized who it was he laughed even harder. He thought of the first time he'd met the man whose elegance was only overshadowed by his reputation as the toughest Japanese negotiator in the film business.

His name was Sam Nanba.

Chapter Four

July 29, 1977

La Costa

Chapter 4. 1977. La Costa

TRYING NOT TO SQUIRM, MARK SAT across from an enigmatic Sam Nanba, who was proving true to his standing as a master at negotiation. Mark, on the other hand, was greener than new money.

He was trying to sell *The Choirboys*, the first Hollywood movie he had produced after living in Italy for fourteen years. But not only did he know little about how to negotiate a deal, he knew nothing about how you dealt with the Japanese. He had no idea that even if you pitched like mad it was almost impossible to push them unless the movie was something they really wanted.

Now, even though Mark had just pitched *The Choirboys* with his heart, his soul and his finely honed acting skills, the only response was silence. Nanba, who was buying pictures for the venerable Japanese distributor, Nippon Herald, took a long puff from his pipe while Mark waited on the edge of his seat.

"The picture sounds interesting," Nanba finally mused. "How much do you want for it?"

This was the moment that Bobby Meyers, an expert at selling movies to international buyers, had coached Mark about . He knew his answer would make or break him.

"$600,000," he quoted.

"Ahhh," said Nanba.

Then he nodded. And looked at Mark. And nodded some more. Like one of those dashboard dolls, Mark thought, unnerved. Long minutes of silence followed while Mark wondered if he had quoted too high a figure. Sweating bullets, he cleared his throat.

"Well, that's what we're *asking...*"

Nanba looked at him impassively and continued to say nothing. Two more interminable minutes of silence passed as he puffed on his pipe and looked at Mark, who was beginning to feel like a worm on a hook.

"You know," he suggested with false bravado, "we could really close it at $500,000."

"Mm-hmmm," said Sam.

More silence as Nanba puffed on his pipe until Mark thought he would scream.

"What about $400,000? Can we close it at that?"

Nanba just kept on nodding and puffing.

"Sam," Mark finally blurted in desperation, "I've never done this before! What do I have to do now?"

"Say yes to $300,000," Nanba replied.

"Yes!" cried Mark. "Yes! I'll take it!"

Later, Meyers laughed when Mark told him what happened. "Sounds like my first experiences with the Japanese. I would say I wanted $600,000 and they would sit and smoke until a number came from them and we were in a negotiation."

"Thanks a lot. Why didn't you tell me that before?" demanded Mark.

"Because it's much better to learn firsthand - with the Japanese, you're negotiating with yourself."

Mark had recently moved back to LA with Maggie after spending eleven years in Italy as an actor and three as a businessman working for PAC, an independent Italian film company headed by two brothers - Piero and Mario Bregni. Although he had been hired to get top American movies for PAC to distribute in Italy, Mark had had little success. Despite his best efforts, he'd soon discovered that Hollywood studios would rather give their 'A-list' movies to their own people stationed in offices around the globe. The long arm of Hollywood, he learned, stretched all through Europe.

During his years with PAC, however, Mark had learned the ins and outs of independent foreign distribution and along the way, learned just how good the independent distributors were. He had helped to organize them into an efficient entity that could rival the studios. But Hollywood studios still refused to give them their movies. Eventually, Mark had realized there was only one way for a foreign distributor like PAC to get an 'A' American movie: they would have to co-produce one. Enter Lorimar Studios, which was looking for money to co-produce *The Choirboys*, soon-to-be-directed by Robert Aldrich. In exchange for PAC co-financing the movie, Mark was made an Executive Producer and authorized to sell the foreign rights around the world. Now, although he had never sold a movie to international buyers before he was determined to do just that, to make *The Choirboys* his calling card back into the industry.

A day earlier, he had driven South to attend a brand-new international event held at the La Costa spa owned by Lorimar Chief, Merv Adelson. It was designed to attract international distributors who wanted to check out top American movies to buy. There, Mark had met with veteran foreign salesman Bobby Meyers, a bright and affable pitchman with a twinkle in his eye. Meyers was considered an expert at selling movies to international distributors, having sold for National General Pictures and First Artists.

Chapter 4. 1977. La Costa

"Mark and I talked about how you structure the deal," he recalled years later. "How you present the movie to a buyer. How you set prices for it based on what the market can bear and how appealing the film is for each country you are selling. We talked about all of the countries (or 'territories' as they were called) and priced *Choirboys* out over each. And we decided what Mark should get from each territory." Meyers had also stressed how important it was to ask for the right amount: "If you ask a number that's unrealistic you lose them right away. They're out the door. It was a crash course but by the time we were done," he later reflected, "Mark being Mark, was off and running."

Soon Mark was literally running when he arrived in Italy for MIFED, a bazaar attended by thousands of film distributors from all over the world.

Mark was racing from room to room like a crazy person while muttering in four different languages: "Molto bene, Fabrizio. Ma non basta..." "Ja, sehr gut, aber ist nicht genug." "Cent mille pour France? Oui, Pierre, c'est ca..." "Mi eres simpatico Jaime, pero tu oferta falta..."

He had just pitched *Choirboys* in German, Italian, French and Spanish, having learned them while living in Europe. Now he was closing deals as he ran into each room where sometimes three people were lined up and waiting for him.

MIFED was a madhouse and Mark loved every minute of it. "I learned so much in those first meetings," he recalled. "Most important of all I learned the importance of leaving with signed contracts in hand." By the time MIFED came to a close he had sold *The Choirboys* most of the way around the world and left Italy with $6 million in foreign sales.

As his plane landed in Los Angeles he looked out at the brilliant blue sky and hills that looked like they were covered with green velvet. For a brief moment he recalled the very first time he had seen them.

Alan Harris

1946 – 1949

The thing that makes you exceptional makes you lonely.
- Lorraine Hansberry

Chapter Five

July 5, 1946

Needles, California

Chapter 5. 1946. Los Angeles

It was early morning when the bus crossed into California from Arizona. Alan stared out the window at the brilliant blue sky and hills that looked like they were covered with green velvet. He kept on staring as the bus sped past deserts dotted with spiky cactus and foothills of pale pinks and purples stretching to sun-dappled mountains. He marveled at the sight of beaches that stretched for miles. He blinked hard at the brilliant sunlight that glinted off the endless stretch of the Pacific Ocean.

"Bobby would love swimming in those waves," he thought. He was hit by an unexpected twinge of loneliness. He remembered last Saturday, before he left Chicago when, as a special treat he had taken his brother to a triple feature at the North Street Theatre: *Gunga Din*, *King Kong* and *The Adventures of Robin Hood*. Six hours later the brothers had staggered out of the theater with splitting headaches. "That was the best day of my life," Bobby had declared breathlessly.

Remembering that, Alan decided it was time to do a puzzle. Puzzles dealt with facts and he preferred facts over feelings. He pulled a newspaper page out of his pocket and started working on the rebus puzzle -- a series of pictures whose letters added up to a word, name, title or expression.

Ever since 1942, when the first crossword puzzle was published, puzzles appeared every day in some newspaper somewhere. Most people did them for relaxation. Alan did them with one goal in mind. "I had to win. I had to be the best in everything I did. I couldn't stand the thought of losing. Plus I needed the money."

As the bus sped through the state he made steady progress on a puzzle that showed a picture of a cap plus a rat minus a car. Alan took the 'c' out, the 'a' out, the 'r' out and got 'tap.' He continued to add and subtract pictures. He worked quickly and was done by the time the bus pulled into downtown Los Angeles. He took the tattered schedule out of his pocket for the last time and checked it against his watch. They were forty-two minutes and twelve seconds behind schedule.

"I won," he smiled to himself. Then he climbed down the steps and set foot in Los Angeles.

"What else did you see on the trip?" Rose Elfman asked as they walked to the car.

"Lots of sweaty people," Alan answered.

31

His grandparents, Rose and Louis and his Uncle Milton (his mother's younger brother) asked more questions as they walked to the light green 1941 Chevy that was Milt's pride and joy. But Alan was too distracted by the warm California sun on his back and shoulders to answer. He felt like it was wrapping him in a golden blanket of light. It felt wonderful.

On the way to their duplex on Orange, in the predominately Jewish Fairfax District, the radio played *The Gypsy* by the Ink Spots. Alan barely heard it. He was too busy staring out the window. Pink and purple bougainvilleas climbed up the sides of houses like jaunty decorations; lawns looked lush and impossibly green; beautiful girls sauntered in bright-colored summer dresses; guys looked clean-cut and healthy-looking. "Everywhere I looked, I saw inherent wealth and a sense of ease," he recalled many years later. It was light years away from the cold, dark tenements of Chicago. By the time Milt pulled up in front of the duplex, on a quiet street half a block from Fairfax and one block from Wilshire, his heart had been won over by Los Angeles.

Uncle Milt smiled broadly as he carried Alan's suitcase into the house. "You and I sleep downstairs. Mom and Pop share the upstairs with Mae (Lillian's sister) and Herb (her husband). Okay with you?"

"Sure."

Alan looked around at the sparsely furnished room. Trying his best to smile, he was struck by how unfamiliar it looked.

"Hey," said Milt, seeing his nephew's expression. "What are the Cubs up to?"

Alan launched into a full report. The moment was broken and his spirits were lifted by his Uncle Milt.

Milt Elfman was red-haired, sharp as a tack and, at thirty-one, only eighteen years older than Alan. He had recently returned from the War where he went over a married man with a child and came back single after getting a "Dear John" letter. By the time Alan arrived, Milt was without a wife, a child or a job and was living with his parents and domineering older sister.

Milt may have needed a project. He certainly felt for Alan, who'd been without a father for the past five years. "Or he might have been considering that Lil was not a good mother," Blossom Elfman, Milt's second wife speculated decades later, "and wanted to step in because he never liked Lil." Whatever the reason, when Milt decided to take over the 'father chores' it was a lucky break for Alan. "By then," he later recalled, "living without a father had affected me deeply."

Milt, recently out of the Army, was strict and military. A disciplinarian with a 'tough love' approach. "There was a list of penalties and demerits and I was penalized if I didn't do something properly," Mark remembered. But his uncle was so good at drawing the line and making Alan understand why it was there that he didn't mind obeying the rules.

Milt also had a terrific sense of logic and Alan loved logic so he warmed to his uncle's pragmatic and unsentimental approach. If he got penalties and demerits for not doing something properly he just worked harder to get it right. If he was rewarded with a driving lesson or some other treat he soaked it up.

Decades later, Milt's son, Rick Elfman, described him as "a great, standard, 'by the books' Dad. He was intellectually sophisticated, artistically sophisticated and a very stable force." Plus, he'd always stand up and do the right thing. "When I was just a kid," Rick remembered, "once we were driving along and saw a gang fight. A kid got knocked to the ground and the others started kicking him. And my dad, who was not physically imposing, pulled the car over and managed to break it up so the guy could scurry off. Any one of these guys could have wiped the fence with my father. But he couldn't drive away. He had to stop and do the right thing, no matter what. That was my dad."

On top of his other stellar qualities, Milt was a born teacher. On Sundays, he took Alan to the park and gave him batting tips. He took him to target practice where they shot real guns (without real ammo.) Then he decided it was time his nephew learned about classical music.

"How do I do that?"

"You listen," Milt answered.

He started taking his nephew through his favorite symphonies, string quartets, concertos, and operas. He identified each by composer, number, name and opus. He devised tests for his young nephew: What symphony was it? What opus? Which opera? Singer? Conductor?

Alan started spending a couple of hours a day listening. The more right answers he gave his uncle, the harder Milt made the tests. And the harder Alan listened. Soon he could identify almost any piece of classical music after hearing the first three notes. He developed favorites -- composers Bizet, Borodin, Stravinsky, Prokofiev and Ralph Vaughan Williams; singers Lily Pons, Igor Gorin, Richard Tucker and Jan Peerce;

operas *Carmen*, *La Traviata* and *Aida*. Within a few months Milt had instilled a lifelong love of classical music in his nephew.

Years later, as a high school student Alan would do his homework to the strains of Bizet or Borodin. As an actor he would prepare for his roles by defining his characters through musical themes. Decades later, as a producer he would be closely involved in the musical score to every movie he produced. (Milt would later instill the same love of music in his talented sons – Richard Elfman, founder of the popular band 1980's band, *Oingo Boingo* and noted film composer Danny Elfman, who has scored countless films and television shows. He recently revealed to *The Hollywood Reporter* that he has never had a music lesson and is entirely self-taught.)

Even though he was living with family, Alan was expected to pay for his keep "and $5 a week is a lot, plus every other expense I have, and believe me they are plenty," he wrote to his mother. He worked odd jobs, supporting himself by mopping floors in a bakery on Fairfax at night and selling flowers on street corners during the day. Whenever he could, he ducked into Canter's Deli to buy himself a treat - a knish or a pickle - with a hard-earned nickel.

By the end of the summer L.A. was on the verge of a growth boom and so was Alan. He had grown three inches, dropped eight pounds, was better in baseball and gained new confidence. Just in time to start junior high.

Alan's stomach tightened when he got off the bus at Wilshire Boulevard and walked down tree-lined McCadden Place to Sixth Street. It was a quiet, family neighborhood until he got to John Burroughs Junior High. Hundreds of kids, hormones racing, swarmed the lawns in clusters, greeting each other with shouts and laughter.

By the time he walked up the wide cement stairs to the front doors of the school with a red brick façade he'd made a decision. "I wasn't going to be called 'Alan' anymore. I was going to be 'Al Harris,' new kid on the block. And I was going to do everything the new kid on the block needed to do to be popular."

He threw himself into the role as he opened the heavy door like he owned the place and walked into his new life.

By November, the new and improved 'Al Harris' was a popular guy, good in baseball and pretty good in football. "I, dorky Alan Harris from

Chapter 5. 1946. Los Angeles

Chicago had become a jock in Los Angeles because I had nobody telling me that I couldn't be." More importantly, he had proved to himself that he could achieve anything through the power of his mind, determination and hard work. It would become a lifelong approach.

Every day when school let out, Al burst out of the doors with the popular kids and hung out on the wide cement steps. He was 'in,' even if he had to work after school instead of hanging with them at Rams on Wilshire and First.

Girls liked him for the first time. They were glad when they spun the bottle and it landed on him. One day, he even made out with bubbly brunette Doreen Bauman in the tunnel of love that ran under 3rd Street at McCadden Place. Then he took the #83 bus to Fairfax and Oakwood where he sold newspapers until dark with stars in his eyes.

On April 22, his fourteenth birthday, he was with his clique when he saw Milt parked at the curb, sitting in the passenger seat of his Chevy. Al went over to the car and asked what he was doing there.

"I thought you might like a ride home."

Bewildered, Al asked, "Who's driving?"

Milt smiled. "You are. Happy Birthday."

Al broke out in a wide grin. He sauntered to the driver's door, casting a glance back at the kids on the lawn. They were looking, all right. Watching him sit behind the wheel like he'd done it every day of his life instead of every so often. As the girls looked on, the Chevy rolled down McCadden Place with Al behind the wheel, feeling like a million bucks.

He wished he could show his father how well he drove, maybe take Bobby out for a spin. Instead, after he drove home he stayed outside until dinnertime, polishing the chrome on the '41 Chevy until it shone like a full moon.

Years later, when he sped through Italy in his little Alfa Romeo he would remember Milt teaching him to drive a stick. And when he raced a Formula 1 Lotus in *The Young Racers* he wrote to his uncle: "Make sure you go and see the movie. And think of me on McCadden Place when I take those curves at 190 MPH, will you?"

When the school year ended, Milt let Alan drive to the bus station to pick up Lillian and Bobby and take them home. This time, home wasn't the duplex on Orange - there wasn't room enough for all of them. Their new home was a small apartment on West Avenue in a poor section of town.

Al would live there with his mother and brother for the next two years. He would hate every day of it. He detested the poverty around him. He missed the firm guidance of his uncle. When he did his homework to classical music he thought of Milt. When he turned fifteen he remembered when Milt had showed up at school. Someday, he promised himself, he would find a way to pay Uncle Milt back.

Chapter Six

September 21, 1949

Beverly Hills, California

Chapter 6. 1949. Beverly Hills

"Just a couple more boxes," Al called to his new stepfather, Ben Gilbert, who stood in the doorway of their new house in Beverly Hills, watching him unload the car.

It was an Indian summer morning and Al would have happily unloaded a moving truck single-handedly. He would have done anything to move out of the apartment on West Avenue with its dingy rooms, dirty streets and ill-clad children. West Avenue meant poverty and he was sick to death of poverty. The new house was the Taj Mahal in comparison. Most important of all – it was in Beverly Hills.

The rich were different and so were their neighborhoods. Al knew that the minute he saw the wide, curving boulevards of Beverly Hills. Sunset Boulevard, Rodeo Drive, Canon Drive, whose palm-lined avenues offered an expansive sense of luxury. Beverly Hills was a far cry from the rest of the city. And light years from all the other places Al had lived.

The new house was on Carson Drive between Robertson and La Cienega, two blocks south of the shopping Mecca's on Wilshire Boulevard. Carson was a quiet street of smaller homes where palm trees shaded well-tended lawns. Mexican tiles blanketed roofs and the air smelled of jasmine and a hint of money. Money remained elusive to Al, who still worked every day after school. Weekdays, he mopped floors in a bakery, worked as a stock boy, dishwasher and soda jerk. Weekends, he ran the kiddy rides at Beverly Park on La Cienega and Beverly.

At sixteen, he'd been self-supporting for years. By now he'd had enough of the stick. He was ready for the carrot. And a house in Beverly Hills got him closer to the proverbial carrot patch. So he hoisted a heavy box onto his shoulder and didn't begrudge his stepfather one whit. Life had just gotten easier thanks to Ben Gilbert, a pharmacist, whom Lillian had met one year earlier at a social for single men and women. He was an older man who'd never married or raised a child. "A strange little man," Mark would later say, "a bit cold and a bit distant but sweet."

When Ben offered to support both of his stepsons, Al graciously declined: "I make enough to support myself. Thanks." Let Ben support Bobby, Al thought. He was young enough to need it and hardly remembered their real father anyway.

Irv Harris had remarried, moved to Washington and had three more boys with his new wife. Years later Mark recalled, "whenever I talked to him on the phone he'd try to impress me with his achievements. Or he'd show off his vocabulary. I started not enjoying time with him. Oh, I loved him very much. But I was fonder of him away from him than with him.

From Cowboy to Mogul to Monster

Over time the memories of my childhood with my father became more important to me than times we spent together afterwards."

Although the new house was comfortable Al planned to spend as little time in it as possible. He was running for Vice President of his Senior class at Fairfax High School, having carefully calculated that he wasn't popular enough to win President. He would strategize to win and he would succeed. Strategy was one of his specialties. Logic was another. Commitment was a third. Whatever he believed in, he pursued with meticulous preparation, efficiency, discipline and hard, hard work.

By now, Al Harris was a master at projecting an image of confidence and ease. So what if behind his bravado lay the outsider from Chicago? If beneath his outgoing manner lay the soul of an introvert, more comfortable in private? No one knew that but Al. He could be icy if he wanted. He could look at you like he didn't see you when he was thinking of something else. But most of the kids at Fairfax High saw him as outgoing, funny and popular. An Honor Student; a member of the Spartans Club. He played third string Center on the football team, pretty good for a Jewish kid. He had even landed the last spot on the softball team which, luckily for him, didn't practice every day after school.

Teachers would remember him for his quick mind and tough questions. For his love of science, which he was convinced held the answers to the mystery of life. For his skills in math, where he calculated numbers in his head at warp speed. On top of all those gifts, Al was growing into his looks.

Girls started to notice his electric green eyes and slicked-back black hair. By the time he was a Senior at Fairfax, "Al was as good-looking as you get," recalled school friend Mal Feinberg. Looking back, Mark didn't agree: "I always wished I were taller and slimmer; that I looked more rugged, and less like what I thought of as a 'pretty boy.'" At the time, he was too busy to make much of his looks. Because aside from all his school activities he was determined to win a jackpot of money in puzzle contests.

Chapter 6. 1949. Beverly Hills

Puzzle contests were a craze in newly prosperous postwar America where people were enjoying guilt-free leisure for the first time in decades. Millions of Americans were newly obsessed with the daily brainteasers in newspapers, which varied between crossword and picture (rebus) puzzles. Newspapers would publish an easy puzzle and encourage readers to send in their answers to win a jackpot of money: "All you have to do is send in fifty cents!" Soon, puzzlers would get a letter from the newspaper: "Congratulations! You're a winner! Now, for only a dollar more you can get the tiebreaker puzzle. It's fun and easy!"

Like most puzzlers, Al fell prey to the come-on. But when the tiebreaker puzzle came in the mail it *wasn't* a lot of fun and it sure wasn't easy. "Instead of a cat, a rat and a tractor, there would be a picture of a stick with a hole in the end of it and some piece of equipment you'd never seen in your life. There were pictures of unknown animals and birds and bushes that nobody in their right mind could identify. It was a bunch of very, very obscure pictures that were supposed to add up to an answer. Plus, there were traps. One puzzle featured an 11-letter picture that started with an 'S' and looked like a 'searchlight' to all but the very few who correctly labeled it a 'stroboscope.'"

Most people who got the 'tiebreaker' would throw it out. Al wanted some of that prize money. So he spent every free hour of his senior year researching obscure pictures in encyclopedias and out-of-date magazines. He became obsessed with winning. He haunted old bookstores, combing through dusty, ancient volumes. He spent most of his Saturday nights at the library, looking through reference books on rare flora and fauna while other kids his age were at parties or on dates. Occasionally he found a picture. Mostly he struck out. Then he realized he was seeing the same people at the library week after week, all using the same books to solve the same tiebreaker. He had a brainstorm.

"I'm Al Harris," he said to a puzzler. "I noticed we're doing the same puzzle. How about trading pictures?"

"What?" The guy covered his answers, suspicious.

"I'll trade you one of mine for one of yours…"

"Are you nuts? No way," answered the puzzler.

Undaunted, Al went to another puzzler and made the same offer. "None of us is winning," he added. "So what's the harm in trading information? Maybe it will help one of us to win."

Eventually, his persistence wore down one puzzler, Ned Manley. "I traded him a picture of a rare form of nettle bush for a picture of a

41

rare form of woodpecker." Soon Al was trading information with a few puzzlers on a regular basis. When he found out that there were a dozen rebus puzzle experts around the country, people who looked on puzzle contests as a living, not a hobby, he got in touch with them and they all started trading pictures by mail. Before long he had loosely organized a 'puzzle contest underground' that exchanged answers. Still, none of them won big money. The puzzles were too damn hard. So Al kept his 'day jobs' during the week and ran the kiddy rides at Beverly Amusement Park on La Cienega over the weekends.

He was working at the airplane ride one Sunday when a man with a thick moustache kept glancing at him. He had two kids with him. The man walked towards the airplane ride, put the two kids on the airplane and casually struck up a conversation. Al was reticent because he thought the man was probably homosexual.

"Have you ever made any movies?" he asked.

"No," Al answered, suspicious.

"Are you interested in acting?"

"I don't know. I guess."

"You've got the face for it. If you like, I could help you get a screen test."

The man stuck out his hand.

"'Name's Groucho Marx," he said.

Al was shocked. Groucho wrote something on a piece of paper and handed it over to him.

"Here's my brother's number. Call him and make an appointment."

Al went home on cloud nine, certain that he was going to become a star. And a millionaire! Later that week he hurried to his appointment with Gummo, the fourth Marx brother who had left the act years earlier and became an agent.

"Hey, kid," Gummo observed, "my brother's right. You do have the looks to be an actor."

"Thanks, Mr. Marx."

Gummo launched into an explanation of what it took to become an actor. Lessons. Auditions. Pictures. The right agent.

"Excuse me," Mark interrupted. "When is my screen test?"

"Slow down," Gummo answered. He wrote down the name of an acting teacher. "Go study acting for a while. Then call me again. You've got potential," he smiled.

42

Chapter 6. 1949. Beverly Hills

Al left, tossing the paper in the garbage on his way out. If he couldn't get a screen test right away, he decided, the whole thing was a waste of time.

He went back to trying to win puzzle contests. With not much success. Then he had another brainstorm. He managed to get the correct answers to the last puzzle contest and paid $13.50 (a fortune) for a mailing list with the names and addresses of the contestants. He plunged every cent he had into sending out postcards suggesting that contestants send him $.25 for a list of the correct answers to the last puzzle. "Knowing the correct answers on a really tough puzzle will help you when you enter future contests," he insisted.

He received over 1,000 letters. He ended up making $250.00 on his $13.50 investment. A *real* fortune. Before long he bought more mailing lists and sent out more postcards with more responses. By the time he was seventeen, he had made enough money to put himself through college. In June, he became the first in his family to graduate from high school. He was headed to UCLA to become a dentist. "A good profession," his mother told him. For young, intelligent Jewish boys, a serious profession was a necessity - a doctor, a lawyer, a judge – "Make something of yourself," the moms insisted.

For Lillian, Al chose dentistry. It would make her happy although he had doubts it would make him happy.

PSO

1978

*The only real voyage of discovery consists
not in seeking new landscapes but in having new eyes.*
– Marcel Proust

Chapter Seven

April 22, 1978

Los Angeles, California

Mark Damon and John Hyde.

Chapter 7. 1978. Hollywood

Mark smiled happily as he read the news in *The Hollywood Reporter*. *The Choirboys* had earned almost $40 million overseas, four times as much as the movie made in the U.S and far more than any major studio projected it could earn. The results proved Mark's point that independent distributors were better than the studios.

Six months later, he launched a company in Hollywood called PSO (Producers Sales Organization). Its mission was to provide a link between Hollywood producers and worldwide independent distributors.

He had two partners: Sandy Howard (a 'B' movie producer) and Richard St. Johns (a producer who was working for Arthur Guinness Son and Company, Guinness Beer, and Guinness Book of World Records.) They all shared a suite of cramped little offices on the third floor of the Playboy Building on Sunset Boulevard.

Mark was back in a tiny office in one corner; Sandy Howard was in another; Richard St. Johns was in yet another office. Another member of the company, who worked in an office so small you could stand in the middle and touch both walls if you spread out your arms, was a man named John Hyde, who worked as a financial and business consultant to the Guinness Film Group.

Sandy Howard was a handsome guy with a booming voice and a ready smile that made people think he was dishing out bullshit. "Actually, he was a very dedicated producer although he had bad business sense and very little creativity," Mark recalled. "But he was a tireless worker who only slept four hours a night and was well-liked by everybody." Richard St. Johns was handsome in an Aryan way. "Blonde," said Mark, "with chiseled features and a smile that made you feel he was putting you down. He was horrid in his dealings with anyone he felt couldn't fight back. He would yell and scream at people in the office." He always knew everything better than anybody else and initially tried dishing out the same shit to Mark. "But I would turn tail and walk out of his office and he would eventually apologize. He needed me because of my growing reputation as a good film salesman." John Hyde was the person that people could talk to if they had a problem with Richard St. Johns. And plenty did.

Hyde, who showed up every day in sneakers, jeans and a tee shirt, had an easy way about him. He liked to say he was "just a po' boy from the Midwest who was trying to make a living" but Mark quickly realized he was even smarter than St. Johns and was playing it down. "His humble, but somewhat practiced exterior as a good little shitkicker worked very well in John's favor," Mark later explained. "It masked a brilliant mind."

Over time, Mark learned that Hyde's eclectic background included degrees in economics and business and he was extremely adept at high finance. He'd made a swift rise from the Universal mail room (working alongside future director John Badham and future studio chief Mike Medavoy) to become the assistant of Vice President Ned Tanen; had owned and run his own film lab, optical house and commercial production company and even made the first two music videos with Marcia Strassman, then Neil Diamond. He and Mark didn't interact often but they enjoyed each other's input on projects.

A lanky young production coordinator named Kate Morris, an organizational whiz with a ready smile and an easy laugh, worked for producer Sandy Howard. When Sandy made 'B' movies like *Meteor*, about a meteor that was supposed to strike the earth and *Jaguar Lives*, Kate worked on them for a year and still couldn't tell what either was about. "All I knew was that every time Sandy got into trouble with *Jaguar Lives* he would borrow satellite shots from *Meteor* and stick them into the other movie." Sandy was also making *The Silent Flute*, a karate movie produced by Paul Maslansky, who was around a lot and living out of his car. (A decade later Maslansky would produce the mega-hit *Police Academy*.) As she recalled years later, "it was a pretty chaotic place and there was a hysterical cast of characters coming in and out of those offices."

Every day, Mark took Hollywood breakfasts, lunches and dinners to sell the concept of PSO. He repeated that the company would neither make movies nor distribute them. It would act as a kind of marriage broker for Hollywood producers and foreign distributors, getting them to work together. "How will you make money?" producers asked him. Mark had a ready answer: "PSO will make its money by taking 10-15% of the advance foreign distributors put up for the rights to a film. And we'll make even more money when a film takes off. It's a win-win all around," he told them. "You want your movie to be a hit. So do the foreign distributors who license it from us because that's how they earn back the money they advanced for it. And PSO *really* wants your film to be a hit because if it goes into overages, that's how we make most of our money."

He stressed how independent overseas distributors would do better than studios: "They're far superior to some guy working for Warner Bros. in France or Italy, who has no incentive to make your movie a hit. That

Chapter 7. 1978. Hollywood

guy gets a check every week regardless of how your movie does. Our distributors, on the other hand, will hustle their butts off to make it a hit. Because they've put up their own money to get it. Give your movies to PSO and you'll see how much more money you make," he repeated. And repeated. And repeated.

St. Johns convinced Sandy Howard and myself that we should allow ourselves to be bought by the billion dollar Guinness corporation. He convinced us that being able to announce to the Hollywood community that we were a subsidiary of Arthur Guinness Son and Company. Would mean we would be taken more seriously, both in the US and abroad.

Mark was convinced.

Having lived in Europe he understood how Europeans did the business of buying and distributing American movies. He knew the culture, the mentality and many of the languages. Having been in the Hollywood 'system' he was able to open doors that other Europeans couldn't. But convincing producers to give PSO their pictures to sell overseas was harder than he thought.

"I had all these contacts and I saw it there - this huge market. But Hollywood still thought of itself as the center of the universe. And the studios had brainwashed producers into believing that their movies made seventy percent of their money in the U.S and only thirty percent in the rest of the world."

Decades before the concept of 'one world' was coined, independent foreign sales just didn't seem like a sexy, money-making proposition. Some in Hollywood were dabbling in the buying and selling of films overseas - there was a small company here and there. But nobody was trying to institutionalize the business of foreign sales the way Mark was. "At the time," said John Hyde, "you'd be lucky if you could find the people who ran the foreign divisions of studios. You'd have to go down a hallway into building B, into building C, into building D and down some dark little corner and there would be the international division, all two people. And some executive was sitting there saying, "Gee, I wonder if I can get to go to Cannes this year?"

Mark showed Hollywood producers the numbers from *Choirboys:* "This is not 70% of business from the U.S.! This is 75% of business overseas and only 25% in the U.S.!" He was a man with a mission and he worked around the clock, fueled by his years in front of the camera as an actor and behind it as a writer, director and producer. He was driven

49

From Cowboy to Mogul to Monster

by his experiences with PAC in Italy, his intricate knowledge of foreign distribution, his love of numbers and puzzles and logic and strategy.

He went out to speak at UCLA, USC, film festivals and conventions. He preached his ideas to everyone who would listen and to plenty who wouldn't. He was determined to awaken American filmmakers to the tremendous amount of money to be made in foreign distribution.

"Mark created the foreign sales model at its fullest," said Eddie Kalish, who worked for Paramount and MGM before joining PSO. "He was a beacon that helped people formulate how to finance and distribute Hollywood movies worldwide." Despite his monumental efforts, his words largely fell on deaf ears. In the late 1970's Hollywood simply did not understand how much money there was to be made in the rest of the world.

If only he could get an 'A' movie for PSO. Mark was convinced that would be his big break. Then his wish came true. And it almost sank the new company.

Chapter Eight

October 17, 1978

Hollywood, California

'Matilda, the Boxing Kangaroo' (actually a man in a kangaroo suit) in the ring with Elliot Gould and others, 1978.

Chapter 8. 1978. Hollywood

MARK STRUGGLED TO HIDE HIS EXCITEMENT as he met with Hollywood veteran Albert S. Ruddy. The affable producer of the Oscar-winning *The Godfather* was making a movie about a boxing kangaroo starring Robert Mitchum and Elliott Gould. "*Matilda* was based on a novel by Paul Gallico about a male kangaroo who was the chief contender for the heavyweight boxing championship of the world," Mark recalled.

Richard St. Johns' company was financing the picture and he had designated PSO the sales company. Still, Mark felt he had to impress such an important producer. So he had just pitched Al Ruddy on all the money to be made around the world by going with PSO.

"You've got yourself a deal," Ruddy decided.

"That's terrific." Mark was elated.

"We're going to make a fortune on this picture," Ruddy enthused. "We'll clean up overseas."

"I agree. So, first I'll sell it at MIFED..."

"How about I come to MIFED with you and meet with the foreign distributors?"

"Wow. That would be great."

"I'll show them pictures of the kangaroo in boxing gloves and talk it up. I'll sell this picture for you!" Ruddy, with his wide smile and twinkling eyes, was a great salesman. The men shook hands on it. Mark left the meeting certain this was the break he'd been waiting for.

In Milan, Ruddy wowed distributors with his Hollywood stories. He showed stills of the kangaroo wearing boxing gloves. He detailed the many weeks of training it took to teach him to box. "It was the real boxing kangaroo that sold them," Mark recalled. After Ruddy finished, Mark told his network of distributors that this was the chance they had been waiting for. "Finally, we have an A-list American movie coming to us, not the studios. How can you pass this up?", he asked. They couldn't. By the time they left MIFED Mark and Ruddy had sold *Matilda* around the world.

The producer went on location to Harrah's in Reno, Nevada. "I'll keep in touch," he promised as they parted. Then weeks passed without a word from Ruddy. Finally, Mark called.

"How's it going down there?"

"Great. Terrific," Ruddy replied.

"When can I see some stills or rushes?"

From Cowboy to Mogul to Monster

"Pretty soon, pretty soon." A few more weeks passed without a word.

"How about those rushes?", Mark asked when he called again. "When can I see something?"

"I'll send you some next week," Ruddy promised. "You're going to love it."

Mark hung up with a bad feeling. Another week. No call. He called again.

"Listen, Al, I just want to show the distributors something. They're so excited about this picture. If they can have some footage to show theater owners, it will help them book it into the best ones."

"Oh. Okay, sure," Ruddy relented. He agreed to meet Mark at a screening room at Warner Bros. in a few days.

When the film rolled, Mark was flabbergasted. Shock set in. Instead of a real boxing kangaroo, the star was a little man in a kangaroo suit!

"What the hell…? Where's the kangaroo?!"

"Oh, he didn't work out," Ruddy explained calmly.

"Why not?"

"He was too lazy. He wasted way too much film."

"Jesus, why didn't you tell me?"

Ruddy patted Mark on the shoulder.

"I didn't want you to worry. I wanted you to see for yourself that the guy in the suit is just as convincing as the real thing. Trust me, we won't tell anyone it's a man in there and nobody will know the difference."

"You're actually going to try to make people think THAT'S a real kangaroo?!! Fuck, Al, his head is three times as big as a kangaroo's!"

"Nobody knows how big a kangaroo's head is. Believe me, it will work."

"No it won't," Mark retorted sharply. "Even a two year-old can see that's a man in a costume."

"What are you worrying about?," Ruddy countered testily. "You already sold the picture."

"Exactly. I sold a picture starring a boxing kangaroo not some guy in a molting costume."

At PSO, Mark stormed into St. John's office. "Have you seen what Ruddy did?"

"Yeah. And he just called and told me you shit a brick."

"So you knew about this?"

"Of course."

54

Chapter 8. 1978. Hollywood

"And you let that happen?!" Mark shouted, enraged.

"Calm down. If Ruddy says it will work, then it will. This is the godfather of *The Godfather* we're talking about. He has a hell of a lot more experience than you."

"Well, I'm not going to be a part of it. I won't deliver this piece of shit to my distributors. I'm canceling their contracts."

"The hell you are!" St. Johns raged. "You're damn well getting every penny they pledged to us!"

"St. Johns went berserk," Mark recalled years later. "He needed the money for the budget and it threatened to put Aspen Films and Guinness in jeopardy if I didn't collect it from all the distributors."

Desperate, Mark begged him . "At least let me into the cutting room. Maybe I can lessen the damage before we have to deliver it."

"Knock yourself out," St. Johns said coldly. "Just remember - your guys are good for the money no matter how it turns out."

Mark spent the next three weeks trimming every shot of the kangaroo to practically nothing. But it was impossible to make a movie about a boxing kangaroo without the kangaroo. He agonized over what to tell his distributors: "These were my guys. They had bought this because I said it was the A-list movie we had been waiting for. Now, here was Ruddy, trying to fool them that it was a real kangaroo. And here I was, fucking them over."

They included distributors like Graham Burke, a young buyer for an Australian company called Village Roadshow, had been singing Mark's praises since they had negotiated a price for the picture in MIFED.

"What are you asking for *Matilda* in Australia," Burke had asked Mark.

"$150,000."

"I'll give you $140,000," Burke countered.

Mark studied his projections thoughtfully.

"That's great," he finally said, "but actually, I only need $125,000. So let's close it at that."

Burke was taken aback. "Okay. Sure. If that's all you really need..."

"Actually, I only needed $100,000," Mark admitted decades later. "But I knew it would look good to St. Johns if I got the extra $25,000. And it would stand me in good stead with Graham Burke (who later became head of the multi-national 'Village Road Show.'")

Now, delivering the travesty of *Matilda* to distributors like Burke was something Mark dreaded. "I swear to you," he kept repeating, "I wasn't trying to fool you. The producers put one over on me, too." But his distributors blamed Mark anyway. After all, he was the one who had sold it to them *and* collected their money.

Matilda was a complete disaster. Audiences walked out of test screenings. American-International, which originally planned a wide release, put the picture into limited release. Critics had a field day: "Matilda looks like a neighborhood prankster on his way to a costume party." "Far from looking like a real kangaroo the star of this woeful spectacle is a ham in a mangy, moth-eaten costume." "According to the production notes the role of Matilda is played by someone named Gary Morgan in a kangaroo suit that reportedly cost $30,000 but fits as if it had been ordered by sea-mail from Hong Kong." "*Matilda* is extremely bad and deservedly one of the biggest financial disasters of the decade."

"It's probably one of the worst pictures ever made," Mark agreed decades later, "yet it was produced by one of our greatest producers. Go figure."

Ruddy took the failure in stride and went on to produce countless other films, emerging decades later with another Oscar win for *Million Dollar Baby*.

Mark barely recovered. After all his distributors took a bath on *Matilda* he had to promise to give them another picture at a discount, to make sure they never lost money again. Still, decades later, whenever he enthusiastically sells a new movie to the same distributors they remind him, "Yeah but you sold me *Matilda*..."

Mark was thrilled when PSO acquired *A Change of Seasons*. The story was co-written by Hollywood veteran Martin Ransohoff (John Hyde's mentor and friend) and produced by Ransohoff and St. Johns. It starred Shirley MacLaine, Anthony Hopkins and Bo Derek. After the debacle of *Matilda*, Mark was more determined than ever to make this one a winner.

When he sold it to a brand new German distributor, *Senator*, he vowed to get the actors to Germany to help promote the movie. After he failed to convince any of them to go, he came up with the idea of promoting it on German TV himself: "Because I used to be an actor… Because Germans know me as a cowboy star… Because I can speak to them in German. Because my ex-wife, Barbara Frey, is German…" Eventually, his ploys got him on German TV where, a decade after learning the language from Barbara Frey, he publicized the movie in fluent German.

It snowed the night *Change* opened but Mark slogged through the drifts and stood outside the theatre, counting the house. "After Germany, I traveled to "every major city in the world where I'd sold the film. I learned theaters, how many seats each screen had, what the cost of the ticket was, what percentage of box office the distributor would get from the theater owner. It got to the point where, when *Change* opened in France on a Wednesday, after the first showing at 2:00 PM I could project within five percent what that picture would do at the end of its run."

In one year he became an expert in all of the forty territories in the world. Then he worked with each distributor on how to market their picture differently in different countries. If a film didn't go well in France he would find something in the Spanish advertising campaign that was different from the French campaign and could possibly work. "Mark is one of the few people in the world who fully understood the potential in foreign sales and he used that expertise to build PSO," said John Hyde. "Soon everyone knew he had a fabulous marketing mind and that frankly, in some cases he made better marketing campaigns than the pictures themselves." "He's one of the only guys who actually knew how to get product placed in the foreign markets in the nascent stages of international sales," agreed noted attorney Peter Dekom, a leading figure in the business of entertainment.

The fiery rise of PSO took all of Mark. But he refused to be daunted by the enormity of his task. He saw the potential and realized he could accomplish it. Before him, no one else had quite seen it that way. (Lew Grade and Dino De Laurentiis saw bits and pieces but they never put it all together.) Mark did just that with PSO and in building the company he built his dream.

Having been an actor for most of his life he had a whole different viewpoint. "Often you get so mired in day-to-day business that you don't see the big picture, you don't see the opportunities," he reflected decades later. "When I quit acting at the age of 40 I didn't know where I would go. All I knew was I had to do something because I had a wife to support. And out of desperation came creation."

As always, he was driven by his lifelong hunger to be #1. "You don't get to be #1 if you think you should be #10," mused Bobby Meyers. "You only get to be #1 if you're totally committed and passionate about what you do. Plus you have to be very good. And if you want to be #1 you have

From Cowboy to Mogul to Monster

to work REALLY hard." "Mark is an out of the box thinker," remarked attorney Kevin Koloff. "Actually, he didn't just work outside the box. He *invented* the box."

At the end of 1978, the Guinness Film Group, including PSO moved from the Playboy Building into nicer offices at 10100 Santa Monica Boulevard in Century City. Until then, producer Sandy Howard, who was always notoriously broke, had been borrowing against his shares of the company for years. Guinness had been buying his piece of the company back piece by piece until, by the time they moved, Howard had no shares left and PSO was down to two partners – Mark and St. Johns.

Mark inherited Howard's assistant, a lovely and smart young woman named Janet Fleming. Kate Morris also began to work for the company as PSO's corporate secretary and they were joined by Arianne Ulmer Cipes, daughter of famed director Edgar Ulmer and wife of Technicolor head, Jay Cipes. Together they formed the nucleus of what would later be called PSO's 'Women Power.'

There were plenty of doubters in Hollywood when PSO inherited their next film from Aspen, *The Wanderers* starring Ken Wahl and Karen Allen. Then Mark came up with a pitch that tied it to *The Warriors*, a hit at the time: "If the Wanderers met the Warriors in a dark alley who would kick bigger butt?" posed the ads in Italy and Germany. They worked so well overseas that the film grossed $10 million versus $2 million in the U.S.

Next, PSO got *The Final Countdown* and it began to look like the company was finally gaining some clout.

Chapter Nine

May 8, 1979

Cannes, France

On December 7th, 1980—The nuclear carrier
USS Nimitz disappeared in the Pacific...
and reappeared December 7th, 1941...
off Pearl Harbor

Nothing in history could prepare you for

THE FINAL COUNTDOWN

© PSO

Chapter 9. 1979. Cannes

"More champagne, sir?" asked the flight attendant of the man in the third row whose green eyes were fixed on the darkened window shade.

"Yes," Mark absently replied, watching the champagne fill his glass. He took a sip and went back to staring at the window shade, although that wasn't what he was seeing. In his mind's eye he was seeing the face of his 'adversary,' the man he was meeting tomorrow at Cannes, the person with whom he hoped to negotiate a deal on *The Final Countdown* for Japan. Mr. Moto Kubotani.

Shooting was slated to begin in a few weeks on PSO's biggest movie to date. *The Final Countdown,* budgeted at $7,000,000 was being produced by Richard St. Johns and starred Kirk Douglas and Martin Sheen. It had a high-concept science fiction plot, which Mark reveled in telling distributors: "The USS Nimitz, America's finest nuclear-powered aircraft carrier loaded with jet warplanes, is caught in a supernatural storm and thrown back from 1980 to December 6, 1941, the day before the Japanese attack on Pearl Harbor. Then the Captain (Kirk Douglas) and his crew have to decide whether to launch a preemptive strike against the Japanese and avert the attack on Pearl Harbor or step back and let history take its course."

One of Mark's selling points was that the movie was being shot on board the actual Nimitz, using the real crew with the cooperation of the Navy. It would be chock-full of special effects and riveting action, he explained. With all that, a fantastic story and a respectable cast of Hollywood veterans, Mark was sure this one would be a winner. But he still hadn't made his most important sale to Japan.

By now he had learned how to deal with the Japanese. He understood that in business, saving face was most important. He knew that you didn't play favorites with Japanese buyers even if you had one. That you gave every important distributor the same opportunity, sending scripts to all of them at the same time. He recognized that rarely would you close a deal with one distributor until you had seen all of them.

Two weeks earlier, Mark had sent out the script of *The Final Countdown* to his three major Japanese buyers simultaneously: Sam Nanba of Nippon-Herald (who had bought *The Choirboys*); Moto Kubotani of Shochiku and Harumasa Shirasu of Toho Towa. "Then I waited for the offers to come in. I was sure this was going to be an incredible auction and we'd get a huge price for the film."

Harumasa Shirasu was the first to call. "Hello Shirasu-San," Mark said eagerly. "Good to hear from you." He picked up his pencil, ready to write down Toho Towa's offer.

"About *The Final Countdown*," said Shirasu, "I am sorry, Mark-san, we just don't think the film's going to work in Japan..."

"Oh shit," Mark thought. He called his old friend Sam Nanba at Nippon Herald.

"*The Final Countdown* could be great for Japan, don't you think?" he said, trying to keep the desperation out of his voice. "Isn't this the kind of film the Japanese public loves?"

Sam replied stoically. "We don't think it will work for us."

Mark hung up with a sinking feeling. By the time he called his third Japanese buyer, Moto Kubotani he was very, very nervous. "What do you think of *The Final Countdown?*" he asked Shochiku's Head of Acquisitions. "Do you think it has possibilities for Shochiku?"

"Actually, we are not terribly excited by it, but maybe..." said Moto.

"Why don't we talk about it in Cannes?" Mark said hastily.

"Fine. I'll see you there."

Mark was puzzled by the reluctance of his Japanese buyers and nervous as hell. One thing he knew for sure. If he didn't sell Japan, it would be a disaster.

So on the way to Cannes, Mark reviewed what he had learned about negotiation – that the first thing was to know the guy on the other side of the table, to understand his psychology and not let him feel he was beaten. Then he thought about what he knew of Moto Kubotani. "Above all, I knew that Moto hated to lose films to the competition." His eyes remained trained on the darkened window shade as he thought about Moto some more. By the time the plane landed in Nice he had come up with a strategy. It was high stakes poker but he hoped it would work. Hell, with two no's and a maybe from Japan, it *had* to work.

"Set up two meetings for tomorrow," he told his secretary when he walked into the PSO suite in the Carlton Hotel. "Sam Nanba at 3:00 and Moto Kubotani at 4:00. And make sure that as soon as Moto arrives you knock on the door of my office and let me know."

The next day, Sam showed up promptly at 3:00. One thing Mark could count on with the Japanese. They were *always* punctual. Sam and Mark chatted about movies, kids, politics, restaurants. Everything but the film. After a while, Sam remarked, "Mark, What's the matter with you? I

Chapter 9. 1979. Cannes

have never seen you so relaxed during a film market. And we've never had a social chat before."

"Sometimes, Sam," Mark replied 'casually,' "you just have to forget business, relax, and get to know your distributors." He and Sam went back to chatting until his assistant knocked on the door signaling the arrival of Moto Kubotani.

When Mark showed Sam out he could see Moto waiting on the couch in the reception area. "Thank you, Sam," Mark said loudly. "It's always great doing business with you."

He shook Sam's hand warmly and watched as a slightly puzzled Nanba walked past Moto Kubotani, whose face darkened. When they got to Mark's office Moto asked, "Did you just sell Sam MY picture?"

"Moto," Mark answered politely, "I wouldn't do that without at least a meeting with you. But you know, you didn't tell me you wanted it. All you said was 'maybe…'"

"Not maybe. Yes. You knew we wanted it. *The Final Countdown* is ours, not Sam Nanba's!" Kubotani interrupted, determined to beat out 'the competition.'

Mark managed to keep his smile to himself as they began to talk numbers and Kubotani closed the deal for Japan. "I got my price from him," Mark laughed decades later, "and thank God for Shochiku, *The Final Countdown* went on to become one of the most successful pictures in Japan that year."

That evening, Mark was talking with Nigel Green and Aurelio De Laurentiis at a cocktail party in the Carlton when he noticed a dark-haired man with sharp features watching them. After the others moved off he approached Mark. "How do you do, Mr. Damon," he said forcefully with a German accent. "My name is Juergen Wohlrabe. Jugend Films."

Mark greeted him politely. The man's name was familiar but he couldn't place it. He knew Jugend Films, however, as one of the oldest German distribution companies, having been around since shortly after the First World War. The company had a reputation as stodgy and specialized in family films (hence the name Jugend [youth] Films). But it had fallen on bad times. "I wanted to speak with you about a film you represent," Wohlrabe continued. "*The Final Countdown*. I am interested in acquiring it for Germany."

"Really? It's not exactly a family film."

63

"I know," replied Wohlrabe. He explained that he had recently become CEO of the company, a family business. "And I was asked to make it an important company again."

"I wish you much success," said Mark. "I assume your background is in business?"

"Yes and no," Wohlrabe laughed, adding that he had served in the German Bundestag for many years. Juergen Wohlrabe, Mark would later learn, was a marketing genius known for promotional campaigns that won him seat after seat in the German Bundestag (the House of Representatives.) Now, taking over Jugend Films was a challenge for the dynamic Wohlrabe and he was a man who loved challenge.

"*The Final Countdown* would make an excellent start for the new Jugend Films," he insisted.

"I'm sure it would," Mark retorted. "But I'm already in negotiations with Sammy Waynberg and Berndt Eichinger for Germany. Why don't you make an appointment with my assistant? Perhaps we have another film for you."

But Wohlrabe, who would later become President of the Bundestag and stand beside Mayor Willy Brandt when the Berlin Wall came down in 1989, refused to take no for an answer. He continued to approach Mark whenever he saw him. One evening, he was emerging from a screening when Wohlrabe came up to him again.

"You owe it to me," he said.

"Why?"

"Because I used to date your ex-wife, Barbara Frey."

"And exactly what does that have to do with my selling you *The Final Countdown?*"

"I'm almost like family," he said with a glint. Mark smiled. He was still not going to sell him the film. Finally, Juergen nabbed him at another cocktail party.

"Look, I don't know what I need to do to get this film but I will offer you more than any other German distributor."

"That's great. I appreciate it. But I'm afraid it's not enough to get you the film."

"Why not?"

"Because I want more than a little more money up front."

"What do you want?"

Chapter 9. 1979. Cannes

"I want *The Final Countdown* to do the best it possibly can in Germany. And you're too new to the business to convince me that you can make that happen."

Juergen smiled at the challenge. "I'll make you a bet. If you give me the movie for Germany and I <u>don't</u> make *Final Countdown* one of the top ten films this year I'll give you an additional $100,000. Is that enough to get Jugend the film?"

Mark smiled back, finally won over by the man's creativity. "You're on."

When shooting began on *The Final Countdown* Mark got permission from Washington to bring foreign distributors onto the U.S.S. Nimitz. Many distributors took Mark up on the offer. Juergen Wohlrabe went one better. He brought all the German press onto the Nimitz, promoted the hell out of the picture and did everything possible before it opened.

The result of his exhaustive work was that *The Final Countdown* was a major success in Germany. Not only was it one of the top ten films that year, it was number one. Beating out all of the films from the major studios was a triumph for the young German politician who never owed Mark the additional money and used the film to kick-start Jugend Film's success over the next twenty years.

In the U.S., however, where it was launched by United Artists as a major movie with a major star, Kirk Douglas, *The Final Countdown* became a major disappointment when it brought in only $6 million at the box office. "Because they didn't know how to market the picture in the U.S.," Mark insisted. Once again, PSO did three times more business overseas than the film did in the U.S.

By the end of 1979, PSO had made $500,000 in profits and word was spreading in Hollywood. But Mark grew concerned that Arthur Guinness Son and Co. was very unhappy with its partner Richard St. Johns, after he attended a Guinness board meeting in London. He worried that if their billion dollar 'big brother' was so unhappy with St. Johns, they might not continue to finance PSO. And what would happen if Guinness pulled out?

Chapter Ten

February 19, 1980

Los Angeles, California

PSO signage at 10100 Santa Monica Boulevard in Century City, Los Angeles, California.

Chapter 10. 1980. Los Angeles

M ARK TRAVELED THE GLOBE, ENTHUSIASTICALLY PITCHING movies to distributors and selling, selling, selling. He sold so much that he began to develop a reputation as "the best pitchman in the business." Meanwhile, John Hyde, who was still working for Richard St. Johns, also heard about Guinness's dissatisfaction with his boss. Simultaneously, he saw PSO grow by leaps and bounds.

"The more films we sold the more people we needed to take care of them," Mark related. He hired more staff to send reports to producers, collect monies and analyze the foreign distributors' reports and correct them. He added a marketing person to get publicity to their distributors, brought in accountants and lawyers and amplified his sales team.

Richard St. Johns' behavior around the office continued to get worse and worse. John: "He was horrid in his dealings with anyone whom he felt couldn't fight back. There were a number of key people in PSO who said they wouldn't stay because of the problems they had with him."

Mark and John started to talk about the skinny they were hearing from Guinness: the company wanted to give St. Johns the boot and was interested in Mark taking over PSO with John as his second in command. The men decided to discuss it further when they were out of the office. John was living in a house owned by St. Johns when Mark came over for dinner. As they talked the men agreed that St. Johns had his own agenda.

"He wants to be a major Hollywood producer," said John.

"And if he can do that and PSO comes along, that would be fine..." Mark began.

"...But if PSO can't be involved that would be fine with him, too," John agreed, finishing Mark's sentence. They were clearly on the same page.

"What if we propose to Guinness to separate St. Johns from PSO and let us run it?"

"Exactly. Let St. Johns keep other parts of the Film Group and do whatever he wants with them."

They figured they had no choice - if they stuck with St. Johns, Guinness would dump all three of them. They talked late into the night and came up with a plan for a newly structured PSO: John would deal with the financial end; Mark would be in charge of sales, marketing and production. They decided to split it 60% (Mark) to 40% (John) and concluded that Mark's titles would be Chairman of the Board and Chief Executive Officer while John would be President and Chief Operating Officer.

From Cowboy to Mogul to Monster

"We shook hands on it and a couple of days later I left for London," John stated.

Mark, meanwhile, began to work on an all-consuming project – dubbing *Das Boot* into English.

Columbia had decided that *Das Boot* should be dubbed before it was released in the U.S. But Mark knew the pitfalls of dubbing better than most people. When his voice had been dubbed by others in movies he made in Europe he had learned that the voices and inflections of dubbers usually didn't fit his mouth movements, facial expressions and body language. "They also missed the nuances that helped make it a real performance." He was duly worried about the fate of a dubbed *Das Boot*.

When he learned that seven of the original German actors spoke English well, he went to see the professional dubbing company.

"Why don't we have some of the original actors dub their own voices into English?" he proposed.

"Because the actors will have German accents!" they answered, shocked.

"So what? They're Germans," he replied.

"But that's not the way it's done," he was told.

"So let's do it differently. If we use the original actors the film might seem like it was shot in English from the beginning."

"Impossible," said one executive.

"Hideously expensive," said another.

"Not doable," said a third.

Mark ignored them all. "What would it take?" he asked simply.

"Weeks and weeks of finding words in English that fit the mouth movements of the actors speaking in German."

"Fine," he said. "What else?"

"Money," was the answer. "A lot of it."

Mark enthusiastically pitched Columbia his idea to make *Das Boot* the best-dubbed film ever and managed to get a budget of $150,000 for dubbing. Kate Morris was sent to London to oversee the arduous process. She would be there for months while John negotiated with Guinness and Mark alternated between running the LA office, flying around the globe and stopping in London to meet with Guinness and supervise the dub.

Kate: "I remember working night and day in a tiny room with a little woman who sat at an old fashioned Movieola. She watched the movie

Chapter 10. 1980. Los Angeles

frame by frame, studying how the mouths moved. Then she helped us come up with English words that would fit the mouth movements of the Germans in each frame."

It was enormously painstaking and Kate knew that Mark was a hard taskmaster "so the night before he showed up for the first time I had a horrible dream. Mark stood up in the middle of a scene and said, 'STOP! STOP! This is the worst piece of shit I have ever seen.'"

She was stressed to the max when he actually arrived. "He was previewing the dubbing when suddenly, just like in my dream, he stopped the film in the middle of a scene and said, 'THIS IS TERRIBLE!' I almost had a heart attack. I thought, 'My life is over, they will put me on a boat to get me home.'" Luckily, it was only one scene. Part of a scene, actually. "The submarine's captain (Juergen Prochnow) was walking to the back of the boat and they hadn't gotten the depth perspective right so it sounded like Juergen was standing in the front of the ship with the rest of the crew. After Mark made sure it was fixed, things got easier."

Kate recalled Wolfgang Petersen coming to London to see the dub. "I picked him up at the airport and noticed he had all of his stuff in a little plastic bag. When we got out of the cab the bag fell out and broke. There went his hair dryer and all his other stuff lying all over the street as he scurried to pick them up. Now, of course, almost thirty years later, Wolfgang Petersen is a mega Hollywood director... although he still blow dries his own hair."

When the film was released, some reviewers thought it had originally been shot in English with some of the actors speaking with heavy German accents. Others called *Das Boot* the best dubbed film ever. It was a major success.

John was also having success in London: "After lengthy negotiations it was our understanding that Guinness was going to break PSO off from the other companies, let us run it and let St. Johns have his own unit: Aspen Productions."

Shortly before Christmas, he called Mark with good news: "PSO is ours!" Years later John remembered that call: "We thought, 'This is great! We've got a 'big brother.' We have a big ownership in the company and plenty of cash flow.'" Elated, the two men went on separate vacations with their families.

John was at the La Jolla Tennis Club on Christmas Day when he got an urgent call from Peter Guinness: "You'd better get back to London right away. Guinness has decided to get out of the movie business. Effective immediately." John quickly called Mark, who said he would fly back and meet him in the morning.

Mark fell asleep that night, deeply worried. PSO had been one of Guinness' most successful subsidiaries. The tiny company had earned two million dollars in its third year of operation. How could they dump it? What was behind their thinking? And what would he and John do if PSO lost Guinness? It would be a huge problem.

He tossed and turned throughout the long night but by the next morning, as he flew to LA, he began to regain his equanimity. "After all," he thought, "it's hardly the first time I've been in hot water."

Al Harris

1951 – 1954

Chapter Eleven

September 29, 1951

Beverly Hills, California

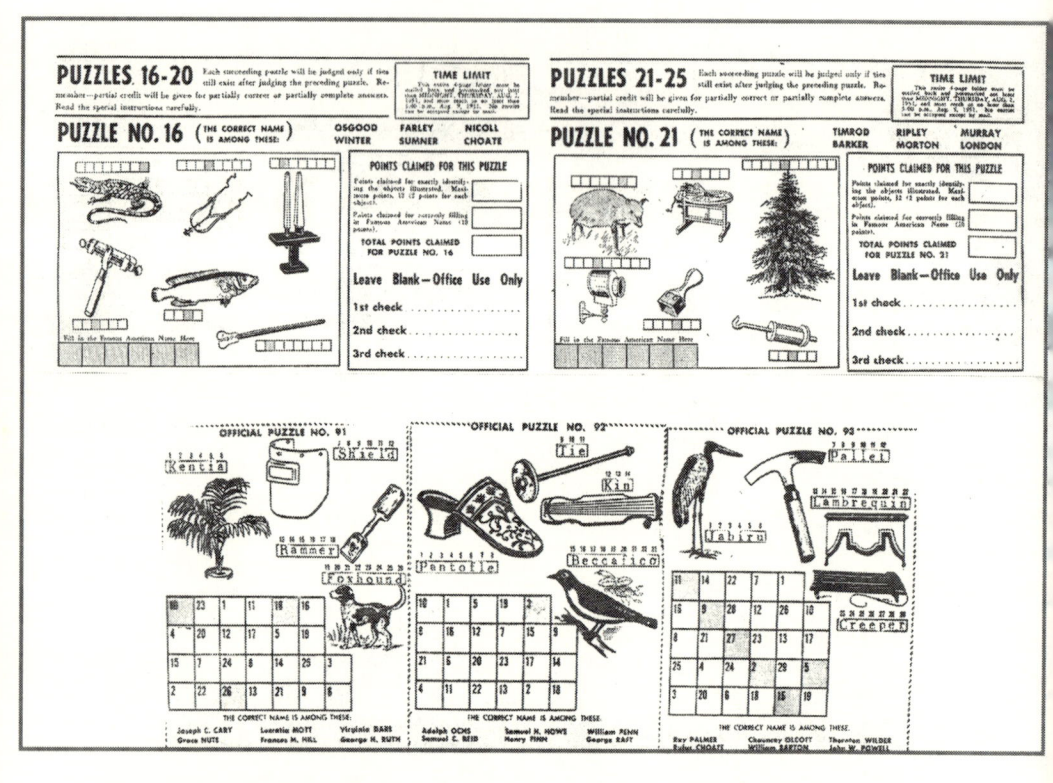

Examples of Rebus puzzles that were popular during the 50s and 60s.

William Caldwell (aka Alan Harris) made his name across the country as a Master puzzle solver and Publisher of CONTEST BOOKS.

Alan Harris (Herskovitz) won first prize in the Disabled American Veterans contest in 1952, reaping a veritable fortune for young Herskovitz/Harris/Caldwell.

Chapter 11. 1951. Beverly Hills

Al was sitting at the kitchen table filling orders for answers to the latest *LA Times* puzzle contest when he heard the front door chime. He looked out the window and saw two men wearing dark suits and an official air. He heard his mother open the door.

"Hello Ma'am, we're from the Los Angeles Times…"

By the time Lillian led them into the kitchen Al had run out the back door, barely eluding them. "This is a warning," the men told Lillian. "Tell your son to stop selling answers to our puzzles."

The Times ran a new, empty box-by-box word puzzle on a daily basis. Every box had a number value (like 'Scrabble') and contestants would come up with the best possible combinations of words to get the most points. Al would do the puzzle, come up with the best answers he could and sell them to people on mailing lists he bought, puzzlers who couldn't come up with answers equally as good.

He was making good money. Then he took the audacious step of taking out advertising space in the LA Times, adjacent to the contest puzzles. The Times provided the puzzles and Al sold the answers, for only $13.00.

After his 'warning' from *The LA Times*, he didn't stop selling answers. He took a P.O. Box in Beverly Hills under another name and sold them through that address. "I became 'William Caldwell' because I thought 'Caldwell' sounded like someone who was solid and adult. Certainly not an eighteen-year-old." Soon 'William Caldwell' and his company, "Contest Books" began to run ads above the daily puzzles: "If you want answers to this puzzle, contact Contest Books, P.O Box 11303, Los Angeles, 48, California."

Next, Al contacted a company on the East Coast and received permission to retail their books on puzzle contests by mail. When he received an enthusiastic response from his mailing list he decided to write his own puzzle books. Before long 'Caldwell' was publishing books titled "Two or More Word Phrases" and "Five Letter Words." Meanwhile, he continued selling answers to his ever-growing mailing list and even wrote a newsletter.

'William Caldwell' became a star in the world of puzzle contests. He even received fan mail. *Dear Mr. Caldwell,* wrote one of his admirers, *"I received your letter with your answers to the Vatican puzzle. How can I ever thank you? The fee of $6.00 that you ask is more than reasonable. Now if I get another tie-breaker back, which will naturally be harder, and I again offer to pay you for whatever help you render me – WILL YOU HELP ME OUT*

77

AGAIN? With your assistance I have a good chance to win a top prize, my first in 10 years. Mr. Caldwell, I can't explain in words what a champion you are. I just can't get over your reliableness. I remain an avid contestant and customer, Martin Whitehead

Before long, William Caldwell was getting so many responses that Al couldn't fill all the orders. He went to see Uncle Milton and his wife, Blossom to ask if they could help with the business. The answer was a resounding 'yes.' "We had no money back then," Blossom explained years later. "My dad wasn't a business man," Rick Elfman confirmed. "He had a liquor store that didn't work out. Then he had a Frostee-Freeze franchise that bombed." By the time Al asked him to help with the puzzle business Milt was delivering milk and mail. (He would soon pursue a teaching degree and become a success as a teacher.) For now, he was eager to work with Blossom and use his brains to make money.

Soon, Milt and Blossom were poring through the Merriam Webster dictionary and making lists of obscure two letter words (ZO, QI); three letter words (DOH, HOO, ISH, UEY); fours (YEUK, TWAE, CUIF, VROW) and lists of five letter words that ended or started with a Y (ENSKY, MUHLY, YIRTH). When "Contest Books" published books with those word lists even Al, Milt and Blossom couldn't fill all the orders. Luckily, Al discovered that a kid he'd known in high school, Mal Feinberg, had followed him to UCLA. When Al learned that Mal, too was trying to win puzzle contests he asked him to join the operation. Mal became 'George P. Simpson' to Al's 'William Caldwell.' "But Al was the brains," Mal asserted decades later, "I was just his helper."

Milt, Blossom, Mal and Al worked around the kitchen table in the house on Carson Drive. Papers were spread out everywhere. The dining room table was covered with old and new encyclopedias and various reference books. Ben didn't pay much attention. Lillian was proud that her firstborn was succeeding "without money, without anything." "But she constantly held me up to my younger brother, Bob as the role model he should be," Mark asserted. "And he resented that," "Al was a hard act to follow," admitted Bob years later, "but I didn't resent him. There was never any question in my mind that my brother was smarter than me."

Even though Al was widely regarded as the genius in the family, at seventeen, he still had the same insecurities and needs he'd had as a boy: to belong, to succeed, to be loved and to love. By now, he had created a fortress around his vulnerability built of intellect, manners and instinct. He knew how to be imperious, even a little intimidating. He knew how

Chapter 11. 1951. Beverly Hills

to keep people at a distance if he wanted. "He has a protective shield that you have to break through," his daughter, Alexis, would say decades later. "He has a test for each person he meets to see who's true and who's not. And he developed that shield because he could get hurt easily."

Somewhere beneath his protective shield lay the mind of a businessman, the heart of a romantic and the soul of an artist. How it all would add up was unclear. But one thing was certain. By the end of his freshman year, Al had decided he wasn't going to be a dentist. He switched his major to Speech because it was easy. And because it left him more time to devote to his growing business.

In March, 1952, the DAV (Disabled American Veterans) ran the Cadillac of puzzle contests. Their ads were in every newspaper: "GRAND TOTAL OF OVER $100,000.00 IN CASH PRIZES! $391,927.35 ALREADY GIVEN AWAY! You may win up to 1,000 TIMES YOUR DONATION!" Hundreds of thousands of Americans took the bait. Literally, a million or more entered to solve the word puzzle with a grid of 100 by 100 empty boxes. Each letter had a number value – so if 'c' was a 2 and 'a' was a 1 and 't' was 3, you'd get 6 for the word 'cat'. The point was to fill in words in all of the boxes and get the highest score out of the entire configuration. In two weeks.

Al was working on the puzzle when his ZBT Fraternity brothers, aware of his puzzle expertise, asked if they could go in on the contest with him. His acceptance into ZBT earlier that year had been very important to him: "ZBT was known as the fraternity of rich Jewish boys. Having come from poverty, it was a coup for me to belong, like getting into the most exclusive country club. Plus, since ZBT boys were seen as a good catch, I thought girls would be impressed." Now, he subjected his would-be helpers to ten of the stiffest examinations he could devise. He chose the group that finished highest and made them a deal - if they won they'd split a piece of the earnings. He stipulated that as the brains behind it all, he'd keep the biggest piece.

Soon Al had three teams of ZBT boys working on the puzzle around the clock. One team consisted of Mal Feinberg (who had followed Al into ZBT), Allan Wilks and Stan Haberman. They worked from eight o'clock in the morning to four o'clock in the afternoon. The next team worked from four o'clock to midnight and the next from midnight to eight o'clock in the morning. Each team would get results and give them to the next team coming on. On top of that, Al worked on the puzzle and had Milt and Blossom working on it, too.

For ten days they never slept. They just worked on the puzzle and tried to come up with the highest score for the words they put in. They were almost at the deadline when Al had an idea. "We're doing this like everyone else, following what we think the rules are. But let's step back - is there any other way to look at this puzzle?"

No one could think of any. Until Al pointed out that they were operating as if all the boxes had to form new words every time they intersected. "But what happens if two columns are side by side and don't form words across but have the highest scores down? Could we do better?"

"That's not playing by the rules," one of the ZBT boys argued.

"But are those the rules?" Al asked. "I read them again and again. And nothing said all the boxes that intersect have to form words."

He was thinking outside the box, as he would for the remainder of his life. Nobody agreed with him. In the end, after he formulated one entry using that theory and came up with a higher score than any of the others, he elected to send that one in as his entry.

He entered once as 'Al Herskovitz' and included a letter to the contest judges: "You'll see that there are certain places where words going down don't always form words going across. I'm not counting them as words and I didn't score them. But there's nothing in the rules that says I can't do this." Then he entered three more times: as 'Milton Elfman,' 'Mal Feinberg' and one of the ZBT boys.

A few weeks later, Al got a call that the DAV Contest was sending people to investigate him because he was up for a prize. The rules had clearly stated that contest officials might investigate potential winners for hours prior to the awarding of prizes. Al had known that contestants were supposed to keep their worksheets. He had made sure they were all in his handwriting. But when the contest officials found out he was only nineteen they didn't just investigate him for a couple of hours. They investigated him for a couple of *days*. They couldn't believe that a nineteen-year-old boy had done such high-level work. But no matter what questions they asked, he provided them with an answer, an explanation and worksheets to back it up. In the end, they went away satisfied.

The next week, letters came from the DAV contest. Al's entry had won 1st prize among a million entrants. Their other entries won 3rd, 4th and 5th prizes. The guys were elated. It was a phenomenal coup. The loot totaled over $30,000, a fortune in 1952 (today that would be like winning

Chapter 11. 1951. Beverly Hills

$5 million dollars). There was just one thing that bugged Al - how on earth did some stranger sneak in between them and win 2nd prize?

He ended up with the largest chunk of the winnings; Mal got a good amount and so did the other boys. Al gave Uncle Milton $8,000, which he used to buy their first house. "And with that money we started our new life," said Blossom. He also bought his stepfather a pharmacy on Third and La Brea. He figured it would make things easier for his mother and be a place for Bob to work after school.

After that, Al became even more of a star at home and in the frat house. But the buzz only lasted until he took a good look at his grades.

Chapter Twelve

December 19, 1954

UCLA

Westwood, California

8 UCLA DAILY BRUIN Friday, May 7, 1954

'Love Thy Coach' Opens
★ ★ ★   ★ ★ ★   ★ ★ ★
Pleasant Comedy Sparks Varsity Show

BY ZENA STANTEN

Providing a thoroughly enjoyable evening of musical comedy is the 1954 student-produced Varsity Show, "Love Thy Coach."

Although getting off to a slow start, the show picks up in pace and is, on the whole, fast-moving, exhibiting a great deal of genuine and spontaneous humor.

The tale, ably written by author-director Vic Schwartz, contains clever dialogue and bright repartee to dress up the story which contributes to the overall success of the show.

Basically, "Love Thy Coach" concerns Christy Adams, the female football coach of Alkali College, Les Mitchell, an egocentric sportswriter, and a host of other assorted characters.

On the verge of an undefeated season, tragedy strikes Alkali's team. Their hearts are broken when Coach Christy starts to fall in love. The inevitable occurs as Alkali loses to the fighting Irish of Notre Dame as love conquers.

Comedy in the production ranged from subtle satire to broad humor, fortunately never becoming slapstick.

Doing an outstanding job was Carol Burnette as Coach Addams. Miss Burnette makes the show sparkle with her fresh and sincere style of acting coupled with an excellent voice and the ability to get her songs over.

Joining her on the roster of excellent performances was Leonard Weinrib who played the part of Eddie, the manager of the team. Weinrib's warm and sometimes subtle comedy adds much to the production.

In the minor roles there were several truly outstanding and humorous characterizations. Max Abrams as Mush Mouth Evans proved a master of broad comedy that could easily have been slapstick and that won the hearts of last night's audience.

Don White as the jazz man, Harry Yiff-Niff, took advantage of his small size to bring roars to Royce Hall. Milton Polsky's portrayal of Ivan the Terrible —he was Alkali's secret weapon because he ate garlic and onions — might have been a bit stereotyped but was done in such a good-hearted manner that only the comedy was remembered.

Some of the cleverest satire in the play was provided by Fred Millstein as the Poet. Cyrano could not have wished for more. Also turning in commendable performances were Alan Harris as Les Mitchell, Jeanne Tabscott as Matilda,

ALAN HARRIS AND CAROLE BURNETTE
For the Coach, a Writer

In his first leading role, Al Harris co-stars with Carol Burnett(e) in the UCLA musical *Love Thy Coach* (1954).

84

Chapter 12. 1954. Westwood

A L STARED AT THE "C" IN acting and it stared right back at him. He was furious. He'd never gotten anything lower than an "A" in his entire life. What the hell did an acting teacher know?! He crumpled the paper with the offending grade and tossed it in the trash. Then he took it out and glared at it some more. And the more he thought about it, the madder he got.

Pretty soon, that "C" started giving him nightmares. "I was destroyed," he later said. "I detested myself for failing. It was a beacon of light to remind me that I was fallible. And I didn't want to be fallible." Because he had to prove he could succeed at something he had failed in, he sought the name of a well-respected private acting coach in Hollywood. He decided to study acting privately and show the UCLA acting teacher how wrong she was.

He landed in 'Estelle Harman's Actors Workshop' alongside young actors Barbara Rush, Karen Sharpe, Jeff Hunter and Race Gentry. And he soon learned why he'd gotten that "C": "I wasn't a natural actor. My talents were math and science -- empirical subjects where a photographic memory served me well."

Estelle Harman, who was tough as nails, agreed with Al's appraisal. Her first evaluation was scathing: "Alan Harris has awkward body patterns; disturbing personal mannerisms; bad vocal habits; jerky personal business; no understanding of stage movement and is too boyish to be appealing commercially. He shows more pretense than truth; no feeling for mood or atmosphere and not enough relationship to other actors."

Al was ready to quit. But that 'C' was still haunting him. So he went back to class and worked even harder on learning to act. In his down time, he started hanging out with some of the other actors, including beautiful Diane Baker. "Our first date was at a coffee house where we sat and talked for about five hours." Meanwhile, his scenes in class continued to be pretty bad. "I forgot lines, I mumbled those I remembered. I generally floundered like an idiot and Estelle Harman continued to hammer at me." Her derisive comments only provoked him to work harder and he slowly began to improve.

A turning point came when he did a scene from "Awake and Sing," the seminal play by Clifford Odets. His partner was Suzy Zanuck, studio head Darryl Zanuck's daughter. "Suzy, like me," he later wrote, "had not yet found herself in acting and we both decided we wouldn't quit rehearsing until we had done all we could do with the scene. Suzy had to give me one good whack in the scene, and by the time we were ready to present it my

From Cowboy to Mogul to Monster

face was raw; my jaw nearly dislocated. But when we finished Estelle said, 'Now you're beginning to know what it means to act.'"

Al wasn't about to go running through the streets declaring he'd found his calling. But when he heard that the lead in the spring Varsity Show at UCLA had gotten sick and they were desperately looking for a replacement, with newly emerging confidence he decided to try out. "In my audition, I sang 'Walking My Baby Back Home' because it didn't have a great range." He sold the daylights out of the song and to his amazement, was cast as the replacement for the male lead in *Love Thy Coach,* the student-penned and produced musical comedy. It centered on a romance between Christy Adams, the female football coach of 'Alkali College' and Les Mitchell, an egocentric sportswriter.

Al was delighted to discover the talent of his energetic co-star, a young theater major named Carol Burnette (who would later achieve stardom as Carol Burnett.) Like Mark, Carol had grown up hard, working her way through school and graduating from Hollywood High School in 1951. Al learned that she was attending UCLA on a scholarship and was planning to go to New York to follow her dream to be an actress.

When they compared acting teachers Carol told him she was studying with a self-effacing coach named Jeff Corey who taught in the garage of his Hollywood Hills home. From his friends in acting class, Al knew that Corey, a black-listed former character actor, was one of the most sought-after coaches in Hollywood. He had no idea that Corey would figure in his own life in a few years' time.

Opening night of "Love Thy Coach" was May 7, 1954. Al stood in the wings of Royce Hall as strains of music from the opening number began. Suddenly, doubt froze him to the spot. He couldn't act. He couldn't sing. How could he go out there in front of 1,000 people including all of his ZBT brothers? He'd never been in a musical before. He'd never been ON STAGE before! Was he crazy? What if they laughed at him? How could he get out of this before it was too late? Then the music started. It was TOO LATE.

"A spotlight came down," he remembered, "and I started singing the romantic ballad that opened the show. But I had no time to get warmed up and my knees were shaking so hard I was sure everyone could see my pants quivering." To make matters worse, when he hit the song's highest notes his voice cracked.

"Oh God! Oh God!" he thought.

Chapter 12. 1954. Westwood

"I became catatonic. I heard snickering. Some of my frat brothers were moaning for me. To this day, when I think about that, I still get the shivers."

When he went offstage, however, one of his fellow actors gave him a nudge.

"Pull out of it. From here on, it can only get better," he advised.

Luckily, by the end of the show Al had conquered his stage fright and had gotten better. Much better. The next day, *The UCLA Daily Bruin* commended him on his performance and Carole Burnett for "her fresh and sincere style of acting." He went back to class and threw himself into scenes with renewed confidence. Over the next six months he tried directing and discovered he loved it even more than acting. Before long he was immersed in the world of theatre.

His next evaluation from Harman came in December. It praised his "marked growth in honesty and believability." She said he was "beginning to experience moments of true release and belief and to make theatrical choices." She even predicted that "his chances for commercial success will improve as he gains greater maturity."

Al read the evaluation with disbelief. He'd actually gotten praise from the great and terrible Estelle Harman? He folded the paper up and carefully stowed it in a safe place.

It made for one hell of a Christmas present.

PSO

1981 – 1983

CHAPTER THIRTEEN

December 26, 1981

Century City, California

Maggie and Mark, the Queen and King of the Cannes Film Festival.

Chapter 13. 1981. Century City

PSO's offices were typically deserted on the day after Christmas. The silence caused the rat-a-tat-tat of John's cowboy boots to echo sharply off the walls as he paced while he tried to explain his urgent call from Peter Guinness. "Apparently, right after I left London one of their stockholders stood up in a meeting and said, 'Guinness has been raped on the proverbial Hollywood casting couch for long enough!'

"What does that mean?", Mark puzzled.

"That Guinness made a pledge to their stockholders that from now on they won't be at risk in the motion picture business. In any way."

"But why would they back out now? We're the only company that's made any money for them!" It was Mark's turn to pace nervously as John perched on the edge of a desk.

"Because they make beer, not movies? I don't know. 'Seems there's a faction that said 'the hell with them, let's just close everything down.' Including PSO."

Neither man said anything for a moment. Overnight, they were losing their billion dollar 'big brother.' It seemed like colossal bad news. But Mark and John weren't giving up that easily. After talking for hours, they decided there was only one way to keep PSO going - they had to buy it back from Guinness. They worked out their negotiating position, coming up with different scenarios before John went back to London. Although it was David going up against Goliath, they believed their bid was based on sound strategy.

Before he left, John appeared in Mark's office. "What if this goes a whole different way?"

"You won't let it. You'll use your wiles," Mark replied.

"I think this negotiation needs more than that."

"What do you suggest?"

"How about the white, the pink and the blue?" John grinned.

Decades later, he explained: "We prepared three sets of cards – white, pink and blue - so we could, without thinking, switch the negotiation at a moment's notice. The white cards were for if they played it straight when they negotiated with us. The blue cards were if we had to get a little tough with Guinness. And the pink cards were for nuclear war."

John left for London in hopes that the giant Guinness Corp might not have it as together as they did. He would be there for the next three months while Mark would embark upon a month-long European sales trip to Paris, Rome, Berlin, Madrid and Zurich where he met with foreign distributors and sold eleven movies with a total budget of over $200 million. He frequently stopped off in London and went to negotiation meetings with Guinness and John. One Sunday, he and Maggie even attended a gala premiere of PSO'S Alec Guinness starrer, *Little Lord Fauntleroy* in the presence of Her Royal Highness Princess Anne before hopping on a red-eye to Los Angeles in time to arrive at the office on Monday morning.

PSO was growing, with an expanding workforce comprised of enthusiastic and savvy young up-and-comers. Some, like Vice President of Sales Kathy Cass, came from studios such as United Artists where "I wasn't allowed to change a light bulb in a lamp. I had to call somebody who had to call somebody else to do that. Everything was specialized and so was every staff member. When I got to PSO, it was the first time I really got to be creative in a business sense." Others began their film careers at PSO "where we were exposed to more aspects of the business than anything I've ever been involved with since," noted Julian Levin, whose first job was in accounting, later graduating to PSO's Vice President of Operations and then to his subsequent position as Executive Vice President of Twentieth Century Fox International Distribution. "My years at PSO were of essence to the creation of who I am today," he said decades later.

Another young accountant, Gary Barber, left his firm to join PSO (subsequently forming a company called Spyglass whose first production was *The Sixth Sense*). Twenty-two-year-old Paul Guay, a budding writer, wrote PR blurbs for the publicity department (and later co-wrote *Liar, Liar*, starring Jim Carrey.) "Because Mark encouraged/demanded that we have our fingers in many pies, I also analyzed screenplays, wrote taglines for posters, re-titled films, wrote trailers and press releases, ghost-wrote some of Mark's bylined articles for the trades, etc. etc."

As John fought Guinness for ownership of the company, exciting growth was afoot at PSO. But the pace was a killer and it left Mark little time for his growing family – Jon, a toddler and Maggie, who was pregnant again and due in April.

Maggie accompanied Mark often, even when it meant traveling with Jon and a suitcase-full of diapers. In city after city, they wined and dined the close-knit 'family' of foreign distributors. Mark marveled at the amount of time Maggie dedicated to get to know all of the distributors' wives and the distributors themselves. "I would always find something special about them," she explained, "something they loved. I would listen to them carefully and bingo, it would always present itself." "Most distributors liked me," Mark explained, "but they *loved* Maggie." While Mark could be

Chapter 13. 1981. Century City

intimidating, Maggie was warm and gracious, genuine and funny. Perhaps most importantly, whenever she was by Mark's side she always made him laugh and distributors liked to see the lighthearted side of the man who usually out-negotiated them.

"Maggie, not to be minimized, has always been a sensational partner for Mark," agreed Bobby Meyers. "She has always been one of Mark's greatest assets," producer David Saunders concurred. "Because she keeps him level, because she's totally wonderful and charming and people just like her. She puts people at their ease and makes it easier to move from a business relationship to more than a business relationship. She's the whole package."

As much as Mark sold PSO he also sold their persona. All of the distributors and their wives knew the mystical, magical tale of how they met. How, in a remarkably short time, they became MarkandMaggie, MaggieandMark. Plus, he was handsome. She was beautiful. To many, they seemed like fairy tale characters.

The truth lay somewhere beneath the fairy tale.

While they were still very much in love, "I sacrificed a lot in those years," Maggie later revealed. "For one thing, I didn't see Mark a lot and when he was with us he couldn't be bothered with the kids' fussing. Sometimes, if any of us made a noise, he got mad. I grew to understand he wasn't blowing off steam at us, he was just saying, 'Let me finish my thoughts. Don't interrupt my thinking process.' But it was very hard."

Mark was at the Los Angeles Film Festival when *Das Boot* opened in the U.S. "We weren't sure how Americans would react to a sympathetic film about the Germans, especially in a city with a large Jewish population." His fears were reinforced when the audience applauded the opening caption saying that 30,000 of 40,000 German submariners were lost in the war. However, when the film ended, the audience gave the film a standing ovation. John, meanwhile, was in London concluding the negotiations. It was a moment of triumph when the two men took back the company from Guinness.

A personal moment of triumph came for Mark and Maggie on April 19, when they welcomed a daughter, Alexis Rose, in the world.

Chapter Fourteen

February 11, 1983

Hollywood, California

Chapter 14. 1983. Beverly Hills

Mark was in the kitchen when he got the call. As soon as he hung up he yelled to Maggie. "Nine Academy Award nominations!"

"For what?!"

"Six for *Das Boot*! Three more for *La Traviata*!"

She screamed with excitement. Mark dialed John in Munich where it was 3:00 AM. After John sleepily answered he woke up Kate. "And we starting dancing around the room, screaming," she recalled years later.

Word spread fast. *Das Boot* had received more nominations than any other foreign language film in Academy Award history - for Best Cinematography, Best Director, Best Effects, Best Film Editing, Best Sound, and Best Screenplay Based on Material from Another Medium.

Wolfgang Petersen was astounded when Mark called him. "When we first screened *Das Boot* in the U.S. we were so nervous. After all, we were showing it to the enemy. But we saw that audiences in the U.S. felt it right away, they understood the humanistic anti-war message." Now, to be lauded with *six* Academy Award nominations - it was beyond his wildest imagination.

Congratulations starting pouring into PSO. From Italy, where Zeffirelli was overwhelmed by the nominations for *La Traviata*. From Hollywood, where "Triumph" (the small division of Columbia Pictures whose first release was *Das Boot*) took out full page ads in the trades. From England, Germany, France, Japan, Australia, where the international family of distributors rejoiced in his success as one of their own.

Mark spent a short time resting on his laurels. Then he got down to the business of "selling" the two movies to the 5,000 voting members of the Academy of Motion Picture Arts and Sciences. He rented theatres to show *Das Boot* and *La Traviata* to every Academy Member he could get. He ceaselessly lobbied for votes, schmoozing everyone he knew in Hollywood and plenty he didn't. Then it was March 29.

Mark, Maggie, John, Kate and Wolfgang stepped out of their limo and paraded down the red carpet alongside Hollywood royalty. They sat amongst 2,900 people in the Dorothy Chandler Pavilion. Maggie sat on one side of Mark; John was on the other.

The all-time top-rated Oscar telecast drew close to 81 million viewers in the U.S. It droned on, overlong as usual and with the usual gaffes. After Matt Dillon and Kristy McNichol mangled the names of the short film nominees, they clowned for the camera to cover their embarrassment.

Maggie whispered in Mark's ear. Actors…" she said, with a knowing smile.

"So dramatic," Mark whispered back.

"Look who's talking," Maggie retorted.

And they both laughed.

Al Harris/Mark Damon

1954

Chapter Fifteen

September, 1954

Hollywood, California

Alan Harris (1954) posing as Nikolai Rostov in De Laurentiis' *War and Peace*. The role was his to lose. And he did.

MARK DAMON

A BACHELOR PICKS HIS FAVORITE GIRLS

Susan Kohner: "She's one of the most feminine girls I know. She has a love of life."

Tuesday Weld: "She's a live, electric person; flirtatious and capricious; appealing."

Diane Baker: "Like the wind, she wants to be everywhere. She's loving, but not aggressive."

Diane Varsi: "She is bright and dedicated; really loves people, hates anything phony."

by JACK HOLLAND

From Cowboy to Mogul to Monster

Onstage at the Players Ring Theatre Al was holding in his laughter as it bubbled up inside him, threatening to explode any minute. "Don't laugh," he ordered himself silently. *"Don't laugh!"* He was onstage in front of a packed house in his first professional stage role, playing opposite Pippa Scott, an emotional actress in an emotional play. They were in a scene where they stood very close to each other and Pippa had just delivered a line with great excitement. And spit right in his eye.

Now, Al was struggling to hold back his laughter and deliver his line when he heard a guy in the audience say to his wife, "Did you see that? She spit right in that kid's eye."

He lost it.

There he was, in a theatre-in-the round where everyone in the audience could see everything. Laughing like a loon while poor Pippa was crying buckets. It was a *bad* moment. Until he remembered, somewhere in his desperation, that when you're laughing it almost seems like you're crying. So he turned his laughter into tears, crying so hard he was practically howling. Pippa was surprised by his reaction but at least they finished the scene without Al disgracing himself completely.

He had come a long way in a short time. He had learned enough about acting to be in a professional production at The Players Ring, a popular little showcase theatre where many actors (including Jack Nicholson) got their start. He had gotten headshots and a resume. He had even secured an agent, an eighteen-year-old kid named Norman Brokaw who became the first mail boy in the William Morris Agency mailroom at the age of fifteen (and would someday become Chairman of the William Morris Agency.) He had also signed with a headstrong PR agent named Helen Ferguson who would have great influence on his career.

She was already planting stories about him in Mike Connolly's *Rambling Reporter* column in *The Hollywood Reporter:* "Al Harris, a good-looking lad discovered in the kiddy playground on La Cienega by Groucho Marx three years ago, gets the Big Break September 23 as a lead in "Pick-Up Girl" at the Players Ring. He's been supporting himself by selling contest answers to contestants."

Variety praised him for giving an "impressive portrayal of a sensitive young violinist marked for a tragic fate." *Los Angeles Times* singled him out as "a very talented boy with fine emotional resources." A female reporter for *NewsLife* gushed, "Alan Harris as Peter is a very good looking boy who registers quickly and reminds me of a young Rock Hudson. Being of romantic inclinations, he may be the answer to the scarcity of leading men in this town."

It was heady stuff but Al had little time to congratulate himself. Aside from his full course load at UCLA and nightly appearances onstage he was still taking acting classes with Estelle Harman. And he was increasingly frustrated with what he felt was his lack of technique. "In 'Pickup Girl,' I had a scene where I was supposed to be upset but I couldn't find the emotion. I would run around the block before going on in order to get breathless and appear agitated in the scene." In another scene, his inability to summon up tears onstage was very discouraging. Especially since Pippa Scott (who would soon garner a Theatre World Award on Broadway) could cry buckets. The smart-looking, reddish haired actress with the unusual name was the daughter of a noted screenwriter and had trained at the Royal Academy of Dramatic Arts (RADA) in London. She had the techniques Al felt he lacked.

Night after night, he tried to produce tears with offstage tricks like cutting onions and rubbing them under his eyes. Until one night, fifteen seconds after he came out on stage, he heard an audience member ask, "Do you smell onions?" Next he tried gargling with Listerine until it burned his throat and tears would start. But he felt pretty silly, backstage in his first professional gig, gargling away until he cried.

He had noticed that one of the older actors, Joe Flynn, was able to cry on cue every night. When he asked how he did it, Joe showed him his trick. He had a little sponge inside his hat where he put a bit of glycerin. When he took his hat off onstage he squeezed the sponge just a little, a bit of the glycerin came down into his eyes and it made him cry. Al was grateful for the older actor's generosity although he couldn't use the trick because his character was hatless. "And it turned out that Joe Flynn didn't show me because he was being kind. He was after me."

He wasn't the only one.

Al was growing into his looks and becoming more and more handsome. He modeled men's fashions in the *LA Times* and swimsuits for magazine ads. He was pictured in casuals, sipping a Pepsi and leaning against a tree with an insouciant air. Next he landed a small part on *Light's Diamond Jubilee*, a TV show that celebrated the 75th anniversary of the electric light. He played opposite a young blond actress named Kim Novak in her first appearance, directed by King Vidor for David O. Selznick.

Soon afterwards he heard that Vidor was directing *War and Peace*. Al was thrilled when he was sent up by his agent for the role of Nikolai

From Cowboy to Mogul to Monster

Rostov. "Dino De Laurentiis was producing and when he met me, he said, 'Okay, you're cast.'" But Al wanted the role so badly that he couldn't leave it at that. He kept pushing De Laurentiis to ask King Vidor about him reminding Dino that he'd just worked for Vidor in a TV show. He wanted to make sure he really had the part. He would later hear that De Laurentiis said to King Vidor, "I'm casting Alan Harris as Nikolai and he keeps telling me he worked with you already. How was he?"

"Alan Harris?" Vidor replied, "Oh, no. He's too inexperienced, much too stiff."

Al's pushiness cost him the role. Although it killed him he refused to give up. He read "War and Peace" over and over, rented costumes to portray various scenes as Nikolai, even hired a photographer to shoot him in different poses in different scenes. He was obsessed with being in *War and Peace* but it didn't matter. He wasn't cast.

He was learning how little power he had as an actor and was drawn to directing where he had more control. Then his acting career got another break – both he and Pippa were cast in *Speaking to Hannah,* a CBS Authors Playhouse production for television. The show starred Ethel Waters of the successful TV series, *Beulah* and the movie, *The Member of the Wedding.* Working with Waters, a terrific performer and only the second African-American actress to be nominated for an Academy Award, was inspiring. Playing opposite Pippa Scott again was challenging and rewarding. By the time the production was over Alan Harris felt he was becoming a real actor.

Pretty soon he would have to become someone else.

When he tried to join the Screen Actors Guild he found out there already was an 'Alan Harris' on the roster and there couldn't be two SAG actors with the same name. (Ironically, the other 'Alan Harris' wasn't really 'Alan Harris.' He had adopted the name as his professional moniker.) Still, Al had to find another name.

After some thought, he decided to become 'Cliff Towers.' He figured it had the same rhythm as other actors in the '50's - Rock Hudson or Tab Hunter or Race Gentry - a one syllable first name, a two syllable last name. When Helen Ferguson thought 'Cliff Towers' "sounded like a pansy" he went back to the drawing board, trying out different combinations of names on his brother, his mother, Helen, his friends.

One day he came up with 'Mark Damon.' 'Mark' came from his middle name, Marvin; 'Damon' from the story of Damon and Pythias because he wanted something classical sounding. Plus, Mark was one syllable and Damon had two like Hudson, Hunter and Gentry.

Thorough as ever, Al devised a sixteen-point test for the name and gave it to his friends and family to take. Some of the questions were: Is it clear and concrete? Is it easily transmitted in introductions, in ordinary conversation, over a loudspeaker system (as in 'Mark Damon's car, please') and over the telephone? Does it have distinction combined with commercial value?

When everyone answered 'yes' to all sixteen questions, Al Harris became 'Mark Damon.'

PSO

1983

Chapter Sixteen

April 3, 1983

Century City, California

Mark and the sales team at PSO's unique Edmond Cara conference table. Left to right: Pattie Zimmerman, Pierre Kalfon, Keith Turner, Janet Fleming, Mark, Arianne Ulmer Cipes, Gregory Cascante, Phil Franzel.

Mark in front of chart showing films PSO was selling that year including *The NeverEnding Story* (1984), *Cotton Club* (1984), *Silkwood* (1983), and *The Outsiders* (1983).

Chapter 16. 1983. Century City

'Mark Damon's PSO.' That was how the company was known in Hollywood and after the Academy Awards it was garnering much more acceptance. Mark was also gaining attention as a smart and savvy businessman known for his charm. But on the Friday after the Oscars he wasn't feeling very charming as his Prada-loafered foot tapped restlessly beneath the redwood conference table.

"Got it?" Mark asked Janet Dammann.

"685," she nodded without skipping a beat.

"Wait a minute," protested Gregory Cascante, madly calculating on his calculator.

It was business as usual at the Friday morning staff meeting.

Every Friday at 9:30 AM, Mark, John and the sales team met around the PSO conference table, a one-of-a-kind piece carved by a maverick. It was the perfect table for PSO - a free-form redwood surface mounted onto a giant wooden-dollar-sign base. That table had been the scene of countless meetings, brainstorming sessions, arguments, discussions and endless jostling for position by the dozens of smart young people who proudly called themselves members of the 'PSO family.' They were mostly women. "The fact that the company was primarily female was a further irritant to the male-dominated world of the studios," Mark gloated years later.

He and John hired female lawyers, accountants and sales people. They promoted women to Vice-Presidents and had an entirely female distribution department. In the 1980's, at a time when women were banging their heads against the glass ceiling, PSO was a place where capable women were hired and inspired to rise to the top.

"Frankly, I think women make much better executives than men," Mark explained. "They multi-task in a way that no man does, they best men in negotiations that men think they've won, they combine their business savvy with compassion and they are not afraid to show their emotions but know how to control them. Women also work harder, longer and better. They're willing to subjugate their egos for the good of the cause and are pretty selfless in terms of the amount of time they put in." Diane Slattery, who described PSO as her 'college,' agreed: "After graduating from high school I found myself working for the office manager. After one month, I was stolen by the sales department. Probably because I had no limits on the amount of time I was willing to commit to the work."

Mark admitted there were other reasons he was glad to be around so many women: "It made me feel good to have bright, attractive young women who were there to carry forward my cause." "Let's face it," laughed Reiko Bradley, a Eurasian beauty whom Mark later trained in sales, "Mark is a very charming man and he loves women, like a lot of Italian men do." Maggie: "I used to get jealous and say, 'Why are you always looking at beautiful women?' It took a while till I understood it was kind of an innocent thing with him. It was a by-product of his Roman days." Reiko: "Mark actually likes and respects women who are strong and intelligent, unlike a lot of men who are intimidated by us."

Because of its attractive female staff PSO became known as the *Charlie's Angels* of the independent film business, hardly a disadvantage in a town built on glitz and glamour. The company was also known for delivering the goods. In the burgeoning independent film world of the '80s PSO was setting the standard for sales, production, marketing, distribution, publicity and delivery. "It was an amazing company at an incredible time," Julian Levin later reflected. "It's really a snapshot of a certain period in the industry." "It was such a high-flying market," Reiko recalled, "we couldn't make movies fast enough and buyers were getting into fights over them. Things were selling like hotcakes."

In order to sell their movies the PSO family worked together, played together, traveled together. They rehearsed sales pitches until late into the night. Everybody had to read every script, had to know all the creative components. Nobody ever went home early and nobody really wanted to. "Sure, it was killer work. Sure, there were people grumbling and carrying on about this, that and the other thing. But we were given license to make it up as we went along and we were learning and creating something new," recalled curly-haired Eddie Kalish, who became PSO's Marketing Director after working for Paramount and UA. "We were proud to be associated with the company that was so different from the studios, the one that everyone was calling the crown jewel," recalled Paul Guay.

PSOers might come to work in blue jeans but they were highly motivated. "They were known as the best and the brightest in the business," said John, "and along with that came competitiveness and some mighty big egos." Now, as Mark waited impatiently at the conference table, Gregory Cascante, one of the 'best and brightest' was scowling at his calculator.

Every week, Mark arrived at 9:00 for the 9:30 meeting; closely followed by Janet Damman, who had a mane of salt and pepper hair, a raspy voice and was Mark's favorite numbers person. Then the sales team trickled in: Gregory Cascante, known as "Mr.-I'm-the-smartest-guy-in-the-world"; VP of International Sales Kathy Cass, Kate, Arianne Cipes, Janet Fleming, Eleanor Powell. Last was John, who slid into his seat at 9:29. "And every week when we came in," he recalled, "Mark and Janet were tossing complicated calculations back and forth. Numbers they'd figured out in their heads. They did it just to put Gregory on edge. And every week it worked."

Now, Gregory Cascante was feverishly working on his calculator.

"Can't we move on?" pleaded the others.

"Wait a minute, I've got it! It's..." He frowned at his calculator as if it had played a trick on him. Everyone waited until Cascante, disappointed, looked up.

"It's... 685."

"Of course," Mark said dryly.

The meeting had begun.

As usual, Mark sat at the head of the table, the king in his kingdom. Randal Kleiser, who would soon direct *Flight of the Navigator* observed: "He always held court at the end of that table, like he was playing Louis B. Mayer. Then again, he was an actor so I guess he was acting like the head of a big studio." "It took me a long time not to be totally intimidated by Mark," remarked an ex-PSOer. "He had a presence that made me not want to say the wrong thing. Not that he ever yelled or anything. I just wanted to do the right thing for him." "Mark had a very commanding presence," agreed another ex-PSOer. "At the same time, he was somebody who inspired respect."

Most PSOers respected Mark from the moment he interviewed them. "I remember sitting in Mark's office in Century City for my interview," recalled ex-PSOer Michael Heuser, a well-spoken young man who had been trained at Paramount. "It was a relatively intimidating meeting because Mark Damon and John Hyde, in particular, are very aggressive individuals. They asked countless questions and the interview went on for ever and ever."

"When I interviewed potential salespeople," Mark recalled, "I would have them read a script, pitch me the picture, then try to sell it to me for a certain amount of money. I would argue as if I was the buyer and negotiate to see how good they were. Then I would give all the reasons, as a buyer, why the price wasn't right to see how they would respond. And I made sure they understood how to calculate distribution fees for the different territories." The process took about an hour and a half and Mark would see candidates more than once, giving them homework to do in between. He might interview ten or fifteen people to get one.

But for all of the rigors he put them through, sometimes he was surprisingly forgiving. "One guy gave me a pitch that should last about five minutes but took forty-five minutes. He told me the whole script from beginning to end instead of giving me the basic story, the highlights and one or two scenes that were interesting. But he was so nervous and he'd worked so hard on it that I didn't have the heart to tell him what he should have done."

Other times, he was not so magnanimous. PSOers sensed that beneath his imperious veneer was a 1000 kilowatt bullshit detector. "He knew when you were telling the truth," confirmed an ex-PSOer, "and he knew when you weren't. Even if he said nothing, you always knew that he knew." "My father is very intuitive," Alexis Damon confirmed decades later. "He'll always notice when something's off and ask about it. Even when he's busy with what he's doing he's aware of what is going on."

"He does not suffer fools well," Reiko summed up. "The thing with Mark is, he can zone in on weaker people. If someone doesn't seem bright enough to get it, he can be scary or intimidating." Paul Guay recalled a staff meeting where Mark asked a staffer to do something and the person was giving all the reasons why it couldn't be done. "After he listened for a minute Mark said, 'I don't want to know why it can't be done. I want you to do it.'" Diane Slattery agreed: "You learned quickly that you didn't just come to him with the problem. You had to come with one or more solutions."

He could be very daunting. "But I don't try to be intimidating. I think that sometimes I come off that way when I'm thinking of something while they're talking," Mark chuckled. "Mark has unusual eyes," Reiko commented. "He has a way of looking at people and you can't quite tell what he's thinking. I think that makes some people feel uncertain and that he's intimidating. But if you keep up with him, if you are right there with him and give him responses that make sense, it's fine. I think that's why we actually got along, because I enjoyed the challenge of always being forced to do my best."

"I feel the way to get the most out of people is to stimulate them to do things on their own and to make their own mistakes. So I gave PSOers a lot of leeway, which is how they grew," Mark explained. Michael Heuser agreed. "I learned a huge amount from him. Mark didn't sit me down in a room and say this is how it's done – I don't think he does that – but it's watch and learn. At the time, a lot of us were very, very young and very impressionable. And so if you were smart, you watched and learned. And the more he saw that you paid attention, I suppose, the more attention he would grant you."

Next to Mark at the Friday morning meeting sat John Hyde, with his easy laugh and 'country boy' manner. He still wore jeans and cowboy boots to the office but all of the PSOers knew that he was smart as a whip. "John Hyde was the great administrator," recalled Heuser. "He could always remember deals to the number and the date when they happened." Kathy Cass regarded him as incredibly decent: "If you had a problem, you could go in and chat with John. He'd always ask, 'What do you need?' You'd lay out your problem and after he came up with suggestions, John would smile and say, 'I'm sure you'll make the right decision.' And if you *didn't* make the right decision, you never heard him talk about it again. That's John."

John, typically modest, was fond of saying there were only two things they needed to make PSO successful: "Cash and/or credit and Mark's sales ability." But Mark knew the business also depended on John's brilliance at business and finance, his creativity in problem-solving and his knack for winning high-level negotiations while maintaining his "good ol' boy" image.

PSO was built on the strengths of both men whose styles were as different as night and day. "They were two very, very smart men who were experts in their particular fields and they did different things 24/7. They were partners and best friends and they complemented each other in a very interesting and beautiful way," observed Michael Heuser.

"We were brothers," Mark and John agreed.

"If I went to the bathroom during a negotiation and came back to find Mark part-way through a sentence, I could finish it," said John.

"If someone had a question for John and talked to me," Mark attested, "I wouldn't have to call him to ask what John would say. I knew what his answer would be. And when the tables were turned, he knew what mine would be."

"We never had arguments, disagreements or screaming sessions. We never had any of the strife that other partners had," both declared. And PSOers counted on their bosses getting along.

"There was this small cadre of people running the company - Mark and John, basically, and Kate and Gregory Cascante and Kathy Cass," said

Kevin Koloff, who joined PSO as in house-attorney in 1983. "And these people appeared, from the perspective of people like me, to be *great* friends. They had dinners together, they went to visit each other—they just seemed to be this fantastic bunch of smart, talented people who loved what they were doing and really liked each other."

In addition to his masterful manner, PSOers also knew that Mark loved to laugh. "My Dad is a goofball," laughed his son, Jon, years later. "He's a lot goofier than any stranger can imagine." "No matter what, whenever Mark was in a social environment, even though he was always keeping his eyes and ears open for things, he was really entertaining," agreed an ex-PSOer.

PSOers also found eating with Mark to be an adventure. Because he knew that much of the staff favored meat-and-potatoes he was fond of taking them to a restaurant, ordering sea urchins for everyone and daring people to try them. "I liked to order exotic dishes for them to try. Partly because I wanted to try them myself. Partly because I enjoyed watching their shock as they were served tripe, lung and heart, goat's brains, bull's balls, lamb tongue. Whatever."

On one such night Michael Heuser looked up from what he was eating.

"What's this?," he asked Mark.

"Why? Is it good?"

"It's okay. What is it?"

"Criadillas."

Heuser looked puzzled. "What does that mean?"

Mark started to laugh. "Let's just say that every time you eat two of them there's one less bull in the world." Heuser gagged and ran to the bathroom to spit it out. All the other PSOers suddenly looked down at their plates with dismay.

It was vintage Damon.

Chapter Seventeen

April 22, 1983

Beverly Hills, California

The NeverEnding Story (1984).

John, Maggie, Mark and Kate at Mark's 50th birthday party.

Chapter 17. 1983. Cannes

It wasn't the pounding rain that woke Mark at five o'clock on the morning of his 50th birthday. He always woke up when Maggie and the kids were still asleep. When the phone wasn't ringing off the hook and the world was quiet. It was the best time to read scripts.

In the quiet, dark bedroom he changed into sweats, grabbed the top script from a large stack and padded down to the kitchen to fire up the Pasquini espresso machine. While he waited for his macchiato he looked out at the hard, driving rain and noted that it was an unusual storm for late April. Then he forgot all about the weather as he settled on the couch to make notes on scenes from the latest draft of the shooting script for *The NeverEnding Story*.

The film was a fantasy fairy tale somewhere between *Alice in Wonderland* and *The Lord of the Rings*. It centered on the quest of a lonely young boy named Bastian who explores Fantasia through a book he steals, *The NeverEnding Story*. As Bastian reads about a young warrior named Atreyu who is trying to save Fantasia from destruction by the Nothing, he realizes that he is part of the story and that only he has the power to save Fantasia.

The movie had started principal photography a few weeks earlier at Munich's Bavaria Studios under Wolfgang Petersen's direction. For months prior, the best special effects experts in England had been hard at work designing creatures such as a swarm-headed monster named Uyulala and a werewolf named Gmork. Meanwhile the original budget of $13 million had swelled to $21 million.

The previous Fall, Mark had committed to raise $8 million of that budget at MIFED, money that wasn't due until production was well underway. Now, even though the film had only been shooting for a month it was hemorrhaging money. In order for production to continue he had to make critical sales on the balance of the unsold territories in Cannes, just a few weeks away. And to do that he needed to sell it to an American distributor, for which he needed a terrific script.

He had worked with author Michael Ende on the first draft, making sure it was close to his best-selling book. Director Wolfgang Petersen collaborated on the next draft with Herman Weigel, with Mark constantly trying to get it closer to U.S. tastes. But he was still not satisfied. Enter young PSOer Paul Guay. "I had been working at PSO for a few years, writing marketing, advertising and publicity material when Mark came to me," Guay related years later. "We need a polish on a script," Mark said. "It reads like it was translated from the German. Would you be interested

From Cowboy to Mogul to Monster

in turning this into idiomatic English?" "It was the first time I actually got my hands on a screenplay," Guay later recalled. He figured he would have two weeks to do the polish. "You have 36 hours Mark corrected." Guay pulled the only all-nighter in his life and polished the whole thing.

Now, as dawn broke on the blustery morning of his birthday, Mark was making notes on a troublesome scene of that script. When thunder and lightning lit up the sky he looked out for a moment. And went back to his reading.

In their bedroom, Maggie woke to a clap of thunder. She looked out at the pouring rain, her heart pounding. Tonight was Mark's 50th birthday party, a surprise she had been planning for months with Kate. They had arranged for it to be held in Producer Bob Evans' beautiful back yard.

"Now what?" Maggie wondered miserably as lightning lit up the sky and the rain fell in sheets.

By ten o'clock, Mark was stepping off the elevator into PSO's offices on the fifteenth floor. By ten o'clock, Maggie and Kate had called twenty alternative restaurants for Mark's birthday bash and struck out with all of them.

Mark, ignorant of the goings-on, called John in Washington, D.C. to update him on PSO business. They talked about a small announcement they both had seen in the trades: Delphi Film Associates, a limited partnership formed by Columbia to provide financing for 15-20 pictures in 1984, had completed funding. "And it won't stop there," proclaimed general partner Lewis J. Korman.

"That would be ideal, wouldn't it?", John speculated.

"To get Delphi to finance PSO-produced pictures?," Mark answered, finishing his sentence. "Definitely."

Neither man was aware that Lew Korman was simultaneously keeping a file on PSO, waiting for the right opportunity to meet with them.

It rained so hard that all the canyons started flooding, including the one where Evans lived. Meanwhile, neither Maggie nor Kate had found a place for the party. At the eleventh hour, Maggie finally got a 'yes' from the Princess Restaurant, around the corner from PSO's office. Then she and Kate frantically called 150 guests to let them know of the change.

Mark came home from work, exhausted. "Let's not go out for dinner," he said as he flopped onto the bed. "Can't we just celebrate at home?"

"Are you kidding?" Maggie retorted. "Of course we're going out. This is a big birthday and we're going to celebrate it."

Chapter 17. 1983. Cannes

"Alright," Mark said. "But I'm going in jeans since it's only the two of us."

Maggie feigned outrage. "It's not important enough for you to dress up for me? You have to, Mark, we should be all dressed up and gorgeous. This is your 50th birthday, for heaven's sake." Mark grumbled.

Maggie finally cajoled him into wearing a tux and enticed him to the Princess Restaurant in Century City. They walked through the dining room where Mark saw his friends Michael Eliasberg and Alan Salke sitting at tables.

"Look who's here," he told Maggie, waving hello.

When he saw four more friends, he remarked, "Isn't it amazing that so many of our friends happen to be at this restaurant tonight?"

Maggie started to laugh and the light bulb lit. All of the PSOers came out of a back room festooned in black and white balloons. Bob Evans wrapped Mark in a bear hug; Dick Clark and his wife offered congrats; David Begelman, Richard and Lauren Donner, Paul Kohner, Terry Semel and Andy Vanja wished him well. Mark beamed. He was only lamenting that his partner was in Washington when John showed up, straight from the airport.

Later that night Eddie Kalish roasted Mark well and thoroughly. Kate screened clips from his old movies that ended on Mark's line from a TV show with June Allyson: "Sometimes I feel like I'm a God." Everyone laughed at the cockiness of the 22-year-old actor. They all agreed he hadn't changed one iota.

"What do we need from Japan for *The Day After*?" Kathy Cass asked Mark at the next Friday morning sales meeting. The Cannes Festival was starting in a week and a grid chart was prominently displayed on an easel, listing 42 territories across the top, eleven movies down the side. As movies found distributors at the Festival, a blue dot would be placed on the grid signifying that the territory had been sold. "By the end of Cannes," Mark told his people, "I want blue dots to cover every box in the grid – no white spaces allowed!"

Mark wanted to target what they needed to close in presales on Francis Ford Coppola's *The Outsiders* (starring Matt Dillon, Tom Cruise, Rob Lowe, Emilio Estevez, Patrick Swayze, Ralph Macchio, C. Thomas Howell and Diane Lane.) Instead, his secretary, Carole Sue Lipman, told him that Jack Valenti was on the phone.

Valenti, the venerable chairman of the Motion Picture Association of America, was a legendary figure in Hollywood. Everyone knew that in the 1960's his PR agency was in charge of press during President Kennedy's visit to Houston. And that Valenti was riding in the motorcade when Kennedy was assassinated. They also knew that he had resigned his post as White House Assistant to President Lyndon Johnson to become the leader of the MPAA in 1966. By 1983, the powerful and well-connected Valenti had presided over the organization for almost twenty years. He was a man to whom others often turned for help. Now Valenti was the one in a jam. And he was calling to see if Mark could get him out of it.

"Did you know that I'm working with the chairman of the Moscow Film Festival?" he asked.

"No, I didn't."

Valenti explained that the slogan of the 1983 festival was "for humanism in cinema and for peace and friendship between nations. Which makes Hollywood's participation in the Moscow Film Festival all the more important."

Mark knew that all the studios had boycotted the Moscow Festival for the past few years. For good reason, from what he'd heard. "After the Festival, apparently the Russians kept films that studios brought over, claiming they had gotten lost or that they shipped them back and didn't know where they were," said Kate. "Then, after studio execs went home, word came back that the Russians were showing them in theaters that ran 24 hours a day, held 6,000 people and paid no royalties." So Mark wasn't surprised when Valenti unhappily pointed out that although 103 countries had entries in the Festival there was not a single one from the United States. Then the MPAA chairman delivered a shocker.

"Since all the studios are boycotting it why don't you give them your pictures and make it a PSO Festival?"

It was a completely unexpected idea. "And a perfect example of how PSO fit into the picture," Mark would later reflect. "There were the majors. And there was PSO. If the studios wouldn't play ball with the Russians, Valenti knew PSO could give them studio quality pictures." The next morning, Mark called back with good news: he and John would go to Moscow personally, with their wives, and deliver a full slate of PSO movies in different categories to the Festival. It was a win for everyone. Valenti saw the egg on his face disappearing. Mark knew that PSO would get a PR

Chapter 17. 1983. Cannes

blitz out of it. Maggie and Kate were jazzed about going. First, however, Mark had to sell *The NeverEnding Story* worldwide at Cannes to plug up the holes in production costs.

As the Festival neared he and John had late-night meetings to calculate exactly how much Mark had to sell. They arranged for John to be standing by in New York, ready to work with the banks as soon as Mark made the sales. "*NeverEnding Story* was financed with our stomach linings," John later quipped. "That movie almost put us out of business. The production was literally eating up money."

When he got to Cannes Mark focused on the task at hand. John: "He was calling me each day and telling me what sales were in place. Finally, with the contracts he had, I flew to Munich to be there on Monday morning to free up the funds so Wolfgang could continue shooting. I literally got off the plane, went to the bank with Eichinger on Monday morning, signed the documents so it went into the drop account, got back on a plane, went to France and collapsed for two days. I think we'd been around the clock for a week by then. That was one of our really great close calls."

"They call Mark Damon 'The King of Cannes,'" wrote *The New York Times,* "but he'll tell you not to envy him the champagne and actresses and all-night parties at the annual Cannes Film Festival. 'Strictly business,' he says: 'As long as all that so-called glamour translates into a healthy bottom line, I'm happy.'" Ever the actor, Mark never let reporters see how stressed he really was.

While his tension was nowhere in evidence PSO's presence was everywhere you looked. Scorsese's *King of Comedy* inaugurated the new Palais du Cinema; three-story banners for Sean Connery in *Never Say Never Again* adorned the Majestic Hotel; ads in the trades for Sergio Leone's *Once Upon a Time in America* and Coppola's *The Outsiders* proclaimed PSO "A Major Force in International Distribution and Marketing." Mark was also selling *The Day After*, the first major TV movie to deal with the aftermath of a nuclear attack.

Months earlier, Brandon Stoddard, head of ABC motion pictures, had called Mark to his office. "This is a picture for television. It's called 'The Day After.'" He threw the script on the desk. "Take a read and see what you think. I don't think it's for movie theaters but you're the expert."

Mark: "I read the script that night and was moved by the intensity and importance of its message. I also felt that audiences around the world would be curious to know what could happen the day after an H-Bomb exploded." The next morning he went back to see Stoddard.

"I think this could be a very important picture for theatrical audiences overseas," Mark said with excitement.

"I don't know," Stoddard countered. "If I give it to our television partners around the world we'll get at least $1 million for it. What do you think you can do with your foreign distributors?"

"No less than $1 and-a-half million."

Stoddard looked Mark in the eye.

"I'm depending on you. If you don't get it, it's your ass… and mine too."

"Trust me," he retorted.

At Cannes, Mark sold the theatrical rights to "The Day After" around the world. For $9 million.

Chapter Eighteen

May 2, 1983

Century City, California

Richard and Lauren Schuler Donner, Unidentified,
Bob Evans and Mark.

PSO team at 'Camp Cannes'. Back row: Mark, Gregory Cascante.
Middle: Eddie Kalish, Kathy Cass, Pattie Zimmerman, Julian
Levin, Eleanor Powell. Front: Barbara Dibbs.

Forbes

How an actor whose career was going nowhere turned into a businessman who knocked the major studios on their ears.

Ronald Reagan is not the only actor who made good

By Ellen Paris

THEY CALL MARK DAMON "The King of Cannes." But he'll tell you not to envy him the champagne and actresses and all-night parties at the annual Cannes Film Festival. Strictly business, he says: "As long as all that so-called glamour translates into a healthy bottom line, I'm happy." Damon (born Alan Harris), an actor turned businessman, has plenty to be happy about these days. In seven years his Los Angeles-based Producers Sales Organization (PSO) has grown from nothing into a power that is equal to the Hollywood major studios in the distribution overseas of independently produced American pictures.

What usually happens is that the producer turns his film over to the distribution arm of a major studio, which handles the overseas and domestic marketing in return for a nice piece of the gross, say 40%. In 1982 Hollywood's ten largest movie companies chalked up gross foreign rentals of around $760 million among them. But upstart PSO now offers the independents an alternative distribution channel. PSO's pictures earned $76 million in foreign rentals last year. Its commissionable revenues for producers were $53.6 million. PSO's gross share of those revenues was $7.4 million, leaving PSO with a net profit of $3.1 million and this year should be even better. Damon owns 60%, and John Hyde, his vice chairman, owns the rest.

Damon, then 26, got off to a good start in 1959 when he won a role in *The Fall of the House of Usher*, opposite Vincent Price. In 1961 he moved to Rome and eventually acted in 41 European films. Mostly it was a diet of spaghetti Westerns and action-adventure movies, brightened by *The Longest Day*. Damon earned a decent living, and the lira was cheap. But he wasn't on the international superstar track.

So in 1975 Damon, then 41, quit

John Hyde (left) and Mark Damon
Good independent distributors are key.

FORBES, FEBRUARY 27, 1984

From Cowboy to Mogul to Monster

IT TOOK THESE INGREDIENTS: PLENTY OF money, some smoke and mirrors and a lot of extraordinarily colorful characters. When you mixed them all together you got the indie film business of the '80's. It was a time when the independent buyer and the independent seller were in economic good health. When Mark could sell a movie on a pitch and make a deal in the hallway on a handshake. When a buyer didn't have to read the script or know who was in the film to commit. When there were no Wall Street characters looking over your shoulder when you made your deals.

It was the '80's. The decade when bumper stickers declared, "the guy with the most toys wins." When colorful, one-of-a-kind mavericks like Mark and Menachem Golan and Yoram Globus of Cannon Films and Mario Kassar and Andy Vajna of Carolco built indie empires based on talent, confidence and charisma. It was a decade when independent film companies had dramatic, quick rises to success and even more dramatic downfalls, ending in bankruptcies and ignominy. It was the time some called the decade of greed. Others called it reprehensible. Whatever else it was, the '80's was a whole lot of fun.

One of the flashiest guys in the '80s was the infamous Bob Evans, whom Mark had known for twenty-five years, since they met when they were climbing the Hollywood ladder as young actors. In December, Evans, the former Paramount head (and producer of *Love Story* and *The Godfather*) had announced a new project he was planning to direct: *The Cotton Club* by Mario Puzo. He called it '*The Godfather* with music.' In March, Evans called to ask Mark to sell the foreign rights to *Cotton Club* at Cannes as a way to finance the movie. Delighted, Mark said yes.

At that point *Cotton Club* had a budget of $23.5 million, was slated to start shooting in October, would be directed by Evans and starred Sylvester Stallone. Acquiring the international rights was one of the most colorful feathers in PSO's new cap.

Then, just as the Cannes Festival was about to begin, Mark had gotten a desperate call from Evans.

"He fucked me over," Evans growled in his typical low-register rumble.

"Who?"

"Stallone. He's playing some joker called Rambo or Sambo instead of doing *Cotton Club*. How the hell are you going to sell it to your guys without a star?"

"I'll figure something out."

Chapter 18. 1983. Century City

Mark hung up, aware that he had nothing to show potential distributors except a striking black and white poster that Bob had spent a lot of time and money to develop. It depicted a full length photo of a man and a machine gun with a trumpet for a shadow. The slogan was "The Cotton Club: its violence startled the nation. Its music startled the world."

It was a terrific image. Mark only hoped it was terrific enough to convince buyers to buy the movie.

At the Festival, trouble started with a phone call from the Carlton Hotel.

"We are confirming that Mr. Jerry Lewis has checked in..."

"Thanks for calling," said Mark, about to hang up.

"There is a little problem, monsieur. Mr. Lewis insists he needs two rooms, not one."

"What for?" Mark asked.

"I don't know, monsieur. He just maintains that he needs them."

"Fine," said Mark, too busy to be bothered. If Lewis needed two rooms, so be it. He needed Lewis to sell *The King of Comedy* (starring Lewis and Robert De Niro) to foreign distributors.

Later that evening he had to stifle his laughter when he found out why he needed the extra room. Apparently, Lewis never went anywhere without his little poodle, Puffy. And he *always* insisted that Puffy have his own hotel room.

"Weird," said John.

"Stars will be stars," Mark shrugged, sarcastic.

He stopped laughing when hotel charges started mounting. Charges for room service meals for Puffy; extra charges for shampooing the carpets. More charges for hotel staff that the comedian hired to stay in the room when he wasn't there because Puffy couldn't possibly be alone.

After several days of this, Mark and John got fed up and sent Lewis home. "But instead of heading for L.A., he went to Israel where Arnon Milchan, the producer of *King of Comedy,* treated him like the crowned head of state he thought he was, with an extra room for Crown Prince Puffy," said John. They later heard that when Jerry asked to see some of the Israeli fighter jets, Milchan made the arrangements. There went Lewis, on a military airbase under tight security, climbing the ladder to look into the cockpits of fighter jets and cooing to the stupid poodle in his arms. "Look at that, Puffy, isn't it great?!"

From Cowboy to Mogul to Monster

In the end, there was more off-camera drama with Lewis and the dog than there was on the screen. In spite of the stars involved, *King of Comedy* would not become a hit and many foreign distributors took a bath on the film. Nevertheless, a movie with Robert De Niro and Jerry Lewis directed by Martin Scorsese was one of the first A-level projects ever offered to overseas distributors by PSO. It looked good in their lineup and few complained about losing money on it.

Armed with only a poster and a pitch Mark pitched *Cotton Club* round-the-clock at Cannes. Green eyes shining, emotions flitting across his face, hands constantly in motion, he told the story over and over again. To an Italian distributor who listened, transfixed; to Australians, Koreans, Germans, Russians, Spaniards, Swedes, Canadians. Chain smoking. Breaking into different languages. Closing one deal after another. His negotiations managed to elicit millions of dollars in guarantees from foreign distributors for *Cotton Club*. "Because he is a superb storyteller," Eddie Kalish explained. "When he pitched a movie, distributors would be leaning across the table, leaning further in and further in as they listened to his story."

Mark acted out all the roles, got the distributors to visualize the film on screen, as he, the narrator, saw it. "We never showed them a promo, we never showed them a script. They'd be mesmerized by Mark and then sign for the best terms anybody could get." (Unfortunately, often the final film didn't measure up to Mark's vision of it and after awhile, some distributors became leery of buying based on his pitch.)

Now, elated by his success, Mark called Evans.

"How much did you get?" Evans asked anxiously.

"Eight million, Bob." He heard Evans' muttered disbelief. "So, what do you think?"

"I think you're a fucking genius, Damon. I love you, kid."

Evans crowed to the press that Mark was a "persistent, hard-nosed negotiator." That only increased the long lines of distributors that flowed through PSO's suite like eager schools of fish. They nibbled on the movies he pitched, took the bait and he reeled them in. "I believe that distributors *want* to be sold," he told his team. "They want to be convinced that the film you're pitching can be great. So go out and convince them!" "At the Festivals I had the opportunity to watch the master at work," said Michael Heuser. "He is the quintessential salesman. I have not met anybody who can sell a product – films in particular – better than Mark Damon."

Chapter 18. 1983. Century City

Some PSOers were in awe of his abilities. Others, like Gregory Cascante, who ran the sales division, felt a mixture of awe and envy. "Gregory was impossible," Mark reflected decades later. "He was very good and very smart but he had some fatal flaws. He felt he was always in my shadow even though I gave him a lot of leeway and let him run the sales division. In retrospect, maybe that only fed his resentment of me."

"You would never put those two men together in the same room if you met them separately," mused Cassian Elwes years later. "Gregory was very flamboyant, outrageous, manic. Impulsive. Not sophisticated or charming, like Mark. Gregory was much tougher and more in your face. Very different from Mark but brilliant in his own right."

When Gregory tried to compete with Mark's ability to sell, he ended up falling short. "That's because a big part of selling is being excited," said Cassian, "and people can tell if you're being fake about it or genuine. Mark really scours material and thinks about what he's going to sell because he has to be genuinely excited about it. He has an infectious enthusiasm about the movies he gets involved with and I think that's what leads so many people to buy them from him."

Another reason for his success was the way Mark treated every distributor, from the smallest to the biggest, with respect. "There is no such thing as an unimportant meeting," he taught the team. "Mark never speaks badly of people," agreed Reiko. "He respects his customers," Bobby Meyers said, "that's why he still has relationships that go back to La Costa."

Cascante, on the other hand, "was very vengeful," according to Mark. "If somebody crossed him, he'd swear he was going to get that person, no matter what. I would say, 'Gregory, it doesn't matter. You're building relationships. You don't have to get back at them. This is going to be your downfall.' But he'd insist, saying 'For the rest of my life I'm going to get back at him. He'll be sorry he did what he did to me.'"

At first all of the new PSOers wanted to go to 'Camp Cannes' in the South of France. They were tempted by pictures of beaches to lie on all day and discos to party at all night. Then they found out what really happened in Cannes.

Every day, Mark met with the sales team at seven o'clock in the morning, went over what had happened the day before and what he expected them to do today. "We were always pissed off about those seven o'clock meetings," recalled Eddie Kalish, "but we all had to be there. And then Mark wouldn't let you order breakfast. Or if you did order it was limited." Mark was always outraged at the costs of the so-called 'Continental Breakfasts.' "They're a total rip-off," he declared. "If we ordered all the same food á la carte it would cost much less money." So he ordered coffee á la carte and a few croissants to satisfy the hungriest. After many complaints he finally allowed staffers to go to the local bakeries at the crack of dawn to buy croissants: "But only because they're still 63% cheaper than the Continental breakfasts."

After the breakfast meetings the staff would go to PSO's three-room suite at the Carlton where, over the next twelve days they would meet with 250 distributors from four dozen countries: Phillippe Hellman, Jean Luc de Fait, Paul Rassam and Pierre Kalfon (France); Nigel and Trevor Green (England); Sammy Waynberg, Hanno Huth, Berndt Eichinger and Kilian Rebentrost (Germany); Aurelio de Laurentiis, Fulvio Lucisano, Vittorio Cecchi Gori and Jacopo Capanna (Italy); Jaime Comas (Spain); Harumasa Shirasu, Moto Kubotani, Hiro Furukawa (Japan); Graham Burke (Australia); Harold Shaw and Vee King Shaw (Singapore); Bill and Edwin Kong, Rigo Jesu, and Crucindo Hung (Hong Kong); Harise Lasmana who had a monopoly in Indonesia; Ugor Terzioglu, our loyal and long-time distributor from Turkey; Paolo Lee, the smartest and most sophisticated of the Taiwanese buyers; Luis Silva, the dean of the Portuguese distributors; and Joe Vincenti, 'the king of the Middle East,' who only spoke to Mark in Italian.

All the distributors knew of Mark's background as an actor. It made him all the more colorful and garnered him respect. "It was a move to be respected," said attorney Kevin Koloff. "When Mark reinvented himself from an actor to a businessman he was doing what some of the most brilliant and successful people in the world do. Many of them are where they are *because* of their mastery of reinvention."

The distributors also knew Maggie and they were all treated as family. "In our business, you have these long-term relationships with certain buyers in every country," said Cassian Elwes, co-head of William Morris Independent, the branch that packages independent films, "and you treat them as your family in a way. If they lose on a movie, you have to make it up to them. You don't want to burn them or shove them out of the business, because they're your buyer. The trick is always to make deals with them but make sure you continue to have a good relationship."

At Cannes, when overseas distributors found out that PSO had the Bond movie, *Never Say Never Again (*a remake of *Thunderball* which

Chapter 18. 1983. Century City

brought Sean Connery back for one more time as James Bond) the sales team had to literally fend them off. "It was a huge event in the life of an independent company," Kathy Cass reflected years later, "and the biggest picture ever offered to independent foreign distributors." Distributors lined up and threw money at PSO to get the movie. "They called me at home at all hours of the day and night, making sure they were going to get it," Mark recalled.

PSO had gotten *Never* through Mark's longtime friendship with Jack Schwartzman (they had known each other since they worked as bag boys in a supermarket.) Mark: "For many years Schwartzman, a former lawyer supreme and nascent film producer had been in contact with a sometime producer named Kevin McClory, who owned a piece of the Bond cinematic rights." McClory, who had been trying for decades to make a Bond movie without Albert ('Cubby') Broccoli, producer of all the others and United Artists (which owned the rights to Bond's onscreen image at the time) finally won a legal battle to produce an independent Bond film titled *Never Say Never Again*.

Never came with some caveats, however. It had to adhere to the storyline of *Thunderball* or it would be tied up in court and never released; it couldn't use the James Bond theme music and the roles of 'M' and 'Q' couldn't be played by the usual actors for copyright reasons. "Plus, McClory was difficult and crotchety," Mark added.

On the plus side, when McClory decided that the best way to get the film overseas was through independent distributors, he went with PSO. The biggest plus was that the film starred Sean Connery, who had been absent from the Bond movies for several years. The cast included Klaus Maria Brandauer as a power-mad villain and Max Von Sydow as the evil SPECTRE chief. Brunette Barbara Carrera played the murderous femme fatale, Fatima Blush, and an unknown blonde actress named Kim Basinger played Domino, who falls for Bond.

The movie literally sold itself, unlike *Misunderstood* and some of the others they were selling that year at Cannes. *Misunderstood*, a remake of one of Mark's favorite Italian movies had originally been directed by Luigi Comencini. Mark: "The original *Misunderstood* was a tear-jerker and a heart-breaker. Now I was excited to be doing the remake with Taraq Ben Ammar, who also loved the original." The sales team watched Mark use his acting skills to pitch the small movie that would be directed by Jerry Schatzberg. PSOers saw tears fill his eyes every time Mark told the story of the businessman whose wife dies, leaving two sons for the man to raise.

They saw the way tears spilled down his cheeks as he spoke about the struggles of the father and son to communicate. How, when the older son lay dying and told his father, "All I ever wanted to hear you say was 'I love you,'" Mark could hardly get the words out without choking up.

His tears seemed so wrenchingly real that when he pitched the film to his old friend from Toho Towa he patted Mark on the arm. "It's okay, Mark," Harumasa Shirasu reassured. "You don't have to cry. We'll buy it."

Some of the PSOers thought Mark's tears were faked. Others thought he had been acting for so long that acting had become a part of him. "But all salespeople become actors," countered Bobby Meyers. "The only difference with Mark is that he came from the other side - an actor who became a salesman." Regardless of their feelings about his methods, all of the PSOers were impressed by the numbers – over the course of the Festival Mark sold *Misunderstood* to every distributor to whom he pitched. "Eventually, we shot the film in Tunisia where Taraq had very strong ties as his uncle was the President," Mark said years later, "but the result was a disappointment because of the poor and labored directing by Jerry Schatzberg."

In between pitch meetings at the Festival the team put on elaborate dog and pony shows for distributors who took a big gamble every time they bought a film. It could take 18 to 24 months before they saw a return on the money they paid PSO. *If* they ever saw it. Distributors needed the films they bought to be successful so they needed to know they were going to get support from PSO once the film got to their territory. As examples, the Carlton suite was jam-packed with posters and showy examples of PSO advertising and pubicity campaigns.

The team gave distributors printed statistics on what a star would do in their territory and stats on how much a certain director's last picture earned at the box office. They explained that PSO had plenty of basic components they could send to distributors to come up with their own campaigns. They emphasized that they did extensive brainstorming to get the title right in a certain language, then worked tirelessly to get the poster that worked in that territory. By the time the sales team was done most distributors were ready to sign on the dotted line. If they weren't, Mark trained his staff to let him step in.

"Okay," he would say, "if this film doesn't work in your territory I've got another one that I think will do great, and I'll drop the price to make up for your loss. And if it doesn't, tell me and we will find a way to help you. I'm not going to let you get hurt." Cassian Elwes: "Part of Mark's success is that he maintained good relationships with all of the people he sold movies to. If they lost money on one movie he made sure to give them another movie they could make money on."

When it came to negotiations for what they would pay for a picture, once again Mark came alive. Although it seemed like a game to him, like all other games he played, he wanted to win. "The interesting thing about Mark was that even though he almost always won in a negotiation, he didn't win by making his opponent feel small," said an ex-PSOer. He had so much fun doing the negotiation that many times the other guy walked away with a smile on his face. Even though he'd lost. "Probably because he didn't think he'd lost," said Mark.

At the end of Cannes the PSOers tallied up the total sales. After 252 meetings, close to 200 contracts, over $100 million in sales. Exhausted as they were, it was an incredible accomplishment. Mark took them all out to a celebration dinner at 'Vignette Haute' in the South of France. Ken Ziffren, one of the top entertainment attorneys in town and PSO's legal representative, Maggie, Kate, Kathy Cass, Gregory Cascante and a few distributors enjoyed a lavish meal and a dozen bottles of wine. The mood was ebullient. Before dessert, Mark hatched the idea to have everyone take turns telling the most embarrassing moment in their life. Then he waited patiently as they all told their stories. Some were lame, some were silly, some were downright awful. Then it was Mark's turn. He had managed to go last, even though it had been his idea.

It happened in the '50s, he said, when he was up for a screen test for *Atlantis, the Lost Continent*, an MGM picture that George Pal was to direct. Pal had met Mark and said, "This is my leading man." All he had to do was take a screen test, said Pal and the part was his.

After waiting all morning in a little trailer on the huge MGM lot, Mark explained he had a bad case of nerves. "What made me really nervous was that this screen test, a love scene, was my first shot at an 'A' studio movie and starring in it could make me a major leading man."

At lunchtime, he walked half a mile to a little restaurant/bar outside the lot, ordered a Bloody Mary and started to relax. Since he wasn't hungry and had time to kill he ordered another. And another. By the time he walked back to his trailer he felt good and ready for the test. First he needed to find a men's room. The Assistant Director told him the nearest bathroom was seven sound stages away and they were going to shoot the screen test in five minutes.

"By the time I went back into the trailer I was desperate. I had to pee, I *had* to pee. I looked over in the corner and saw a little bowl with dirty water. I thought to myself, 'no one will ever know.' And I peed in the bowl. Then I donned my toga and the makeup man walked in."

"Time for body makeup," he announced.

Before he could stop him, the makeup man grabbed the bowl Mark had just peed in, put a sponge in it and started slathering it all over his body. "Pretty soon that bowl was empty and I was covered with pee-pee soaked makeup. Then I was sent out to do the love scene."

Everyone at the table was howling as Mark described how he started to sweat as soon as he got under the hot lights, which only made the smell worse. How he had to play the love scene with Joyce Taylor (with whom he starred in *Beauty and the Beast*) knowing that he reeked: "She had no idea why I wasn't more passionate in the scene. While I knew if I had held her tight she would have smelled urine all over me! I was just stinking awful," he told the table, "and awful stinking! P.S. I didn't get the role."

Chapter Nineteen

July 10, 1983

Moscow, Russia

Mark, MPAA Chairman Jack Valenti, Marc Spiegal, Head of European Office of MPAA at the Moscow Film Festival.

Mark emulates Lenin, whose birthday he shares.

John, Maggie and Mark in St. Petersburg,
the Hermitage in the background.

Mark wears Maggie's nightgown for breakfast after
all his luggage disappeared 'into Finn Air.'

From Cowboy to Mogul to Monster

As soon as they boarded Aeroflot to Moscow, Mark, Maggie, John and Kate realized they were in for something different.

"There's no carpeting," Maggie noticed.

"No first class," said John.

"No classes at all," Mark agreed.

"And no flight attendants," Kate pronounced.

Row after row of tiny, uncomfortable seats were crammed into a small cabin. But the foursome rolled with the punches, reminding each other that they were on an adventure. Maggie was happy to be traveling with Mark and he with her. Kate and John were excited about the trip. While they waited for lunch, the threesome teased Kate about the suitcase she had packed chock-full of Rye Krisp, licorice and other good stuff to eat. Kate hotly defended her stash. "Everyone knows there's nothing to eat in Russia. Believe me, I'm the only smart one."

"It was incredible to be going there," she later confirmed, "at a time when people just didn't get into the U.S.S.R." But even their eager anticipation couldn't overshadow the fact that as the hours wore on, their stomachs were growling and there was no meal in sight. And no flight attendants to serve one.

Finally, a plainly dressed woman starting walking down the aisle with a metal tray, like they used in prisons. It had no doily, no napkin, no peanuts, pretzels, drinks or a meal. The tray was just piled with bananas from Cuba, courtesy of Castro. And one banana apiece was all they were allowed. By the time they landed in Moscow Kate's stash had never looked so good. They would eat it all in the next few days and mourn that it was gone.

After going through grim passport control they were met by their Russian guide, an unsmiling woman who would take them to locations approved for tourists. She confirmed that they had Deluxe accommodations at the Rossia Hotel (with 3,000 rooms, the largest hotel in the world) situated near Red Square on the Volga River. On the way, Maggie and Kate were thrilled by the prospect of seeing Red Square. Mark was struck by what he saw out the car window. "The men wore gray, heavy suits and they had an air of ugliness about them. And no one smiled. Ever." In July 1983, there was not much to smile about. On top of overarching repression and constant food shortages, Russians were frightened that the United States was getting ready to attack them.

A few months earlier, President Reagan had declared the USSR "the focus of evil in the modern world." US-Soviet relations had quickly

Chapter 19. 1983. Moscow

deteriorated as each side accused the other of violating the spirit of détente while stockpiling nuclear weapons. By the time Mark et al. arrived in Moscow, relations between the two superpowers were at an all time low. (Mikhail Gorbachev would later confirm that the situation of the world was never as explosive as in the first half of the 1980's.)

When the foursome was taken to their Deluxe rooms at the Rossia they found "the rooms had two tiny twin beds, one on either side of the room, with a little nightstand in the middle. That was it," Kate recalled. "And when we showered and dressed for the gala opening ceremonies I found out I had dishtowels that were bigger than the bath towels they gave us. *And* they felt like sandpaper." Plus, they were told not to drink the tap water but to brush their teeth with beer.

By the time they arrived at the Opening Ceremonies of the Festival, they were rattled. They calmed down when they were seated among visiting dignitaries Melina Mercouri, Greece's minister of culture; Raj Kapoor (India); actresses Monica Vitti, Claudia Cardinale and actor Nino Manfredi (Italy); Annie Girardot (France) and Richard Attenborough (England). How bad could Russia be if all these luminaries were there?

The Festival opened with a speech in the name of Kremlin Premiere Yuri Andropov: "Let the film-makers' voices all over the world be raised in the name of the triumph of truth, good, social justice, confidence and peace among nations." So much for the hype. Despite being presented to the West as a closet liberal who spoke English, read American magazines and danced the tango, Andropov, a former KGB chief, had ruled with an iron fist during his first year in power. He had strengthened controls of the border to stop "unwanted" literature from entering the U.S.S.R. He had antagonized the U.S., persecuted political dissidents, disdained Western propaganda that made a fuss about 'human rights' and deliberately isolated the U.S.S.R. By the time Mark and the others arrived in Moscow, Russians were deeply fearful of outsiders, especially Americans. Especially Americans who spoke their minds and were not afraid to question authority.

The next day Mark became a victim of Andropov's efforts to isolate the Kremlin from the world. Chaos reigned when he tried to get hotel operators to call Italy, France, Germany *and* the U.S.

"Impossible," he was told.

Mark protested. He insisted that he talk to the manager. "He's not here," he was told dismissively. Despite his immense frustration, nobody could explain *why* he couldn't call. Everyone simply shrugged and said it was impossible. Mark later learned that a few months earlier Andropov had ordered the direct-dial telephone link between the Soviet Union and the rest of the world to be disconnected. Calling other cities had become very difficult. Calling other *countries* was virtually impossible.

Despite these detractions the foursome found the Moscow Festival interesting. It attracted directors from all over the world who assembled after hours in the nightclub of the Rossia, where the food may have been scarce but the vodka flowed like water. One evening, at Mark's urging, Robert De Niro made a surprise and crew-cut appearance. Another night, French distributor Jean-Luc DeFait, a friend of Mark and Maggie's, drank so much vodka that he danced on a table with his son. Meanwhile, the Festival screened films day and night.

Ten PSO movies meant a lot of screenings for Mark and John to attend. Especially when they had to juggle screenings between meetings with representatives of hundreds of foreign film and television companies registered at the film market. Maggie and Kate were dying to go sightseeing with them. "There we were," Kate recalled years later, "blocks from Red Square and the guys were either at a screening or off with some Russians talking about doing a Soviet-American picture." The women went together, with Kate snapping photos of St. Basil's, Lenin's Tomb and the Kremlin. Their sightseeing was soon curtailed, however, when it became clear that John and Mark couldn't go to all of the PSO screenings AND the film mart. It was decided that Maggie and Kate would go to some of the screenings without them.

"It will be an adventure," they thought.

They took turns going up to the stage, where one of them was introduced before the screening of a PSO film. Kate: "We would be presented with a rose and we'd hold it and smile while someone droned on in Russian. Of course, we had no idea what they were saying or how long we had to stand there until somebody signaled that we could get off that stage." Over the next ten days, they continued to attend Festival screenings without incident. But on the eleventh day they attended a seminar on détente, where Kate suddenly stood up and talked about the new PSO picture that would be aired on TV in November: *The Day After*. It was not the most tactful move considering that the implication in the film was that the U.S. was at war with Russia. "But I found myself going on about the future and what would happen if we didn't all work together," Kate remembers. Afterwards, John and Mark yelled, "YOU DID WHAT?!! You're not supposed to say anything political!"

Chapter 19. 1983. Moscow

In the evenings they all went out to eat at the "approved" restaurants where food shortages abounded. They learned that if one restaurant didn't have tomatoes on one night, all the restaurants didn't have tomatoes. The next night it might be chicken or green vegetables or fruit. "Eventually, we learned to read down the right side of the menu. If there was a price next to something, you knew that they had it. Then you had to figure out if it was anything you might eat." Maggie and Kate entertained themselves by learning how to spot the ubiquitous presence of KGB at the 'approved' restaurants. "We noticed that there were always certain Russian men with razor cut hair, leather jackets and nice Italian shoes." When they asked their guide she said it was the unofficial KGB uniform.

After twelve days the Festival was coming to an end with only nine out of ten PSO films screened. The Russians had decided *not* to show *Das Boot* and when Mark and John demanded a reason, they claimed it had 'technical difficulties.' "Which was what?" Kate asked many years later. "The sprocket holes didn't work?" When they realized that the Russians had simply decided they weren't showing a film that showed Germany as human an angry Mark told *The New York Times,* "The Russians wouldn't show *Das Boot* but they didn't mind showing a film like *King Of Comedy* that denigrated the American way of life."

On that memorable note the Festival ended and the foursome went on to St. Petersburg before returning home.

They were met by a guide who made sure they only went to approved sites and only ate in approved restaurants. They played along. Until the repression got to them and rebellion kicked in. "We were tired of only going to restaurants that were 'approved' for foreigners." Mark recalled. "So on our last night we decided what the hell -- we're going to a real Russian restaurant. One that's off limits."

They slipped away from the guide. When they passed a busy restaurant and heard a Russian band playing knock-off versions of American '50s rock 'n' roll they decided this was the place. In they went, the only Americans in a restaurant brimful of Russian couples, families, even a wedding party. It was a lively scene with couples gyrating on the dance floor. Maggie and Kate were busily people-watching while they ate, noting the usual presence of KGB (or 'cabbage', as they dubbed them) at the bar. But the vodka was flowing and they were feeling no pain.

A little Russian man in military uniform approached their table.

"Want to dance?" he asked Kate.

"No thanks," she answered, thinking it was obvious that she was with John.

He went away. But soon he sent a bottle of vodka over to the table. Then he came back and asked her to dance again.

"Go on, dance with him," Mark urged.

"Do it," said Maggie.

"Sure," John added. "Just don't run off with the guy."

Kate finally said yes.

"So I'm out there dancing with the guy," Kate recalled, "when Maggie decides it would be cool if she got a picture of us."

Kate always carried a tiny camera in her purse, taking it out often to snap a quick picture. Now, Maggie aimed it at Kate and the Russian. One click. One flash. And it almost became an international incident.

The Russian in uniform started screaming, "FILM, FILM, FILM!" The entire restaurant stopped talking. The music ceased and people froze on the dance floor. Everyone stared as the military man ran over to Maggie and grabbed the camera out of her hands, quickly joined by the KGB guy.

"FILM!" they screamed, trying to open the camera.

Kate tried to stay calm as she pried the camera open. The men ripped out the film, gave her back the camera and walked away. Then the music started up and everyone resumed talking and dancing as if nothing had happened.

Mark, Maggie, Kate and John were shaking in their boots. Mark signaled to the waiter to bring the check and he came immediately. "No check," he growled. "Out!" He pointed to the door. As they walked back to the hotel they kept looking over their shoulders. "We were sure a KGB van was going to pull up any minute and take us to some Russian prison." Needless to say, no one slept that night.

The next morning, they confessed their adventure to their guide on their way to the airport. After scolding them she speculated that the military officer was supposed to be on base, not in a restaurant. Same with the man from the KGB. The last thing they wanted, she lectured, was to show up in an American photograph that could cause them trouble.

Having stayed up all night listening for footsteps in the hallway, the foursome was relieved that it had nothing to do with them *personally*. They began to feel a little giddy as they made their way to customs at the end of

Chapter 19. 1983. Moscow

a long line. Then Kate found out that Maggie was about to smuggle out four pounds of caviar in her carry-on bag. "I still don't know how she got through customs," noted Kate.

When they disembarked at the Helsinki airport to make their connection with Finn Air, relief washed over them. They ate hot dogs and drank beer until they were ready to burst. Giddy, Kate started laughing when she saw passengers walking up the walkway and into the Finn Air plane. "Look," she exclaimed, "they're disappearing into Finn Air!"

It turned out that Mark's luggage also disappeared into 'Finn Air.' Deprived of his clothes, he ended up wearing Maggie's nightgown to breakfast on their stopover. All four declared it a fitting end to the trip.

On November 20, 100 million Americans (including President Ronald Reagan) watched *The Day After* on television. According to J. Walter Thompson, the broadcast reached over 38,500,000 homes, not to mention schools, churches and organizations that gathered to watch the show as groups. The show's 46 rating and 62 share made it the 12th-highest rated program ever shown on TV.

The drama extended to the reviews: "The Orioles win; the Phillies win," wrote *The Los Angeles Times*. "It rains today; it doesn't. You get the raise; you don't. Home computers are the rage; they aren't. None of it matters compared with ending the threat of nuclear obliteration. That is what you carry away from *The Day After*, a shocking, horrifying, utterly bleak and highly controversial ABC movie about the lethal impact on Lawrence, Kansas, when nearby Kansas City is destroyed by Soviet missiles. Forget about *Psycho, Friday the 13th* and *Halloween. This* is a horror story." Russian Minister Marshal Ogarlov confirmed that the movie was screened privately for Soviet officials who went on record stating that "the danger shown in the film really exists."

On the same day it aired, *The New York Times Magazine* published a five page article titled "Selling American Films Abroad." "The days when foreign sales agents like Mark Damon were considered 'upstarts' are over," they wrote. "The half-dozen biggest independents have offices, life styles and $250,000-and-up incomes, rivaling those of major studio executives. Their success is impossible to ignore."

By the time Mark and John raised their glasses in a toast to the New Year, 1984, they saw nothing but promise in the bubbles of their champagne. PSO was fast becoming an empire and they were still friends, partners and brothers. They were certain that what lay ahead was more money, power, prestige and world travels.

Chapter Twenty

August 8, 1983

Hollywood, California

Artwork and Photography ©1984 The Ladd Company;
DVD Package Design ©2003 Warner Bros. Entertainment Inc.

Chapter 20. 1983. Beverly Hills

It was ten o'clock on a sweltering summer's day when Mark parked his Jaguar and swaggered into PolyGram Pictures wearing a shit-eating grin. He struggled for a poker face as he walked into producer Peter Guber's office and slapped a check made out to PolyGram onto the surprised man's desk.

"Happy birthday," Mark grinned, sprawling in the chair across from Guber.

Peter was confused. It wasn't his birthday. He wasn't expecting Mark. And he'd never seen a grin that size on Mark Damon's face.

"Go ahead. Take a look."

Guber picked up the check.

"$632,000?" he gasped.

"Umm hmm," Mark nodded, thoroughly enjoying the shock on Guber's face. "It just came in."

"For what?"

"*Endless Love.* Overages from Japan."

Peter's jaw dropped.

"In the studio system, that $632,000 would have never been seen," Mark exulted. "It would have gone into a big pot and balanced out losses from some other territory." Unlike PSO, studios still thought of 'foreign' as one entity with the plusses and minuses in one hopper instead of 40 different territories.

Guber, like everyone else in the business, knew that it could take up to a year for theatre owners to get an independent's box-office figures on the books. Yet the check had arrived at PSO only thirty days after the film had been released in Japan. Remarkably, in one month the movie had earned back its guarantee of $500,000; its print and advertising money; a complete fee to the Japanese distributor *and* phenomenal overages. It was terrific promotion for PSO.

Later that morning, Guber wore his own shit-eating grin when he drove onto the Universal lot and strode into the office of studio chief Ned Tanen. He slapped the check down on his desk. "Look what I got, man," he boasted. Gleefully explaining Mark's little visit to his office, he added "you guys lost a fortune by not selling the film overseas. I was right going with those independents you don't believe in."

Tanen, who had a reputation for wild mood swings, was furious that PolyGram had just walked away with $632,000 that could have gone to Universal. After Guber left he called his international division. "You'd better make sure that never happens again!" he screamed. Then he slammed down the phone and vowed to kill PSO.

Meanwhile, Peter Guber was calling his pals in the business, a bunch of young, entrepreneurial producers. After he told them about the check, pretty soon some of those producers were knocking on PSO's doors. The team put on their best dog and pony shows. "Everyone was involved," Kate recalled, "every department head and one or two people under them would come in and do a presentation." The foreign rights department explained the contracts; the accounting department explained how they kept track of box office revenues in forty foreign territories. The delivery department laid out how PSO kept track of moving the elements so exhibitors could use them in France, then Spain, Germany, Italy. The legal department clarified how much time it took to turn the contracts around after a deal memo was signed.

It was an amazing feat for an indie company. Studios had whole buildings for people doing what they were doing with their little group. And throughout, Mark and John made their pitch: "Look, you can go to the studios and have fourteen people carry your briefcase, open the door and take you on their jet. Or you can save all of that overhead and go with us. We run a real tight ship but we'll make sure you'll get more money out of Israel or Brazil or wherever your picture plays." On top of that, they would carefully explain that PSO would report to them like the studios.

Producers left with a head full of ideas and a packet of materials including samples of "computerized" reports. "This is great," they said to each other. "Here's a company that gets us more money overseas and they even give us computerized reports!" "We didn't use computers," John laughed decades later. "I mean, this was the early '80s, when computers were weird things that sometimes worked and sometimes didn't. Instead, we had people working all night, manually duplicating those reports to make them look like they had just come out of a computer."

Soon, some of those producers started taking a tough line with the studios: "Either you make a better deal with me or I'm taking the foreign rights to my movie to PSO."

Mark and John hoped they would start lining up to give PSO their "A" movies to distribute overseas.

"Or are we dreaming?" they wondered.

They were.

John was having lunch with his good friend and mentor, Ned Tanen when he began to rant. "You pricks are not going to skim the cream off my milk anymore. I'll never allow the studio to make another deal with a producer like the one we made with Guber on *Endless Love*. Never again."

Mark called Frank Mancuso, CEO of Paramount, who confirmed their worst fears: "Your success is going to become your failure. Once studios see you as a competitor, they're going to bury you."

"Screw that," Mark retorted.

But Tanen remained true to his word. He redid his deal with Guber and every other producer on the lot. From then on, Universal owned the foreign rights on any movie it distributed. Other studios soon followed suit.

To eliminate the advantage PSO offered (by un-crossing the money from foreign territories) studios started to offer producers 'gross points' on their movies – a direct cut of money without deductions for print and advertising costs or studio distribution fees. The change dramatically bettered the position of independent producers. Making their pictures at a studio became one-stop shopping.

"So in an indirect but meaningful way," mused John, "that one $632,0000 check helped to improve the independent producer's position at the studios." It also made life much more difficult for PSO. Just as they were on the verge of winning over studio producers to go with them they lost those "A" films to studios. But Mark refused to be discouraged.

"So we hit a few bumps," he told John. "Roads have bumps. It may make it a little slower but we'll still get to the finish line."

In early October, Mark and Maggie arrived in Munich on their way to MIFED. They were having dinner with one of PSO's top distributors, Sam Waynberg, a Polish Jew who had survived a concentration camp and remained in Germany, managing to build one of the most successful film distribution companies in the world while hating the Germans. At age 58, Sammy was a bit of a legend, sharp as a tack and a favorite of Mark's.

It was starting to snow when Mark and Maggie arrived at the Conti Hotel with just enough time to unpack, shower and change before dinner. He was reading a script when he heard a scream from the bathroom.

"Mark! My hair dryer doesn't work!"

When he went into the bathroom he found Maggie in a robe, her long, long wet hair dripping on the floor, a useless hair dryer in her hand.

"What happened?"

"I don't know – I plugged in the adapter and it burnt out."

Mark tried plugging it in again but the hair dryer was toast. Meanwhile, Maggie's thick Rapunzel-length hair was sopping wet. Outside, snow was covering the sidewalks. They had less than an hour before dinner. Maggie was going to freeze if she went out with wet hair.

Mark picked up the phone and called the concierge.

"Excuse me, do you have a hairdryer in the hotel?"

"One minute," the concierge said promptly. "I will connect you."

"Got one!" Mark called to Maggie as the phone rang and rang until someone answered.

"Ja. Hallo…"

"Hello, I'm looking for a hairdryer," Mark repeated.

"Ja, *I'm* Herr Dreyer," said the man.

Mark's jaw dropped.

"Herr Dreyer here," the man repeated impatiently. "Hallo…?"

Mark managed to sputter an excuse and hang up before he started to laugh. Maggie found him doubled over. When she asked when the hair dryer was coming he laughed even harder. When she heard what happened, she started laughing until they were both hysterical.

Between a hamper of towels and a steaming radiator they managed to get her hair dry. When they went to dinner with Sammy, they told him the story of 'Herr Dreyer.' He roared. And he bought Mark's pictures.

"It's because I know how to talk to actors…" Mark told reporters when asked how he persuaded them to go on the road for PSO's movies. "I talk to them as a former actor not a businessman. I tell them I've been there myself so I know that overseas reporters are more reverential and don't bait you. I also tell them that if you're a star foreign reporters ask fewer questions about your personal life and more about the filmmaking process. And that foreign publicity travel can be eye-opening."

Mark worked hard to get stars to trumpet PSO's movies overseas because he knew that the success or failure of a picture often depended on personal appearances by actors or the director. Now, as MIFED neared, he had his eye on Sean Connery to do a publicity tour for the Bond movie.

After Mark and Maggie stopped off at a castle on the French Riviera to visit the set of *Never Say Never Again,* they took Connery out to dinner with French distributor, Jean Luc de Fait. Mark ordered duck á l'orange for everyone and chose a 1964 Chateau-Neuf du Pape. After dinner, when Mark proceeded to tell the story of 'Herr Dryer' Maggie chimed in. Soon everyone was hysterical, including Connery. He was laughing heartily, his belly full, his glass filled to the top when Mark turned to him.

Chapter 20. 1983. Beverly Hills

"By the way, how about doing a publicity tour for *Never?*"

"Depends," Connery replied.

"On what?"

"How much do I get paid?"

"Nothing."

"So, why should I do it?"

"Because you owe it to your foreign distributors. They put up a lot of money and I need you to go to protect their investment."

Connery arched an eyebrow. "How does that concern me?"

"You get 15% of the gross from first dollar. That should earn you about another $10 million the way I see it."

That got a rise out of Connery. "But I'm not going to wear my rug," he said, somewhat defiantly.

"It's up to you. But that means your $10 million will only be worth five." Being a stingy Scotsman, Connery thought for half a second.

"I'll wear my rug."

(A highlight for PSO would later occur when *Never Say Never Again* opened one month after *Octopussy* (with Roger Moore) and the press declared it "The War of The Bonds." Despite the dire epithet, both Bond movies became phenomenally successful with reviewers lauding the return of Connery, who looked more fit than ever.)

When MIFED opened, *Hollywood Reporter* proclaimed Mark "the kingpin of the Los Angeles independent foreign sales community." PSO was selling movies with big names attached: Francis Ford Coppola's *The Outsiders* and *Rumble Fish;* Sergio Leone's *Once Upon a Time in America;* David Begelman's *Mr. Mom* and *The Adventures of Buckaroo Banzai Across the 8th Dimension*. *Variety* claimed PSO would provide "a touch of glamour" by hosting a cocktail reception for David Begelman: "Damon's bash on a yacht for the notorious former Columbia chief will be the biggest event in MIFED history."

Several years earlier Begelman, then head of Columbia Pictures, had been caught forging Cliff Robertson's name on a $10,000 check. The incident shook Hollywood and rattled Wall Street but Begelman had resurfaced to form Sherwood Productions with former LA Kings owner Bruce McNall and the Texas billionaire Hunt brothers. All of them, colorful mavericks of the '80s.

From Cowboy to Mogul to Monster

Mark was meeting with Berndt Eichinger, President of Neue Constantin *(Das Boot)* when he noticed how hard the man was sweating. Eichinger had brought storyboards and paintings of costumes and sets for a new movie called *The NeverEnding Story,* based on a German bestseller by Michael Ende. "The boards look terrific," Mark concluded. Very imaginative."

"Good. Very good."

Mark tried to ignore Eichinger's sweat-soaked shirt as they continued.

"So what's the budget?" he asked.

"$13 million."

"Wow. That's high."

"I know. But this movie has a built-in audience that loves the book. And it's a fantasy so we need to use the best special effects men in the business." Eichinger paused to nervously clear his throat. "I was hoping to make a deal with PSO to raise some of the budget in exchange for foreign rights."

The more they talked about the project the more interested Mark became. But he still wondered why Eichinger looked so worried.

"Okay," Mark said, finally. "We'll commit to provide $8 million of the budget. In exchange for the foreign rights. And PSO becomes production partners with Bavaria Studios and Neue Constantin."

Eichinger smiled with relief and the men hugged. Mark felt Berndt shaking. It would be much later when he learned why his German friend was so desperate: "He had sunk so much money into the picture that if I didn't say yes Neue Constantin was finished."

At the time, neither man knew that by the time it was done the budget for *The NeverEnding Story* would almost double to $25 million, making it the most expensive German film ever made. And they had no idea that it would gross $125 million worldwide and spawn two sequels and a TV series, becoming one of the most beloved children's films ever.

That year, the high point of MIFED for Mark was watching his old friend, director Sergio Leone, now a major star, pitch *Once Upon a Time in America* to foreign distributors.

"You have to let me sell your next film in Milano," Mark had insisted when he called Leone months earlier, speaking in Italian, the only language Leone spoke. It helped Mark's cause that he was fluent.

"I do?"

"Absolutely. You owe it to me," Mark maintained lightly. "I worked my ass off to get you Clint Eastwood for *A Fistful of Dollars.* And this is how you're going to thank me."

154

Chapter 20. 1983. Beverly Hills

"Oh... okay. Va bene. Che devo fare?" (What do I need to do?)

"Just come to Milano. I'll put the top distributors in the world in a room with you."

"And then what?"

"Then you tell them your vision for *America*. That's all."

Mark arranged for Sergio and a translator to meet with distributors in a small basement room where the director began to talk about *Once Upon a Time in America,* his gangster epic starring Robert DeNiro. "We jammed eighty distributors in there and it was very hot. It was physically uncomfortable, which made Leone's telling even more powerful. At the beginning, however, it was painful because he spoke in Italian," Mark recalled, "and the translator translated every sentence, literally."

Once he started, Sergio didn't stop. He went through the entire three-hour movie, describing every shot and camera angle in every scene. Although his pitch lasted for four hours and fifteen minutes, although it was hotter than hell in there, nobody moved. Nobody went to the bathroom. The distributors sat, rapt with fascination at listening to a director who had the whole movie in his head. By the time they signed up to distribute the movie they felt it was an honor.

When *America* was released those same distributors were blown away. What they saw on the screen was what Leone had pitched. Exactly. They thought it was brilliant. "Until the U.S. distributor, Warner Bros., fucked it up," said Mark. "Alan Ladd, Jr. recut the picture, making a linear story out of the one Sergio told in flashbacks. Laddie was a good filmmaker but he miscalculated on this one. He took the brilliance out of the movie and it bombed in the U.S. while it succeeded everywhere else."

In early December, John appeared in the doorway of Mark's office.

"I just finished the numbers and PSO did $2 million in profits this year."

"Damn," said Mark with joy and admiration. What do you want ?"

"A gold Rolex," John shot back casually.

On December 31, Mark put a small box on John's desk. "Go ahead. Open it."

John was astonished to find a gold Rolex with an inscription on the back: "John Hyde, December 31. $2,000,000."

It took a second before John remembered what he had asked for. Both men were laughing happily as the year came to an end.

Mark Damon

1955

Chapter Twenty-One

March 15, 1955

Burbank, California

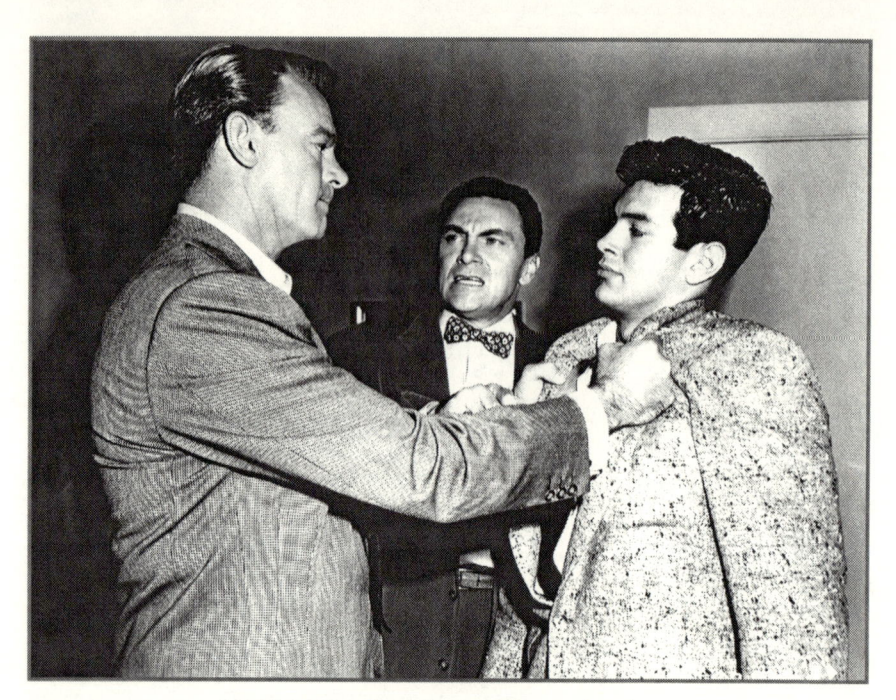

Mark in his first feature for Columbia,
Inside Detroit (1956) with Dennis O'Keefe.

Between Heaven and Hell (1956, Fox),
Mark, Broderick Crawford, Robert Wagner, Biff Elliot.

It's a Date!

★ When the phone rang early one Saturday morning in Natalie Wood's apartment, she immediately thought, "No! Whoever it is and whatever they want, I'm not stirring out of the house today. I'm straightening closets and bureau drawers and that's it!" With determination in her voice, she picked up the phone. It was handsome screen newcomer, Mark Damon, with a fine idea. Natalie and he would take off for a day at Santa Monica. The weather was gorgeous, the sun was shining and let's go. Natalie immediately told him of her unshakable decision to stay home all day long. But Mark wouldn't take "no" as an answer and Natalie soon made another unshakable decision. She would straighten closets and drawers some day when it was raining. Almost before Mark could finish eloquently stating his case, she interrupted with a laugh and said, "It's a date!" A happy Mark turned up almost immediately on her doorstep and they were off for a day of fun on the glamorous beach at Santa Monica.

Mark and Natalie Wood.

Natalie and Mark were so thrilled to be on the beach on such a glorious day that they had to release their energy somehow—and horseplay seems to be the order of the day.

CIGARETTE SMOKE LINGERED ABOVE THE DARK red leather booth of the Smokehouse Restaurant where Pat O'Brien, mid-fifties and a big star, was happily drinking his lunch as he spun another colorful Hollywood yarn to the spellbound young actor across the table. Twenty-one year old Mark was exhilarated to be lunching with O'Brien on his first day in his first movie. Although he'd only played small roles in TV shows, Columbia's casting director had remembered him and wangled an audition with producer Sam Katzman, who had surprised Mark by casting him as O'Brien's son in *Inside Detroit,* an expose of the auto industry.

By 1955, O'Brien, the popular actor whom Hollywood called "The Irishman in Residence" had worked in movies for two decades. He was beloved for his 1940 role as Knute Rockne, the Notre Dame coach who urged his players to "win one for the Gipper." Now he was playing 'Gus Linden,' a powerful and corrupt racketeer whose murder of the brother of a union leader (Dennis O'Keefe) motivates O'Keefe to revenge. He becomes determined to bust O'Brien, whose wife and two grown kids (Mark and Margaret Field) are in denial about Dad's brutal career and ignorant of his involvement with a flashy prostitute (Tina Carver.)

Mark's big scene featured him breaking into O'Keefe's apartment, drunk and determined to defend his family's honor and it was too bad the scene wasn't shooting after the first day's lunch. Because by the time the check came, O'Brien was nicely juiced and Mark was dealing with a dead battery.

They were late getting back to the set, no big deal for O'Brien, who'd been at Warner's since 1940. Not so good for Mark, who was supposed to smoke nervously as he argued with his sister. 'Problem was, he'd never smoked before. Oh, he had practiced in front of the mirror, cigarette dangling from his lips like Marlon Brando. And he had written notes on his script, earnest reminders from his acting classes: "Trust senses." "Maturity is you." "Release tension before scenes – exercise!" "OFFBEAT – Don't do the expected!" "Move from the brain." But by the time the cameras rolled Mark was in a stupor from those three martinis O'Brien had encouraged Mark to drink. It was hard enough to remember his lines let alone manage a cigarette. When he saw the finished film, Mark was mortified to see that he had smoked with his pinky held high in the air.

From that day on, Mark stayed on the lot for lunch. He ate in the commissary and flirted with the leading lady, Tina Carver. By the time the movie wrapped he had accomplished two 'firsts': his first movie and his first leading lady. From then on, in almost every movie or TV appearance

Chapter 21. 1955. Burbank

he did, he made it his business to 'get' the leading lady or somebody else. When it was released *Inside Detroit* proved to be a career changer for Mark when O'Brien proclaimed, "The kid's got electricity" and the quote was circulated widely by Helen Ferguson. It would be printed and re-printed in countless fan mags and stick to Mark like glue for the rest of his Hollywood career.

Between Ferguson and his mother, Mark had plenty of strong female figures in his life. So he decided to stop studying with yet another overbearing woman, Estelle Harman. She was discouraging in his final evaluation: "Your work habits are not up to standard despite the fact that your professional career is getting started! Excuses or not... you must not let down now!" Mark had no intention of letting down although he was more and more convinced that he preferred directing to acting.

His next role was playing one in a lot of soldiers along with Tom Tryon, Jan Merlin, Alvy Moore, Martin Milner and Robert Blake in a WW2 picture, *Screaming Eagles*. The high point for Mark was when his character was killed and Alvy Moore proclaimed: "You die good, kid." They were words Mark would always be proud of. And all he would ever remember about the film.

In February he was about to graduate UCLA, having gotten a B.A. in Speech and an MBA in Business Administration. He was also working on his Doctorate in English Literature, having done it all in 5 ½ years on top of acting and directing. He was directing a new play when his lead actor fell sick on opening night. Mark stepped into the role, unaware that a talent scout from 20th Century Fox was in the audience. After the show he offered Mark a six month contract with the studio.

It was an actor's dream. But Mark wasn't sure he wanted to be an actor. He preferred directing to acting. He mulled it over and finally decided that if he took the contract he'd learn more about acting. And if he learned more about acting he'd become a better director.

He accepted the offer.

In his first role under contract Mark played opposite a sixteen-year-old actress named Lili Gentle in Twentieth Century Fox Hour's TV show "In Times Like These." The cast included Macdonald Carey, the Beverly Hills High School Choir and Fay Wray. Mark thought that Lili, Tallulah Bankhead's 2nd cousin, was cute. She thought he was more than cute. "She was -- in those days we called it a 'nymphomaniac.' She met me, we acted together, next thing I knew she wanted to make love." Mark gladly obliged.

From Cowboy to Mogul to Monster

But a while later he found out that he had gotten Lili pregnant. And that she had caught the eye of Richard Zanuck, son of powerful studio head, Darryl Zanuck. "There we were, under contract to the studio that was grooming her for stardom. I was sure that when they found out that underaged Lili was pregnant my career would be over and I'd end up in jail."

Desperate, Mark went to see his stepfather at the pharmacy he had bought for him with his puzzle winnings. After he poured his heart out, Ben ducked into a back room and came out with a bottle of pills. "It was called 'Apiol and Ergol' or something like that," Mark recalled. "I gave it to Lili, who took a pill and amazingly, it worked." The pregnancy was terminated and Lili continued to date Richard Zanuck, whom she would later marry.

Next, Mark was cast as 'Private Terry' in *Between Heaven and Hell*, a WW2 picture starring Robert Wagner as 'Sergeant Sam Gifford,' an arrogant plantation owner who marries the Colonel's daughter, played by bosomy blonde Terry Moore. Buddy Ebsen played a loyal private and Broderick Crawford was a scary psychopathic Captain named 'Waco.' 'Private Terry' was only a small part. But Mark still managed to drive the director, stalwart Richard Fleischer (son of animation pioneer Max Fleischer) crazy.

In one scene, he was in a ragged platoon of soldiers bushwhacking through the Pacific jungle as they listened for sounds of the Japanese. One after another, five of the six soldiers filed past the camera framed in profile. Then the last soldier (Mark) walked past the camera, stopped, turned and "looked" all over for the enemy. Which "just happened" to get his full face in the camera. "Cut!" yelled Fleischer. "What the hell are you doing?"

"Checking to see if any enemy soldiers are following us," Mark answered 'innocently.'

"Did I tell you to do that?" Fleischer demanded.

"No, but… "

"THEN DON'T DO IT AGAIN!"

Fleischer stalked back to his chair. When the cameras rolled again all the soldiers filed past the camera framed in profile, including Mark. He seemed to have learned his lesson. So the director figured. He figured wrong. In his next scene, Mark was one of the soldiers in Robert Wagner's platoon when Wagner caught up with his men from behind, passing them in the jungle. Fleischer had told them all to face forward when Wagner passed. But when the cameras rolled Mark turned to look at him, once again managing to get his face in the camera.

Chapter 21. 1955. Burbank

"Cut!" Fleischer screamed. *"Now* what are you doing?"

"Nothing. I turned to look at him," Mark protested.

"I told all the soldiers to face forward!" Fleischer yelled.

"But that's not natural."

Infuriated, Fleischer ordered him to cut it out or he'd have him fired.

When they resumed shooting, Mark was on his best behavior again. Until his next scene, when he would pull something new. "I was impossible as an actor," Mark would later reflect. "I was always sure I knew more than the director and was constantly changing the blocking or telling him what to do." No surprise, after Private Terry died because he disobeyed his Sergeant, Fleischer threw a small party on the set.

Soon Mark had no new roles lined up at Twentieth. No matter to Helen Ferguson, who planted stories that made him seem like a rising young star: "The parts have been snowballing around Mark ever since his first teleplay and his bank account's been rising like a yeast cake. To top it all off, the guy just happens to be handsome, intelligent and talented," declared fan magazine *Screen Gems*. In truth, he was grappling to get a foothold in a town that was grooming him to become a star in the old-fashioned sense of the word. At the same time, it was falling under the spell of a whole new approach to acting.

The "Method," an acting technique that was taught at Lee Strasberg's New York Actors' Studio, was based on the innovative techniques of the Russian master Constantin Stanislavsky. It involved a series of physical and psychological exercises meant to break down the actor's barrier between life on and off the stage.

Over the next few years, while Mark struggled to find his place in Hollywood, the "Method" launched the careers of Montgomery Clift, Marlon Brando, Marilyn Monroe, Karl Malden, Shelley Winters, Rod Steiger and many others. There was also a buzz about actors who attended Sanford Meisner's celebrated Neighborhood Playhouse School of Theater in New York - Gregory Peck, Geraldine Page, Grace Kelly, Joanne Woodward, Steve McQueen, Eli Wallach and others. These New York-trained-actors brought authenticity and depth to the screen. They were not afraid to show their sensuality or their sensitivity. And they were not afraid to show their vigorous contempt for Hollywood with its focus on profits over authenticity.

Strasberg and Meisner advocated authenticity and disdained phoniness, which Mark agreed with. The problem was, the Hollywood ladder he was

From Cowboy to Mogul to Monster

trying to climb demanded he become one of the phonies he detested. So he went to all the right parties and sweet-talked and glad-handed the right people. At restaurants like Ciro's, Trocadero, Scandia, The Brown Derby and the Polo Lounge at the Beverly Hills Hotel he showed up with a beautiful starlet and flashed his 1000 kilowatt smile as photos were taken to be sent to the fan mags. His name appeared regularly in gossip columns, linked with one nubile starlet after another. But throughout, his acting career was not where he wanted it to be. "I was playing the game but I wasn't getting the roles I wanted. I was being type cast as a pretty-boy juvenile and there seemed to be little I could do to change the situation." To top it off, after six months 20th Century Fox chose not to exercise the option on his contract.

When Mark was dating Elaine Aiken, a respected New York actress and member of the Actor's Studio he complained about his hunger to learn more about acting. She insisted that he would never get anywhere unless he studied with Strasberg or Meisner. "You have to go to New York," Elaine pronounced over long cups of coffee. "It's the only place for a serious actor." Mark knew she was right. But the idea of moving to New York, where he knew nobody, was daunting. He put the idea on the back burner.

Soon, however, he was sent on a 'set-up date' with Natalie Wood which would provide the catalyst for his move to New York.

"It was a sunny Saturday in Los Angeles when the phone rang in a beautiful girl's apartment and a man's voice suggested a day at Santa Monica," wrote *Screen Life*. "Soon Mark Damon and Natalie Wood were off to spend this perfect Saturday at the beach."

It was the epitome of the set-up date, arranged by Natalie and Mark's PR people. They were photographed in a convertible on their way to the beach, looking like two beautiful, wind-blown young people without a care in the world. In reality, Mark was clawing for recognition in Hollywood and eighteen-year-old Natalie had been caught taking a shower with Nick Ray, the forty-three year old director of *Rebel Without A Cause*.

But Mark's attraction to Natalie was real. He was entranced by her big brown eyes and natural beauty. She liked the way he made her laugh. They frolicked in the sand all afternoon as photographers captured them playing a mock game of touch football, pretending to go for a swim (despite the

Chapter 21. 1955. Burbank

fact that Natalie was deathly afraid of water) and playing cards on a beach blanket. It made for a terrific spread in the movie mags.

During their breaks, Mark asked what it had been like to shoot *Rebel Without A Cause* with James Dean. Natalie confessed to having a serious crush on him. "But she complained that everyone on the set was carrying a copy of Stanislavski's *To an Actor* and using phrases like 'sense memory' and 'emotional memory.' Mark sensed a vulnerability beneath Natalie's groomed "Natalie Wood" image. He wondered if, like him, she felt inferior to anyone with Studio training.

He confessed his insecurities about "Method" acting and they began to talk in earnest. And somewhere between the makeup touchups and posing for the cameras, a friendship between them began.

One month later, Natalie told him she was auditioning for the producer and writers of *Diary of Anne Frank,* about to be launched on Broadway. "She was reading for the part of Anne and thought I should read for Peter, Anne's boy friend." She said she had spoken to the star, Joseph Schildkraut, who would be playing Anne's father, Otto Frank about him. Soon, Mark received a call asking him to come to Schildkraut's Beverly Hills home the next day. "I'll never forget the strange response I received when I walked in. He looked me up and down, slowly circled around me with appropriate 'hmmm's' and 'yes, yes'es', looked at my shoes to see if I was wearing lifts (I was not) and then carefully placed his hands on my shoulders, and pushed down. 'You might be too tall,' he said while he pushed."

Schildkraut, an elegant and cultured Viennese actor, was the son of the great German actor, Rudolph Schildkraut,. He introduced himself and sat Mark down before regaling him with his feelings about playing Otto Frank and its importance in his life. He 'confessed' that he hoped the role would fulfill his deceased father's expectations of him. As he talked, his eyes filled with tears. Mark was enthralled by the older man's culture and sensitivity. He had no idea that Schildkraut was renowned for working a room.

After an hour, the actor said, "Call me 'Pepi,'" and told Mark that despite his being too tall, he should come to read a few scenes for the Hacketts (the writers), Mr. Kermit Bloomgarten (the producer) and Schildkraut. In a week. Mark left with the script and a wonderful sense of excitement. One week later, he walked from the sunny gardens of the Beverly Hills Hotel into the deep cool of a ballroom. The play's "brass" sat at tables on the dance floor as Mark read a few scenes. When he was done, they conferred quietly among themselves while he waited nervously. Finally, Pepi (Schildkraut) came over to him.

From Cowboy to Mogul to Monster

"We were very impressed with your readings but my boy, everyone thinks you are just too healthy-looking for Peter."

Mark was crushed.

"But you have much talent," Pepi continued, "and I strongly advise that you move to New York. I will take you under my wing. I will even recommend you to Sanford Meisner's acting school. Think about that, would you please?"

What was there to think about? "I knew that I was headed for trouble if I stayed on in Hollywood," Mark would say years later. "I was afraid I would fall flat on my face if someone made the mistake of casting me in a demanding leading role." In August, 1956, Mark took a huge leap.

On a blistering L.A. morning he left Hollywood to study with Sanford Meisner at the Neighborhood Playhouse in New York.

PSO

1983

Chapter Twenty-Two

March 7, 1984

Beverly Hills, California

THE COTTON CLUB
ITS VIOLENCE STARTLED THE NATION-
ITS MUSIC STARTLED THE WORLD.
ROBERT EVANS presents
RICHARD GERE
GREGORY HINES
THE COTTON CLUB
Principal Photography July 11, 1983. Release June 1984.
© PSO

Chapter 22. 1984. Beverly Hills

It was a blistering morning in LA when Mark's secretary told him he had a call from Bob Evans. "They're a bunch of dumb fucks but they've got billions," Evans barked when Mark picked up the phone. It was vintage Evans. Start in the middle of a thought and figure you can follow. After knowing him for decades, Mark was used to it. So he listened while Evans boasted that he'd met some Texans who were going to invest in *The Cotton Club*.

Ever since Mark had raised millions for the picture from foreign distributors and a commitment came in from Orion Pictures to distribute the film in the U.S. and Canada, Evans had been searching for private investors to finance the rest of the picture. With him as director.

He had no idea that his search would ultimately take four years to make a movie that would cost a staggering (at that time) $58 million, die at the box office and lose money for every single investor except PSO. Nor did he know that the making of *The Cotton Club* would involve shady Mafiosi, a slew of lawsuits, a murder and the ruin of his career. (Although Evans would later re-surface in the '90's with a tell-all memoir, "The Kid Stays in the Picture" and in 2003, become more famous for that movie than any he'd ever produced.)

On the warm March morning when he called Mark, Evans was beaming. "These Texans are even talking about investing in the studio I want to start with PSO!," he exulted in his gravelly growl. It was the first Mark had ever heard about PSO forming a studio with Evans. "But the truth was, most of the time Evans was coked out of his mind and you didn't know what he was talking about anyway." One thing Mark *did* know - there was always something happening with Bob. So he wasn't surprised when Evans added that the Texans were flying in on their Lear jets and he was throwing them an old-fashioned Texas barbecue at the house that night.

"Bring Maggie. Tell John to bring Kate."

This being the early '80's, at the height of oil money, Mark and John figured Evans could be right about the Texans. So that night the foursome headed to Woodlands, his majestic Tudor home. They were ushered into Evans' backyard by his English butler, where little lights twinkled in all of the branches of the large trees and a small train ran on a track lit by hundreds of candles. A live dance band played Beatles songs while the Texans, large, loud and looped, crowded onto a small dance floor, raucously two-stepping. Liveried servants bobbed and weaved, desperately trying to keep French hors d'oeuvres from flying off their silver trays.

The perennially tanned, fast-talking Evans greeted the foursome beneath an enormous Chinese Elm. "Is this one hell of a Texan barbeque or what?" He laughed loudly in his characteristic low-register rumble. They all agreed it was.

"So how do you like this tree?" he asked, gazing at the towering Chinese Elm above them. He boomed loud enough for the Texans to hear, "Isn't it a beaut?"

"It is. And perfectly symmetrical."

"You think so?," Evans crowed. "That damn tree was lopsided 'till I fixed it. See that branch up there? The big one? It's a fake. A phony."

"What?"

Some of the Texans gathered near, craning their necks to see the branch. "I tell you, that branch is a sham." Evans gestured to another group of Texans. "C'mere. Take a look. I had the props department at Paramount build me that phony limb. And I made sure it looked real, right down to the grain in the wood. So there it is, the only one of its kind in the world."

Everyone looked up with amazement.

"Listen," he went on, "it's just like the movies. Everything in a movie is fake, right? But when you see it all put together it looks real. You know what I mean?"

"It better look real after I paid five bucks for my ticket," yelled one of the Texans.

"Of course," Evans laughed. "But everything on that screen is an illusion. Just like that branch up there. Just like *The Cotton Club* will be. The only thing that won't be an illusion is how much money we're all going to take to the bank. That's going to be God damned real."

Of course, the whole point of the fake limb was that it was supposed to pass for real. But Evans was always showing it off. Despite the popular 1980's TV slogan - "It's not nice to fool Mother Nature" - men like Bob Evans knew that all it took was money to do just that.

After making sure the Texans were thoroughly soused, Evans had his staff usher them into his screening room, a separate building with gorgeous inlaid wooden floors. He screened a little film starring Dustin Hoffman in a hilarious take-off on Bob Evans. Hoffman's mockery made Evans seem even larger than before. After making sure the Texans had endless refills of Kristal he stood up and pitched *The Cotton Club*. "Evans was a great pitcher and a fabulous salesman," recalled John Hyde. Indeed, by the end of his spiel the Texans were in for millions.

Chapter 22. 1984. Beverly Hills

Later that night, after everyone left, the toilet overflowed into the screening room. Turned out somebody had thrown a tampon into it. The water ruined the inlaid floor. But Evans swore the money it cost to replace it was a trifle compared to what the Texans were putting into *Cotton Club*.

Eventually, the Texans and their money disappeared. Evans was pissed. For a little while he thought he'd give up. Then he became more determined than ever to get the funding. Unfortunately, his real problems began *after* he finally had the $23.5 million budget in hand.

The film was slated to star Richard Gere, Diane Lane and Gregory Hines. But it was a disaster from start to finish. After all his failed attempts to raise the money, Evans realized he wasn't going to get it with him directing. After he was told over and over again that he'd have to bring in a top director, despite hating his guts, Evans offered the picture to Francis Ford Coppola.

Coppola and Evans had an adversarial history from *The Godfather*, which Coppola had directed and Evans produced when he was head of Paramount. After Coppola signed on to direct, their fighting resumed with their respective roles on *The Cotton Club*. "It was not a good script," Mark recalled, "and Coppola continued to play with it. Meanwhile, it took forever and got worse and worse."

The plot revolved around The Cotton Club, a famous Harlem night club. It followed the guests who visited and performed at the place as well as the gangsters who ran it and the jazz that made it famous. The rambling story included crime, drama, music and dance. But it lacked cohesion.

Pulitzer-Prize winning novelist William Kennedy was brought in to do a ten-day polish. But the legendary fights between Evans and Coppola kept on delaying the shoot. After it finally started, it went on for the next twenty-two months. Kennedy's ten-day polish lasted eighty-seven days, the length of the production, at $12,500 a week. He wrote twenty-eight drafts while the $10 million budget swelled to $48 million. Payrolls were missed. Further delays sent the budget skyrocketing to a staggering $58 million. Evans scurried to find more investors to put up more money for him to finish the film. With little success.

One day, John got a call from Bob. "Oh God, we got all the money," he enthused. "These guys are going to finance the rest of the *Cotton Club*. They're a sure bet!"

"Great," said John, not mentioning that this was the 12th set of "sure bet" financiers.

"You've got to get over here right away, man," pleaded Evans. "And remember, you guys are doing *Sheena, Queen of the Jungle.*"

"What?" demanded John.

"Just tell these guys we're doing a movie together called *Sheena*. Please," Evans pleaded in a gruff whisper. "The money depends on it."

John went over to Woodlands that night. "I was introduced to a couple of guys and a minute later a blond girl came in," he recalled, "and Bob said, 'Tell me, John, isn't she *Sheena*?!'" An enthusiastic Evans showed John pictures of the girl with a snake wrapped around her body. "Apparently, she did some kind of Vegas lounge act with animals, kind of like Siegfried and Roy's younger sister."

Evans introduced John to Sheena's 'friends,' Fred Doumani and his brother, Ed, wealthy Las Vegas casino owners. John quickly discovered that on the promise that Evans was going to put the girl in the fictitious *Sheena of the Jungle* he had gotten the Doumani brothers to put their money into *The Cotton Club*. "Who am I to quash the deal?," John decided. He went along with Evans as he described the 'movie' they were going to make together and the Doumani's wanted in.

As time passed, they put more and more money into *The Cotton Club* until their investment added up to $24 million. Along with such a large venture came the Doumani's watchdog - a spindly little guy named Joey Cusumano - a Vegas associate with reputed Mafia ties. When *Cotton Club* shot in New York, Cusumano was on set all day every day. When Evans went back to L.A. he hung out at Woodlands. He was around so often he became one of the 'gang.' "One day when I was over there," recalled Hyde, "Cusumano, a little guy who didn't look at all athletic, was watching Jack Nicholson and Bob play tennis in their tennis whites."

"Stop running around in your underwear, guys. Let's go have a drink," he yelled.

"No, come play tennis with us," they yelled back.

"Are you kidding?" Cusumano laughed. "I don't know how."

Eventually, Nicholson got tired and Joey was pressured to play with Evans. Hyde: "When he said he had nothing to wear Nicholson said he'd lend him some shorts. We all laughed when Cusumano came out of Evan's pool-house wearing black socks and a pair of white shorts that were about 14 times too big. "

It was no big surprise that he was terrible.

"Tell you what," Evans said charitably. "You always play better when you bet. Bet me something."

Chapter 22. 1984. Beverly Hills

"Oh God, okay," said Cusumano, "I'll bet $500. That's all I can afford to lose."

Evans agreed. And from that moment on, he didn't win another point. Turned out Cusumano was a great tennis player. He beat the shit out of Evans who lost the $500 while Nicholson watched, loving that he had been taken by Cusumano. It would later turn out that Evans was taken by Cusumano and the Doumani's in more ways than one.

In time, the Doumani's were investigated by the Gambling Commission and lost their gambling license because of their association with Cusumano and his ties to organized crime. Despite their insistence that they didn't know him, the Commission pointed out that Cusumano was on the set of *The Cotton Club* every day as their watchdog. (Cusumano would later spend four years in prison only to resurface, claim he'd found money to finance films and disappear again.) As a result the Doumani's were forced to sell their stock when the market was at a low. With so much of their cash in *The Cotton Club* the only way they could recoup their losses was for the picture to be a hit.

They turned on Evans, blaming him for everything that had gone wrong. But their venomous accusations were only one of many nails in the coffin of his career. After being conceived by Evans as his crowning achievement he ended up being banned from the set of *The Cotton Club* by Coppola. "I want to pick him up and throw him, the fat fuck, outta the fuckin' window," Evans roared. But he was helpless to change things. "When I visited the set," Mark affirmed, "Evans was lying on a couch in a fetal position. There he was, a beaten man."

All of that drama paled in comparison to the charges the LAPD leveled at Evans when an associate, Roy Radin, was found murdered. Although it was rumored that after LAPD investigators interviewed Evans for four hours they emerged with autographed copies of the Chinatown script in their hands, the murder investigation added more fuel to the fire of his highly public demise.

By the time *The Cotton Club* was finally released, Evans was a beaten man. The film tanked. Four months later the film hadn't even recouped half of its $58 million budget and lawsuits began piling up.

Everyone sued everyone else. Most U.S. backers never saw a penny from *The Cotton Club*. PSO became the only investor to make money on the cursed film. Still, like everyone else involved, Mark and John got burned.

From Cowboy to Mogul to Monster

Although they had gotten the original $8 million for the foreign rights based on Bob Evans as the director, when Coppola came on Orion wanted PSO to put up a bigger foreign guarantee. Mark refused, making an enemy of Orion. The studio didn't invite him or John to the Hollywood premiere of *The Cotton Club,* a film they had helped to finance.

The men had to throw a fit in the lobby just to get in to see it.

In the end, although Bob Evans was able to one-up Mother Nature by buying a perfect fake tree limb, even a showman like him couldn't buy his way out of the mess of *The Cotton Club.*

Mark Damon

1956 - 1961

"Take it from a director: if you get an actor that Sandy Meisner has trained you've been blessed."
- Elia Kazan

CHAPTER TWENTY-THREE

August 19, 1956

New York City

Sanford Meisner Acting School.

Chapter 23. 1956. New York

WHEN MARK EMERGED FROM LA GUARDIA he was hit by a wall of hot and humid August air. It was the month when most well-heeled New Yorkers vamoosed to the beach or the country. But as everyone else was busily rushing to escape the city he was heading right into it, sticking to the vinyl seat of the taxi and wondering if he had just made a huge mistake. "I realized that the work I had done in Hollywood meant nothing and the people who had guided me were 3000 miles behind me," he later wrote.

As they crossed the Triboro Bridge he had his first glimpse of the city he hoped to conquer, a Mecca for artists of all types. In Greenwich Village, Beat poets mingled with jazz musicians; on Broadway, Barbara Bel Geddes was starring as Maggie in "Cat On A Hot Tin Roof;" Jason Robards was in rehearsals for Eugene O'Neill's "Long Day's Journey into Night"; Charles Laughton, Eli Wallach and Burgess Meredith were about to open in George Bernard Shaw's "Major Barbara." It was a thrilling place for a serious actor. But as he climbed up the stairs of the sixth floor walkup he had rented, Mark was questioning whether he would ever become one.

The next morning he took two buses to Sanford Meisner's Neighborhood Playhouse School of the Theatre at 340 East 54th Street and enrolled in Meisner's two-year intensive course in all aspects of theatre. The course was open to a maximum of 110 students, most in their early twenties. It included, besides acting, classes in speech, dance, fencing, makeup, etc.

Later, he met Elaine Aiken for dinner at Downey's, a hangout for New York actors. "If you went to Downey's," commented Susan Strasberg, "you didn't need to read the gossip columns. You found out everything that was happening and to whom."

Standing in front of the restaurant Elaine, in her trench coat and Levis, looked very New York-Actorish. Mark, in his broad-shouldered sport coat and tie, didn't. "At that time in Hollywood if they groomed you for stardom you were supposed to wear suits, ties, sport jackets. It was part of the whole studio system about teaching kids how to dress, how to act. But when the Method came in, suddenly it was 'cool' to dress down and fight the Hollywood image."

Elaine greeted him with a hug and kiss.

"Let me look at you," she exclaimed. "I can't believe you're really here!"

"That makes two of us."

"How does it feel to start all over again?" she asked.

"Scary."

"So let's get a drink. 'Scary' is good."

She put her arm through his and they walked into Downey's where she was greeted by actors as they headed to their table. As soon as they sat down someone yelled, "Since when are you dating Hollywood actors?"

"Lay off, Marty, he's OK," she shot back.

"Oh, yeah? But can he act?" the voice laughed. Others joined in.

"Ignore it," she told Mark.

But the barbs kept coming throughout dinner and after a fast burger they left. Outside, Elaine reassured him.

"Don't let those assholes bug you. You're here to learn, not impress the Downey's gang."

"Yeah."

She gave him a friendly kiss on the lips and headed in the opposite direction. As Mark walked home alone he passed couples who strolled hand in hand, a group of dancers giggling at a private joke, a gaggle of attractive young party-goers coming out of a restaurant, drunk on champagne. By the time he climbed the stairs to his sublet on West 67th Street he'd never felt so lonely in his life.

The next day he reported promptly to Meisner's class at 1:00 PM, a good thing since the doors locked as soon as class started. He would have done well to heed the sole quote on the wall of Meisner's office: "I wish the stage were as narrow as a tightrope wire so that no incompetent would dare step upon it." Instead, he walked into the classroom, unaware that he was about to have a life-changing encounter.

The Meisner classroom was large, cold and bare. No stage, just a few props on one side of the room where they were to act. On the other side of the room, Sandy Meisner sat at a small desk surrounded by sixteen hard wooden chairs where students sat quietly, either staring straight ahead or trying to take in Sandy or the other students with side glances.

He recognized Gwen Verdon, who was starring as Lola in "Damn Yankees", John Frankenheimer and a few other actors. Several class members were called to do scenes and Mark nervously waited his turn as he studied Meisner, a small man with an intense presence.

"We called him Sandy," recalled Sidney Pollack, who studied with Meisner for six years after graduating from high school and became his assistant, "but it felt daring and dangerous, like ordering a martini in a nightclub when you were sixteen and trying to pass for twenty-one. He was too awesome a presence for the familiarity of a first name."

Chapter 23. 1956. New York

Meisner, formerly an actor, had been a founding member of the Group Theatre, a cooperative ensemble which became a leading force in the '30s. He had performed in many of the group's most memorable productions before forming the Neighborhood Playhouse School, where he taught his unique approach to acting.

Meisner felt the actor's job was simply to prepare for an experiment that would take place on stage. The best acting, he believed, was made up of spontaneous responses to the actor's immediate surroundings. His approach centered on improvisations designed "to eliminate all intellectuality from the actor's instrument and make him react to where he is, what is happening to him and what is being done to him."

Mark watched the other students work until Sandy finally called on him, assigned him a partner, outlined a situation and told them to go ahead and improvise the scene. "I became pretty emotional," he later wrote, "and when it was finished I felt pretty good and awaited Sandy's praise." There was a long pause. Finally, Sandy said: "You're not in Hollywood anymore. You're really going to have to work."

New York wasn't going to go easy on him, Mark reflected as he walked home through Central Park. But what was his alternative? Go back to minor roles in TV and 'B' movies? Berate himself for not having learned techniques he desperately needed? No, he would stick it out in New York. He was going to become a serious actor no matter what Meisner or anyone said.

For the next couple of months he attended class five days a week and worked on Meisner's exercises. One was 'spontaneous repetition': two actors looked directly at each other while one described a feature of the other, then the actors said the phrase back and forth. Because the phrase (such as "You have sad eyes") came from a physical reality apparent to the actors, Meisner believed the statement retained its meaning no matter how many times it was repeated. Another exercise was to have two actors enter a room and play specific roles without specific lines. As they spoke the plot was formed out of nothing but their surroundings. The actor's only concern was to stay in character.

Meisner's goal was to strip actors of everything, to just force them to react. It was all action/reaction. It was all foreign to Mark and difficult for him to surrender to. Meanwhile, Sandy remained unimpressed with his

183

efforts as well as his Hollywood credits. "Today, most actors simply want to be famous," he expounded. "But being an actor was never supposed to be about fame and money. Being an actor is a religious calling because you've been given the ability, the gift to inspire humanity. Think about *that* on the way to your soap opera audition."

"Nothing prepared me for the intensity of the experience," said Pollack. "It wasn't that Sandy was harsh or mean; it was only that he was so frighteningly accurate. You felt he knew every thought, impulse or feeling in your head, that he had an ability to x-ray your very being and there was absolutely no place to hide." "Above all," said Gregory Peck of Meisner, "what he wanted from you was truthful acting."

"What Meisner taught was going from moment to moment," Mark recalled. "And I found that very hard to do." So Meisner criticized him for being too mannered, too phony, too *too*. "Stop being false! Be honest," he barked. "Don't think about what you're about to say. Really listen to the other person." "Relax, and respond to everything the other actor does."

He was a tough critic but he did so with purpose. "I like to think that I prepare artists to survive in a world that doesn't always want them," he explained.

As promised, Pepi Schildkraut took Mark under his wing. One afternoon, after watching Mark read a scene he was preparing, the older actor leapt to his feet. "Not like that, my boy," he exclaimed, taking the 'sides' out of Mark's hands. "Like this." He read the lines with his typical flamboyance and an entirely different interpretation. Mark started to laugh as he realized what he had missed in the scene.

"Wonderful," he praised. "Okay, let me try it again."

But Pepi held onto the 'sides.'

"Shall we do it a little later?" he suggested smoothly. "After we go have a coffee? All that emoting made me hungry."

"Sure." By now, Mark was used to this. As usual, they walked to a local restaurant and lingered over coffee, talking and laughing until one cup of coffee turned into two, then drinks and dinner.

"You see that girl over there?" Pepi said. As usual.

Mark played along, following his gaze. "You mean the little brunette? The one who's smiling?"

"She's been smiling at you for the last hour. Why don't you smile back at the poor dear and invite her to join us. And tell her to bring her little friend."

Chapter 23. 1956. New York

That was how it went whenever he saw Pepi. Mark would invite the women and Schildkraut, a superb raconteur, would hold court for the rest of the evening, sometimes wangling a good night kiss from a pretty young thing. It was Schildkraut's ulterior motive for mentoring him. Although devoted to his wife, Marie, he had an insatiable eye for young women and he knew that wherever Mark went, women were sure to follow. It was a harmless tradeoff, Mark decided, for Pepi's helpful acting tips and good advice.

By the end of October, Mark's routine was to go from class to the unemployment office to one theatre audition after another without ever getting cast. One afternoon he read for *The Dark at the Top of the Stairs* with a teenage blonde actress named Tuesday Weld. He thought she was a cute kid and later heard she got the part of Theresa Wright's understudy.

Other than that he spent a lot of time alone. "Mark never needed a lot of friends," said his brother Bob. "I don't think he needed someone to talk to all the time, a best buddy-type." Instead, Mark often walked through Central Park alone, stopping to write notes to himself on his old "Contest Books" letterhead: "I want to say what is individually mine. I want to find the essence, the specialness, the feeling and believing and meaning of *my own* truth."

But even as he searched and probed for his essence, Sandy kept after him to dig deeper. "I didn't realize that he might have a purpose in doing this. That maybe he sensed I responded well to a challenge and picked my Hollywood background as a vulnerable point so he hit at it again and again."

As the New Year approached, Mark had been living in New York for almost six months with no sign of progress. He began to wonder if Sandy was constantly criticizing him because he disliked him. Should he leave the school? But who would he study with? Who could possibly top Sandy Meisner?

On New Year's Eve, 1956, Mark scowled at himself in the mirror as he took another stab at tying his bow tie. He gave up, shrugged into his tux coat and eyed himself warily. He didn't look like he was going to a New Year's Eve party. He looked like he was preparing for battle.

He was. Because he wasn't going to just any New Year's Eve party. He had wangled an invite to *Lee Strasberg's* New Year's Eve party: "And I was afraid it might be another repeat of the Downey's scene with digs about me being too Hollywood. Only ten times worse, because the cream of the New York crop of actors would be there." Despite his misgivings he was determined to meet the legendary Strasberg in his own home, maybe even talk about working with him. Mark also knew that his daughter, Susan Strasberg would be there and he'd wanted to meet the dark-eyed young actress since he'd been struck by her beauty in *Picnic*.

As he took one last look in the mirror a light bulb went off. "What am I thinking?!" Going to the party in that tux would be like waving a red flag at the Strasberg crowd. "Haven't you learned anything in New York?" he chided himself. He threw off his tux coat and dressed down in an open shirt and jeans.

When he got off the elevator on the tenth floor of the Strasberg's building on the Upper West Side he heard loud music and raucous laughter coming from down the hall. He followed it and stepped into an apartment filled with a hundred people in animated conversations framed against the largest collection of books he'd ever seen.

He knew hardly anyone but recognized Shelley Winters, Ben Gazzara, Tony Franciosa, Cliff Robertson, Kim Stanley, Judy Holliday and others. As the party raged on with drunken singing, yelling and laughter he met Strasberg, a small, intense man with piercing eyes behind glasses. The revelry was so loud they couldn't talk.

"At that by-now famous New Year's Eve party," Susan Strasberg later wrote in her memoir, *Bittersweet,* "my brother, without consulting anyone, invited his entire school football team: thirty-five fourteen and fifteen-year olds. My mother banished them to a back room, where Judy Holliday and Maureen Stapleton spent much of the evening with one of the best audiences they ever had."

The high point of Mark's evening came when he was sandwiched between Paula Strasberg's generous spread and the guests who were demolishing it. He was in the dining room when he was introduced to the small and lovely Susan, who was starring on Broadway in *The Diary of Anne Frank,* having beaten Natalie Wood for the role.

"Hello, Mark Damon," she said saucily. "Do you want to make small talk or do you want to really talk?"

"Everyone around me faded away," he later recalled. "I was struck by her laugh, her openness and her intense, fun way of talking."

"It depends," he shot back. "How real do you want to get?"

Chapter 23. 1956. New York

She smiled, took his hand in hers and led him to her bedroom (which she sometimes shared with Marilyn Monroe.) There, they talked and laughed into the wee hours of the New Year 1957.

A week later he showed up backstage at the Coronet Theatre to walk her home. First he ran into Pepi, who was playing Susan's father, Otto Frank.

"My dear boy," Pepi exclaimed, embracing him.

Over his shoulder, Mark glimpsed Susan gazing at him with distinct coolness. He disentangled himself from Pepi and followed her to the door.

"Can I walk you home?"

Susan paused for a moment.

"Okay."

They walked up Broadway chatting uneasily before she turned to him.

"How long have you known Pepi?"

"Not that long," Mark answered, explaining their connection. "Why?"

"Because he's making my life miserable!" Susan vented.

"What is he doing?"

"The other day, he pinched me onstage," she protested. "And another night during a scene where I kiss him good night, he opened his mouth! He's a complete letch!"

"I'm sorry," Mark said, not surprised. He knew that any female was fair game to Pepi.

"And another time he came into my dressing room without knocking," she continued hotly, "and when I protested that I wasn't dressed he said, 'my dear Suzileh, I saw you when you were a baby.'" She was close to tears. "He's known me all my life!"

"What a shit!" Mark said. "I'm so sorry."

As he sympathized with her, Susan began to thaw. From then on Mark often walked her home from the theatre. Sometimes they stopped for coffee, sometimes they talked late into the night before kissing at her front door. He was falling for the slender, sensitive young brunette. "But Susan wasn't falling in love with me," he lamented. "She was in 'like' with me. So we were just friends."

Mark was still thinking about asking Lee Strasberg to work with him until Susan discouraged him. "My father can be completely unmerciful.

Sometimes he'll tear into someone's work. Rip it apart. He says he does it to get results. And sometimes it works. But he can be brutal."

"I suddenly realized maybe that was what Sandy had been doing with me," Mark later wrote, "and that if I were to learn anything switching was not the answer. I would just have to let down my Hollywood defenses and buckle down to work."

He returned to Meisner's class in early 1957 with renewed vigor. He began to follow through on the out-of-class exercises. One called for what Meisner dubbed 'critical seeing': a student was supposed to make a habit of looking at things and recording what he saw, liked or disliked.

On a gray and wintry day Mark began to do just that as he was walking through Central Park. Alone, as usual. "There was a light drizzle in the air but I stopped to watch a flock of pigeons. It was the first time I ever really noticed how they eat," he later wrote. "How, when pieces of bread are too big to consume in one peck, they shake their heads violently until the bread breaks off, then scurry to find the pieces they've flung.

Nice, these pigeons. No arguments. If another pigeon picks up on their meal before they're finished, they just calmly search for another morsel. No bickering about rightful possession. I wondered why I had never noticed this before. Then I realized that in New York I had seen many things I hadn't allowed myself time to notice. Just as I had while I was trying to get a foothold in Hollywood. I realized that for a long time I've been so concerned with movie lots, trade papers, producers, directors, scripts, etc. that I didn't even notice that the most important thing, living fully, was getting a bypass."

When he read the passage aloud in class, Meisner for once, had no criticism. A month later a miracle occurred. After Mark presented a scene he'd worked on with an actress named Karen Chandler he held his breath, waiting for Sandy to criticize it. He was frowning. "Here it comes again," Mark thought. Then Sandy began nodding his head slowly up and down and a wonderful thing happened. He actually *smiled* at Mark.

"You know," he said, "Hollywood just might be proud of you when you return."

Irving Harris, age 39, in front of his grocery store with his brother Alvin Harris.

Lilian Elfman Harris, age 22

Alan Harris (nee Herkovitz, later to become Mark Damon) age 3 years, 8 months

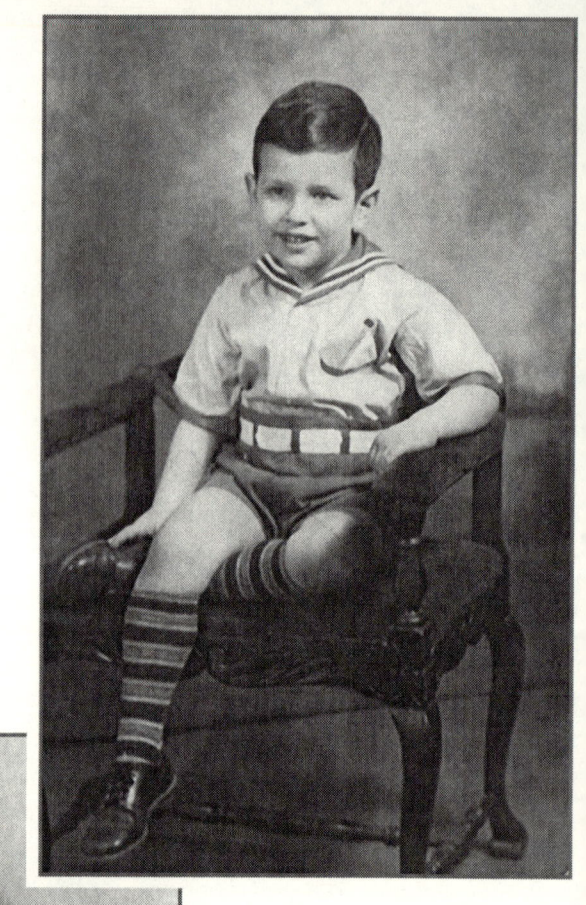

Alan Harris, age 5 with mother and baby brother, Bobby in Chicago.

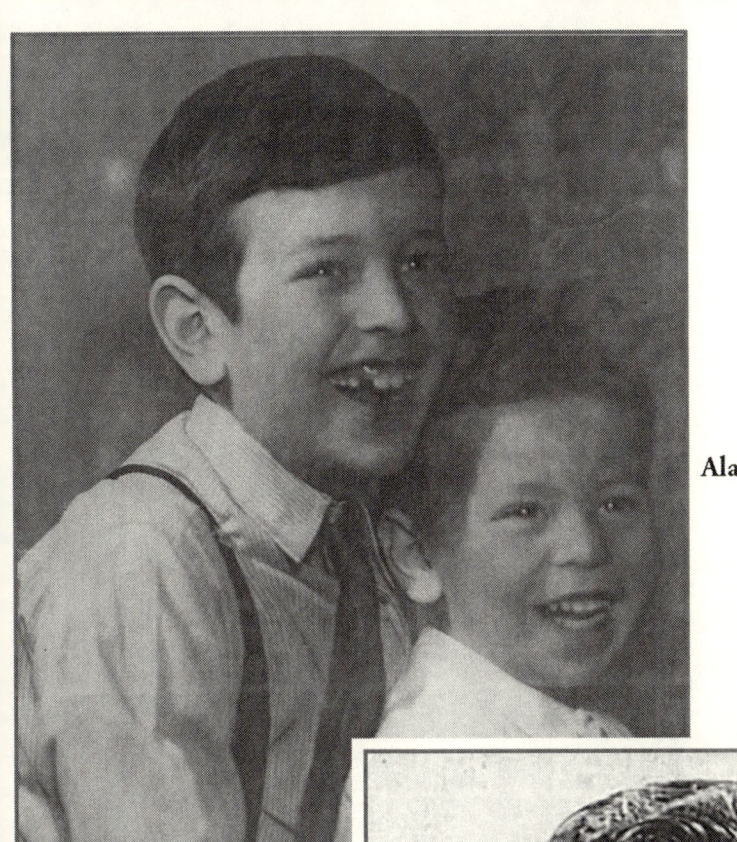

Alan and Bobby, ages 7 and 2

Alan, age 13

Graduating Fairfax High School (1950).

Age 18, at college prom with Barbara Marks.

192

Al Harris, age 21, sips a Coke in ad for clothing line.

Modeling swimwear.

Beefcake shot.

Starring with June Allyson in *June Allyson Show* (1956).

Coming to blows in *Young and Dangerous* (Fox), 1957.

Embracing Lily Gentile in *Young and Dangerous* (Fox), 1957.

With Connie Stevens in *Party Crashers* (Par), 1958.

Flexing his biceps for *Party Crashers*.

On American Bandstand to promote *I Don't Wanna Go Home*.
With Dick Clark.

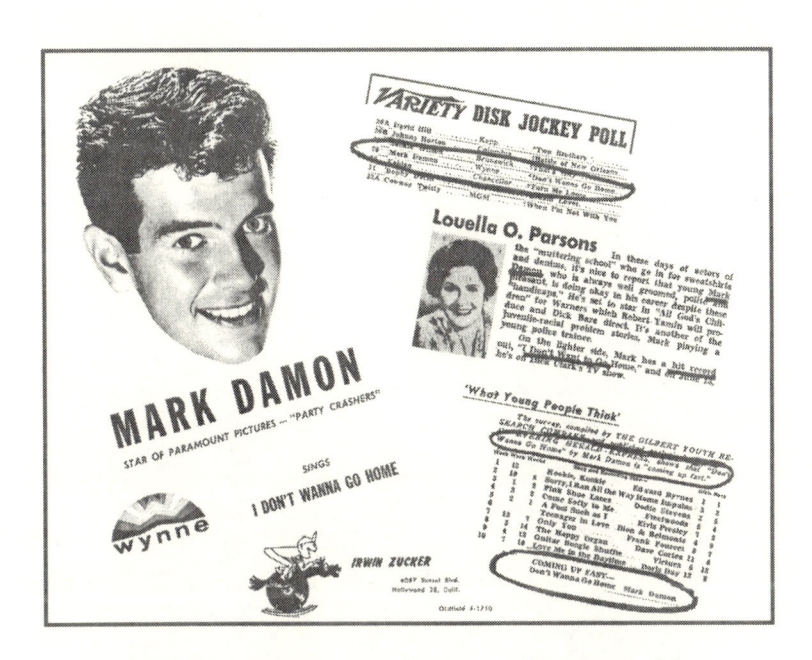

Mark's recording career begins, and ends quickly.

With Dyan Cannon frolicking on the set of *This Rebel Breed* (1960).

With Susan Kohner out on the town.

With mom, Lillian, and his date, Madlyn Rhue.

With Myrna Fahey, theater exhibitor and Roger Corman on the set of *The Fall of the House of Usher* (1960).

202

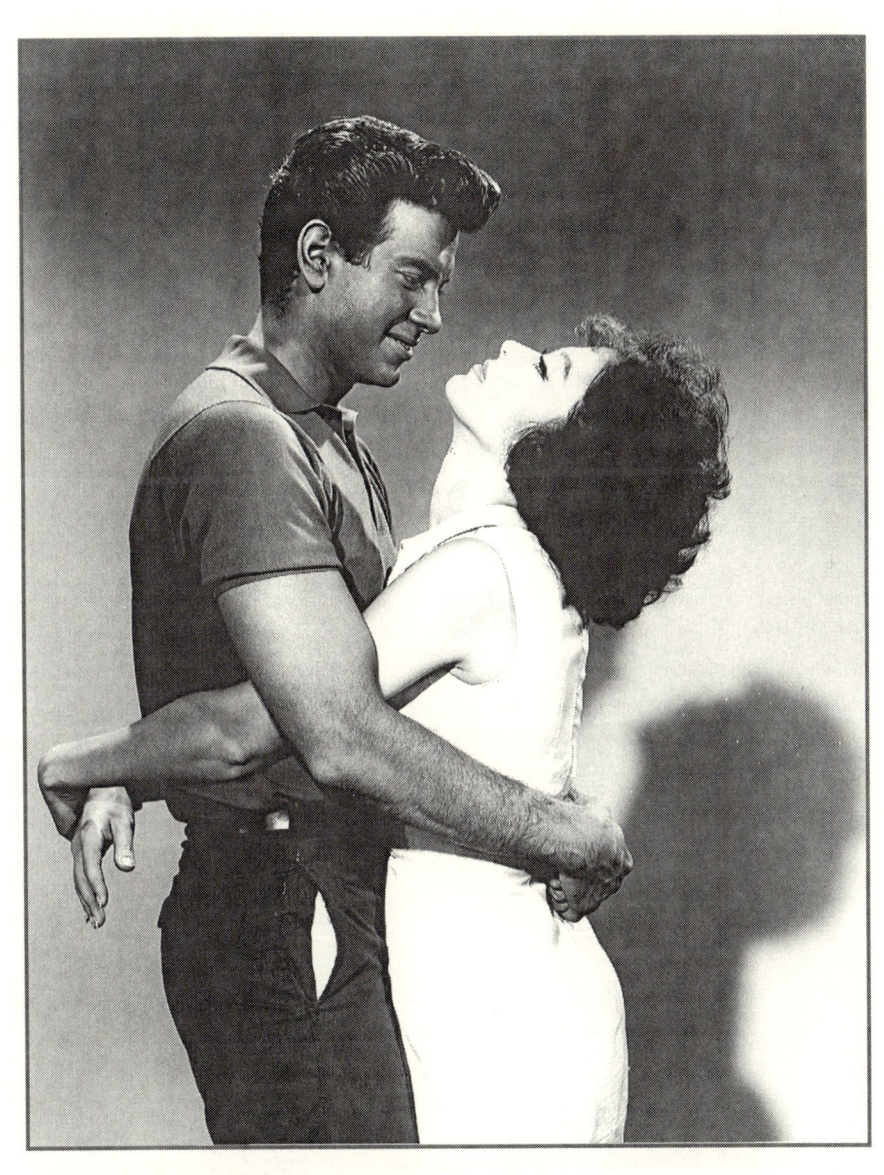

In dark makeup, as the half-Black/ half – Mexican hero with Rita Moreno, in *This Rebel Breed* (1960).

Mark Damon's fan club.

Marked Man

Heading the growing list of Hollywood's hot newcomers, Mark Damon's talent and determination are destined to carry him far.

WHEN Mark Damon was very young he wanted to be a cowboy. A few years later it was an astronomer and still later a professor. Then one day Mark made a startling discovery. He could be *everything*! How? By becoming an actor. From that day on Mark never swerved in his determination to meet his fate. He felt sure he was destined to become an actor and nothing was going to stand in his way. Carefully he laid his plans. If he wanted to be everything he would have to know a little about everything. He studied hard in school, reading every book he could find. After classes he worked at an assortment of jobs from delivering newspapers to washing dishes. There were sacrifices involved because there simply wasn't time. At 17 he went into business for himself, selling books on winning puzzle contests. By the time he was 18 he had netted $10,000 and also won an $18,000 first prize in a puzzle contest. Financial pressure relieved, Mark was able to enter college and take an active part not only in dramatics but in sports. When he was graduated from U.C.L.A. he set out, with the same determination, to carve his niche in the professional world. An amateur production won him TV offers and a film role in Inside Detroit. Since that time he has been seen on Author's Playhouse, Light's Diamond Jubilee, Hallmark Playhouse and many others. Each time his dynamic acting and good looks have attracted wide attention. Although the parts are coming in nicely now, Mark doesn't believe in sitting back and waiting for luck to come to him. He feels you should make your own breaks by working hard and being ready for the opportunities when they come. His favorite quotation, quite appropriately, is from Julius Caesar: "The fault, dear Brutus, is not in our stars, but in ourselves, that we are underlings." Mark knows, as do all who have seen him act, that he has an appointment with destiny to move on to acting fame, but you can be sure he's going to meet destiny halfway. ★★

Karen Sharpe's phone rings constantly but it's a real treat when Mark Damon calls her for a date.

TV Star Parade July 1960

HE HAS EVERYTHING BUT THE GIRL TO SHARE IT WITH; FROM MARK DAMON'S HEART, COMES AN . . .

open letter to THE GIRL I'LL MARRY

Mark often dates Susan Kohner (rt.) and Diane Baker (below). His most important role yet will be in Poe's Fall of the House of Usher *for American International.*

M y dearest,
"I tried to think I was a woman's man." Mark Damon's green eyes twinkled as he wrote. He was remembering how it felt to be 15, to have a "steady girl," to be in love for the first time—and was laughing just a little at the image of himself as the ardent young lover. This was a letter to a very special girl, the girl he would marry. Conscious of his 27 years, thinking of all the girls he had known—and some whom he had loved—Mark continued hesitantly. He wanted this girl to know all about himself, yet he didn't want to sound like a know-it-all playboy.

"In the past seven years I've dated many different types of girls, I guess depending on my tastes and needs at the moment. In high school it was the external things that attracted me. I wanted everyone to see me out with the most popular girl, the girl all the other guys wanted to date. I went steady for a while, but found that soon there wasn't much to talk about.

"When I was 18 and in college, I dated the rah-rah girl, the gal who was the most fun at football games. As a graduate just starting to act, it was the sophisticated glamour girl—young starlets just coming up like Lori Nelson or Susan Cabot—that fascinated me. I thought I was in love a couple of times, *(Continued on page 65)*

TV STAR PARADE 45

Every move is carefully planned—
and try holding that pose while the
photog takes a light reading.

You can't pigeon-hole Mark. He's both rebel
(as in **Young and Dangerous**) and nice guy,
and confesses he changes roles almost daily!

Pals like Luana Anders understand Mark's yen to
be "exotic without shaving my head." And he
does succeed, too! Mark's in **The Party Crashers**.

DAMON!

PART TWO

Making a movie is like a stage coach ride through the old west.
At first you hope for a pleasant journey.
Then you simply hope to reach your destination.
            -Francois Truffaut

Chapter Twenty-Four

April 25, 1984

New York City

9½ Weeks

Chapter 24. 1984. New York

"Being a Hollywood producer is definitely *not* all it was cracked up to be," Mark thought as he stood on the set of *9 ½ Weeks*.

Food was everywhere. On the kitchen floor a blindfolded, bath-robed and bobby-soxed Kim Basinger sprawled in front of an open refrigerator. Her eyes were closed as Mickey Rourke hand-fed her black olives, spoonfuls of juicy red cherry jam, a chili pepper, a carafe of milk that poured down her face. After Rourke drizzled honey onto her thighs and rubbed it in they began to make love.

On the sound stages, director Adrian Lyne manned one of the cameras, cheer-leading his actors while cinematographer Peter Biziou silently manned the second one. The few crew members who were allowed in watched, unsure what to make of these two sexy young stars who were cavorting with food. Mark, least of all.

Just that morning, in his new role as producer, he had come into Kim's dressing room and found her curled up in the fetal position, unable to function. "She was a basket case," he said of the actress who was so shy that her mother used to beg her grade school teachers not to call on Kim in class. "Plus, she hated Mickey and he hated her." "And they both hated Adrian Lyne," confirmed casting director Mary Jo Slattery.

Yet there they were, sensuously enjoying each other on the sound stage. And their chemistry was incredible.

PSO's first production began with a desperate phone call from Gary Hendler, Chairman and CEO of Tri-Star Studios.

"We have a big problem with *9 ½ Weeks*," he confided. "It's about to shoot in three days and the studio decided it's too risky to make. Do you guys want to take over and finance and produce the picture?"

"Send me the script right away," Mark replied.

"By then, *9 ½ Weeks* had been around for years and every studio had turned it down," recalled John. Most studios feared American audiences weren't ready for a film featuring sadomasochism, female masturbation and plenty of kinky sex.

But three things were in Hendler's favor on the day he called: John had just closed a deal for a $50 million PSO picture fund with Sidney Kimmel, the successful New York businessman who was the founder of Jones Apparel Group and the newly formed Jonesfilm Productions. Mark

From Cowboy to Mogul to Monster

and John were eager for a film to produce. And Mark had always wanted to make an erotic movie.

He loved the script and within 48 hours they had a deal with Tri-Star to distribute the first PSO/Jonesfilm Production. Adrian Lyne was already set to direct, fresh off his success with *Flashdance*. Two hot young actors were playing the leads. Rehearsals had been going on for two weeks in New York by the time Mark flew in, eager to work with Lyne and the actors.

Adrian Lyne had gotten his start as a director of TV commercials. He had directed only one feature before *Flashdance,* the breakout film that showcased his dazzling visuals in a story about an aspiring ballerina who works in a factory by day and dances at a club by night. When his visuals were paired with innovative dance sequences and an exuberant score by Giorgio Moroder, Lyne had a hit on his hands.

Offers began to pour in for new projects. Lyne was mesmerized when he read the novel, "9 ½ Weeks." The title of the sexually explicit work by Elizabeth McNeill referred to the length of time of an affair between Elizabeth, a beautiful, uptight art dealer and John, a mysteriously compelling and dangerous financier who becomes her lover. As the plot unfolds John takes Elizabeth on a sensual journey in an ever-deepening game of sexual dominance while unlocking the doors to her hidden passion.

The script was written by newcomers Zalman King, his wife, Patricia Louisianna Knopf and Sarah Kernochan. "All kinds of people warned me not to do it because it was a sadomasochistic love story," Lyne later recalled. "But I thought it had fascinating possibilities. 'It will be like committing professional suicide,' said some of my friends. To be honest," he later laughed, "it almost was."

His troubles began when he offered the role of John to Mickey Rourke, a young actor whom some Hollywood insiders saw as 'the next Brando.' He had blown critics away with his performances in *Body Heat, Rumble Fish* and *The Pope of Greenwich Village.* Lyne thought the sullen-looking former boxer was perfect for the part. But when Rourke agreed to the role Lyne was unaware that he would prove to be a mouthy, undisciplined, streetwise Hell-raiser who would be perpetually late and terrify Kim Basinger. Or that he would cause so much trouble on the shoot that Mark would be the first of many in Hollywood to call him a "first-class prick."

Chapter 24. 1984. New York

Lyne's search for the perfect Elizabeth involved testing hundreds of actresses until Kim Basinger's screen test convinced Lyne to go with her. "She displayed an incredible range of emotions – from composure to self-confidence, from child-like vulnerability to a bundle of nerves with all her imperfections on display."

But when he offered her the part the long-legged, full-lipped blonde beauty turned the role down. "In fact, she turned it down nine different times," according to casting director Mary Jo Slater. "Basinger hated the script. She didn't want to do it. I just kept saying to the director, Adrian Lyne, 'She's the one. Make her an offer she can't refuse.'"

Eventually, Basinger was persuaded to take the role. Once again, Lyne had no idea of the trouble ahead. That the very mood swings that convinced him to cast Basinger were daily occurrences in the life of the gorgeous, unpredictable, agoraphobic actress.

At first, everyone was jazzed about doing the movie. "We are very excited about doing *9 ½ Weeks*," Mark told the press. "I believe it will make a terrific picture."

"I want to make films… that people care about…" Lyne added, "and I'd love our audiences to walk out of the theatre wondering what it would be like to encounter John or Elizabeth."

"I think this is a movie that means something and says something – and a movie that will allow me to stretch and grow," Rourke expounded.

Everyone was feeling optimistic about the project. Then they started shooting.

On the first day, Mark discovered that "Adrian's way of directing was to *not* direct the actors. He would just let them go and shoot and shoot and shoot." Lyne, once a trumpeter in an amateur jazz band, liked his actors to improvise. "As long as I have a basic structure, I like to film the unpredictable moments between actors," he explained, "the bits and pieces."

"While that 'bits and pieces' approach might have worked with some actors," Mark countered, "by the time I got there Mickey had taken over as the director since Adrian didn't direct the actors much. Mickey was directing himself and trying to control Kim, who wasn't easily getting into the role. Rourke would run lines with her before the cameras rolled and do really sick things to her. In one of my first days on set just before Adrian yelled 'Action' Mickey suddenly slapped Kim in the face. When she burst out crying Adrian started shooting."

Mark was appalled. He soon learned that Kim was frightened of the role, frightened of Mickey and a basket case on set. "Most mornings I would come into Kim's dressing room and she would be lying there, helpless to fight her fear. I didn't know anything about agoraphobia back then. All I knew was that I would have to sit and talk with her for a couple of hours just to get her to even come on the set."

"In those days I was so scared of my own shadow that it was difficult for me to cross the street," Basinger later said. "I was often flat-out paralyzed by fear and self-consciousness... so insecure that I was out of my mind. All these eyes were on me and I felt like, 'Whatever you do, please don't look at me!'" As for her sexpot persona, "I was fighting my own image tooth and nail every day. I rebelled against it. I don't consider myself sexy. I have to <u>act</u> to be sexy."

Yet every evening as Adrian and Mark watched dailies, Kim's explicitly sexual scenes with Mickey portrayed an intimacy between them that was stunning. Despite the fact that "they hated each other" the footage showed the two of them in an incredible relationship onscreen.

Despite Kim's insistence to the contrary, Lyne's relentless close-ups captured her sensuality. Her blue eyes were rimmed with mascara-blackened lashes, her blonde hair was tousled and free, her beautiful face expressive and open. Perhaps her on-screen vulnerability was partially due to the tension between what Kim was playing and how much she hated playing it. Certainly her sensuality was enhanced by Lyne's lush and moody visuals. Whatever the reason, his voyeuristic camera made looking at Kim a compelling act on the part of the viewer. It would help to turn her into a world-wide icon after *9 ½ Weeks* was released.

As the shoot continued, Mark had increasing conflicts with Adrian. "He was always running behind schedule because he wouldn't block out scenes with the actors in advance. Then, after hours of free-wheeling improvisations he wouldn't get the shots he needed." So Mark insisted that he block scenes the night before. Adrian hated that. "I'm sorry," Mark said, "we don't have time anymore. This picture is costing us $16 million. We're way over budget." Adrian was put off by Mark's interference. "An executive's every instinct... is to iron out the bumps and it's always the bumps that are the most interesting stuff," he said. "You have to go to war on those things. And you never cut your losses."

Lyne thought Mark's methods were changing his movie for the worse. Mark thought producing a movie was the way you controlled it. "I didn't

Chapter 24. 1984. New York

care if I had to force him to block out scenes before he shot them. Every day that Lyne improvised on the set, dollar signs mounted." Soon they were locked in battle. Mark was growing desperate for a solution.

One afternoon after they wrapped, instead of arguing with Lyne he decided to use his experience as an actor. "I acted out the lines in the scenes we were shooting the next day. I played Kim, I played Mickey. Adrian picked up moves of mine that he liked and laid out others for the actors. I even *improvised* the actors' lines while we blocked out the scene. It gave Adrian at least some small sense that he was not being deprived of his freedom of improvisation."

Being the producer, Mark grew to realize, meant being the heavy. Especially when it meant dealing with Mickey Rourke, who sported seven tattoos, rode Harleys and was rude and surly. "I'm a night person," he liked to boast.

Mark soon found the problems that created. "Mickey would always show up late then spend about three hours on his hair. It turned out that often he had been out the whole night and got home at seven o'clock in the morning. Then, if he had a nine o'clock call he'd sleep till eleven o'clock."

One morning, Mark was waiting for Mickey in his trailer when he finally showed up, several hours late. "Mickey," he said evenly, "you know I'm funding this picture out of my own pocket, basically. When you miss three hours in the morning, do you know that it costs me about $40,000? I'm not rich. I've worked hard for everything I've got and I need your help."

"Oh man," Mickey apologized, "I didn't realize. I'm so sorry. Oh man, that's terrible. Yeah, I understand."

Then the next morning, same thing. Mickey Rourke couldn't have cared less whom he kept waiting or how much it cost. Decades later, he would admit, "I was getting a reputation for showing up late - which I did – and having a bad attitude – which I had." But at the time, he shrugged off all criticism. "This town is made up of people who have inherited their positions," he sneered. "I've earned my right to be whatever I am."

Unlikely as it seemed, Mickey and Mark had much in common. Both had grown up poor before becoming actors; both had worked at menial jobs to support themselves. Both took acting seriously and studied at the Strasberg Institute. But their common backgrounds didn't make for common ground.

Unlike Mark, Mickey was explosive, unruly and uncontrollable. He was surly and disrespectful to everyone, spewing venom in all directions. "If you cross me or disrespect me, you should get a bus ticket out of town," he liked to threaten. "Acting is a very unmanly business - it's woman's work," he scoffed, prompting Kim to call the chain-smoking Rourke nothing but "a human ashtray."

Mickey also offended Adrian: "A lot of directors are so brainwashed by the level of garbage they make that they can't see beyond their noses." He ridiculed critics: "I don't give a fuck about what any of the critics in this country say." Rourke was a walking minefield who would ultimately confess in 2000: "I've led an extreme life and it's taken a toll." But he was only one of the challenges on the troubled set.

Mark and Adrian's next battle was waged over one paragraph in the script: "Elizabeth does a strip tease for John." When it came time to shoot the strip, Adrian refused. "He felt it mirrored something he'd done in *Flashdance* and he didn't want critics to say he was repeating himself."

"You're going to do it," Mark insisted.

"No, I'm not," countered Adrian.

"It's in the script," Mark argued, "and you signed off on the script so you have to do it."

The more Adrian objected, the more Mark insisted. When Adrian realized he was making no headway with Mark he started to convince Kim and Mickey not to do the scene.

Kim told Mark she wouldn't do it. He repeated his mantra: "The scene is in the script. It has to be done." Soon he got a call from Rick Nicita at CAA, Kim's agent. "Mark, she just doesn't want to do it."

"Sorry. She's got to."

"What if she refuses?"

"We'll fine her. We'll take away her salary. I'll see that SAG suspends her." Mark had no idea whether SAG would do such a thing but he felt he had to show assuredness and determination. Nicita promised to talk with Kim.

Mark was on set when Kim and Mickey came in to rehearse the strip scene. They were dragging their heels. Adrian reluctantly started to lay it out. It was clear they all hated what they were doing. Mark started throwing out ideas. They were all rejected.

"Why not have her do the strip tease behind the blinds?" he finally suggested.

"Maybe that's not bad," Adrian reluctantly agreed.

Chapter 24. 1984. New York

The director started to lay it out. He began to see that they actually might do something interesting. His excitement caught on with Kim and Mickey. The scene began to come alive. Eventually she started to strip, silhouetted behind the blinds as Mickey sat on the other side, a bowl of popcorn in his hands, laughingly encouraging her.

Kim was electrifying from the moment she first appeared behind the blinds wearing a hat, a silk robe and high heels, teasing a set of handcuffs at the long end of a whip. Her gyrations to the music were inspired. She managed to look sexy and comical as she wrapped herself in a phone cord and slowly peeled off her long gloves and fishnets. The scene ended with Kim dropping her robe and running upstairs, nude, with Mickey in hot pursuit. When he found her dancing in the nude they began to make love.

Mark: "I didn't really think that Kim would take off her robe and dash upstairs nude but it was her idea. Once she had gotten into it she had no problem showing off her body. And no, despite the rumors, we did not use a body double for her."

In the end, the scene became one of the set pieces of the movie. When *9 ½ Weeks* was released and Basinger stripped to Joe Cocker's "You Can Leave Your Hat On" you could practically see the steam rising in the theatres.

By August, the troubled shoot was coming to an end just as they were running out of money. But Adrian still desperately wanted to shoot a scene where Elizabeth goes to the country to talk with an elderly painter, Matthew Farnsworth. Kim also wanted to do it. Mark thought "it had no purpose whatsoever. Adrian just loved the texture of it."

"It's just one scene. Can't we squeeze it in before we wrap?" he pleaded with Mark.

"I wish we could but we don't have the money."

"Come on, how long can it take to shoot?"

"Three days and lots of overtime," Mark replied.

Adrian kept pushing for it. Mark kept saying they didn't have the money. A producer, he had learned, may not have much creative control once shooting had started. But he still controlled the purse strings. When Mark was certain they had gotten all the scenes needed to make the movie he pulled the plug. Literally turned off the electricity.

"Movie's over," he pronounced.

Adrian came up to him. Furious.

"We still need that scene. We have to do it."

Alan Salke, Sidney Kimmel's tough, but able, production executive, came over, arms crossed, waiting to see if Mark would relent. Mark glanced at Salke, then said, "OK," surprising the hell out of Adrian, who grabbed Mark in a hug to thank him. Mark whispered in Adrian's ear, "But <u>you</u> have to pay for it."

Adrian looked at Mark to see if he was kidding. He wasn't. "The amazing thing was that Adrian shot one of the most gorgeous scenes in the movie on his own money and in twelve hours. Because it was costing him. Suddenly, a director saw how economy could work when it wasn't somebody else's money."

When the shoot wrapped Mark flew to Munich to see the rough cut of *NeverEnding Story*. The film had been almost two years in the making, its budget of $25 million rendering it the most expensive German picture ever. Next he planned to go back to running PSO and developing their next films. He had no idea that he would spend the next fourteen months in post-production, supervising the cutting and re-cutting of *9 ½ Weeks*. Twenty-three different times.

Hollywood

1957 – 1961

Chapter Twenty-five

August 24, 1957

Hollywood, California

Co-starring with Lily Gentle in Fox's *Young and Dangerous* (1957).

With Connie Stevens and Bobbie Driscoll in
Party Crashers (1958).

Causing a ruckus (*Party Crashers*).

With Luana Anders and Tommy Ivo in *Life Begins at 17* (1958).

Chapter 25. 1957. Hollywood

"WHAT'S THE MATTER WITH YOU?!" THE angry pedestrian yelled at 'Tommy Price', a young punk who had almost hit him with his hot rod. On the soundstage at Twentieth Century Fox, Mark was starring as Tommy, the tough, hormone-driven teen who terrorizes parents, defies cops and engages in nasty street brawls.

The movie, ironically titled *Young and Dangerous,* co-starred Lili Gentle as innocent, upstanding Rosemary whose pure love tames Tommy. Luckily, Lili was now seriously involved with Richard Zanuck and wanted nothing more than a friendship with Mark. He breathed a sigh of relief and hung out with two young actors who were making their debuts in the film: blonde and bubbly Connie Stevens and Edd Byrnes.

Billed as "the story that will shake every home in town!" *Young and Dangerous* was a classic 1950's cautionary tale. Teenagers were obsessed with hot rods, gangs and drive-ins. Parents were hopelessly old fashioned and ineffectual. It was only one of many teen rebellion movies Hollywood was churning out and the first in a succession of 'B' teenflicks that Mark would star in over the next three years.

He threw himself into the role of the rebellious leader of a gang of hoods, using what he'd learned from the Meisner Technique. He played reckless and tough, then tender and vulnerable with Rosemary. He had newfound range and he reveled in showing it. But returning to Hollywood proved to be a challenge.

When he tried to share Meisner's methods with other young actors on the set they balked. When he contradicted director Bill Claxton with his newfound knowledge the director walked off the set. "In New York they thought I was too Hollywood. Now that I was back in Hollywood they thought I was a New York snob."

He complained to Helen Ferguson that he felt like an outsider but she saw an opportunity to cash in. She began to pitch Mark as 'a Hollywood type with New York training.' Not exactly Jimmy Dean but not Troy Donahue either.

Screen Gems soon took the bait: "A distinct departure from recent discoveries Mark Damon, like George Hamilton, is helping to bring back the well-dressed gentleman-actor who looks the way a film hero is expected to look. He shuns the blue-jeans-sweatshirt set and deplores the "muttering school" of 'method' actors. Entirely dedicated to his profession, Mark does not however disapprove of 'Method' acting. He defends it strongly, adding that he owes much to the fact that he recently studied under that well-known instructor, Sanford Meisner."

Mark intrigued reporters with his Meisner-inspired insights: "I react as I feel at any given moment. When I feel like laughing, I laugh. When I'm annoyed, I sometimes pop my cork. When I'm depressed, I don't bother to put on a Punchinello act. After all, the right to be natural – without violating the other fellow's rights – is the essence of freedom."

Interviewers were impressed with his energy: "In addition to being brilliant and imaginative the handsome young actor is restless," wrote *Photoplay*. "When he becomes deeply interested in a conversation he paces up and down the room; finds a high-backed chair and leans across it, gesturing now and then with sweeping grace. He extracts a ballpoint pen from his breast pocket, snapping and unsnapping the point. Or he taps his forehead or chin with the pen, using his left hand. Physical activity seems to stimulate his mental agility."

Despite the image he presented of feeling at home in his own skin, Mark was unsettled. He was still trying to find himself and his year in New York was having a profound effect. He had absorbed some of the New York snobbery about Hollywood and often found himself looking at his acting through the eyes of Sandy Meisner. It was an unexpected paradox: just as his Hollywood career was beginning to take off he was having mixed feelings about Hollywood. Some of the fan mags began to note his confusion: "You can't pigeon-hole Mark. He's both rebel and nice guy and confesses he changes roles daily."

As soon as *Young and Dangerous* was in the can he decided to go back to New York and resume working with Meisner. He was there when the reviews for *Young and Dangerous* came in. *Variety*: "Promising newcomer Mark Damon is undoubtedly destined to make his mark"; *Hollywood Reporter*: "Mark Damon, who is starred in this drama, deserves his stardom."

Despite feeling pretty good about his press, Mark was still struggling to find his identity when he went to an interview with Max Arnow, talent head at Columbia. "For that interview I had combed my hair to look like another star, even dressed like him."

Arnow took one look at him and shook his head.

"Don't be a second anyone else," he advised. "Be a 'first Mark Damon.'"

Everyone in New York was telling him the same thing, Mark realized. Be yourself. Be authentic. Be a first Mark Damon. Meanwhile, in Hollywood Helen Ferguson continued to build the "Mark Damon" persona, mixing truths with half-truths. "Black-haired, green-eyed Mark was born in

Chapter 25. 1957. Hollywood

Chicago," she wrote in his bio, "and after an early and intense desire to be a cowboy... in turn he determined to be a geographer, an astronomer, a scholar and a professor. Always hovering in the background, however, was the image of himself as an actor. An actor could be *everything*!

"His favorite authors are Shakespeare, Jonathan Swift, and Tolstoy. He considers *War and Peace*, Chaucer's *Canterbury Tales* and the Bible the greatest books ever written and lists the five greatest characters in history as: Jesus, Mohammed, Buddha, Moses and Confucius." Decades later, Mark laughed at his mention of the Bible. "I only said it to impress people. Although "War and Peace" really *was* my favorite."

Helen's next concoction was even more fanciful: "MARK DAMON doesn't claim to know all the answers—well, not quite all—but he can tell you things like how many women in the U.S. bought the Kinsey Report or how many legs a velocipede has. He can also make a pretty good guess as to where he'll be five or six years from now... With self-assured green eyes, jet black hair, a terrific quick smile, plus one of the sharpest minds on anybody's shoulders, Mark feels you should make your own breaks by working hard. His favorite quotation, quite appropriately, is from Julius Caesar: "The fault, dear Brutus, is not in our stars, but in ourselves, that we are underlings."

It was lofty stuff but teen girls ate it up. "Mark Damon Fan Clubs" began sprouting up across the country, filled with girls who were dying to date 'dreamy Mark Damon.' Meanwhile, while in New York Mark was busily dating 'the four Susans': Susan Oliver, an actress and one of the first female pilots; Susan Cabot, an actress who would go on to star in the Roger Corman movie, *The Wasp Woman* (and would later be killed by her son); Susan Strasberg and Susan Kohner, about whom his feelings ran deep.

"Susan Kohner was my first true love," Mark reflected decades later. "She was smart, well-educated, European in feel, very talented and I admired her. She was also wealthy and the daughter of one of the most important agents in town. She was beautiful, precocious, jasmine-like and I was her first love as well." The gorgeous brunette's performance in Douglas Sirk's *Imitation of Life* (playing a young woman trying to cope in the white world while hiding the fact that she's black) had earned her an Academy Award Nomination and a Golden Globe Award. She was a talented young actress on the rise. Mark: "We were very, very close until one day, on the set of *All The Fine Young Cannibals,* she met George Hamilton. He swept her off her feet and I was devastated." (She and Mark would continue to see each other off and on until 1964 when she met the man she married, John Weitz.)

Mark returned to Hollywood to play 'Russ Lippincott' in *Life Begins at 17*, a saga of a rich frat cad (Russ) who is determined to get a small-town beauty, played by Dorothy Johnson to dump her steady, played by Edd Byrnes, and fall for him. After Russ pretends to be interested in her tomboy kid sister Carol (Luana Anders) to make Elaine jealous, Carol discovers his deceit and Russ makes no apologies: "Maybe I'm not very nice. But maybe the heir to the Lippincott steel fortune doesn't have to be a nice guy." Eventually, Carol seeks revenge by falsely claiming Russ got her pregnant and all hell breaks loose. The movie was yet another depiction of the alienation of 1950's teenagers who were so much wiser than their parents that they had no one to turn to but each other. In his poignant scenes with Luana Anders, a very good actress who became a close friend, Mark pulled out all the stops. His new-found assurance shined in scenes with his country-club father whose values Russ has learned and detests.

When the film was done, Mark returned to study in New York. But the contrast in attitudes of actors on the two different coasts began wearing thin. In some interviews his frustration with the Hollywood publicity mill began to show: "Mark Damon's early success at puzzles may account for a current inclination to baffle interviewers. Deadpan, he likes to confess on occasion that he is Melanesian. Or that he was born in Baltaslavia. When taxed with these flights of fancy, he defends himself with the innocent explanation that 'I like to be exotic without shaving my head.'"

Others lauded his clean cut image. "In this day of actors of the 'muttering school' who go in for sweatshirts and denims, it's nice to report that young Mark Damon who is always well groomed, polite and pleasant, is doing okay in his career despite these 'handicaps'"- wrote Louella Parsons. Columnist George Christy gushed: "What a pleasure it is to meet an actor who isn't a beatnik or a sicknik (sickniks are jokers with a 'sick' sense of humor). Mark Damon has already received considerable comment from West Coast preview audiences and is neither a beatnik or a sicknik. He's a romantic after the manner of Julian Sorel in Stendhal's *The Red and the Black*."

Mark stopped reading his publicity after being scorned by his New York cronies. He was re-focusing is energy on acting classes when he was cast in yet another starring role, his first as a 'heavy' in *The Party Crashers*, with Frances Farmer and Bobby Driscoll. This time his New

Chapter 25. 1957. Hollywood

York acting buddies were impressed by the cast. In the summer of 1958, Mark returned to Hollywood for good.

The Party Crashers would turn out to be the last role for Frances Farmer, whose stardom in the 1940's had crossed with her 'wild' behavior to land her in an asylum where she was given a lobotomy. She played the mother of Bobby Driscoll, for whom this would also be his last role. (He would die eight years later of drug abuse.) Mark was 'Twig Webster', the son of an ineffectual father and a deceitful, cheating mother. Connie Stevens was 'Barbara Nickerson', a good girl who is bored by the conformist life she is leading with her good guy boyfriend, (Driscoll) and drawn to Twig.

Party Crashers ("Who are the delinquents–kids or their 'respectable' parents?") featured the sleazy goings-on of Twig's teenage gang, which gets its kicks by 'crashing parties' and ruining the fun. From the start, 'Twig' is shown as an angry outsider looking through the window on the 'good' kids dancing at a party like miniature adults.

Later, when Twig and his gang crash a party of grownups he discovers one of them is his own mother (played by Doris Dowling, a dark-eyed former chorus girl.) After Twig finds her drinking and flirting, having lied to her spineless husband about her evening plans, they have an angry confrontation. In a horrific twist, Twig accidentally causes his mother to fall down a flight of stairs to her death. Everything is wrapped up in a tidy ending, however, when his father meets him at the hospital, assures Twig that it wasn't his fault and promises to be a better father from now on.

The role allowed Mark to show more depth than he had ever demonstrated. He was also more of a pain than ever on the set. "Now that I thought I knew so much about acting I was *really* a problem for director Bernie Girard." Eventually, the director took his revenge. "It was just after I was in a fight and I was supposed to pass out on a couch, keep my eyes closed and hold my breath for a count of '5' until he yelled 'Cut.'"

In the first take, Mark was gasping for breath by the time Girard got to '3'.

"Hey, you're not supposed to breathe till I say 'Cut!" Bernie yelled.

"That's the best I can do. Why don't we shoot it differently…"

"Can it, Damon. Take two!" he yelled. "Action."

The cameras rolled and they did the fight again. Mark lay on the couch again, holding his breath, his eyes closed, for what seemed like an eternity. He was completely breathless when he finally opened his eyes.

"Jeez, Bernie, that was a long…"

The stage was dark. Everyone was gone. "Bernie?" he yelled, looking across the cavernous soundstage. Suddenly, he heard distant laughter. As he peered through the darkness he spied the director, the cast and the crew cracking up at the other end of the soundstage. 'Turned out that while he was holding his breath, eyes closed, Girard had the lights turned off, and had everyone tiptoe off, leaving Mark alone.. From then on, the director took his second-guessing in stride. "You do exactly what I say… or what Damon says!" he would yell at the actors.

In the evenings, Connie, Bobby and Mark hung out at Cyrano's on Sunset or Barney's Beanery. They met up with other young actors at Scandia, the Cock 'n Bull, Schwabs's Drugstore, the Formosa Café. For a while Connie and Mark were just good friends. Buddies. "Until one day we were in New York together and I took her to see *West Side Story*. Connie was so moved that I moved her into my bed for the first time in my New York hotel, The Warwick. As far as I remember, it was also the last. I wasn't that attracted to Connie. But I had to have her. Just like I had to have almost any woman I was dating."

By the time the shoot was over, Stevens was on her way to becoming a recording star. Mark soon followed suit. "I was approached by a music producer from Philadelphia named Sid Pastner who thought that since I was becoming a movie star I should become a singing star as well." They went down to Nashville and Mark recorded "I Don't Want To Go Home," "Party Crashers," a cross promotion for the movie, and "Oooh, What You Do To Me." "With all the bells and whistles they made me sound pretty good," he commented.

Over the next several months he visited radio stations from Santa Barbara to Bakersfield and sat in with all the DJ's, making them his buddies and making sure they played his records. By May, *Variety's* 'Disk Jockey Poll' put Mark Damon's "I Don't Wanna Go Home" at #29 – above Bobby Darin's "Dream Lover." In June he toured the country as a singer, appearing on Dick Clark's American Bandstand twice. In July, "Kookie, Kookie, Lend Me Your Comb" (Edd Byrnes and Connie Stevens) was #1 on the charts. Elvis Presley's "A Fool Such As I" was #5. Mark's "I Don't Wanna Go Home," was #20 and 'COMING UP FAST.'

By the time *Party Crashers* opened in September, Mark was being called "a promising new actor who has far more to offer than romantic good looks and an infectious grin – he has a major singing career as well." He took his 'infectious grin' to meetings across the country of 'Mark

Chapter 25. 1957. Hollywood

Damon Fan Clubs' where adoring girls lined up to meet him. "And at some of those Fan Clubs I knocked off all the groupies I could, one after the other."

Soon he was receiving stacks of fan mail (which his mother took to answering) and was mobbed by teenage girls. After all his years of competing in contests, movie magazines began running contests about him, offering readers a chance to get their picture taken with Mark Damon if they sent in a ballot explaining why he was their favorite star. He was cast in one TV role after another. Finally, he seemed to finally be getting what he wanted, only to discover that he was too private a person to enjoy it. When he had a quiet moment he reflected on the existential questions he had sought to answer in New York.

Was his emerging fame making him any happier? Was he taking time to 'live fully'? Was he being authentic? When he looked back at notes he'd written to himself in New York, it seemed like a long time ago: "It's hard to find yourself... it takes time... but how can you produce anything real if you don't know who you are...?"

Mark decided to study acting again, hoping it would help him recover what he had felt in New York. Some of the kids who'd studied with Sandy and moved to Hollywood needed a place to work. "So we all got together and I became the teacher, teaching the 'Meisner technique' I'd picked up at the Neighborhood Playhouse." He also started going to acting classes with Jeff Corey in his garage on Cheremoya in Hollywood.

Corey was one of Tinsel town's best kept secrets. The former actor had been blacklisted since the early 1950s after being summoned to the House Un-American Committee where he not only refused to name names but offered an acting critique of the previous witness. By the time Mark joined his class Corey was one of the most sought-after acting coaches in town. Studios that wouldn't hire him as an actor sent their young talent to take classes with him.

Corey charged ten dollars for two classes a week which were always full even though he never promoted himself. There, Mark re-connected with Robert Blake, the former child star of "Our Gang" (whom he knew from *Screaming Eagles.)* Blake often played handball before class with a dark-haired, skinny would-be young actor named Jack Nicholson, known as 'Jocko.' Other classmates were Shirley Knight, would-be actor Robert Towne, exotic Latina Rita Moreno, Abby Dalton, green-eyed and red-haired Dolores Hart, classic blonde Diane Baker, Bert Convy and striking Diane Varsi.

From Cowboy to Mogul to Monster

Mark found Corey, who was well-versed in Stanislavski, to be an eclectic and challenging teacher. He soon encouraged a friend he'd met through Susan Cabot, a tall good-looking director named Roger Corman, to join.

"You'll never be a good director unless you learn about acting," Mark insisted.

"I think you may be right," Corman agreed.

"By then I had directed two dozen low-budget films for American International Pictures, using my degree in Engineering to sort-of learn the use of the camera and all that," Corman later said, "but I had no background in acting so it was difficult for me to work with actors."

So Corman came to class with Mark and went up to Corey, explaining that he was a director who wanted to learn about working with actors.

"Can I just come and observe?"

"Sorry. Not possible."

"Why not?"

"The only way you're going to learn about acting is to act. My class is for working actors only. So either you participate or don't come."

Corman ended up joining Corey's class and kept coming back for the next couple of years. "I learned a lot and met some talented actors there," he recalled, "including Jack (Nicholson)." "I was a nobody until Roger started using me in his movies," Jack Nicholson commented. "I am eternally grateful he stuck with me because I didn't have anything else going for me." "I was also impressed with Mark in class," Corman added. "I thought he was a very good actor and a very handsome guy."

Plenty of the actresses in class agreed and Mark began to juggle dates with some of them along with other starlets he was seeing, including a young blonde actress who was called "a lethal mixture of Shirley Temple and Jezebel."

Her name was Tuesday Weld.

Chapter Twenty-six

October 25, 1958

Hollywood, California

Mark and Tuesday Weld in a photo layout.

LOS ANGELES EVENING MIRROR NEWS

Vol. XI — No. 279   PART II   3*   TUESDAY, SEPTEMBER 1, 1959   Largest Afternoon Home Deli

TUESDAY WELD'S WILD ABOUT MEN FRIENDS

Her Mother Is Confidante, Not Adviser

Second of three articles

BY LEE BELSER
Staff Writer

By her own admission, Tuesday Weld, moviedom's newest sex kitten, is just crazy over men.

"I love them," said this 16-year-old combination Shirley Temple and Jezebel. "I like all types and all ages and I like to keep a variety going.

"I even like some 10-year-old boys. But whatever age they are they must have something to say.

"They should know their way around. And they should know where to take a girl. They must be stimulating conversationalists and no just talk about business all the time."

Although both deny that they are dating, she and 44-year-old actor John Ireland have been seen together many times in restaurants, night clubs, at private parties and driving down Sunset Blvd. But she insists:

"John is just a good friend. I happen to like to learn from people, and the older they are, the more experienced they are and the more they can contribute.

Ireland explains a Weld-Ireland restaurant rendezvous this way:

"I was waiting for Marsha Ford. Tuesday is a friend of Marsha's so she was invited to dinner, too. It just so happened that Tuesday arrived before Marsha and

TUESDAY LOVES BOYS—AND HERE SHE IS WITH JUST TWO OF THEM
The sex kitten is flanked at a preview by Dennis Hopper (l) and Mark Damau.
—Globe photo

Tuesday Weld flanked by Mark and Dennis Hopper.

236

Chapter 26. 1958. Hollywood

"Faster! Faster!" Tuesday screamed as Mark drove through thick clouds of smoke into the canyon. Mark obliged, heading for the little house off Beverly Glen that he was sharing with Robert Towne. Up ahead, through the smoke he saw a sign: ROAD CLOSED. He slowed momentarily.

"Hurry!" Tuesday shrieked. "I want to make love with you so badly!" Mark swerved around the sign, gunned the engine and headed right into the fire. Tuesday threw her arms around him and covered his face with kisses as he drove.

"What we were doing was sooo dangerous," Mark later recalled. "And it's not that I was heroic - I was just afraid that if I didn't get home really quick, she wouldn't make love with me. So I drove through fire for a great lay. It's pretty stupid in retrospect, but at the time it was hard to argue with testosterone."

By the time they arrived Tuesday was completely entranced with Mark's heroics. She started to kiss him passionately as soon as they got out of the car. "I practically fell through the front door and we didn't make it as far as my bed. We made love for the first time right there on my living room floor."

Tuesday was all of sixteen.

Baby-faced, erotically angelic Tuesday Weld had moved to Hollywood with her mother/manager after being cast as 'Comfort Goodpasture' in *Rally 'Round the Flag, Boys!*, a satirical comedy by Max Schultz. (Tuesday's chemistry with co-star Dwayne Hickman would soon result in their hit TV series, *Dobie Gillis*.) In her next role she was convincingly innocent as Danny Kaye's polio-stricken daughter in *The Five Pennies*. But her racy reputation trumped her performance. By the time the film was finished Kaye was calling her "15 going on 27."

The gorgeous young blonde had the smile of a child and the measurements of a woman: 36-19-36 according to fan mags. The rags loved to write about the lurid details of her early life: how Tuesday was born in a Salvation Army hospital and raised in a tenement on New York's Lower East Side; how she took over the role of the family breadwinner at a young age, becoming a successful child model after her father died. How she suffered a nervous breakdown at the age of nine, started heavy drinking at ten, began having love affairs at eleven and attempted suicide at twelve. It made for one hell of a resume.

From Cowboy to Mogul to Monster

By the time Mark re-met Tuesday in Hollywood she was gaining household fame as Thalia Meninger in *Dobie Gillis*. Decades before Britney Spears, Tuesday's wild antics were reported daily in some tabloid. She danced provocatively at parties and swigged Scotch-on-the-rocks, ignoring the law forbidding minors to drink in public. She said whatever she pleased: "I hate clothes. I'd never wear underwear if I didn't have to, and sometimes I don't. I like to sleep in the raw with just a light blanket of eau de cologne."

She dated whomever she chose: Dennis Hopper, Tab Hunter, Tommy Sands, Tony Perkins, Edd Byrnes, Elvis, Frank Sinatra, 44-year old John Ireland and others. "I love men," she gushed. "I like all types and all ages and I like to keep a variety going." She was a petulant, ripe young siren and Mark fell for her siren song.

Soon after their wild ride through the fire Tuesday asked Mark to take her to a premiere. He drove through the Hollywood Hills to her plush modernistic home above Sunset, where Tuesday greeted him with a sexy kiss at the door.

"Come on in," she purred as she put her arm through his. "I have a surprise."

She ushered him into her living room where Mark was astonished to find a tuxedoed Dennis Hopper already sitting on the couch.

"Mark, Dennis – I want you both to meet 'my other date.'"

Dennis fumed. Mark laughed. Tuesday playfully took both men's arms and whisked them off to the limo. The next morning the Hollywood headlines blared: "TUESDAY LOVES BOYS—AND HERE SHE IS WITH TWO OF THEM." Photos depicted the smiling sex kitten dressed in innocent white chiffon and flanked by Dennis Hopper and Mark.

"It's never dull when Tuesday's around," he told reporters. "She's a live, electric person, she's capricious and she's a flirt. No guy will ever change those things about her." There was no getting serious with Tuesday, he realized. She was utterly fickle, alighting from man to man like a butterfly on flowers.

After a while, she decided she didn't feel like making love with Mark anymore. But he wasn't going to leave it at that. "I knew fear was an aphrodisiac for Tuesday so I'd drop by around bedtime, sit on her bed and tell her tales of terror: Poe's *The Black Cat* and *The Cask of Amontillado*. I would frighten the shit out of her. Then when fear turned to 'wetness,' I would sink into delicious lovemaking with this little sixteen-year-old nymphet."

Chapter 26. 1958. Hollywood

He also continued to date many other starlets: Beverly Garland, Susanne Pleshette, Diane Baker, Madlyn Rhue, Connie Stevens, Luana Anders, Dolores Hart and Susan Cabot.

He was sitting with Dolores Hart in Jeff Corey's acting class when he was struck by a new girl sitting next to her. She was dressed in a sweat shirt, a pair of khaki shorts and chukka boots."

"Who is she?" he asked Dolores.

"Diane Varsi. You know, the girl in 'Peyton Place.'"

Varsi's performance as dreamy Alison in *Peyton Place* had earned her a Golden Globe and an Academy Award Nomination for Best Supporting Actress the year before. She was seen as one of the brightest young stars in Hollywood. She was also known to be unconventional and unglamorous.

True to her reputation, as soon as every class was over, Diane was always the first to leave, sneaking out quietly. Mark was taken with her presence and her extraordinary work in class; by her singular aloofness and the fact that she seemed to be incapable of being a phony, something he admired. He began to develop a serious crush on her. But she never lingered long enough to talk to him. So he started to send her flowers. Secretly.

"At first it was a single long-stemmed white rose. Then a bunch of orange tulips. Never anything extravagant. Just touches." He never signed his name but enclosed a quote by one of his favorite poets with every bouquet. A bunch of yellow daisies bore a card: "not even the rain has such small hands" by e.e. cummings. Rainer Maria Rilke's "Waiting is nothingness..." accompanied blue irises. Meanwhile, Mark waited for a sign from Diane.

One day Hart confided, "Diane called me after you sent the last one. She said she danced around the room." That night, Mark called Varsi.

"Hi Mark," she answered as if he'd been calling her for weeks. "Thanks for the flowers and poems."

"You *knew* it was me?"

"After awhile I figured it out. So, what do you want?" she asked nicely.

"I'd like to see you," he said.

"When?"

"Tonight."

"Come on over."

She opened the door wearing Levis, sandals and a baggy sweater. Mark entered a homey living room and was surprised to find toys lying around.

"Those are my son, Shawn's," she said. "He's sleeping so I got a babysitter. Want to go for a walk?"

They walked on the beach for hours, talking about writers and poets and life in Hollywood and how much they both disliked living in a fishbowl. They talked about how hard it was to cope with the hundred and one other things that were part of an acting career — the publicity, the probing interviews, the endless parties and premieres you had to attend. They talked about the meaning of life and whether or not God existed. She read him some of her poetry. He sang her his favorite song. Diane had no use for small talk and Mark talked with her as he rarely talked on a Hollywood date. Hours later he drove home, entranced.

From then on they saw each other often. Diane liked to stay home to be with her son, to sit around and talk to Mark. She told him how she had started her career as a folk singer and drummer, was married twice and had barely enrolled in Jeff Corey's class when she was discovered and cast in *Peyton Place*. "I wasn't going anywhere in particular when I started," she explained. "It was more like a religious mission." But after the premiere of *Peyton Place,* producer Jerry Wald predicted that Diane would be a big star with a great future in films.

"She's different," Wald remarked. "Fresh and original. She doesn't act like anyone else or think like anyone else. That's what comes across on the screen."

"I don't know about that," Diane answered. "This is just another experiment for me."

Her performance in *Peyton Place* turned her into an overnight sensation. Louella Parsons called her Hollywood's "Female Brando." Others compared her to James Dean. 20th Century-Fox began to groom her for major stardom. But Varsi wasn't convinced she wanted to stay in movies. "Shawn is the only real thing in my life," she insisted.

At a time when Mark was questioning his place in Hollywood, talking with Diane was eye-opening. She was a bigger star and she was miserable. She had more life experience than any other woman he knew yet she would rather talk about spirituality and her longing for the truth than anything else. Mark admired her for her honesty and integrity. For the way she refused to play the Hollywood game. How, when she was called a "movie star' she replied: "I don't understand the term. It just doesn't mean much

Chapter 26. 1958. Hollywood

to me." She was what he was struggling to become - entirely authentic. "She was very rare, very fragile, and very deep," he reflected many years later, "and Hollywood was very destructive for her."

After starring in *Compulsion*, based on Meyer Levin's play about the Leopold-Loeb murder case, Diane became more unhappy. The studio kept pushing her to do more movies and Diane kept turning down scripts. One night, when Mark came over he found her even more quiet than usual.

"What's wrong?" he asked.

"The studio just put me on suspension," she answered.

"How do you feel about that?"

Diane said nothing for a moment. Then she handed him a poem she had just written.

"Go away and don't bother me," he read, "can't you see I'm lonesome?"

"What does that mean?"

"It means I can't see why I should stay here and be miserable. Just because other people think I should go on with my career."

On March 20, 1959, Diane Varsi announced that she was leaving Hollywood. She was going to Bennington, Vermont, she said, to be with her son, attend classes and write poetry. She refused to do any stories on why she was leaving but she did make a statement: "It has nothing to do with the studio (20th Century Fox) itself. I just don't want to act anymore, or to be a part of this business. I don't like some of the ways of Hollywood. But my reasons go much deeper. It is the performing itself I object to. I find it too destructive. If I have any talent I will try to find some other outlet for it that will make me less unhappy."

Mark was saddened but not surprised to see her go. Hollywood was unforgiving. The press called her a beatnik and a copout and claimed she didn't know how to handle success. They ran articles about the mysterious young girl who seemed to have such a bright future in movies only to toss it all away.

Publicly, Mark defended her: "I wasn't surprised when she decided to give up all the success she'd earned and leave for a quiet, uncomplicated place where she could meditate on her life and future without distractions. No one knows, I'm sure, all of the emotional conflicts she must have experienced in making such a sudden, unexpected and drastic departure from the business."

Privately, Diane's departure had a strong impact on him. Not only did she take his heart with her, her decision to leave Hollywood made him question his reasons for staying.

On the one year anniversary of Varsi's departure, Bob Hope closed the Academy Awards ceremony with: "Goodnight Diane Varsi...wherever you are." Hollywood published a rash of sensationalized articles about her in the fan mags. Mark countered by writing an open letter to her titled "Please Diane, Don't Come Back to Hollywood." Years later he explained his reasons: "I knew she was healing in Vermont and that if she came back she would just be destroyed again."

Mark's struggles to be authentic in Hollywood became more difficult. He began to hate the endless PR appearances and the invasion of his privacy by screaming teenage girls. By the time he starred in his next 'B' movie, *This Rebel Breed,* his quest for stardom seemed more and more meaningless.

Filmed in East Los Angeles, *Breed* focused on the brutal clashes of young gangs of African-Americans, whites and Mexicans in a local high school. Mark played Frank, an undercover cop of mixed African-American and Mexican parentage who infiltrates the gangs to stop narcotics trafficking. Rita Moreno, one of his Corey classmates, played Lola, a Latina high school student who starts to fall for Frank after her boyfriend is killed in a gang fight. (One year later, Moreno would land a similar part, the Oscar-winning role of Anita in *West Side Story.*) A young blonde actress named Dyan Cannon played "the come-hitherest gal in the high school" who earns herself the title of 'Wiggles.' (Mark and Dyan started dating and remained close friends for years. She later caught the eye of Cary Grant, 35 years her senior, whom she married in 1962.)

Directed by Richard Bare, *Rebel* was released in May, 1960 with the usual lurid poster campaign: "With Blazing Impact The Screen Looks Squarely Into The Face Of Today's Wild Teenage Emotions Caught In The Cross-Fire Of Love And Hate!" The movie caught the eye of Bob Hope, who penned a long letter to the *Baltimore News-Post*: "Here is a picture which has something important to say and says it in a dramatic, exciting way. *This Rebel Breed* is all about young people who think it really matters whether a man's skin is brown or white, his eyes blue or his speech strange. They're angry and confused, and they don't make much sense but they do make plenty of trouble. It's time for us to do something about it."

Chapter 26. 1958. Hollywood

At the time, when Mark was interviewed about *This Rebel Breed* he cited the film's "controversial subject matter and honesty." Decades later, when asked what it took to play part African-American/part Mexican he replied with a laugh: "A lot of silly dark makeup to cover up the Jewish kid from Chicago. I did my best in the role but even Method acting wouldn't have helped."

CHAPTER TWENTY-SEVEN

February 11, 1960

Hollywood, California

Mark, as hero Phillip Winthrop in *The Fall of the House of Usher* (1960), walks away from the burning Usher house.

Challenging Vincent Price (Roderick Usher): "You have murdered your sister and I will see that you hang for it!"

Chapter 27. 1960. Hollywood

"**D**AMN YOU METHOD ACTORS!" VINCENT PRICE yelled as Mark sent him flying across the room. He fell, breaking a chair. "It was part of the action but I hadn't controlled the move," Mark recalled years later.

"Take all your New York training and shove it!" Price quipped, trying to appear good-natured, as Mark helped him to his feet. Luckily, Vincent wasn't hurt.

Mark was co-starring with Price in the Edgar Allen Poe classic, *The Fall of the House of Usher*. It was a big break that had come through his friendship with director Roger Corman. Mark: "We'd been in Corey's acting class for about a year when we were having lunch and started talking about the stories of Edgar Allen Poe."

"They would make great movies," Mark suggested.

Roger nodded enthusiastically. "Poe's one of my favorites. I remember reading "The Fall of the House of Usher" in Junior High and asking my parents for Poe's Complete Works for Christmas."

Soon, Corman was having lunch with Jim (Nicholson) and Sam (Arkoff) of American International Pictures (AIP) to talk about making two more black-and-white horror films for them.

"What's the budget?" Corman asked.

"$100,000. Each."

"Sorry, I'm going to have to pass," the director replied.

"What? Why?"

"Because I'd really like to make *one* horror film. In color. Maybe even CinemaScope."

"Sounds pricy," Arkoff frowned. "How much would it cost?"

"Maybe double the budget. $200,000. The price of the two pictures. And we'd go to a three-week schedule."

"So tell me," Arkoff challenged, "what kind of picture deserves such special treatment?"

"The Fall of the House of Usher. It's a great story. By Edgar Allen Poe."

"Who wants to see a movie by Poe?" Nicholson scoffed.

"Kids do. He has a built-in following with them," Corman argued. "He's read in every high school. Plus one quality film in color is better than two cheap films in black and white." He briefly outlined the story of *Usher* for them but when he was done Arkoff was frowning.

"Where's the monster?" he asked.

Roger thought fast.

247

From Cowboy to Mogul to Monster

"The house. The house is the monster."

Arkoff and Nicholson left, skeptical. But Corman refused to give up. He kept pursuing the project until AIP gave him the go-ahead for a fifteen-day schedule and a production budget of over $200,000 for *House*. It was a coup for Roger and the most money AIP had ever gambled on a film.

Vincent Price was cast as Roderick Usher, the strange, white-haired owner of the creaking, mysterious house where he lives in seclusion with his sister, Madeline (Myrna Fahey). Mark was cast as Phillip Winthrop, the handsome love-struck suitor who travels to the House of Usher to marry Madeline. But Roderick refuses to let Phillip marry Madeline. He informs him that he and his sister are the last of the Ushers and that they suffer from a bizarre madness that must not be transmitted to another generation.

When Philip refuses to leave the spooky house strange accidents begin to befall him. Then Madeline falls ill and Roderick tells Phillip that she died of a heart attack and he had her entombed in the family chapel. Phillip, heartbroken, is about to leave when the butler informs him that his fiancée has suffered from periodic blackouts and may have been buried alive by her brother. When Roderick blocks Phillip's desperate attempts to rescue his beloved, he challenges: "You have murdered your sister, Mr. Usher, and I intend to see that you hang for it." In a grandiose climax, the House of Usher burns to the ground as Phillip rides away on a white horse, the sole survivor.

Mark was interviewed by *The Los Angeles Times* before shooting began. "Black-haired, green-eyed Damon co-stars with Vincent Price and Myrna Fahey in *The Fall of the House of Usher* and he believes this film will be his biggest break. 'I am in every single scene of the film,' he remarked excitedly."

His excitement paled when they began to shoot and he discovered that being in every scene of a film (shot out of sequence) proved to be more than he'd anticipated. On the third day he told Roger, "I'm lost."

"OK, Mark. Remember the circumstances and just play moment to moment," Corman quipped, quoting Sandy Meisner.

"Gee thanks, Roger. Thanks a lot."

Realizing that Roger would be of little help, I designed a protective strategy. "I ended up doing a different card for every setup to remind me of what went before and what went afterwards; what I was supposed to *feel* in a scene, what my props would be, what I was supposed to wear, etc." His methodical approach got him through the rest of the challenging shoot. But the filming of *Usher* presented serious production challenges for Corman.

The movie opened on Philip riding through a twisted, burned-out forest to the house of Usher. "The forest was supposed to have a stark fantasy look," the director later recounted. "But I was worried - where was I going to find that? Then, as 'luck' would have it, I heard about a forest fire in the Hollywood Hills on my car radio just as we were going into production. I turned my car around and drove to the scene. I watched the firemen put out the tail end of that fire." The next day, Corman went back to the burned-out hills with a skeleton crew, Mark and a horse. "It was perfect," the director recalled. "The ground was gray with ash, the trees were charred and black. We threw a little fog in to add some effect" and Corman got exactly what he wanted. No green grass. No leafy trees. No organic signs of life. "It greatly enhanced a film that was about decay and madness."

Decay and madness also permeated Vincent Price's performance. In his thoroughly Gothic presence as Roderick, he rarely spoke above a whisper. His was a masterful depiction of a madman. But when he came to the line, "The house lives, the house breathes," Price was baffled. "What does that mean?" he asked Roger.

"It means I promised the producers that the *Usher* house was the monster."

"Yes, but what does it *mean?*"

"It means that's the line that made them make this movie," Corman replied.

Vincent nodded sagely. "I see. Well, I suppose I can breathe some life into it then."

"Vincent breathed plenty of life into that and all the other lines," Corman concluded. When his performance was combined with the director's moody and atmospheric use of color, yards of musty cobwebs and groaning sound effects the *house* actually did seem to be the cause of all the madness. "But the real star of the show was my art director Danny Haller," Corman insisted. Haller, who stayed in a trailer on the lot, was there around the clock while the crew built the sets for *Usher*. Corman: "He'd sketch things on the back of napkins as we'd sit at night and have a drink to discuss the look of the film. All told, Danny did an incredible job of creating the claustrophobic, haunted atmosphere within that house."

Another stroke of luck gave Corman the spectacular fire he needed for the film's climactic ending of the House of Usher burning to the ground.

"Just by chance we located an old barn in Orange County that was going to be demolished by developers," he recalled. Roger went to see the owner. "Instead of demolishing it, how would you like to burn it down at night and I'll be out there with fifty dollars and two cameras rolling? 'Sure,' they said. And that's how we got the incredible long shots of the Usher house burning. I think we tossed some gasoline on the damned thing to get it going out in the middle of a field." The footage of the fire was highly dramatic, with burning rafters falling and flames shooting higher and higher. (In fact it was so dramatic that Corman would re-use the same fire footage in several of his later films.) As the house went up in flames the portraits of the Ushers (painted by Danny Haller) also looked like they were burning. (With the help of special effects, audiences would later hear them moaning and groaning as if every ancestor had come to life when he was being burned to death.)

Before the movie opened, Haller's *Usher* portraits were hung in a restaurant on Sunset for a couple of months. In a strange twist, on the night of the premiere of *The Fall of the House of Usher* a fire broke out in the restaurant. While the audience was being scared out of their wits at the burning of the House of Usher, the restaurant itself burned to the ground, along with all the portraits. "It was like the Ushers took their revenge that night. Eerie," Damon later commented.

The movie was a hit. Vincent Price was heralded for his performance. Roger Corman was vindicated with AIP when the house indeed proved to be a monster and *Usher* became the first of the director's several 'Poe' films. Girls, including a twelve-year old blonde named Margaret Markov, fell in love with Mark as he walked away from the burning house costumed in a long-sleeved Edwardian white shirt. When it was over, Ms. Markov told her mother, "I love him. One day I'm going to marry that man." Betty Jo Markov patted her daughter's hand. "Yes Margaret, of course you will." Margaret Markov's words would prove prophetic.

Today, almost fifty years later, if you channel-surf at any time of night or day, on any day of the week, you are bound to find *The Fall Of the House of Usher* playing on some channel, somewhere, worldwide. The movie has become a cult classic, is considered a first-rate horror movie and continues to entertain millions of fans.

Chapter Twenty-Eight

March 5, 1961

Hollywood, California

I'm very, very grateful

MARK DAMON

INTERNATIONAL STAR OF TOMORROW

Hollywood Foreign Press Association
18th Annual Golden Globe Awards

Mark thanks the Hollywood Foreign Press after winning a Golden Globe Award in 1961 for *The Fall of the House of Usher* and *This Rebel Breed* (1960).

Chapter 28. 1961. Hollywood

WHEN LORETTA YOUNG ANNOUNCED THE NAMES of the nominees for "Most Promising Newcomer of the Year" at the 18th Annual Golden Globe Awards, Mark was sitting at a small glass table at the Coconut Grove, trying to remember to breathe.

"Inhale," he told himself, hoping to claim an Award in the next few minutes. Hadn't he romanced every member of the Hollywood Foreign Press Association, taken them out to lunch and dinner, sent them articles about himself? Hadn't he wined and dined and schmoozed all the right people, been seen at the right parties, appeared in the right gossip columns? Hadn't he left no stone unturned in working the Hollywood system? Plus, he'd given his all in *The Fall of the House of Usher* and *This Rebel Breed*.

Judging from the throng of screaming young fans in front of the Ambassador Hotel, Mark was on his way to becoming a star. There was just one thing that still eluded him: a solid, meaty role in an 'A list' movie. But Mark willed himself not to think about that. He was up for an award that Hollywood designated for young up-and-comers like George Hamilton, Susan Kohner and James Garner.

Loretta Young read on: "The nominees are: Peter Falk, Brett Halsey, Mark Damon, David Janssen, Mickey Callan. And the winner is…"

Mark drew in a long breath and inhaled a dose of the strong perfume of the woman sitting next to him: Barbara Stanwyck. When he started to cough, Stanwyck looked over and raised an amused eyebrow. Then he heard: "Mark Damon! Mickey Callan! Brett Halsey!" and went up to claim his Award with the others. As he looked out at the luminaries who were applauding him he felt, for the first time, like he truly 'belonged.'

At the 'after party' he swilled Scotch and rubbed shoulders with Fred Astaire, Liz Taylor and Burt Lancaster. Nearby, Sophia Loren was talking with Tony Curtis; Rock Hudson was laughing at one of Lucille Ball's jokes. Mark was feeling great as Barbara Stanwyck caught his glance from across the room and shot him a sultry look. Mark found it all intoxicating. At the end of the evening Stanwyck sidled up to him.

"Would you escort me home?" she asked seductively.

"Of course," Mark answered.

"As soon as we walked into the house, she pulled me to her and said, 'Fuck me,'" he recalled. "And I did it on the living room floor and didn't like it at all."

Winning the Golden Globe was supposed to be the highlight of his career. But the day after the Awards was just like every other day. And the weeks and months that followed brought more of the same. Despite his win, he still wasn't offered any important roles. Meanwhile, his self-criticism of his acting increased: "I would watch my performance from the outside. There were times when I would really lose myself in a scene but usually I was aware of what my performance should be and wasn't. I was always self-conscious."

"It was not his fault," commented Titian-tressed Italian actress Luciana Paluzzi (who would soon meet Mark) many years later. "He did the best he could. But it was a style that was in vogue at the time. If you look at old movies you see that even when the actors were good, every move looks calculated. That's because actors had to be much more stiff than they are today. At that time you were not allowed to totally be yourself and just let go. You were *supposed* to be self-conscious."

Mark's discontent grew after he starred in his next 'B' movie, *Beauty and the Beast* (opposite Joyce Taylor.) It was tough going to throw himself into the role of a young prince who turns into a hairy beast every night. When the movie met with mediocre reception it reinforced his need to get out of Hollywood. Then, out of nowhere, his younger brother, Bob was diagnosed with Hodgkin's Disease at the age of twenty-two.

"At the time, Hodgkin's was a death sentence," Mark recalled. Bob, who was about to go to dental school, was given five years to live. Maximum. Mark visited him in the hospital where he was undergoing radiation and Bob looked defeated.

"Looks like I'm not going to dental school after all," he said, trying to be matter-of-fact.

"Why not?"

"What's the point? I'm going to die anyway so I might as well enjoy the rest of my life."

"But you're *not* going to enjoy it."

"Sure I am. I'm going to go to parties and listen to music and spend my days at the beach..."

"And you think you'll enjoy that? You'll hate it."

"You're joking, right?"

"No, I'm not. You'll hate every minute of it because you're accepting the fact that you're going to die."

"I *am* going to die. So what do you suggest?!"

"That you live your life like the Hodgkin's doesn't exist. If you do that, you can make it NOT exist."

Chapter 28. 1961. Hollywood

Bob shook his head. His brother obviously didn't understand. But Mark argued the same point when he came back the next day. And the day after that. Over and over again he argued that if Bob exercised his will he could defeat the cancer.

"You're not making any sense," Bob argued. "This isn't something I can beat with my will."

"Why not?" Mark countered. "Of course you can."

As always, Mark believed in the power of the mind. He was certain Bob's mind could heal his body. Every time he went to see his brother, he hammered away at his point until eventually, he got through. They were both crying when Bob agreed to go on with his life as if nothing ever happened. (Bob went on to UCSF Dental School, became a dentist and his cancer went into remission. Decades later, he still credits Mark with saving his life.)

But after Bob's brush with death, becoming a star seemed more superficial to Mark than ever. "I had to be honest with myself," he recalled. "I wasn't living fully and I had a film career that wasn't going anywhere. Sure, I was well known among U.S. teenagers, I was on the cover of fan magazines, I was dating young starlets. But my career was more advanced from a publicity stand-point than an actual career stand-point."

Then he got a call from his agent, Phil Gersh (founder of The Gersh Agency.) "Get over here fast. You just got a telegram from Luchino Visconti. He wants you to go to Rome. Right away!"

PSO

1984

Chapter Twenty-Nine

June 23, 1984

Munich, Germany

PSO ad fronting the Carlton Hotel at the Cannes Film Festival.

Chapter 29. 1984. Munich

"Well, I think it's awful," Mark told a stunned Wolfgang Petersen. The director looked at him stonily, waiting for an explanation. They had just had the first screening of *The NeverEnding Story* to a packed audience in a large screening room on the Bavaria Studio lot.

"You're only talking about the music, wahr?" Berndt Eichinger interjected diplomatically.

"Right, wahr. This is a good film. The special effects, the visuals, the acting, your direction, it's all working, except for the music."

"What's wrong with it?" Wolfgang demanded.

"It's too heavy for the subject matter. It will never play for the kids."

"The composer, Klaus Doldinger, had scored *Das Boot* for Wolfgang," Mark recalled years later. "But Doldinger, brilliant as he was, had written a very serious score for *The NeverEnding Story* and I realized it was not going to work."

He tried to explain that to Wolfgang but he was unmoved.

"I'm sorry," Mark insisted. "We have to re-do it."

Wolfgang turned and walked out of the room. Mark immediately called Giorgio Moroder, with whom he had worked on the updated *Metropolis*. Moroder was about as hot as any film composer could be at the time. (He had done *Midnight Express, American Gigolo, Fast Times at Ridgemont High, Flashdance* and *Scarface*.) It was still early in LA when Giorgio picked up.

"I need your help," Mark said, and explained the problem. "Can you do a new score?"

"I'm very busy," Giorgio replied, "but I'll try to squeeze it in between some other gigs. I'll need to finish it in five days," he warned.

"Great. The sooner, the better, and Giorgio, I need an incredible title song." "D'accordo," said Giorgio. Mark and Giorgio often spoke in Italian. Giorgio agreed he would do his best.

Two weeks later, Mark's foot was tapping to the beat of Moroder's running bass line in the new title song (with lyrics by K. Forsey, co-writer of the theme song for "Flashdance".) A young Brit named Limahl warbled: "Reach the stars, fly a fantasy, dream a dream and what you see will be. There upon the rainbow is the answer to the NeverEnding Story...Oh-oh-oh-oh-oh-oh-oh...the NeverEnding Story...oh-oh-oh-oh-oh-oh-oh..."

When the last exuberant notes faded out Wolfgang turned to Mark.

"So, do you hate it a little less now?"

Mark grinned broadly. "I hate it a LOT less."

The NeverEnding Story had the biggest opening in the history of German movies. Moroder's soundtrack became a hit in 17 countries where over four million copies were sold worldwide. The single reached the Top Ten in numerous countries. Savvy marketing helped the film's success when replicas of Rock Biter and Night Hob appeared on television shows throughout Europe.

Once again, in every territory where PSO's independent distributors had the picture it went through the roof. In the territories where Warner Bros. released it outside of the U.S. the film tanked. The results caused Terry Semel, President of Warner Bros. (and future Yahoo! CEO) to restructure his foreign division from top to bottom.

The NeverEnding Story went on to gross $125 million worldwide and to spawn two sequels. Reviewers hailed its 'astounding visual effects' (although they were animatronics) and called it a near-perfect film. Others predicted it would assure Wolfgang Peterson's place in the cinematic firmament, and it would establish German producer Dieter Geissler, Mark's old friend from his acting days, as an important new international filmmaker. For Mark, the movie's success was a validation of his hard work and creative decision-making. But he had no time to rest on his laurels.

Tinsel town was buzzing about PSO'S next production, *Clan Of The Cave Bear*, financed by Warner Bros. and Sydney Kimmel and starring a young actress who was fast becoming a breakout star. "Darryl Hannah is set to make an even bigger splash then she did in *Splash* and without a fishtail," *Variety* revealed. "The blonde actress has been signed by Jon Peters, Peter Guber, Mark Damon and John Hyde to star as a prehistoric cave woman in *Clan*."

The project had originally been conceived as an NBC miniseries until Guber and Peters decided to make it a film with PSO. Now, Mark was pleased with the press coverage but very concerned about the script. Written by John Sayles in colloquial English, it was based on the 1980 novel by Jean Auel which had blazed to the top of best seller lists and sold millions of copies worldwide.

Readers had been drawn to the struggles of Ayla, a Cro-Magnon orphan in Ice Age Asia who joins the Neanderthal clan after her mother is killed in an earthquake. They sympathized with Ayla's plight as an intelligent outsider, a misfit who is punished for challenging male-dominated Neanderthal traditions and taboos as she grows and matures.

They were hooked by the time Ayla matures into a young woman of intelligence, spirit and courage. She finds herself caught in a fierce and dangerous power struggle that includes her brutal rape and the jealous bigotry of Broud (the clan's leader.) By the end of the book, when Ayla leaves the clan to set off on her own, readers were cheering the courageous heroine, willing her not just to survive but to thrive.

Auel was revered for her creation of Ayla, described by one reviewer as "Cleopatra, Marie Curie, Mother Teresa and Tarzan's Jane in the same person." Mark was well aware of the power of the character as a modern-day feminist heroine living 35,000 years ago. *"Clan of the Cave Bear* will be a highly unique picture," he told the trades, "since it deals with, perhaps, the first liberated female."

But casting Ayla was a tall order to fill. Luckily, long-limbed, lean Darryl Hannah would prove to be an inspired choice. So far, her two film roles had featured her playing a believable outsider - a creature from the sea (*Splash*) and a replicant (*Blade Runner*.) Unbeknownst to the producers, Hannah's personal history would contribute to her depiction of Ayla. Hannah: "I grew up on the 47th floor of a building in downtown Chicago. I was so disassociated and alien to the world that by the time I was seven my teachers suspected I was autistic… until my father decided to send me to a summer camp in the Rockies… where I found my center. Things always made more sense to me when I was in nature."

When Mark made arrangements for Hannah to live in remote Okanagan in British Columbia for four months he was unaware that they were returning her to her natural roots. Once they started shooting, however, it was clear to everyone. Despite her modern-day beauty, the actress was completely at home in nature. Her childlike innocence and wonder aided in making her a believable and unaffected Ayla. The solid cast included Pamela Reed (Iza), Thomas G. Waites (Broud), Curtis Armstrong (Goov) and John Doolittle (Brun). They would be joined by a 9 ½-foot-tall, 1420-pound Kodiac bear named Bart, Kibor the lion and a pack of wolves. Acclaimed makeup artist Michael Westmore and Michele Burke, winner of a 1983 Oscar for her makeup for *Quest for Fire*, would create special tribal makeup for the film, assisted by dozens of other makeup people.

Mark was not worrying about any of those production details when he walked off the elevator and was enthusiastically greeted by PSOers. He was musing over how to translate the book to film. In the novel, readers were able to get into the heads of the characters because Auel described their thoughts and reactions in detail: "Before dipping in and disturbing the mirrored surface Ayla leaned over and looked at herself. She studied her features carefully; she didn't seem so ugly this time, but it wasn't herself she was interested in. She wanted to see the face of the Others." But even a simple passage like that would be difficult to translate to film. How would the audience know what Darryl Hannah was thinking as she stared into the water? And how on earth would she and the ape-men and women communicate with each other? "We had decided we couldn't have them speak English because that would suspend all believability. We also thought that if they communicated to each other with random noises and grunts it would sound silly."

"What is the answer?" Mark wondered as he walked into John's office. Obviously, they couldn't just yell "yabba dabba doo!"

He put the problems with *Clan* aside as John told him the latest on the negotiations with Delphi. "They're talking about giving us access to millions of dollars to make movies. Hundreds of millions," he added with a grin.

"Fantastic."

Both men let that thought settle for a moment.

"If this goes the way I think it will, we'll be in a joint venture with Delphi before the end of the year."

"What would we call it?" Mark asked.

"I don't know... Delphi/PSO?"

"No way," Mark replied. "Has to be PSO/Delphi. Delphi is so much bigger than us that if our name comes second the industry will think we've been swallowed up by them.

"You're right."

"We have to show the world that PSO is in control."

"I agree. But will Lew Korman?"

"I'll make him. Or no deal. We've worked too hard to establish ourselves in this town to take a back seat now."

That night, Mark awoke at 4:00 AM, worrying about *Clan*. He looked over at Maggie, who was sleeping. At 36, she was still as beautiful as the day they met. She had the same girlish innocence that had attracted him and the same inner strength, enthusiasm and loyalty. As he watched her sleep he felt a twinge of guilt that she had given up her career for his, that he was home so rarely that he never had enough time for her. Or the kids. Then he stole into the bathroom to sit in an easy chair and go over the script for *Clan*.

As he read, he was reminded of his doubts about the director whom Guber recommended for the project, a cinematographer named Michael

Chapman who had photographed *Raging Bull* and *The Last Detail*. "I know he's only directed one movie, *All The Right Moves*. But I swear to you, he's the one," Guber had insisted.

"What makes you so sure?"

"You'll see. He's a *shtarker*," Peter alleged.

Mark didn't see what being a *shtarker* (Yiddish for a strong guy) had to do with it. On a project like this Chapman's inexperience could only be a hindrance. What they really needed was an experienced, hands-on director who would be able to marshal the cast through a very tough shoot.

It would take months of struggles for the actors to imitate life as cavemen; to learn to talk using false teeth that made them look the part; to act with prosthetics that made them into believable Neanderthals and to move comfortably clothed only in loincloths and skins. Most difficult of all, nobody had figured out how these actors were going to talk to each other.

In the silence of the early morning Mark was hit by a sudden thought. He woke up Maggie at 7:00 AM. "How would you like to work on our next movie?" he asked excitedly.

"What?!"

She became flustered when Mark told her he wanted her to create a 'caveman dictionary' for *Clan*. "What we need is a language of grunts, hand signals and sounds. Certain gestures that always mean the same thing in a limited vocabulary of caveman "words." Sometimes they can sound like what they're meant to be. But, of course it can't be English."

"Why me?" she protested. "What do I know about how cavemen spoke?"

"Nobody knows. That's the beauty of it. We can make up our own language because nobody was there to hear it."

"I can't do it alone," she complained.

"So put together a team," he suggested. "Who better than you? You were an actress. Use your creativity. It can really be fun. There's a whole language to invent. Who better than us to do it?"

"How much time do we have?"

"Three days."

Mark sold the idea until Maggie finally relented and called her friends, actors Deborah Kramer and Toni Montenaro. They started on the 'caveman dictionary' that day. With Mark's help they set about inventing a language. "The next step was to translate the script into this primitive 'language.' If that worked, we would only need minimal narration and subtitles in the film to translate the Neanderthal gestures and language for the audience," Mark later explained.

By the time they went up to Vancouver to teach the 'language' to the actors there was little time left for them to learn it before they started shooting. It took hard work for the cast to convey the entire script in a totally different language *and* manage to keep it consistent without it restricting their acting. "Plus I had to make certain that Michael Chapman was on our side on this. But he was so happy just doing the film that he agreed to almost anything."

In late July, after being home for less than a month, Mark left again to oversee the start of production on *Clan of the Cave Bear*. He would be gone for the rest of the summer. "Things changed when we went into production," recalled Eddie Kalish. "Mark would leave with a briefcase bulging with papers. But the thing is - he *left*. The paper was just that. It was the people who felt neglected."

"I had all of my correspondence telexed to me every night and I was running the office from whatever set I was on," Mark insisted. But the deeper he got into production, the less involved he was in the day-to-day life of PSO. And the loss of his constant presence as boss, guiding light and father figure began to erode the harmony of PSO. Mark had not appointed lieutenants to take his place while he was gone. He was sorely missed. He was also running into problems on the second PSO production. After the first week Mark realized, "Michael Chapman was a total lox. He knew how to move the camera but had no idea how to stage the actors or direct them." Mark was ready to fire him. First he called Guber, who pleaded, "Give him another chance. I swear he'll come through."

By the second week Mark realized that Chapman wouldn't be able to overcome his inexperience as a director. He went to see him. "I don't think you can cut it on this project," Mark said with typical bluntness.

"Give me a chance," pleaded Chapman. "I can do this."

"I'm sorry. I don't think you can."

"I was pretty direct, probably even brutal," Mark said years later. "Chapman had tears in his eyes as he begged me to let him continue. He swore he could pull it off if I were there to help him."

In the end, he had no choice but to keep Chapman as director. It was simply too late to make a change. "I did try to show him how to block the actors in a more natural way, to rehearse with them and let them take the lead instead of just giving them their places to stand. Work your camera movements during the actors' rehearsals," he instructed Chapman. "Let them guide your camera through their instinctual moves."

Overall, it was an extraordinarily difficult shoot. The actors had a hard time communicating consistently in the primitive language of hand movements and grunts. "Although it was beautifully shot by Chapman, between them talking in a strange caveman language and giving stilted performances, the picture never quite congealed."

By October, Mark was back in L.A. He was supervising a $150,000 featurette on *The Making of Clan* to take to MIFED, overseeing the editing of *9 ½ Weeks* after Lyne's first cut came in at four hours and twenty minutes and prepping PSO's next production, *Short Circuit*.

John was in New York working with Lew Korman on finalizing the merger between PSO and Delphi. He had been spending so much time there that he and Kate thought about buying a place in the city. But after seeing some real estate possibilities she told John, "You know that ad you've been carrying around in your briefcase forever? The one for the ranch in Visalia."

"What about it?"

"I think we should buy it."

John was floored. "Are you serious?"

"I am. Look, we could buy that whole ranch for less than a studio apartment in New York where you have to stick your head out the window and look four blocks up just to see the river."

John was absolutely delighted with her logic. One week later, they were back in L.A. and they drove three and half hours north to tiny, remote Badger in the foothills of Sierra Nevada. They saw the ranch, bought it on the spot and named it 'Fairlea,' after John's grandfather's farm. Although they vowed to visit only once a month, soon they were heading north every Friday for the weekend.

In November, while John was returning to his country roots in Badger, California, Mark was returning to his in Rome.

He had stopped there on his way to MIFED with PSOer Michael Heuser, who had gone to high school in the city. Many years later, Heuser recalled their experiences there: "Mark and I walked around Rome together. I remember how emotional we both were when we would look at a particular spot and remember what we had been doing there. The highlight was looking up at an apartment where he used to live in Piazza

Margana. Standing there brought tears to his eyes. You know," Heuser reflected, "it's hard not to love a guy with whom you share an experience like that."

After MIFED, Mark and John finalized the agreement for PSO/Delphi. Mark, it was decided, would become head of production, sales and marketing of the new company. John would focus on business matters as before. Lew Korman would utilize his ties to Wall Street to raise money for the new entity.

On November 14, 1984 the news hit the trades. "Producers Sales Organization and the Delphi Companies Merge and Commit $350 Million to Production Financing. Hollywood is buzzing about the creation of the new studio formed by Producers Sales Organization, a group of foreign film investors and Wall Street's Delphi," wrote *USA Today*.

"Producers Sales Organization, a leader for years in licensing independently produced films to foreign distributors, has just evolved into a production company that insiders are now calling an independent major" proclaimed Martin Grove in *Hollywood Reporter*.

At the end of December, John, Mark and their families welcomed in the New Year at Fairlea Ranch in Badger where everyone slept in front of the living room fireplace in sleeping bags "because we had no furniture yet," Kate laughingly recalled.

At midnight, Mark and John raised their champagne glasses high, certain they were riding the tail of a comet. In the wee hours of the New Year, while everyone else was sleeping Mark was wide awake, imagining the bright future of the company he had started. In less than a decade PSO had grown into an entity that would take him back to his creative roots. After becoming a businessman he was about to become a full-fledged producer with a full slate of movies. The prospect was thrilling. By the time he finally fell asleep, a smile of triumph was spread across his face.

ITALY

1961-1974

*Sometimes a man hits upon a place to which he mysteriously
feels that he belongs. Here is the home he sought and he will settle amid
scenes that he has never seen before among men he has never known as
though they were familiar to him from his birth.
Here at last he finds rest.
- W. Somerset Maugham*

Chapter Thirty

April 20, 1961

Los Angeles, California/Rome, Italy

Tor Margana, Rome, circa 1300.

Chapter 30. 1961. Los Angeles/Rome

A SMILE OF TRIUMPH SPREAD ACROSS Mark's face as he read the telegram: SAW PHOTO MARK DAMON GOLDEN GLOBE *STOP* INTERESTED IN MEETING *STOP* POSSIBLE ROLE *STOP* PLEASE RESPOND *STOP* LUCHINO VISCONTI. He couldn't believe he was being approached by one of the most important directors of the time.

"Cable him back. Tell him I'm coming to Rome right away," he informed Phil Gersh.

Within a few weeks he was on a plane with visions of international stardom dancing in his head as he winged his way through the night, reading what he had dug up on famed director and former Count Don Luchino Visconti di Modrone.

He learned that the fifty-five year old Visconti was known as one of the most complex and contradictory figures in Italian cinema. That after being born into one of Northern Italy's richest families (one of seven offspring of the Duke of Modrone) Visconti spent his twenties as a dilettante dabbling in art, music and racehorses and began his film career after meeting French director Jean Renoir at a party.

He read that Visconti followed Renoir to Paris where he discovered film and became influenced by Marxist ideology, returning to Rome after the War a filmmaker and an avid leftist. When Visconti started to make films with an emphasis on the plight of the poor and oppressed, using nonprofessional actors and natural settings, his movies were declared masterpieces and he was hailed as the pioneer of a new style of Italian cinema: Neo-Realism, also espoused by his friends Vittorio De Sica and Roberto Rossellini.

In the years since, however, Visconti's style had changed several times and his latest film, *Rocco e i suoi fratelli* (*Rocco and His Brothers*), while hailed as a masterpiece by some, was seen as "overly lush and operatic" by others. As he flew to Rome, Mark learned much about the man he was about to meet. Unfortunately, it was what he *didn't* learn that would have helped the most.

That in the last decade the openly bisexual Visconti had become passionately involved with several young men, including the star of *Rocco,* the breathtakingly good-looking Alain Delon. And that Mark himself was a dead ringer for Delon.

He knew none of this as his plane landed at Fiumicino airport. He entered the terminal with two suitcases and a bundle of expectations, pushed his way through the pushy crowds and hailed a taxi that screeched to a stop. Luckily the driver seemed to understand the name of the hotel. Luckier still, Mark was arriving at the height of a golden age for American actors in Italy. It was called La Dolce Vita (the Sweet Life.)

Long before it became the name of countless restaurants, perfumes and chocolate, La Dolce Vita was the name of an Italian lifestyle lived by the glamorous and the beautiful from 1950 through the mid-60's. It was a time when the glitterati of the film industry were living in Rome, then known as the movie capital of the world. It was also a time when the greatest Italian films were created, including Federico Fellini's brilliant and scandalous *La Dolce Vita*.

The Vatican immediately placed the film on its "Excluded" list. Catholics were forbidden to see it. Nevertheless, moviegoers lined up at theatres worldwide and it became a mega hit.

By the time Mark arrived, Rome had been a Mecca for American filmmakers for a decade. Production was cheap and the facilities of Cinecitta' Studios were terrific for large-scale spectacles like *Quo Vadis* and *Ben-Hur*. Hollywood stars Joseph Cotten, Broderick Crawford, John Ireland, Guy Madison, Ben Gazzara and others ended up staying in Italy, working in 'Spaghetti Westerns' (or 'macaronis,' as they were called in other European countries) when their domestic careers flagged. By 1960, so many of these American ex-pats (writers, directors and actors) were living in Rome that it was dubbed 'Hollywood on the Tiber.'

Immediately after his taxi arrived at the Hotel Hassler at the foot of the Spanish Steps and he checked into his room, Mark set out to explore the famed city that was pulsing with life. "It was almost midnight when I headed down the Via Veneto, passing crowds outside Harry's Bar and the Cafe de Paris. I saw the biggest stars sitting outside Doney's having dinner and drinks: Marcello Mastroianni, Anita Ekberg, Federico Fellini, Annette Stroyberg, Vittorio Gassman. They were laughing, drinking, talking, smoking and pairing up till all hours."

He stared at the elegantly dressed Italian men in hand tailored suits who strolled down the streets with magnificent-looking women hanging on their arms. He laughed at the guys on the make who wove in and out of the traffic in convertible Fiats, slowing when they passed a pretty woman and calling out until she answered, zooming off to find another if she didn't. He marveled at the intricate maze of ancient streets that opened to

Chapter 30. 1961. Los Angeles/Rome

spacious piazzas. By the time he made it back to his hotel he had fallen under Rome's intoxicating spell.

"Welcome to Roma," said the elegant and handsome Luchino Visconti the next morning, kissing Mark on both cheeks.

"Thank you, Mr. Visconti. The pleasure's all mine."

The director's hair was slicked back. He was dressed in a red velvet smoking jacket. A perfect Continental gentleman, Visconti took a seat on a stiff-backed couch, patting a place beside him. "Please. Sit down and tell me, how was your flight? Long, so they tell me. Although I have never flown it, thank God."

Mark was much relieved that this perfect Continental gentleman spoke perfect English and they chatted for a while about movies, restaurants, music and stars. Visconti told him a scandalous story about 'La Magnani' (Anna Magnani, who starred in his *Bellisima*). "Absolutely volcanic sex drive," the director concluded.

While they were chatting Mark noticed that occasionally Visconti touched his shoulder or kicked his foot playfully. He realized the director must be gay. Then Visconti started talking about his next movie and Mark forgot all about it.

"It's called *Bocaccio '70* and based on some of his writings. Actually, it's four small movies in one, each directed by a different director."

"Who are the other directors?"

"Vittorio (De Sica), Federico (Fellini), Mario (Monicelli)," Visconti smiled.

"Good God," Mark thought, trying to act normal at the sound of those names. They were legends, all. "And... are the actors set?" he managed to ask.

"Some. We have Anita (Ekberg), Romy (Schneider) and Sophia (Loren). Among others..." Visconti said, smiling with great charm.

Mark smiled back. His mind was reeling. This was a Ferrari of a movie. Was he really going to get a role in it?

"Aspetta, my dear boy -- do you like opera?" Visconti suddenly exclaimed.

"Yes. Very much."

"Excellent! How would you like to come to *Tosca* tonight as my guest?" His hand lingered on Mark's shoulder for a long moment.

273

"I'd like it very much," he beamed, ignoring the hand.

That night, Visconti strolled into the opera house with legendary diva Maria Callas on one arm and an awed Mark on the other. They walked up to a small group of elegantly dressed men. "Franco, Paolo, please welcome Mark Damon from Hollywood."

Visconti beamed at Mark as he met legendary directors Franco Zeffirelli and Pier Paolo Pasolini. They were soon joined by producer-director Franco Rossellini (nephew of Roberto) and author Gore Vidal.

The men gathered around Mark and complimented him on his looks and charm. He relished the attention as they laughed at his stories and insisted on fresh Hollywood gossip, raising their eyebrows and tut-tutting when Mark obliged.

Suddenly, Franco looked towards the entrance. "Delon," he murmured to Visconti, whose expression hardened. He put his arm through Mark's and laughed loudly.

"So amusing," he laughed again as he looked into Mark's eyes.

Mark laughed, too. Partly from embarrassment. "I wasn't sure what to make of it. Suddenly, I was surrounded by a glamorous and completely open clique of homosexuals."

He was flat-out astonished by their openness. He didn't know that in Italy many gay men were completely candid about their liaisons. That although the term 'homosexuality' was never mentioned in public it was common knowledge and widely accepted that Zeffirelli, Pier-Paolo Pasolini, Visconti and many others were openly gay.

Coming from America, where the McCarthy era had exacerbated homophobia, Mark felt like a stranger in a strange land. Coming from Hollywood, where Rock Hudson, a closeted gay man, was currently playing a straight man pretending to be gay in *Pillow Talk*, he was very uncomfortable: "I realized I was an object of prey." But he also drank in the approval from these glamorous, successful men.

By the time he'd spent a week of elegant evenings in their company he was overwhelmed by their culture and elegance. Even if they all seemed eager to sleep with him. Meanwhile, Visconti dangled the part in *Bocaccio '70* in front of Mark's nose.

"Don't you think he and Romy (Schneider) would make a beautiful couple?" he asked at a dinner party.

"Absolutely," said the others. Visconti beamed at Mark, who felt like he was in a dream.

Chapter 30. 1961. Los Angeles/Rome

When he invited Mark into the "Dolce Vita scene" he eagerly said yes. Soon he was enjoying three hour lunches with Visconti or Rossellini; drinking vino with Pasolini and Gore Vidal; partaking in midnight dinners at Al Moro, Bolognese, Piccolo Mondo, Gigi Fazzi, Casina Valadier: "Although every man in the clique was betting each other on who would be the first to get me in bed I decided if my access to work meant hanging out with them, that was fine with me."

It was more than fine. He reveled in their flamboyance and the sensual grace in the way they moved, laughed, talked, argued. They were playful, not repressed and he became more playful in response. He began to live for today, something he had never done before. "I felt I was becoming more 'Continental.' And I loved that everybody was talking about me playing the lead in *Bocaccio '70* opposite sexy Romy Schneider. I decided I wasn't above using my looks to get what I wanted. I just wouldn't go to bed with any of them."

When he wasn't with the clique, Mark explored Rome's heterosexual nightlife. He danced into the early morning hours at Jackie O's and Club Ottantaquattro (Club 84) where luscious Italian beauties were eager to go home with the handsome young American.

Luchino couldn't have cared less that Mark was sleeping with one woman after another. He knew Mark wasn't gay and would only have cared if he had slept with another man since Visconti hoped to become the first man to seduce him.

One night, at a party thrown by Annalena Limentani, an agent with Kaufman/Lerner, the most prestigious agency for foreign actors in Rome, Mark was introduced to a sexy French brunette named Dominique Boschero. She was a fireball of an actress who had started as a fashion model. Mark thought she was gorgeous, wild and impossibly sexy. "Later that night when we made love it was incredible. She was a hellcat who spoke no English so I kept a dictionary close by. She really accelerated my learning Italian, especially phrases you wouldn't find in the dictionary. On one of our first nights together, after a particularly wild bout of lovemaking (and bouts they often were) Dominique shrieked, 'Ho goduto, Ho goduto!' I looked at her, surprised by her choice of words. I knew that 'Ho goduto' meant 'I enjoyed.'

"You enjoyed?" Mark asked. "You *enjoyed?!* "How could you scream like that and only just *enjoy*?"

Dominique looked at him innocently. "Che cos'e *enjoyed*?"

It was then that Mark learned (and not from the dictionary) that 'ho goduto' also means 'I came...' "So on and off over the next two years I really 'enjoyed' my relationship with Dominique." One night, they were lying in bed after making love when she asked why he came to Rome. "I got a telegram from Luchino. He saw a photo of me and wanted to meet me. He's going to put me in his next movie... "

Dominique started to laugh.

"My poor naive American idiot," she said in Italian.

Mark sat up on his elbow.

"What do you mean?"

"Darling, don't you think there are enough good actors in Italy? Luchino didn't bring you here to *act*. He only wanted you here because you look like Alain (Delon)."

"And...?"

"And Alain had just broken up with him. So he wanted to make Delon jealous!"

It made sense, Mark realized. But by now he didn't care why he had gotten to Rome. What was important to him was getting the role Visconti continued to dangle in front of his nose.

In June, Luchino invited Mark to accompany him to the premiere of *Salomé*, an opera he was directing at the week-long Festival of Two Worlds which showcased new works by composers, dancers and artists. The Festival, in its second year, was held in tiny Spoleto, a medieval town in Umbria. Mark rented a Fiat 500 convertible and drove through the winding hills of Umbria, past ancient groves of olive trees and into the heart of the gay community of Spoleto where the Festival took place. He guided the little car through the crowded streets, a Marlboro dangling from his lips. His suntan brought out the green of his eyes, his white tee shirt and black jeans were the height of 'hip.' He was the beautiful new boy someone was sure he was going to get.

At the Festival he accompanied Visconti to the premiere of *Salomé* (conducted by Thomas Schippers) where the audience went wild, covering the stage with red roses. Visconti was hailed as a genius (although his direction was later called "the height of artifice and a terrific example of 'camp'" by Susan Sontag). Outside the Festival, nightlife throbbed on the tiny, ancient streets. Every night there was a new performance and a

Chapter 30. 1961. Los Angeles/Rome

new round of parties with Luchino and the gang. Mark went to them all, managing to maintain the competition for his affections as well as his proposed lead in the film. Until the night he played 'the game of truth.'

"The 'game of truth' was very popular in Italy at the time," said Italian actress Luciana Paluzzi. "It was a party game. Anyone who wanted could ask you any question. And you had to tell the truth."

Mark was playing it with Visconti, Rossellini and the others when Pietro Notarianni, Visconti's trusted producer, suddenly asked him a question.

"Tell us, Mark - would you 'do it' with Luchino (Visconti) if you were on a desert island and no one else could ever find out?"

From across the room Visconti's eyes bored holes into Mark's. Everyone grew silent as they all waited eagerly for his answer. Mark froze. It was indeed, the moment of truth.

"No," he blurted, "I like Luchino a lot but I just won't do it with a man."

Some of the men started to laugh. Visconti gazed at him with a look of amusement but his eyes were cold. "I felt I had to be honest," Mark added decades later. "I was still very American. Later, as the European mentality began to seep into me and I learned that no one ever said what they meant, I would have acted like it could have been possible." Now, the silence in the room was deafening. Until another actor, Cuban-born Tomas Milian piped up.

"I would," he said.

He smiled at Visconti, who smiled back.

Milian got the part.

The next morning, Visconti wouldn't return Mark's calls. Rumors flew through the gay community as the Festival came to a close. Zeffirelli boasted to Rossellini that maybe Visconti didn't get Mark but he, Zeffirelli, did. "And Rossellini believed him. After accepting that I had rejected him because I was straight, now not only was Visconti angry and humiliated, Franco was destroyed because he thought I had lied to him."

Suddenly, Mark was a pariah. No one believed that he had simply said no to all of them. "They always assumed that any good-looking guy would drop his pants somewhere, somehow, for whatever reason. To them it was no big deal. So you go to bed with somebody? So what?" By the time the Festival was over he was no longer the darling of the homosexual set.

Back in Rome, Mark was shunned by his former group. He also fought with Dominique constantly and broke it off. "She was totally nuts," he recalled. "She was always losing it, hitting me, screaming hysterically. But after I broke up with her I came back. Then I would break up with her again and come back again. I probably did that half a dozen times. It was tough to let her out of my life, the physical attraction was so strong. And way down deep, I really cared for her."

During one of their break-ups he started seeing Luciana Paluzzi. They had met in Hollywood a few years earlier when she was under contract to Twentieth Century Fox and married to Brett Halsey. After starring in *Return to Peyton Place* and the TV series, *The Five Fingers*, Luciana had broken her studio contract, divorced Halsey and returned to Rome with her mother and infant son. (She would later co-star as Domino in the James Bond movie, *Thunderball*.)

Luciana was smart, classy and a total knockout. Mark fell for her hard, and they began an intense relationship that lasted for the next several months. Meanwhile, he had no paying work and, without the role in *Bocaccio 70*, no prospects. He wondered if he should go back to America but Luciana urged him to stay and see if he could forge a career in Rome. He began by hiring an Italian PR agent to get his name in the press.

"Who do you know in La Dolce Vita scene?" the man asked. "Someone glamorous that you can be seen with?"

"Let me see..." Mark couldn't mention anyone from Visconti's clique. None of them were talking to him. "I just met Annette Stroyberg at a party."

The PR agent's eyes lit up. "Molto bene."

Danish-born blonde Annette Stroyberg was Rome's sexpot-of-the-moment. Newly divorced from Roger Vadim, she had everyone gossiping about her notorious lesbian sex scenes in his vampire-erotica movie, *Blood and Roses*.

"Ask her out," urged the PR agent. "If she says yes, I'll take care of the rest."

A few nights later Mark took Stroyberg to Jackie O's where they danced and drank into the wee hours. When he suggested they end the evening at his place she was delighted that he had succumbed to her charms. Until they were mobbed by the perfectly positioned paparazzi as they left the club and she realized that Mark had set her up. Stroyberg's furor was

Chapter 30. 1961. Los Angeles/Rome

captured by the flashbulbs of a dozen cameras and the next morning she was depicted in the Italian tabloids, steaming, alongside Mark. The tell-all photos even made it into U.S. fan mags where Mark was quoted: "This friendship has done more for my career than anything that has happened to me in Rome yet."

It wasn't his most chivalrous move. But the coverage helped him win his first role in an Italian movie, *Peccati d'Estate (Sins of Summer)* with a much-needed salary of one million lire a week ($1,620) for ten weeks. He would be playing a poor country doctor opposite Daniela Rocca, another Italian sexpot.

In August he skipped off to the island of Elba, where they were filming. Where he was in for a rude surprise.

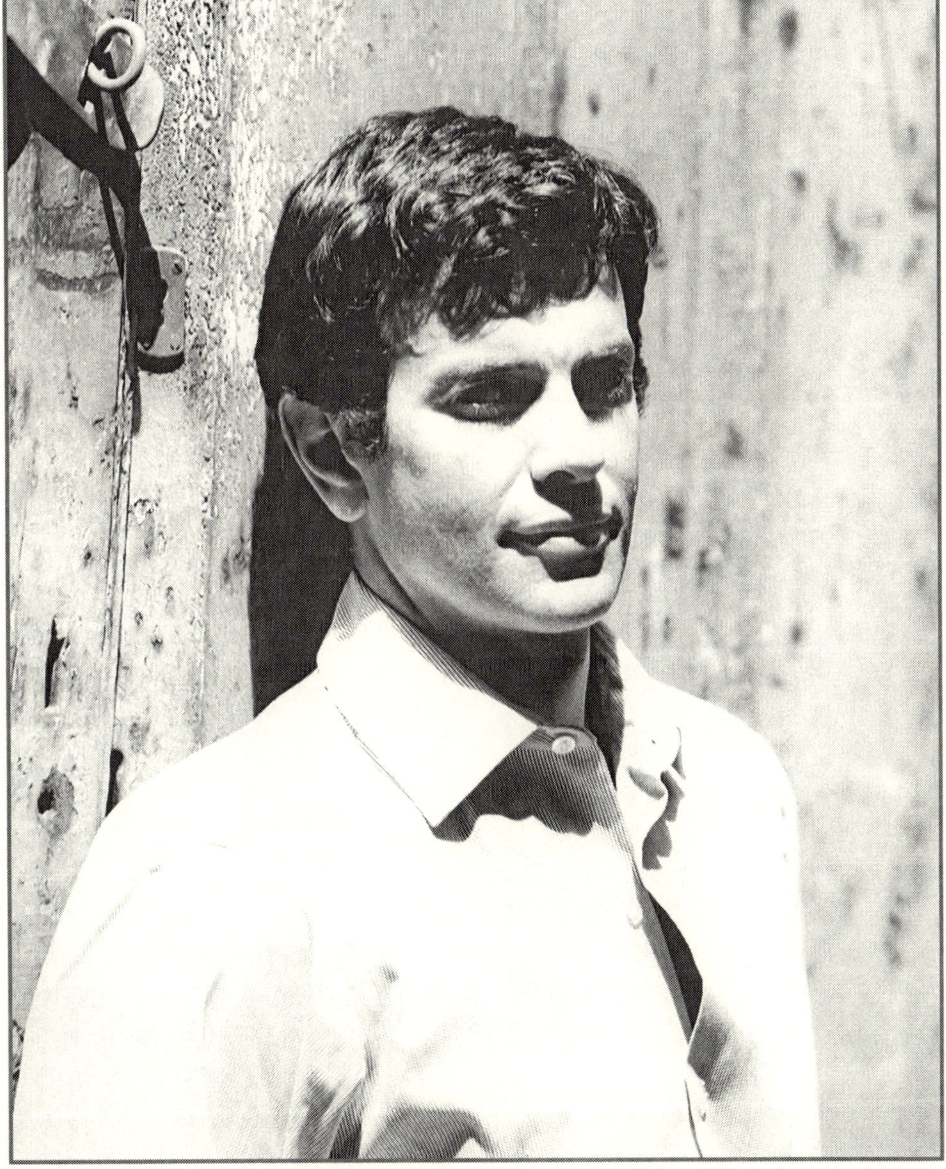

LE FILS DE CLEOPATRE
MARK DAMON
SCILLA GABEL
ARNOLDO FOA'
ALBERTO LUPO
TECHNISCOPE-TECHNICOLOR
REGIE
FERDINANDO BALDI
DE ZOON VAN CLEOPATRA

SALOON
THE GREAT CHIHUAHUA
TREASURE HUNT
(MONTA IN SELLA FIGLIO DI !...)

Mark costars with then girlfriend Dominique Boschero in *I Killed My Husband* (1962).

With Antonella Lualdi in *100 Horsemen*, (*I Cento Cavalieri*) (1964).

Mark shows his versatility by playing six roles in *The Golden Chameleon* (1966).

E' IL NUOVO DIVO DELLA HOLLYWOOD SUL TEVERE

Mark Damon monarca del western italiano

ROMA, 12 — Gran da fare per gli attori americani in Italia: l'imprevisto successo dei nostri western (da «Per un pugno di dollari» a «Un dollaro bucato») ha reso necessaria la loro presenza, specie se si tratta di attori giovani, fisicamente prestanti, e di buon nome. Fra questi, Mark Damon: uno dei migliori giuntoci da oltre Oceano, attuale «re della Hollywood sul Tevere» per le simpatie e la popolarità che ha saputo assicurarsi anche da noi.

La «Hollywood sul Tevere» ha visto di volta in volta, dallo inizio del dopoguerra in poi, diversi «monarchi»: il povero Tyrone Power, Orson Welles, Jack Palance, Van Heflin, Anthony Quinn, Clint Eastwood, una interessante proposta di Lattuada, ma prima di parlarne devo essere sicuro della cosa».

Le note biografiche di Mark Damon ci dicono che è stato straordinario fin da bambino. A due anni già leggeva e scriveva; a quattro anni risolveva problemi di aritmetica quasi impossibili per un bambino di quell'età; a nove aveva letto tutti i libri della biblioteca della scuola. Di lì a poco vinse un concorso di quiz radiofonici, primo tra cinquecento ragazzi di tutti gli Stati Uniti.

«Debbo molto alla mia capacità di risolvere quiz — ci ha detto lo stesso Damon con un sorriso compiaciuto — ho potuto mantenermi agli studi sino all'Università ed aiutare nello stesso tempo la mia famiglia, perchè ho preso parte ed ho vinto innumerevoli competizioni agonistiche, guadagnando molto denaro. Il mio ingresso nel cinema lo devo però a Groucho Marx, il grande comico, che un giorno incontrandomi in un Luna Park mi consigliò di presentarmi a una casa di produzione. Da allora ho percorso molta strada, ed ora eccomi qua».

Mark Damon, che ha appena trent'anni, ha tutta l'aria di voler restare a lungo il «re della Holywood sul Tevere».

Alberto Crucillà

Italian article – naming Jack Palance, Van Heflin, Anthony Quinn and Clint Eastwood as previous "Kings of Hollywood on the Tiber" – crowns Mark Damon as the reigning monarch of the Italian Western.

Three faces of *Johnny Oro* (1966).

287

Charming his fans at a *Johnny Oro* press day.

Damon squares off against baddies in *Johnny Oro* and *Pistol Packin' Preacher* (*Posate le Pistole Revelendo*) (1971).

Injecting humor into his Western roles.

Trying his hand at comedy, and playing a gunslinger posing as a woman in *Pistol Packin' Preacher* (*Posate le Pistole Revelendo*)(1971).

Mark Damon marries Barbara Frey in Rome, 1971.

La Spada Normanna (*Ivanhoe*) (1971)

Devil's Wedding Night (1973)

Margaret Markov, age 21

THE NEW YORK TIMES, SUNDAY, MAY 25, 1980

He Sells Hollywood to Europe

By SUSAN HELLER ANDERSON

CANNES, France — Mark Damon is a tall, dark former actor whose well-modulated baritone voice and finely tailored cashmere wardrobe immediately set him apart from the jeans-and-sandals hypesters operating on the terrace of the Carlton Hotel, the nerve center of the Cannes Film Festival, which ended here yesterday.

Ensconced in a suite at the hotel, Mr. Damon possibly never saw the terrace. For every day, from 6 A.M., when he would dream up innovative contracts in the bathtub, to 10 P.M. and often later, when he retired to nurse a streaming cold, fever and laryngitis, he did only one thing — sell.

Mr. Damon, 47 years old, is the founder and president of the Producers Sales Organization, a three-year-old Los Angeles-based company that licenses foreign distribution rights of American films and then baby-sits each film through the duration of the license, normally five years. The company, the biggest of its kind, oversees release dates to assure the buildup of enthusiasm for a picture, coordinates worldwide advertising campaigns, smooths problems with censors and keeps track of box office revenues in 40 foreign territories. Thus, the deal at the Cannes festival is only the beginning.

During the two-week-long pressure cooker of the festival where everyone is hungry only for American films, Mr. Damon consummated some 238 deals in more than 40 countries for the rights to American motion pictures with budgets totaling $75 million. In two weeks of round-the-clock dealing, he contracted $18 million in advance guarantees for seven pictures made and unmade, with a potential of 40 percent more in future revenues.

Since foreign revenues account for an average of 45 percent of a movie's gross intake and can often exceed revenues in America, foreign distribution is vital for a financial success. Traditionally, the distribution of American films was done by the major studios through their offices abroad. But the recent flourishing of the independent producers — often savvy businessmen backed by large corporations, investment groups or joint ventures — has led to a demand for a more sophisticated approach to the foreign market.

"We're dependent on Cannes for most of the year's revenues," Mr. Damon said. "We spend four months planning for it. We reserve advertising space a year ahead." Mr. Damon's company is a subsidiary of Arthur Guinness Son & Company, of London brewery fame. But while Guinness owns the majority share of Mr. Damon's company, he is not obligated to take on films made by Guinness's motion-picture subsidiary. In fact, Mr. Damon is choosy about all the films he takes on, accepting only 5 percent of the 200 films offered him over the last year.

He has also built up a loyal clientele. "We talked to many key distributors and other producers before we came to P.S.O.," said Larry Spiegel, the co-producer of "Phobia." "The organization builds futures. Producers who do business with Mark return." For Mr. Spiegel's $5.2 million picture, Mr. Damon negotiated $2 million in advance guarantees.

Producers also come to Mr. Damon for evaluation of a film's potential in foreign markets. Often the film is not yet made, perhaps with producers needing distribution advances to assure production. "Even if you don't need the money, I think it's better to sell a picture up front," Mr. Damon stated. "People buy hopes."

Japan is the most important foreign market, accounting for 20 percent of a film's foreign revenues. Next is Southeast Asia at 10 percent, then Britain for 7 to 8 percent.

But producers often prefer to forgo a maximum advance for higher shares of the box office take. "If the producer doesn't need the money up front, it's better," Mr. Damon explained. "Eventually you can make much more money."

Indeed, his fee structure is based on that theory. He gets a percentage of the advance guarantee paid by the distributor plus a percentage of overages, the money divided between the distributor and the producer after the former has recouped his advance. Mr. Damon's commissions range from 10 to 20 percent of advances and from 15 to 25 percent of overages.

Having been an actor, a distributor and a producer, Mr. Damon exhibits a formidable knowledge of the financial elements of movie-making. Born in Chicago, he grew up in Los Angeles. After earning a master's degree in business administration at the University of California at Los Angeles, he studied acting in New York. By 1956, he was under contract with the 20th Century-Fox Film Corporation, a handsome heart-throb often pictured in fan magazines. In 1961, he moved to Italy and stayed there until 1976, when he returned to produce "The Choirboys." A year later he founded Producers Sales Organization.

Fluent in Spanish and Italian and competent in German and French, Mr. Damon copes daily with cultural differences in doing business from one country to another, educates American producers to foreign-currency fluctuations and confronts a panoply of specific problems that vary with the country. "In Israel I can sell pictures that will be ready soon," explained Arianne Sipes, Mr. Damon's assistant. "But what's hard is asking for big money for films two or three years away. They don't even know what their inflation will be in two years."

While Guinness, the parent company, does not break out figures of subsidiaries, Mr. Damon says that this year the company will begin to see considerable income from films sold at previous Cannes festivals.

"We've been in business only three years so we have few films actually in theaters," he said. "But we've got some potent ones coming down, and that will make a huge change in our profits." Among them are "The Final Countdown," a science-fiction picture filmed aboard the U.S.S. Nimitz, starring Kirk Douglas and Martin Sheen, and "A Change of Seasons" with Shirley MacLaine and Bo Derek, sold before her rise to fame. "Low advance and high overages," Mr. Damon said, grinning.

At the Carlton Hotel, the walls of his suite were plastered with posters for only six of the seven films he's handling. The seventh has no script, no publicity, no press leaks. But a top director, a top actor and a few well-placed whispers brought the world's leading distributors clamoring to Mr. Damon's door. "At Cannes you puff and you hype," he reflected, "but sometimes the most important business is done quietly."

Elliot Erwitt/Magnum
Mark Damon

LOS ANGELES HERALD EXAMINER

Section D / Page 14
Los Angeles Herald Examiner
Monday
October 22, 1984

It takes the right accent to sell U.S. films abroad

PSO succeeds by adjusting strategy to suit country

By Richard Natale
Herald staff writer

Mark Damon entered the motion picture distribution business on little cat's feet. But after only seven years, his Producers Sales Organization is behaving like a tiger, with more than $10 million in revenues and $4.2 million in profits for 1983, vs. $7 million in revenues and profits of $3.5 million for 1982.

Last year, the major Hollywood studios combined did less than $1 billion in total overseas rentals, while PSO alone did $120 million.

PSO is on the verge of becoming a full-service entertainment company, possibly including ownership of radio and television stations and its own record label.

Rumors that Damon and his partner, John Hyde, intend to take the company public in the near future, selling stock to fund this expansion, are met with an assured nod of the head from the 50-year-old entrepreneur. "It's only a few months away," he says.

Damon began PSO in 1976 as a foreign sales operation, providing American films to foreign distributors for viewing overseas.

There was a five-year interlude not long afterward when the company was owned by the Irish brewing concern, Arthur Guinness Son & Co. Ltd. Damon bought out Guinness in 1982. He now owns 60 percent of the company, Hyde 40 percent.

While most foreign sales agents merely sell films to overseas territories, PSO operates more as a producer's representative. It creates marketing and advertising strategy for the films.

The company also provides partial financing before production ever starts by getting overseas distributors to guarantee funding beforehand — PSO gathered the first $8 million for the production of "Cotton Club."

Damon and Hyde recently formed a production subsidiary, PSO Presentations Inc., which provides full financing of films through a $100 million revolving line of credit from First Boston Corp. and partnerships with other companies.

For instance, PSO is allied on a number of projects with Jonesfilm, the motion picture arm of the successful Jones Apparel Group consortium, which includes Jones New York, Christian Dior and Norma Kamali.

Foreign distribution of American films has always been the domain of the major Hollywood studios, which for better or worse represented the top American films abroad — and to Damon's mind it was usually for the worse.

"Hollywood tended to treat all foreign countries alike," he says, "without regard for individual tastes."

Damon realized there were a number of good foreign independent distributors not allied to the Hollywood system who were eminently successful with films made in their own countries, and whatever American product they could get their hands on — usually low-budget B-grade movies.

The independents' strengths, as Damon saw it, were being in sync with different national audiences, knowing the kind of films they wanted and understanding how to sell those films. Hollywood studios, in contrast, sell movies as a block, with the same advertising campaign used for American release.

To persuade producers in the Hollywood community to change the way they'd been doing business for the past 50 years, Damon needed to prove his theory. His zeal got him through a lot of doors, but it wasn't until Damon turned a number of domestic box-office disappointments into overseas hits that people began to take notice.

"The Choirboys," based on a Joseph Wambaugh novel, did a modest $6 million in rentals in the United States and Canada, and a whopping $16 million overseas — on the average, an American film brings in only half as much money overseas as it makes in this country and Canada.

Similarly, "The Wanderers" made $11 million abroad and only $2.5 million domestically.

Damon perceived that both films needed hard-sell marketing approaches, emphasizing strong action elements, which he helped design.

"The Wanderers" was marketed as a comedy domestically, but the foreign campaign was closer to that of 'The Warriors," a movie about street gangs that was popular overseas as well as in the United States.

Damon helps distributors tailor marketing to their countries and sometimes has three or four different approaches to appeal to various tastes.

"A film's success overseas can be determined just by a change in title," he says. "'Young Doctors in Love,' would not work as a title overseas. So in Argentina it was called, 'Where's the Doctor?' because the film 'Airplane,' had been a success there under the title 'Where's the Airplane?' In Spain, it was 'Those Crazies with The Scalpels,' because films with 'Those Crazies,' in the title had done well in the past."

Mark Damon
Capitalizing on sale of films overseas

Mickey Rourke and Kim Basinger are stars of PSO-financed "9½ Weeks."

"A film's success overseas can be determined just by a change in title."

Mark Damon
partner in PSO

In the case of "The Final Countdown" ($6 million in the domestic market, $20 million overseas), the key sales tool was the film's star, Charlton Heston.

Damon has enlisted Heston and such notoriously publicity-shy stars as Paul Newman and Robert DeNiro to do extensive foreign stumping for their films. "The success or failure of a film overseas," he says, "often depends on personal appearances by the star."

Damon's background as an actor stood him in good stead when it came to persuading reticent actors to endure the rigors of foreign publicity travel.

"Also, actors get a whole different feeling from overseas journalists," says Damon. "They find the reporters are less blase, more reverential, and don't bait them. They tend to ask fewer questions about the actor's personal life and more about the filmmaking process.

"In Europe, an actor may be noticed on the street, but he is never, ever molested," Damon maintains. "They truly respect his privacy."

Damon's market-by-market approach also changed the profit participation structure for producers.

"Hollywood studios 'cross-collateralize' film revenues in overseas markets," says Damon. When an American film is released abroad, the producer's share of any possible profits is based on its overall box-office performance.

"All the monies are thrown into a pot," he says. "So if a film is a roaring success in Italy but a flop in Sweden, the profits are canceled out by the losses."

PSO's move into financing and production has been intermittent. While owned by Guinness, the company financed "The Wanderers" and "Final Countdown." After those films, however, it concentrated on foreign sales and partial financing.

That gave PSO little voice in the final product. "But we found that we were raising up-front monies for movies in which we were ultimately disappointed," Damon says.

PSO returned to full finance as a better way of controlling its own destiny. Among its upcoming films are "9½ Weeks," "Clan of the Cave Bear" and "The Navigator."

As the next logical step, Damon foresees a long-term domestic distribution arrangement with one of the major studios for the six fully financed productions PSO is planning annually.

A videocassette tie-in is also in the planning stages.

Foreign representation of independent and partially financed movies is still PSO's backbone, however, and Damon figures the company can handle a dozen films each year.

Although Damon and Hyde are still considering a number of options for financing the company's expansion, including limited partnership offerings, a public stock offering is the most likely route.

Besides motion pictures, a public PSO would also investigate television syndication sales, a record label (the company already has a music publishing division), merchandising, cable-TV, and buying radio and television stations.

With director John Huston.

Matthew Photographic Services

With renowned indie film financier Lew Horwitz

Matthew Photographic Services

With Spanish distributors Jose Hueva, Felipe Ortiz, and Luis Ortiz of Tripictures, S.A. at the Michael Jackson party.

Matthew Photographic Services

With Frank Agrama

Matthew Photographic Services

With Maggie and Raju Patel

Matthew Photographic Services

Mark, Michael Jackson, and Raju Patel sign partnership agreements at Mark's house.

Lexi and Maggie

Jon and Lexi

mark damon 50th SEPTEMBER 21-27, 2004

A Life in Pictures

Selected scenes from the life and career of **Mark Damon**

From his childhood years in Depression-era Chicago to his teen years in Beverly Hills, Mark Damon's colorful life plays out like something from a Hollywood novel — the only difference being, it's all true! Herein are excerpts from the upcoming biography of Damon by Linda Schreyer.

AMUSEMENT BUSINESS

"As a teenager in 1949, I ran rides at the Beverly Amusement Park at Third and La Cienega. One afternoon, a man with a mustache put two children on my airplane ride. He asked me if I'd ever made any movies, and said if I would like to take a screen test, he could get me one. Then he told me his name — Groucho Marx! I was so excited, I barely got the kids to the ground safely. He gave me his brother Gummo's number. Gummo — the fourth Marx brother who'd performed in vaudeville but left the act before they started making movies — was an agent. Gummo was swell and honest. He told me a screen test wasn't easy to get for a guy without any acting training. He advised me to study acting, then call him again. I thought about it a few days, then decided the whole thing was a waste of time. It was a while before I realized that Mr. Groucho had planted a seed that would keep on growing."

GLOBAL PAC

In 1974, Damon started working for the Bregni brothers — Mario and Pietro — and their international sales firm, PAC. Observing the intricacies of global film sales first-hand, Damon says, "I learned there was no such animal as 'foreign.' The foreign market was not a single entity but dozens of countries, each with their own tastes and needs. So, I learned how to sell movies differently to each market and how to tailor advertising and promotional campaigns differently, depending on the market's tastes and cultural needs."

As he familiarized himself with the international network of independent distributors, he realized they could do a much better job of selling American movies in their territories than the major studios.

S-18 www.hollywoodreporter.com

© 2008 Nielsen Business Media, Inc. All rights reserved.

Hollywood Reporter feature on Mark's 50th anniversary in show business.

Chapter Thirty-One

August 28, 1961

Elba/Rome, Italy

Mark and Dominique Boschero at Jackie O's.

Co-starring with fiery Dominique Boschero in
I Killed My Husband (1962).

With Luciana Paluzzi on the set of *The Reluctant Saint* (1962).

Chapter 31. 1961. Elba/Rome

NOBODY SPOKE ENGLISH. NOT THE DIRECTOR of *Peccati d'Estate*, Giorgio Bianchi, the actors or a single member of the crew. Mark understood only a little Italian and spoke even less. Until then, everyone he knew in Italy spoke passable English. On the first day of rehearsal, every time the director gave him a direction Mark had to look it up in his dictionary. It was a nightmare for an actor who didn't trust American directors, let alone Italians. Luckily, Bianchi was a funny guy with a great sense of humor who specialized in directing comedies.

There was one scene that everyone thought was hysterically funny. Everyone but Mark. It opened on a street cleaner sweeping up the piazza after a long night of reveling. Mark: "Bianchi would call action by saying '*Scopa! Scopa!*' which meant 'start sweeping.' Then he looked off at me and said, '*Beato lui*' meaning 'lucky bastard' and the whole crew laughed."

Mark looked up 'scopa' in his dictionary. The verb *scopare* meant to sweep and *scopa* was simply the command to start sweeping. He remained mystified until Luciana Paluzzi arrived in Elba to be with him. They were having dinner when Mark asked, "Why does everyone laugh when Bianchi says, 'Scopa!?'" To his annoyance Luciana started to laugh, too.

"Because *scopare* is also slang for 'to fuck,' she finally explained.

Mark laughed, finally getting the joke. "That night in our little hotel room, in the middle of our making love, Luciana yelled '*Scopa! Scopa!*' Then she murmured '*Beato te*' (lucky you) and we really exploded in laughter."

By the time he finished shooting *Peccati d'Estate* Mark had earned enough lira to live on. He returned to Rome and threw himself into learning Italian, "mostly to protect myself against directors." He chose an apartment in an Italian section of town, Piazza Margana 39 (otherwise known as Tor Margana), in a building that was a minor palace dating back to the 1300's. "And I refused to hang out with the American ex-pat colony. I spent my time with Italians. It was difficult because I didn't understand what they were saying. But it forced me to learn the language."

His romance with Luciana was going strong when they were both cast as young lovers in veteran Hollywood director Edward Dmytryk's (*The Caine Mutiny, Raintree County*) *The Reluctant Saint*, starring Maximilian Schell as a 17th-century peasant who grows up to become St. Joseph of Cupertino. The film proved to be a disappointment but his romance with

Luciana was in full bloom when she went back to the States for several months. So Mark was shattered when she wrote that she had fallen in love with somebody else, a wealthy man who could provide for her, her mother and young son, Cristiano (today known as Christian Solomon Halsey, a film executive in Europe): "He can give me the financial security I need, even if my feeling for him is *amore* with a small 'a' not a capital 'A' like ours."

Mark still had strong feelings for her when Luciana returned and called him. "Can I please come over and see you?"

"What for?"

"So we can talk," she pleaded. "Please..."

He was waiting for her in his apartment when she knocked. He had planned a lovely seduction that included the timely playing of *their* song, *Che Cosa C'e* (*What's Happening to Me*), sung by Gino Paoli. "She melted. But at the end of that song as she bent in to kiss me I pulled back and slapped her. I had been hurt and angry. Now I was just angry. It was the only time I ever hit a woman." Decades later, Luciana admitted, "I deserved it. I know that I hurt Mark. But I forgave him and we stayed friends through the years. It just wasn't meant to be. But I was very fond of him and always respected him because he has a very good soul."

As consolation, Mark resumed his explosive affair with Dominique. "It only lasted so long because of the absolutely incredible sex." At the same time he continued to seduce every beautiful woman he could. "During those years," he later commented, "I often slept with three or four women a week. When I multiply that by the number of years I did it, I probably slept with a thousand women."

There were other rewards for Mark in Rome besides the draw of Italian women. "Back then, to be an actor in Italy was really a lot of fun," remarked Luciana decades later. "Especially to be a handsome American actor like Mark. Today, when an actor walks into a restaurant, people hardly take a look. Back then, when Mark walked into a restaurant in Rome everyone would exclaim with great excitement: 'Marco Damone!' Believe me, it was a thrill."

Mark was excited to be cast in the star-studded *The Longest Day,* even if it was a small role. The film was the epic recreation of the Allied invasion of Normandy, a PR bonanza with 42 international stars including Henry

Fonda, John Wayne, Robert Mitchum, Richard Burton, Sean Connery and others. It was divided into four segments: American, British, French and German. Each had its own director and Zanuck was directing the American segment of the lollapalooza he was also producing.

Mark was on set when he noted that Zanuck, his perpetual cigar clamped between his teeth, was listening to their line readings while staring at his shoes. "He was an amazingly bad director," Mark remembered. "He wouldn't even watch us perform. He would just listen to our line readings and when the lines were over he'd ask the cameraman, 'Did they hit their marks? Everything okay for the camera?' And if the cameraman said 'Yes,' Zanuck would say, 'It's a print.'" No surprise - *The Longest Day* was the first and last film Zanuck would ever direct.

Next, Mark played a small role in *The Shortest Day*, an Italian-made spoof of *The Longest Day* directed by Italian writer-director Sergio Corbucci, a very good director with a great sense of humor. The plot centered on two goof-ups who enlist in the Italian army in World War II and somehow manage to help win a crucial battle. "It didn't pay much," Mark quipped, "but it made me the only actor in the world who played in both *The Longest* and *The Shortest Day*."

The picture featured its own cast of celebrities including Jean-Paul Belmondo, Walter Pidgeon, Vittorio Gassman, Simone Signoret and Mark's old pal, Susan Strasberg, who had fled to Rome after American critics skewered her for her over-the-top performance in *Stage Struck*. She was staying with Josephine Baker around the corner from Piazza Margana and the threesome often dined at Vecchia Roma. Mark talked with Susan about the difference between an actor's life in Europe versus Hollywood. "It's so much better here," he reflected. "You can live as a whole person, not just another Hollywood hopeful." Susan heartily agreed. Their evenings always ended on a fond note "but although I adored Susan, to my chagrin, she still wasn't in love with me." Whenever they appeared in public, however, eager paparazzi surrounded them and their photos were regularly splashed across Italian tabloids with enticing (false) headlines like "Mark Damon is engaged to Susan Strasberg!"

Despite his glamorous PR, another period of unemployment soon followed. Mark was despairing of ever working again when his PR agent suggested he send "Louella (Parsons), Mike (Connolly), Hedda (Hopper) and Sheila (Graham) little notes saying 'hello' and giving them some news about yourself. It's important that they feel that you still have a personal relationship with them."

Mark played along, eager to keep his connections with Hollywood. When he was cast in *I Shot My Husband* (with Dominique) he penned a short note that soon appeared in Sheila Graham's Hollywood column: 'Mark Damon writes from Europe: 'I feel that my current picture is a floating U.N. The script girl is Spanish, the lead actress is Romanian, the producer is Polish, the director is Hungarian. I am an American. And here we are, in Yugoslavia, speaking the only language common to all of us – Italian!'"

Once again, the Mark Damon public persona revealed only adventure and excitement while his private life was far more tumultuous. After shooting on location in Bled, Yugoslavia with Nadia Grey in *Husband*, Dominique showed up and caught him sleeping with Grey. "She slugged me, more than once, then grabbed the platinum watch that she had given me and threw it outside in a snow drift. It took me days to find it." He broke up with Dominique (again) and had just returned to Rome when he got a call from her.

"I'm desperate without you," she cried.

"Sorry," Mark replied. "I'm desperate *with* you."

He was about to hang up when Dominique moaned softly.

"I just slit my wrists because of you, you bastard. You'd better come over here before I die..."

He sped over to her house and found her in the bathroom. Her cuts weren't deep but there was a lot of blood. Panicked, he looked for something to clean the wounds. "Not knowing any better, I poured iodine on her wrists and she practically passed out from the pain." Mark became concerned that if he left Dominique for good she might try it again "until I walked into her apartment one afternoon and found her in bed with some guy named Franco. That absolved me of guilt."

When their mutual agent, Annalena Limentani, found out Dominique tried to kill herself over Mark it was all over for him with Limentani. "Annalena, who was gay, had a big thing for Dominique and was very jealous of my relationship with her." Mark quickly found another agent - twenty-one year old Rossana Pelliccia - a former assistant to Annalena who was starting her own agency, Continental Management. (After Mark became her first client she represented him for the rest of his career in Italy. The agency still exists today.)

Despite his efforts to secure the right agent and to rev up his PR, the vagaries of non-union European filmmaking began to catch up to Mark. "I did a costume picture in Italy but I am still owed $12,500 for my work,"

Chapter 31. 1961. Elba/Rome

he wrote to his family in December, 1961. "I think I will collect some of that because the film can't be released before my money is paid. But getting the $4,000 that is owed to me for another movie, *I Shot My Husband,* is dubious." As 1961 turned to 1962 he was practically broke and wondered if he should stay in Italy.

At the time Mark would never have bet that he would stay abroad for the next fourteen years and make movies in seventeen different countries: Belgium, Bulgaria, Andorra, Egypt, England, France, Germany, Italy, Lebanon, Luxembourg, Monte Carlo, Poland, Romania, Spain, Switzerland, Turkey, and Yugoslavia. He had no inkling that he would become an action movie hero and star in forty-one Spaghetti Westerns, sword-and-sandals, horror and detective flicks; work with famed Italian directors Mario Bava *(Black Sabbath),* Vittorio Cottafavi *(The Hundred Horseman),* Carlo Lizzani *(Requiescant)* and Sergio Corbucci *(Johnny Oro).* Or that he would direct and write three films of his own and produce four others.

After the failure of his early attempts Mark could not possibly imagine that one day he would become more famous in Italy as 'Marco Damone' than he'd ever been in the U.S.

PSO

1985

*Any time you think that you've made it,
get ready to fall.*
- Mark Damon

Chapter Thirty-Two

January 29, 1985

Century City, California

DAILY VARIETY

VOL. 705 No. 53   32 Pages   Hollywood, California 90028, Friday, November 16, 1984   Newspaper Second Class P.O. Entry   50 Cents

PSO, DELPHI COMPANIES MERGE

Combined Resources Total $350 Mil Over 5 Years; CBS/Fox Homevid Distrib Deal

By JAMES GREENBERG

Culminating seven months of intense negotiations and the natural evolution of both companies, Producers Sales Organization and The Delphi Companies have merged to form PSO/Delphi with combined resources of $350,000,000 over a five-year period for the financing, distribution and marketing of motion pictures.

Announced at the same time and a major component of the new company's financing is a longterm distribution deal with CBS/Fox Video for domestic homevideo rights to all titles and worldwide rights for selected films under the newly formed PSO video label.

Exact dimensions of the deal, which includes up to 80 films over a five-year period, were unavailable, but Mark Damon, chairman and chief executive officer, stated that it was, to his knowledge, "one of the biggest deals ever between a video company and an independent production entity."

Rounding out the structure of the PSO/Delphi affiliation is a domestic distribution deal with Tri-Star Pictures for a five-year period.

PSO/Delphi is expected to produce between five and eight films annually for domestic release through Tri-Star, but unlike the video deal with CBS/Fox, Tri-Star is not initially entering co-production pools.

PSO/Delphi is backstopping both production and distribution costs, with Tri-Star receiving a gross percentage which exceeds the distribution fee they in turn pay to Columbia Pictures for sales and booking services.

Neither CBS/Fox nor Tri-Star has a say in production decisions, but all parties indicated a spirit of cooperation will prevail. With the addition of the new products, Tri-Star stands to up its release schedule to some 25 films a year, thereby securing its relationships with distributors.

Though the distribution arrangement with Tri-Star is nonexclusive and PSO/Delphi product could go out from other distributors, the lion

(Continued on Page 26, Column 1)

THE WALL STREET JOURNAL.

© 1985 Dow Jones & Company, Inc. All Rights Reserved

WESTERN EDITION   TUESDAY, APRIL 16, 1985   RIVERSIDE, CALIFORNIA

Making Movies

Overseas Distributor Takes On Big Studios By Doing Own Films

Mark Damon Joins Forces With Financing Expert; Seven Pictures in Works

By LAURA LANDRO
Staff Reporter of THE WALL STREET JOURNAL

LOS ANGELES — "The Cotton Club" has died a slow death over the last four months in U.S. theaters. The jazz-era gangster movie hasn't recouped even half of its $54 million cost, and most of its backers will probably never see a penny from it.

Except for Mark Damon.

Three years ago, when "The Cotton Club" was just a script, Mr. Damon's company, Producers Sales Organization, invested $8 million in the Francis Ford Coppola epic in return for rights to distribute the movie overseas. Now, following PSO's carefully orchestrated publicity blitz in France, Italy and West Germany, "The Cotton Club" is a success overseas and PSO is reaping the profits.

Mr. Damon, a former actor in B movies, Italian Westerns and horror films, has become one of Hollywood's most successful entrepreneurs by turning American movies—including turkeys like "Endless Love" and "The Wanderers"—into big hits overseas. Last year, PSO sold more tickets overseas than any of the major U.S. studios. Now Mr. Damon has bigger ambitions. If PSO can successfully market U.S. movies overseas, he figures, there is no reason it can't muscle into the ranks of the major studios and produce movies, too.

Mark Damon

314

Newsweek

JUNE 24, 1985

Is There Life After Spaghetti?

Is there life after an unremarkable acting career in even less remarkable spaghetti Westerns? Maverick movie mogul Mark Damon made sure there was. At the Cannes Film Festival three years ago Damon and his five-year-old film-distribution company, Producers Sales Organization (PSO), bargained against the big boys and raised $8 million to help produce a major American film in exchange for exclusive overseas distribution rights. The movie was Robert Evans's "The Cotton Club." It ultimately bombed in the United States, but now is expected to gross $50 million abroad—more than double its domestic take.

Now in its eighth year, PSO ranks with the major Hollywood studios' overseas distribution arms, with more than $300 million in box-office receipts last year. Its success is largely attributable to what the 52-year-old Damon calls his "instinct" for what will play, not only in Peoria, America's bellwether, but in Paris, Palermo and Prague. "Knowing what works in a picture is international," he says. "What's important is having a gut instinct for what the public likes. I think, for whatever reason, I have that instinct."

Flirtation: Damon—born Allen Herskovitz in Chicago—was fresh out of the Graduate School of Management at the University of California, Los Angeles, when his flirtation with acting became serious. Seeing a photograph of Damon, Italian director Luchino Visconti invited him abroad to audition for one of his films. Though Damon didn't get the part, he decided to stay in Italy (and adopted, though only briefly, the Italianate version of his name: Marco Damone). During the 1960s and '70s Damon acted in 50 grade-B Italian films and wrote, directed or produced another half dozen. He introduced his friend, director Sergio Leone, to Clint Eastwood, then known for his role in the American television series "Rawhide." Leone cast Eastwood in the lead in his film, "A Fistful of Dollars"—launching the career of one of Hollywood's all-time box-office superstars.

Damon's final acting role, in the American film "There Is No 13," propelled him into the distribution business. The film was artistically successful enough to become the U.S. entry in the 1975 Berlin Film Festival, but it wasn't commercial enough to entice distributors. Realizing that distribution can make or break a hit, Damon set out to learn the tricks of the trade—and invent a few of his own.

In the course of his training, Damon learned that, even though it was foreign distributors who had their fingers firmly on the pulse of regional cinema audiences, most American producers preferred to deal with the overseas distribution arms of the major U.S. studios. Damon thought the American attitude was shortsighted. "I noticed that independent companies were often more successful in the marketing of the product that they handled than major American studios," says Damon. "They were entrepreneurs, nationals to the marketplace [who] understood that marketplace better." Damon brought his 15-year experience abroad, his command of five languages and his international connections in the industry back to Hollywood.

In 1977, his one-man, two-secretary office turned a $50,000 profit in its first year of business. Eager to back a comer, the Irish-based brewery, Arthur Guinness Son & Co., acquired PSO, and the following year Damon's profits increased tenfold. Two years later, banking on such films as "An American Werewolf in London," "Endless Love" and "Fort Apache, The Bronx," PSO logged $2 million in profits. And the company took on a new challenge: marketing foreign-made films in the U.S.

By the time PSO bid for the rights to "The Cotton Club," Damon had acquired a business partner, former independent producer John Hyde, and bought PSO back from Guinness. Late last year, PSO became an "independent major." Last December PSO merged with the Delphi Organization, a highly respected New York-based film-financing company. PSO Delphi has committed $350 million over the next five years to the production of its own original films—and has already signed some of the industry's most sought-after talent, such as "Flashdance" director Adrian Lyne and Daryl Hannah of "Splash."

Foundation: The firm has also negotiated an agreement with Tri-Star Pictures to distribute its films in the United States and has closed a deal that gives CBS/Fox worldwide video-cassette distribution rights to any films PSO produces. Damon says his lackluster years in the spaghettis—and his exposure to the industry overseas—provided the foundation on which his current success is built. "If I had been in Hollywood the whole time, I wouldn't have had the benefit of the experimentation I had overseas. I expect that PSO will be in this business to stay. We've been a maverick, we did it with our own money and we did it slowly—but with a lot of panache."

MARILYN ACHIRON with PETER McALEVEY in Los Angeles

Damon: A maverick mogul with 'instinct'

Scenes from 'Cotton Club,' 'Fort Apache' and 'Werewolf': A distributor that knows how to turn bombs into hot properties

315

From Cowboy to Mogul to Monster

THE NEXT TWO AND A HALF years passed in a flash. One minute PSO was a small company. The next, they were an entity.

In January, *Variety* reported: "PSO Delphi will produce five to eight movies a year which will be distributed domestically by Tri-Star Pictures. CBS/Fox video will distribute a PSO home video label."

In February: "PSO Delphi stands a chance of having the kind of financial clout in Hollywood that only major studios have been able to muster in the past," predicted Enrique Senor, director of Allen & Co., one of the leading investment banking firms in the entertainment industry.

In March: "Lewis Korman, Delphi's co-founder and CEO stated, 'Independent filmmakers who fought for years to get financing, domestic and foreign theatrical distribution and home video deals will now come to PSO Delphi, a one-stop shop.'"

Ads began to appear with the company's new slogan: "PSO Delphi – The Independent Major." Hollywood insiders jumped on the bandwagon, taking out full page ads congratulating Mark and John on the merger: "Good people make good partners."

Overnight, the company Mark and John had built had money to make movies, domestic distribution for them, even their own video label. It was astounding.

"The merger wasn't just front-page news in the trades," Kevin Koloff recalled. "It was banner-headline front-page news. Everybody at PSO was feeling real good, like we're in on the ground floor of this thing that's about to take off." "At that moment, there was this enormous swell of optimism," another ex-PSOer agreed. "The Delphi merger brought in a ton of cash. We were in the middle of making a bunch of movies. We had no idea that we were gonna crash and burn."

The merger involved a drastic restructuring in the organization of the company. "Up until then, ever since we went into business together Mark owned 60% and I owned 40% of PSO," said John, "minus a small percentage spread out between key employees." Now they would share ownership with Delphi and Allen& Co., which would own about 45% of the new company. In PSO Delphi, Mark would be the CEO, generally focusing on marketing and production, development of projects, deals with producers, directors and actors, etc. John would be the Vice Chairman, overseeing West Coast operations and financial matters. Lew Korman would be President, covering East Coast business from New York.

At least, that was how it was supposed to work.

Chapter 32. 1985. Century City

"The reality is, after the Delphi deal, there were three people running the company," said Eddie Kalish. "Lew Korman's entry into the picture was the beginning of the end of PSO. The merger politicized the company because now there were factions that had never existed before, new leaders, new people to deal with."

"We were a great combination until we brought in our 3rd partner," Mark agreed decades later. "When you bring in a 3rd party he will start to align with one or the other and Korman caused a lot of strain and tension between John and me."

"Korman was based in New York," John explained, "so now you had a group in New York who thought PSO should be run one way, you had Mark, you had me, you had all these different viewpoints and you had politics for the first time."

They also had an influx of new staff. "We went from being half a floor of a building to occupying the entire floor," Michael Heuser recalled. "Suddenly, you'd walk down the hallway and there'd be office after office after office. We went from knowing one another intimately as friends to not even knowing who somebody was in the corridors."

With the influx of additional manpower from Delphi and Allen & Co. "we became an entirely different company," Kathy Cass agreed.

"For the first time there were Wall Street people looking over your shoulder all the time," said Kate.

"After Lew Korman caused the bank to loan us $350 million PSO was never the same," agreed Kalish. "You could feel the pressure mounting from the minute the deal was made." "The bank loan blew things out of proportion," agreed an ex-PSOer. "It took Mark and John out of their element which was guerrilla marketing, guerrilla sales, being in the trenches. Suddenly they were in a completely different realm."

"The mistake, if there was one, was probably because of *hubris* on both of our parts," John speculated decades later. "In retrospect, maybe it was foolish to think that we could jump-start to the next level by bringing in a partner and financing. What we probably should have done was continue to run a very successful company and been satisfied with producing two or three pictures a year instead of suddenly deciding we could now make six or eight."

When an article in *California* magazine included Mark, John and Lew Korman alongside studios as the most powerful forces in Hollywood, Mark exuberantly crowed: "We are on our way to becoming the largest 'independent' movie company in Hollywood!"

"It seemed ideal but maybe it was too ideal," John reflected decades later. "Going back to where we started, Mark was the first to institutionalize foreign sales and to say we can do this for fifteen different producers and do it on a business level. Then PSO was the first to say we can do marketing equal to a major studio. Then we were the first to say that the distribution will be just as good and the reporting just as good. Finally, we said, 'Gee, we can even finance like a major studio.' And that was where the trouble began." "Very few can make those kinds of quantum leap developments," noted Eddie Kalish. "You have to build towards things and we didn't do that. An analogy of how PSO evolved was that we took a giant step across a big chasm and didn't have the legs to reach the other side."

Some industry critics were dubious about the sudden growth of PSO. Powerful agent Jeffrey Berg, President of International Creative Management (a leading Hollywood talent agency) told the trades that PSO would be better off continuing to do what it did best - selling movies overseas for other movie producers instead of producing them. "When you go from being a foreign sales agent," he said of Mark, "to becoming an executive who is selecting projects, hiring producers, writers, directors and actors, you're casting yourself in a whole new light – and competing with some very sophisticated guys at the studios who have been doing it for 20 years."

Other insiders disagreed. Mark Canton, Executive Vice President of worldwide motion picture production at Warner Bros. told *Hollywood Reporter*, "Mark has a big future in this town. He has established great relationships with American movie makers by doing well with their movies overseas, and in turn there are a lot of doors open to him now that he wants to build PSO into a production company."

Overnight PSO Delphi was deluged by writers, agents, directors and producers eager to proffer services and projects. Mark's desk was covered with stacks of scripts that he took home nightly, waking at 3:00 AM to plow through them. He was developing six movies that PSO would produce within the next eighteen months; they were in pre-production on *Short Circuit* and post-production on movies already shot -- *The NeverEnding Story, 9 ½ Weeks* and *Clan of The Cave Bear.*

John, meanwhile, continued to fly back and forth to New York where he was actively engaged in high-level negotiations for multi-million dollar credit lines to finance these movies. Both men were so consumed with fulfilling the next stage of PSO that they didn't realize the distance that was growing between them. Between their hectic schedules and the input of their divisive 3rd partner, Lew Korman, the harmony they had always enjoyed was becoming strained.

Publicly, Mark was confident that he'd made the right move into production: "I spent twenty years in front of the camera and behind it, writing, directing, cutting – doing everything in the motion picture business. When filmmakers come in here, I know how to talk to them. I know what they're going through. I'm familiar with every phase of a movie because I've been there." Privately, the first movie to bear the PSO Productions stamp — *9 ½ Weeks* — was testing all of Mark's skills.

They had recently begun to preview a two hour cut and each screening was worse than the last one. "At a research screening, you have a successful picture if 80% of the audience marks the top two boxes as excellent and very good. If you get 60% saying they would definitely recommend it to their friends, you also have a good chance for success." At the first screenings for *9 ½ Weeks,* only 7% marked the top two boxes.

Mark: "People hated the movie. Because of the length. Because of Mickey's sick character, which made him dislikable. Because the movie didn't have a through line. Because of a hundred reasons."

Meanwhile, according to Mark, Adrian Lyne was becoming more and more desperate as each successive research screening went from bad to very bad. "Finally, at about the fourteenth research screening, Adrian listened to the boos and taunts of the audience and went white in the face. He turned to me and asked, 'What are we going to do?' I responded, 'I'll do the next cut. I think I know how to fix it.'"

Working with editors, they cut scenes that Adrian had taken from the novel depicting graphic sadomasochism and other dark moments. Then they set about re-doing Mickey Rourke's performance. "Mickey had a very sick take on his role so we worked on finding every moment of charm that we could. A giggle here, a shy grimace there, a cute shrug of his shoulders. We even took footage after Adrian had called 'Cut' and Mickey was just goofing around. We reconstructed his performance practically frame by frame, so that he became warm, vulnerable and cute instead of the prick he had set out to play. And we tried to add some fun to the piece." It was painstaking work that took a lot of Mark's time.

From Cowboy to Mogul to Monster

On a blustery Wednesday in March, he drove up to the entrance to Hillcrest Country Club, grabbed the script for *Short Circuit* from the passenger seat and walked into the dining room at 12:35 for his 1:00 lunch with the producers and potential director, John Badham. Mark was making script notes when a tall, dark-haired man strode over to the table.

"Mark Damon?" he asked with a crisp British accent.

"Yes."

"Hello. I'm John Badham."

The English-born director of the box office smash hit *Saturday Night Fever, Blue Thunder* and *War Games* had only just read the script for *Short Circuit* that morning. "It originated in a screenwriting workshop and eventually made its way to me. I loved it right away," he recalled. "I was running around the house, going 'This is great! This is great! So delightful and funny!'"

The script centered on a robot named Number 5, one of a group of experimental military robots built in a top-secret defense laboratory. Equipped with deadly lasers, Number 5, the ultimate killing machine, undergoes a sudden transformation after being struck by lightning. When he escapes from the top-secret laboratory and becomes a peacenik who no longer wants to kill or, in robotese, "disassemble" anyone, he is pursued by scientists eager to catch him.

Mark and Badham, who started in the Universal Studios mailroom alongside John Hyde, liked each other immediately. By the end of their meeting (with producers David Foster, his son, Gary [who found the script] and Larry Turman) Mark gave *Short Circuit* the 'green light.' Mark came on as Executive Producer. "And from then on," John Badham remembers "there was a lot of contribution, from start to finish, from him."

Most of the script was already in place. "But Mark and I thought there's more fun to be had with it," Badham reflected. "With his support and blessing I worked with the original writers (Brent Maddock and S. S. Wilson) until we brought in another writer, Jay Tarses, to make what they had even funnier. The writers and the other producers were kind-of upset by this but Mark was very supportive. He kept saying, 'Let's try it. If we get something better it would be silly to say we're sticking with this because it's what we started with. We'll just have to make sure that what we're doing is better and not just different.'"

In fact, the rewrite by Tarses helped to create one of the funniest characters in the movie, after Number 5: an Indian scientist named Ben

Chapter 32. 1985. Century City

Jabituya, a master of malapropisms who is the best friend of Dr. Newton Crosby, the scientist who created Number 5. Badham: "We were thinking that we get so many clever scientific people from India and English is not necessarily their second language but maybe their language-and-a-half, so things can get a little mixed up. It was supposed to be a bright kind of funny as we didn't want to be making fun of anybody."

Tarses contributed such comic lines as: "With excitement like this who is needing enemas?"; "Oooooh. Her pants are blazing for you"; "Goodbye crazy lady, I enjoyed repeatedly throwing you to the ground" and "I am standing here beside myself!" As Badham recalled, "the more we worked on it, the more we realized it didn't matter how funny we thought the script was, we could always add more jokes for Ben or Number 5 to say." The robot's best-known line came after Number 5 bursts into the bathroom where Stephanie is taking a bubble bath: "Nice software."

During the rewrites they also worked on the design of the robot. Badham: "We all knew the audience had to fall in love with the little guy to make the story work. So we made a committee composed of the designer, the production designer, our special effects man (who had some experience in building robots) and Syd Mead, the renowned Futurist who had worked on *Blade Runner*." After they came up with a prototype they showed it to Mark. He looked at it for a while and mused, "I think it's really good, but there's something lacking in the expression. Somewhere in the face."

The team looked at the robot critically. How could it be more expressive? "I remember being at a bullfight in Madrid," Mark continued, "and there were a couple of bulls that had big eyelashes. When they stopped to catch their breath and blinked their eyes at the crowd those beautiful long lashes made me feel so much more for them than the matadors who were trying to kill them." Suddenly, Badham had a flash: "You know how movie cameras have matte boxes to keep reflections from the sun off the lens?" he asked excitedly. Everyone nodded. "And you know how there's another shade in front of the matte box? Well, if we put two of those bill-type-shades on Number 5, one on each lens, we might get the same effect as the eyelashes on those bulls." They went back to the drawing board "and that's what we did," said Badham, "and it made a big difference in terms of the expressiveness of the robot."

They cast Steve Guttenberg (fresh off his success in *Cocoon*) to play Dr. Newton Crosby and Ally Sheedy (recent star of *The Breakfast Club*)as Stephanie, the young woman who drives an ice cream truck, ends up sheltering Number 5 and falls in love with his creator while convincing him that the robot has truly become alive.

By the time *Circuit* was ready to go PSO Delphi's movie slate was looking good: *Eight Million Ways to Die,* a police drama based on a book by popular author Lawrence Block with a script penned by Oliver Stone, was scheduled to shoot in the summer. Other projects included *Flight of The Navigator,* a science fiction fantasy and *The Lost Boys,* a dark comedy/thriller about young boys who become vampires, to be directed by Richard Donner.

In April, the Damon's moved to a new house on Benedict Canyon, a sprawling Tudor manse on two acres up a long, winding driveway. Formerly owned by uber-manager Sandy Gallin, (whose client roster included Dolly Parton, Kenny Rogers and others) Mark and Maggie had first seen the house eighteen months earlier.

"The minute I walked in I fell in love with it," Mark recalled. "Maybe because it felt like a European house. The high ceilings in the living room reminded me of my first apartment in Rome. The rolling green hills by the swimming pool could have been Baden-Baden, Germany or Lucerne, Switzerland or the hills of Tuscany, even Ireland." Maggie loved it, too: "It was more than we could afford but we decided we had to have it."

They started negotiations but after nine months, Gallin pulled out. Mark: "His business manager admitted privately to us that Sandy never had any intention of selling the house. He had just wanted to get an idea of what it was worth. So, with heavy hearts we decided to forget about it."

Six months later, the business manager called again. "Would you still be interested in the house? Sandy has decided he's ready to sell."

"I don't know. Is he serious this time?"

"Dead serious."

Mark met with Sandy. "What I really want is to be able to move out of this house with just my toothbrush and sell everything in it," Gallin declared.

Mark clarified. "Including your wine cellar? All your furniture, everything?" He loved that furniture.

"Yes."

Sandy asked for a price. Mark countered. Gallin finally agreed. Mark: "But when I put out my hand to shake his, Sandy suddenly pulled his hand away."

"Are you one of those guys whose handshake means the deal is closed?"

Chapter 32. 1985. Century City

"Absolutely."

Gallin put his hand in his pocket. "I need to think about this," he said.

He called his friends, David Geffen and Barry Diller for advice. "Grab it," they both said. So Gallin finally told his business manager to close the deal with Mark.

For the first time in their marriage, Mark gave Maggie complete control over furnishing their home. "Before that, I had to be part of every decision. And I had to win. It was a painful process for Maggie."

"This is your project," he told her. "Consult me if you want, but the final decision is yours."

"Boy, was that a welcome change," Maggie declared years later. She went to town, transforming their home into a world of light and air and grace, a reflection of lives lived on a grand scale. When she was done the place was even more exquisite. "But it had taken everything I had, basically, for the down payment," Mark added. "I went far beyond my means for us to get that house."

Nobody suspected that on the first weekend in April, when Mark threw a celebration party at the new house. PSO Delphi had just acquired the foreign rights for *Prizzi's Honor* starring Jack Nicholson and Angelica Huston, directed by John Huston and produced by the newly formed ABC Motion Pictures.

The scent of orange blossoms filled the air as Mark stood in the doorway of his lavish new home and greeted Angelica Houston, Sherry Lansing, Richard Donner and Lauren Schuyler-Donner, Terry Semel, Brandon Stoddard and others.

"What a magnificent house!" they exclaimed.

"The furnishings are incredible."

"Great taste," people remarked.

Maggie glowed. Mark beamed.

He had no idea how soon that beautiful home would become a millstone around his neck.

CHAPTER THIRTY-THREE

June 24, 1985

Beverly Hills, California

Chapter 33. 1985. Beverly Hills

Chaos reigned. On the set of *Eight Million Ways to Die*, Jeff Bridges and Rosanna Arquette were saying and doing whatever they wanted while director Hal Ashby nodded his approval. "Wonderful," he applauded. "Keep it up!"

Mark and Kate stood off to the side, confused.

"Where the hell is the script?" Mark quietly asked.

"Beats me."

Mystified, they looked around for it. But the script, penned by Oliver Stone with a rewrite by Robert Towne, was nowhere to be seen. Meanwhile, the actors continued to improvise the scene. They seemed to have complete conviction. But what exactly *were* they saying and doing and how was it part of the story? Mark and Kate had no idea. Even the crew looked confused. Worried, Mark looked over at Ashby, who couldn't have been happier. As usual, he was barefoot and dressed in threadbare jeans and a rumpled shirt. His eyes were deeply sunken and long fringes of unwashed grey hair hung around his unshaven face.

As usual, Mark thought the director looked like a cross between a Beatnik and a Bowery Bum. But he didn't give a hoot about Ashby's appearance. He only cared that the director he had hired had thrown out the script, was letting the actors improvise and had turned them all against him. While the movie he and John were funding out of their pockets was going down the tubes.

It was a far cry from the way it began.

On a brilliant morning in late April, fifty-five-year-old Hal Ashby drove up the long driveway to the Damon's new home on his motorcycle. Mark, curious, watched from inside his office as Ashby got off his motorcycle and took off his helmet. His long grey hair tumbled to his shoulders. He sported large, rose-colored glasses in wire frames, wooden beads, a plaid flannel shirt that revealed his rail-thin shoulder-blades and threadbare corduroy pants and sandals. As he walked towards Mark, his first impression was of an aging flower child. Despite Ashby's outfit, it was his face that made the strongest impression on Mark. Hollow-eyed and gaunt, the man looked completely ravaged.

As he went out to greet him Mark couldn't help remembering the stories he'd heard about him and his doubts about hiring the man surfaced.

In the 1970s, Hal Ashby had been one of the hottest directors in Hollywood. He had hitch-hiked there from Ohio at the age of eighteen, having grown up on a Mid-West dairy farm where Ashby survived the loneliness and isolation after his parents' divorce (when he was five) only to find his father's dead body in the barn when he was twelve, a suicide victim after he lost the family farm because he refused to allow the milk to be pasteurized. By the time he arrived in Hollywood, Ashby had been traumatized, abandoned, married and divorced. By the age of seventeen.

After starting as a clerk at Universal Ashby had worked his way up to become an editor, forging a friendship with and editing for acclaimed director Norman Jewison, culminating in an Oscar win for Ashby's editing of Jewison's *In the Heat of the Night.* Over the next ten years Ashby went on to direct *Harold and Maude, Being There, Shampoo, Coming Home* and *The Last Detail.* He had a phenomenal run. But along with his success came self-destruction.

Over the next decade Ashby's life became increasingly consumed by drugs and alcohol. In 1983, his notoriously erratic behavior was topped by an incident while he was making the Rolling Stones concert film, *Let's Spend the Night Together.* By then it was rumored that Ashby, who smoked two packs of cigarettes a day and countless joints, was getting deeper into cocaine, freebasing and smack. After a night of hard partying with Mick Jagger and company he proved the rumormongers correct when he OD'ed and collapsed at a stadium in Phoenix. When photos of Ashby being wheeled out on a gurney with an I.V. in his arm hit the trades the next morning his career officially went into the toilet.

Ashby's downward spiral continued with his uninspired direction of a string of flops in the next few years. He developed a reputation as an unreliable director who spent so much time in the editing room that his movies were taken away from him and given to someone else to cut, especially sad since he was such a talented editor.

By the time he drove up Mark's driveway Hal Ashby was considered to be unemployable by most of Hollywood. So why was Mark even considering him for *8 Million Ways To Die?*

"I'd heard about Ashby being a cokehead and I knew his last couple of pictures were dreadful. But his earlier movies were terrific and he was also known as a director with whom actors loved to work." Cassian Elwes of William Morris added, "Mark constantly talks about how he wants to make big commercial, studio level films. But really, his heart is in smaller, more meaningful films with interesting directors and material." "And

Chapter 33. 1985. Beverly Hills

there was the fact that Jeff Berg, his agent, was pushing him on me," said Mark himself. "Berg had been Ashby's agent for many, many years and was desperate to get him a job. He pushed me really hard, almost to the point of bullying." With PSO newly spreading its wings as a production company it was important to have good relations with top talent agencies like ICM (where Berg was recently named Chairman as well as President.) "So after Jeff called me every other day for two weeks, I finally agreed to meet with Hal."

Now, Mark greeted Ashby cordially. They discussed the script, which had been adapted by Oliver Stone from the popular books by award-winning author Lawrence Block, centering on 'Matt Scudder,' a tough New York vice squad detective and unlicensed P.I. who had been around for twenty-five years and had a built-in audience of fans.

"Eight Million Ways" began with Scudder accidentally killing a suspect during a drug bust, then taking to the bottle to relieve his guilt while his marriage and career fall apart. After Scudder meets a prostitute who asks for protection from her pimp so she can get out of "the life" he agrees to help her. After she is murdered by 'Angel,' an evil Latin drug dealer, Scudder's investigation into her death leads him into an underworld of prostitution, drugs and shoot-outs.

In their first meeting, Mark told Ashby how he visualized certain scenes. Ashby enthusiastically agreed: "That's exactly how I see them, too." "We went over three, four, five scenes and he saw eye to eye with the way I saw them. He seemed enamored with me and I was flattered," Mark recalled ruefully years later.

After Ashby left, Mark called Berg and said he would take a shot with the director. "I also told him, 'If he gives us any trouble I'm going to depend upon you to straighten him out'." Jeff assured Mark that he'd make sure Ashby did his job and PSO signed him as the director of *8 Million Ways to Die*.

The script needed a re-write, they decided. "As we threw out different names, Robert Towne (*The Last Detail, Chinatown, Shampoo*) was the one that most appealed. Partly because of his past work with Ashby, partly because I'd been roommates with Bob so many years before." While Towne rewrote they cast three-time Oscar nominee Jeff Bridges as Scudder, took a chance on a young actor named Andy Garcia, who had never been in a movie but gave an incredible reading as 'Angel' and cast Rosanna Arquette as 'Sarah,' the hooker with a heart of gold.

With so many award-winning talents (Bridges, Block, Stone and Towne) the project seemed to have been born under the right stars. According to author Lawrence Block, however, troubles began long before they started to shoot: "Stone had come to see me and wanted to work with me on the original script. But I didn't think I could stand it. I saw one script that he did and didn't think much of it. Then I never heard anything of or from Towne."

Block, who had chosen the title, "Eight Million Ways to Die" from the phrase about New York: "There are eight million stories in the naked city" was shocked to learn that the rewrite set the story in LA rather than in New York. Years later Mark explained, "Having recently finished shooting *9 ½ Weeks* in New York, we knew that union prices there were incredibly high. When we learned that the $16 million budget would have gone up by $3 or 4 million if we shot in New York we decided to do it in L.A."

Excitement was high when the film started shooting on location on July 15. Mark: "Then, on the first day I found out that they didn't start shooting until 5:00 P.M. even though there was a call at 8:00 A.M. Second day, 4:00 P.M. rolls around and they didn't have their first shot. I went down to the set and discovered that Ashby had thrown out the script and was having his actors improvise." Mark hit the roof. "How could he throw out a script written by one brilliant writer, Oliver Stone, and re-written by another brilliant writer, Robert Towne?!"

"Hal always had his actors improvise," said Ashby's longtime friend, producer Charles Mulvehill. "He created an atmosphere for the actors on a set that was totally permissive. He'd stroke them and let them try anything they wanted." In the past, this approach had led Jack Nicholson, who starred in Ashby's *The Last Detail*, to call him "one of the greatest <u>non</u>-directors of all time."

Now, when Mark confronted him on tossing the script for *Eight*, Ashby replied: "Don't worry, these actors are good enough to come up with great performances."

"I don't care how good they are," Mark countered. "Actors aren't writers. Certainly not writers who should be replacing Stone and Towne!"

Ashby was unmoved. "Trust me," he answered. And walked away.

The problem was, Mark didn't. For good reason. "Ashby would come on the set in the morning and say 'we have to rehearse today,'" Kate recalled. "I was like, well, excuse me... We have $60,000 dollars worth of crew and equipment and everyone in here waiting. So Mark would come

Chapter 33. 1985. Beverly Hills

in and say 'the time for that is over.' And that would make Ashby dig in his heels and want to rehearse for *two* days. With no script in sight."

"I went into production on *Coming Home* with only a handful of pages of shooting script," Ashby once recalled proudly in an interview, "and I remember that just before we started shooting, Jane (Fonda) said to me, 'Have you ever started a film knowing no more about what we're going to do than this?' And I said, 'No.' She looked at me and said, 'I hope it works.' I said, 'So do I.'

On *Coming Home,* Ashby further recalled, "during the first two weeks of shooting I had Rudy Wurlitzer, a writer, working on the screenplay. I would come home at eleven at night and we would work until about two in the morning... But I had a big problem with the actors," he admitted. "They would say, 'When are we going to get some pages?' And I would say, 'I'm going to give you a whole bunch in about ten days or two weeks.' But it really ended up, 'What are we going to do for tomorrow?' or, even, 'What are we going to do today?' Despite his actors' concerns Ashby was proud of his approach. "I think overall that having no script helped give the film that sense of reality and honesty," he said about *Coming Home.*

"Maybe so," Mark retorted. "But that was a decade ago, when Ashby could still direct." Now, with each passing day, it became clear that Ashby was simply not there anymore. "He was able to stay behind the camera and encourage the actors but he had no sense of story or anything else."

"Ashby was nuts," Kate confirmed.

Even his longtime friend, Haskell Wexler, concurred, "Once he was on the set Hal went crazy... Something flipped."

"He would never pressure the performers or provoke a clash on the set. He left his dramatizing to clashes with producers", said Mulvehill. "Ashby was rarely angry in public, but he would come to a slow boil and get back to some private space, like a car, and fucking explode, start cursing."

True to form, when Mark went to the set, "Ashby and I would take the 'long walk' talking and talking for half an hour, forty-five minutes. I would tell him the problems, suggest solutions. He would say, 'I understand what you're saying. I'm going to do it this way. Okay, okay.' It was wonderful, hugs, kisses. I later heard that as soon as I walked off set, Ashby would kick tires and scream, 'That fucking asshole!'"

"He could be gentle and soft-spoken one minute, loud and abusive the next," agreed Haskell Wexler, recalling the day Ashby had fired him off a movie: "Hal was snorting and all of a sudden he said, "You're fired." 'Whaddya mean I'm fired?' 'You're fired.' Then he started to scream and

From Cowboy to Mogul to Monster

stomp. I went to Hal and I said, 'You're not the Hal Ashby I love and respect. You're the Hal Ashby who's doing something to himself up his nose, and I'm not going to accept it.'

Ashby, according to Mulvehill, "had a lot of rage that he didn't know how to handle and never dealt with. He particularly disliked creative producers who brought scripts to him. It really frustrated him that he couldn't originate material. By getting rid of them, he could assert authorship over the project." As Jerome Hellman, producer of *Coming Home*, recalled, "Hal tended to view any comment from a producer, or a suggestion even, as criticism, an incursion into his domain." On the set of *Eight Million Ways* Kate concurred: "Ashby despised all of us. It was ugly."

Perhaps one problem for Ashby was that "Mark is much more of a hands-on producer than most," noted Roger Corman. "Having been through all the different aspects of the business, he knew what he was talking about." Now, Mark was at a dead end. With Ashby casting him as the heavy some of the actors hated him: "Jeff Bridges was always cordial to me but Andy Garcia and Rosanna Arquette were another story. They wouldn't talk to me." Mark knew that the actors, loyal to Ashby, would have mutinied if he tried to fire him or overstepped the director's authority. So he called Jeff Berg, told him what was going on and asked for help. "Berg was a brilliant agent but he was heartless. He knew that Ashby was not in a position to do this picture. He also knew the director needed money desperately. So Berg did absolutely nothing."

By the time they went into the 4th week of photography the production was taking more and more of Mark's time and draining every bit of cash from PSO. It was way over budget and weeks over schedule. "The problem was, Ashby never did a thing that he agreed to do," Mark lamented. "He improvised that entire script. Maybe because he was burned out and his brain was fried from too much coke."

While Mark was desperately trying to hold the production together in LA, John was in New York, desperately trying to close the loans with the two New York banks, who kept stalling and stalling. John sensed that something was happening under the surface. But he had no idea how deep it went. Meanwhile, both partners' responsibilities kept them away from PSO.

Mark: "What kept me working twenty hours a day was that besides overseeing production I still had fifty, sixty, seventy PSOers to supervise. I read all of their mail. I had to see everything that came in and went out.

Chapter 33. 1985. Beverly Hills

There was no way I could pull out of the rest of PSO, due to my busybody nature. I continued to stick my nose into sales and marketing and every other aspect of the company." "Of course he did," laughed Reiko Bradley. "Mark defined micromanagement. He created the 'art of'."

Micromanager, control freak, perfectionist. Mark freely confessed to being all of them. He needed to be in control of PSO as he had always needed to be in control. Of his acting career. His marriage. Of PSO's movies. But it was a losing battle. By the time Ashby finished shooting, the script had been decimated. Scenes that were filled with tension now had none. The plot was completely muddled. Nothing that happened was clear to anyone, least of all Ashby. Mark was exhausted from fighting with him and it was a relief when shooting ended and editing began.

Normally, a director is allowed ten weeks to do his cut. Mark went back to running PSO, eager for a break. Then Ashby disappeared. "He wouldn't take any of our calls. We sent telegrams to him but got no answer." Mark started asking around about Ashby's editing on recent films. He heard one chilling story after another: how Ashby had disappeared for two months after production ended on *Lookin' to Get Out,* leaving the editors unsupervised; how after he returned he spent weeks cutting a dozen versions of eight-minute montages that would never be used in the film; how Lorimar tried to seize the film from him but Ashby carried the reels around in the trunk of his car for a month until he finally gave them up.

Once again, Mark appealed to Jeff Berg. "Will you please find out exactly what your client is doing?" Berg had no luck. "More often than not," he later said, "you couldn't reach Hal. You left a message, the guy didn't call back." "By then Hal was so zonked out of his mind," mused Peter Bart, longtime Hollywood writer, producer, former studio President and Editor-in-Chief of *Daily Variety,* "that he didn't need any help self-destructing."

More weeks went by with no word from Ashby. Meanwhile, the cost to PSO in dollars, stress and Mark's time was enormous. Finally, PSO formally protested and the film went to the DGA for arbitration. Soon, as Chuck Mulvehill recalled, "A five-ton truck pulled up with a couple of palookas, they came up to the editing room and they took the film away from him – the best editor in Hollywood – for the third time in a row."

Ashby's denial was as strong as his addictions. He refused to take responsibility and cast himself as the victim to his friends: "I give up. I can't fight it, they're scumbags," he told Bruce Dern, who lived down the Coast and had stayed in touch since *Coming Home.* "Hal said, 'I can

333

From Cowboy to Mogul to Monster

understand anything except not letting me edit something, particularly something I shot.'

At first Mark counted himself lucky that Ashby hadn't driven around with the film in his trunk for months. "Then we got all the footage and discovered that what Ashby shot was unreleasable." Mark began to work around the clock with new editors. "We had to cut around a lot of unusable footage and did the best we could. Then Andy Garcia and Rosanna Arquette tried to refuse to do the ADR work (post-production sound) because it was not Ashby's cut. The Guild forced them to do it but Arquette was in tears when she saw some of the shots. 'Hal Ashby would never have allowed me to look like that,' she wailed.'" Little did she know. "The movie you see today," Mark said years later, "is very flawed although it has some brilliant scenes."

The ill-fated *Eight Million Ways To Die* was Ashby's last directorial effort. He was diagnosed in early 1988 with a cancer that spread rapidly to his liver and colon and to which he succumbed at the age of fifty-nine on December 27.

To Ashby's friends, it was a sad passing of a once-brilliant director. To audiences everywhere, he left behind a legacy of work, some of it excellent. To PSO, he left a legacy of pain, problems and bitter memories of a shoot that dealt them a mortal blow.

"If anything brought down PSO in my mind, it was making the movie *8 Million Ways to Die,*" Kate Hyde recalled twenty years later. "When we did *8 Million Ways to Die* we found the 8 Million and 1st," John ruefully agreed.

Italy

1962 – 1973

CHAPTER THIRTY-FOUR

April 16, 1962

Rome, Italy

Mark confers with legendary race-car driver Bruce McLaren in the film *Young Racers* (1963).

With Boris Karloff in Mario Bava's *Black Sabbath* (1963).

As a 14th c. Spanish king, *Peter the Cruel* (1964).

On the set of *100 Horsemen* (1965).

As *Son of Cleopatra* (1964).

Chapter 34. 1962. Rome

An April breeze was blowing through the open windows of Mark's apartment in Piazza Margana. It ruffled the paper in the rented Royal typewriter where he was typing a letter to Roger Corman. *Dear Rog; Today I woke to the marvelous sounds of Rome: the pleasant roar of motorcycles, the mellifluous tones of two peasant women screaming at a butcher, the dulcet sounds of a would-be tenor of 65 singing the "Italian Street Song" from the floor above me, sempre off-key, and the always soothing screech of two cats in the street, fighting each other for a discarded veal bone. Stretching myself languidly, savoring every one of these morsels of ancient Roman charm, I thought to myself how marvelous it is to be here in my 13th century "palazzo" in the heart of Rome, and how delightful it will be to just live this day fully."*

Mark's breezy letter was designed to put the best face on his life in Italy before he got into the heart of the matter - negotiating the salary the notoriously cheap Corman had just offered him: *"I was pleased to hear that you want me to be one of the co-stars of* THE YOUNG RACERS.*" Then Sandy told me what you were offering to pay me..........! Now, Roger, I know that you were joking, and you know that you were joking, but none of the agents in the agency knew that. They were very embarrassed, and that made me embarrassed and that made my poor Sicilian maid embarrassed, who thereupon gave her five-year old boy a slap (out of embarrassment) and, of course, he started crying! What could I say to everybody? They thought you were insulting me."*

Mark, like others in Corman's circle, liked to kid him on the "sadistic glee you take in offering actors a fraction of their worth." As Chuck Griffith (screenwriter of *Little Shop of Horrors* and a Corman 'regular') wrote to Mark: "Can you believe Roger had the audacity to offer me another job at the old rates? If I have to get out of this business completely I'll never work for Corman at his cheap figures."

Despite his grumbling, Griffith, like Jack Nicholson, Robert Towne, Jonathan Demme, Francis Ford Coppola and Marty Scorsese had gained his career in the movie business as a direct result of working for the low-budget "Corman Graduate School of Film." Now, Corman's budget for *Young Racers* was even lower than usual. "AIP only had a hundred and some thousand dollars for that movie," the director reminisced decades later, "but I was determined to make it. I had always thought a Grand Prix film would be fun to shoot."

The director had offered Mark the co-starring role of 'Stephen,' a former race car driver-turned-writer who is covering the European circuit when he discovers his fiancée is having an affair with a womanizing Grand

Prix champ. After the writer exposes the champ as a dirty driver, he challenges the writer to a climactic driving duel.

Mark wrote back: *"Please, Rog, make me a fair offer on The Young Racers,"* Mark wrote, *"then increase that new offer by at least 25%. (I mention this 25% increase because only then will your idea of a fair offer begin to approximate what is really a fair offer, right?) And then we can start talking seriously. I look forward to hearing from you as soon as possible and Rog, do exert yourself to be fair, if only for Auld Lang Syne. Ciao, Mark and my maid, and her son..."*

Time was on Mark's side. The Grand Prix races started in a couple of weeks and Corman needed to shoot them. So he upped his offer (a little) and gave Mark first billing and a small percentage in exchange for his casting some beautiful European actresses. *"Welcome back to FRANTIC PICTURES,"* Roger penned when Mark accepted. *"We start "Young Racers" in Monte Carlo on June 3 for the Monaco Grand Prix and follow the racing circuit to Spa in Belgium, Rouen in France, and Aintree in England. Incidentally, we will not be taking a make-up man so it will be best if you came equipped with a good suntan."*

Mark summarily rented his apartment to American actor, John Saxon for the summer and used his salary advance to buy an Alfa Romeo. Then he drove the little beauty to Monte Carlo with the top down the whole way, fulfilling Corman's request for a tan.

In the US, Corman was calling on all his old friends "to put together one of the all-time great crews. I offered them low money but round-trip airfare and room and board along the circuit. I told everybody, 'Don't think of this as a motion picture. Think of this as an all-expenses paid trip through Europe." His ploy worked.

Bob Towne agreed to fly in as Roger's third Assistant; Chuck Griffith came on to be an A.D; Menachem Golan (a USC film school student who would later become co-president of Cannon Films) agreed to be Roger's second assistant; his wife, Rachel, came along to do wardrobe. Last to join was a young would-be director named Francis Ford Coppola (fresh out of UCLA film school) whom Roger had recently hired as his assistant for $90 a week. As Coppola later recalled, "One day, Roger asked me if I knew a good soundman for the European shoot of *Young Racers*. I said, 'Gee, yeah, sure I do. I'll do the sound.' So I immediately got the Nagra (tape recorder) out of the closet at the office and went home to read the manual."

Chapter 34. 1962. Rome

At first, Mark was happy to be re-united with his old Hollywood buddies Roger, Chuck, Luana and Towne. Then, to his surprise, after living and working in Italy for the past year he felt a growing distance between himself and the others. "Chuck was my buddy but other than him I felt pretty much like a loner." He started to hang out with the world-class race-car drivers, charting their speeds on each lap during the day; drinking with them at night. He got close to Graham Hill and sandy-haired New Zealander Bruce McLaren, the legendary race-car designer, driver, engineer and inventor (who won the Monaco Grand Prix that year.)

When they shot the climactic scene, a racing duel between Stephen (Mark) and Joe (played by Bob Campbell) Roger put Campbell and Mark in cars on the track. McLaren gave Mark a couple of pointers about driving a Formula One racecar. Mark: "It was dangerous because they have a very low center of gravity so you feel safe in them even when you're taking curves at 190 per hour. It lulls you into a false sense of security that you can do anything in the car and get away with it. Which, of course, isn't true."

Corman attached his cameras to the front of Mark and Bob's cars and had other cars, driven by real race drivers, dodge in and out. Corman: "The racing footage turned out great. It was a lucky break because I didn't have much money for 'process shots.' In the end, not having the money actually made it look more real."

After they wrapped in Monte Carlo, everyone took a week off to travel before meeting up North in Spa, Belgium. Mark headed off with Norwegian actress Margrete Rubsahm, one of four beautiful European women he had cast in the film. (The others were Christina Gregg [England] Marie Versini [France] and Beatrice Altariba [Italy.] They provided terrific eye candy and would ultimately be billed as "The International Playgirls.") Chuck Griffith drove off in one of the production cars, a fast little Sunbeam but didn't get far. Griffith: "My girlfriend, Irena and I had just left Monaco when we hit a bad rainstorm and an English camper plowed into us." They flipped over five times and Griffith was hospitalized for the rest of the shoot.

Mark and the others met up in Belgium where they all resumed their roles, then everyone moved on the British Grand Prix. True to Corman's words it was a cross-European adventure, which most of the Americans loved. Mark loved driving the Formula One Lotus. More than he liked playing Stephen. "I found the part to be very uninteresting."

From Cowboy to Mogul to Monster

When they wrapped, Corman (as he often did) decided to piggyback the shooting of another film onto *The Young Racers*. Despite having failed to work the Nagra (all the sound tapes would have to be junked) Coppola gutsily volunteered to direct a second film. "Please let me take the equipment and some of the cast and make a low-budget psychological thriller," he pleaded.

"Show me a script," replied Corman.

Coppola: "So I went home that night and wrote a Hitchcock-type ax murder sequence." The next day he showed it to Roger, who agreed to let Coppola direct the movie. "As long as you do the rest of the script like that and shoot it for $20,000." Coppola turned around and cast Bob Campbell and Luana Anders in his first movie, *Dementia 13* (which turned out to be a solid success.) Mark was a little hurt that he wasn't included. "But I think he felt I was too much of a star, too self-centered and perhaps not talented enough."

Young Racers was released to poor reviews. *Variety* claimed the American International Picture "simply doesn't have what it takes." Critics blasted Campbell's "contrived, affected, pretentious scenario with its stilted and artificial dialogue" and said "Damon is rather wooden." "I was not good in that movie," Mark agreed. "It was done so fast that I didn't care about anything in my performance. Also, I found nothing in the character to build on." Plus, all of the dialogue had to be looped because of Coppola's Nagra fiasco.

When Mark's voice was replaced by a then-unknown actor named William Shatner, "I was offended and angry with Roger for not inviting me to dub myself. Not that he could have afforded to fly me to LA… but I would have sprung for my own ticket just to have my voice on there. I think that being dubbed just added to my 'wooden performance' because there's a flatness in a dubbed voice that takes away from an actor's personal line readings."

In Mark's next movie, *Black Sabbath (I tre volti della paura)*, an American-Italian trilogy of horror stories directed by Mario Bava (later dubbed "The Maestro of the Macabre") he played opposite Boris Karloff in "The Wurdalak", one of three segments supposedly taken from a story attributed to a Russian count named Alexei (not Leo) Tolstoy. Karloff starred as a creepy but sympathetic 'wurdalak,' a vampire doomed to drink the blood of those he loves. Mark was Vladimir, a young horseman who wanders into a countryside beset by 'wurdalaks' and stumbles upon

Chapter 34. 1962. Rome

a family waiting for their patriarch (Karloff) who has ventured outside to kill one of the terrible creatures. Upon his return his family undergoes a horrible ordeal.

Mario Bava bore the reputation of a legendary director of horror cinema but the director's genius made little impression on Mark: "He was very funny and always making jokes. But he never directed his actors. I mean, he would tell us where to move and stuff like that, but he'd never say one word to us about the performance. It was all about images."

Mark, however, found working with Boris Karloff, in one of his last great roles in a horror film to be terrific: "He was a very gentle soul, giving, generous, and quiet. I remember a wonderful softness about him. He seemed amazed by his success in horror films."

Today, *Black Sabbath,* known as Bava's personal favorite, has been celebrated by directors Martin Scorsese, Joe Dante, Tim Burton and John Carpenter. They praise the director's cinematography and use of "film as dream." Critics laud his lavish use of color: "In *The Wurdalak,* Bava fills the frame with deep blues, purples, and reds. The film glows with color and remains a stunning achievement.

After another dry spell, Mark was cast as the King in *Peter the Cruel,* a powerful Castilian monarch who was known as the leader of the Christian world in the mid-1300's. Although he was one of Spain's more controversial kings, Peter the First of Castile was nonetheless seen by many of his subjects as a defender of the rights of the commoners. Especially the Jews.

Mark traveled to Toledo, Spain, where they shot in a centuries-old synagogue. He was struck by writing that was intricately carved into the sparkling white plaster walls. And he was thrilled when he realized that it was in Hebrew and he could read it. "I discovered that Peter the First had built that synagogue for the Jews and they were thanking the king, whom they called 'Peter the Just' for everything he did for them." *"I am really enjoying PEDRO, THE CRUEL,"* he wrote to his family. *"I think it may be the best role I've ever had."*

By the time he made his next movie, *The Son of El Cid (The Hundred Horsemen or I Cento Cavalieri),* he was beginning to have a grand time in European cinema. Directed by well-respected director Vittorio Cottafavi, the picture was shot in Castile and set in the year 1000 AD amidst the Spanish-Arab Wars. Mark played Don Fernando Herrero, the buffoonish young son of Don Gonzalo (played by the great Italian actor, Arnoldo Foa.) "The image I used for my character was L'il Abner, a big, goofy, good-looking but kind of buffoonish guy. Always eating. Always trying to emulate his father, learning to be brave from him." The plot centered on the growth of Don Fernando (Mark) who is reluctant to assume the mantle of leadership which is his birthright. Eventually, he rallies the peasants to overthrow their cruel Moorish occupiers in medieval Spain.

The Moors' cruelty involved a unique punishment: a man was stripped to the waist and hanged by his wrists from a tripod built over the well in the town square, then he was dropped down into the well until the rope binding his wrists brought him to a sudden, socket-wrenching halt. When Mark was 'dropped' into the well "they really dropped me. I fell directly on my hip, got a bruised kidney and was in the hospital for three days." It was his first injury but "it was important for me to do my own stunts in those movies. It made me feel macho." (It also led to him getting hurt in almost all the action movies he did in Europe.)

Antonella Lualdi, one of Italy's most popular young actresses, played one of the female leads. "I had a crush on Antonella," said Mark, "but even though we tongue-kissed during our love scenes she was happily married and nothing was going to happen between us. So I waited patiently for the second female lead to arrive, a German actress named Barbara Frey. I remember the first time I saw her from the back as she was checking into the hotel. She had the cutest little butt. I think I fell in love with her butt before I even saw her face."

Long-haired, sweet-faced Barbara Frey was a minor star in Germany where she became known as the 'Sandra Dee of Germany' after co-starring with Horst Bucholz in a film called *Endstazion Liebe (Last Train Stop Love.)* She and Mark soon began a passionate romance. By then he could speak Italian, French and Spanish. But Barbara only spoke German. As with Dominique Boschero, once again it was "love by the book." Mark kept his German-English dictionary close by. "I didn't know how long or how serious our love affair might be so I decided at least I was going to get a language out of it."

As the shoot continued they fell deeply in love. "Because we couldn't talk to each other we communicated by touches and caresses and deep soulful looks. That's when I learned that people in relationships often hide behind words. They talk *about* their love and talk *through* their love and don't always mean what they say."

The Hundred Horsemen opened to excellent reviews. *L'Osservatore Romano* raved over the climactic battle scene which began as a grand, glorious spectacle in full color, then started to lose color and went to black and white as people began to die. Critics wrote: 'In contrast to the rest of the film, when the battle loses color it ends in black and white that dissolves into the colors of the women's costumes who are now cutting grain in the same fields we previously saw used for battle." The music, which began as a triumphant march, also became heavier and slower as the battle raged until it became a dirge. "The battle scene made the point that there is nothing glorious or honorable about war. That war is just death and killing. Slaughter," Mark later reflected.

Director Vittorio Cottafavi was proclaimed "a shining light in Italian cinema." Mark was declared "a very talented and engaging young American actor who is beginning to make an important name for himself in European cinema.' (Decades later *I Cento Cavalieri* was lodged in the venerable Cinematheque Francais. At the Venice Film Festival 2004 it was feted as an example of an outstanding and innovative Italian genre film of the 60's and 70's. Mark flew there to present the movie to a packed house of fans including Quentin Tarantino, Joe Dante, and Taylor Hackford.)

Barbara Frey came to Rome to live with Mark at Piazza Margana. At first, he was enchanted by her fragility and vulnerability. There was a naiveté about her that made her seem little-girlish. She trusted him completely. "The more madly in love with me she was, the more I cared about her. And the more she needed me." Barbara felt like a nobody in Rome, where she knew no-one and couldn't speak the language. "So I was her hero, protector and lover, her rock and her security blanket. But as soon as she learned my language and I learned hers, words became barriers to the deep communication we'd had when we couldn't speak each others' language."

Over time, Barbara started to tell Mark how she resented him. How she felt that she'd given up her career for him. How she was living in his shadow and walking timidly behind him while feeling totally overshadowed by him. When Mark's brother, Bob, came for a visit he noticed her insecurity: "One night, the three of us went out to dinner and Mark, of course, knew all the best places to eat in Rome. There was one restaurant in a cave where they greeted him with big shouts and served us lamb's head and we both ate it, eyeballs and all." As they walked home, Mark was recognized by passersby who made much of him. He was full of life, exuberant and happy. Bob was thrilled to be there. Barbara complained, "I feel like a mouse between two elephants." "It was a situation that had to have its downfall sooner or later," Mark said years later, "but I was far too self-involved in pursuing my own career to spend much time dealing with her insecurities."

He went on to star in *The Son of Cleopatra,* a low-budget 'sword and sandals' epic that featured impressive desert tableaux of armies marching across desert scenery. Mark played the leader of a desert tribe in 1st-century B.C. Egypt who leads a revolt against the corrupt Romans. "In one of the sword fights one of the gladiators whacked my hand with his sword and blood spurted everywhere. I had to do the rest of the film in a cast and had a scar for years." When the film was released, women responded eagerly when Mark's bare torso was put on display as he knelt down and was given a lashing by horsemen wielding whips.

After living in Italy for four years he was beginning to become a little more known, although he wasn't exactly on the international superstar track. Then he was cast in his first Spaghetti Western.

Chapter Thirty-Five

July 28, 1965

Rome, Italy

In his first Spaghetti Western as Johnny Oro
(*Ringo and His Golden Pistols*), 1966.

Chapter 35. 1965. Rome

After six years in Hollywood, Mark played his first cowboy in *Johnny Oro (Ringo and His Golden Pistols)* and the irony was not lost on him. "I was a nice Jewish boy from Chicago's West Side who had to go East to become an Italian Western star," he later quipped.

Although he had never been in a Western and had rarely been on a horse he was recommended for the lead by his old friend, producer Franco Rossellini. He had forgiven Mark for his supposed perfidy but was still in love with him. After Rosselini talked to writer-director Sergio Corbucci about him, Mark was cast as the hero in Corbucci's fourth Spaghetti Western, "not because of my acting skills but because they thought it would make an easier sale to America if the Spaghetti Western starred a Hollywood actor."

Italian (or 'Spaghetti') Westerns got their start in 1960 after imports of American Westerns, although wildly popular in Italy, had mostly dried up. When a director named Sergio Leone and his assistant (the same Sergio Corbucci) were filming *The Last Days of Pompeii* in Almeria, Spain they realized how similar the landscape was to the Mexican border where many American Westerns were set and the idea for making Westerns in Italy was born. (A few years later, Leone and Corbucci would become "rivals" as the two masters of the genre.)

Over the next fifteen years many other directors and producers jumped on the bandwagon. European film production companies made nearly 600 of these Westerns. Mostly financed by Italian companies critics dubbed them, derisively, 'Spaghetti Westerns.'

Contrary to Hollywood Westerns, which starred upstanding cowboys who cleaned up the West, the Spaghetti's focused on heroes only slightly less evil than the villains. Drawing from genres as diverse as Japanese Samurai movies and Italian opera, Italian writers and directors created cowboys as anti-heroes who were often only motivated by vengeance or money. Their unscrupulous methods led them into spectacularly violent gunfights with high body counts and Spaghetti's often ended with all of the main characters dead.

Plots were thin and often had little purpose except to lead the characters from one shootout to the next. Women were of little use, usually featured as widows, whores or punching bags. Music played an important part,

From Cowboy to Mogul to Monster

whether it was classic hoof-beat rhythms or a man whistling a foreboding tune as a mysterious stranger rides into town.

All of these elements were unique to the Spaghetti's. Together, they combined to make them a genre of their own. They became wildly popular in Europe. Over time, the Spaghetti's even garnered respect from critics. Eventually, they influenced decades of filmmakers and gained the love of millions of fans worldwide.

When Mark was cast as 'Johnny Oro' he realized he had a lot to learn in a little time. "Because I still thought of myself as a serious actor I was determined to become a top horseman and pistol slinger." So he practiced for hours in front of the mirror, learning to quick-draw and twirl a gun like a gunfighter and to shoot so that he looked natural. He learned how to shoot a gun in three different ways in the space of three seconds. He trained at twirling a lasso until he mastered it. His final task was to learn to ride a horse like he'd been born in the saddle. Eventually, he could jump on a horse without putting his feet in the stirrups. But he wasn't done yet.

Playing the hero in a Spaghetti Western also meant fighting all the bad guys. So Mark got together with stuntmen and learned how to punch, kick, throw chairs and break bottles over their heads. "All the while, I knew that the whole idea of getting into action pictures was contradictory to everything I'd learned. I mean, I still thought of myself as a serious actor, a Meisner-trained actor. I was the least inclined person to become an action hero." But he learned to be a good cowboy just as he had learned to be a good athlete and a decent actor. "I didn't have great talent for any of them. I just worked hard until I mastered them."

Johnny Oro (or 'Ringo' as he was later dubbed to capitalize on a successful series by director Duccio Tessari) was a typical Spaghetti Western anti-hero, a bounty hunter who sees killing as business, a gunslinger who won't even draw his solid gold pistol unless he can profit from it.

The film begins with Johnny gunning down a gang of bandits while letting their brother live because there is no price on his head. When the brother swears lifelong revenge on Johnny the action is set in motion. By the time the movie is over, Johnny has fired countless bullets from his golden pistol and joined with a local sheriff to defend 'Coldstone City,' demolishing half the town with dynamite and a cannon in the process.

Chapter 35. 1965. Rome

The movie opens on a long shot of the hero (Mark, sporting a Rhett Butler moustache and sideburns) on horseback, riding down from the hills. He was dressed in black from his hat to his boots, a cigarette dangling lazily from his gold cigarette holder, a studded black gun belt holding his golden pistol. In the action-packed film, Mark proved to be completely convincing as the mercenary cowboy who never hurries and never loses his cool or a gunfight or a woman. As the insouciant Johnny, he ducked and rolled, double punched and back-fisted the villains, threw them over balconies and broke bottles over their heads. He looked good on a horse, despite falling off at one point. And he learned that he loved playing a cowboy. "In Hollywood I was an intellectual. In Italy I became physical. It was a whole new sense of being. I had to constantly remind myself to sit tall in the saddle because I was the hero."

He was happy to work with Corbucci, whom he called "a great comedy director. He was one of the only Italian directors I worked with who would show me what he meant and how to do comic takes." By the time the film wrapped, Mark and Corbucci had become fast friends.

Colorful posters of *Johnny Oro* hit the streets of Rome, depicting Mark in his black gunfighter outfit, his golden pistol pointed at the viewer. Fans flocked to see the movie. Italian newspapers ran headlines: 'IL VERO VOLTO DI MARK DAMON' (the true face of Mark Damon.) He was dubbed 'Il dandy killer' because of his natty outfit. He was declared 'Western sexy' and 'Capellone autentico' (the guy with the big ten gallon hat).

Reviewers praised Mark's acting and Corbucci's skillful directing. The director wanted to collaborate with him on another Western he was writing, titled *Django*. The two men began to work on a screenplay for Mark to star in. But when he was cast in *Dio Como Ti Amo* (*God, How I Love You*) Mark and Corbucci agreed to finish writing *Django* when *Dio* wrapped. Overnight, Mark went from playing a rakish cowboy to co-star as the boyfriend of a sixteen-year-old Italian singing sensation named Gigliola Cinquetti who had never been kissed. It would be quite a change of pace.

CHAPTER THIRTY-SIX

August 17, 1966

Rome, Italy

In *Dio, Como Te Amo* Mark becomes a household word in Italy as the first man to kiss teen sweetheart singer, Gigliola Cinquetti.

Headlines across Italy blazened the scandal of the kiss.
The song for the film *Dio, Come Te Amo* remains an Italian classic.

356

RICORDATE QUESTO NOME!
JOHNNY YUMA
Presto sentirete
parlare di lui!

From Cowboy to Mogul to Monster

It's hard to think back to a time when a kiss from a sixteen-year-old starlet could cause a national scandal. Before Britney. Long before Lindsay Lohan. Way back in the 1960's, when Mark co-starred with Italy's sweetheart, sixteen-year-old Gigliola Cinquetti, famed for the innocence she proclaimed in her hit duet with Domenico Modugno (of "Volare" fame), "Non ho l'eta" ('I'm not old enough to love you'.)

Singing that song, Gigliola had recently won the Festival di Sanremo Music Competition and the Eurovision Song Contest. The song became an instant classic in Italy. "And there was a lot of publicity about the fact that she had never been kissed," Mark recalled, "and that she was supposed to kiss me in the movie." Then Gigliola said to the press: "I like Mark, but I don't want my first kiss to be in front of the camera. I want it to be private. This kiss will have to be done by my double."

Mark responded by talking to the press, too: "If it's going to be her double doing the kissing then it's going to be my double, too."

Overnight, the scandal of the kiss/no-kiss made it to AP wire service news: 'Cinema lawyers are searching through their books to determine if a star should be required to kiss a double. The situation has arisen in the Italian film, *Dio, Come Ti Amo* in which Mark Damon was asked to kiss a double because his leading lady insisted she had never kissed a man and would not begin with a film kiss. Damon is ready to kiss or not to kiss Miss Cinquetti but will not kiss a double before the cameras under any circumstances. The ultimate decision in the Mark Damon case may well go into the books.'

Banner headlines in Italy declared it "The War of the Kisses." (LA GUERRA DEI BACI DI MARK E GIGLIOLA.) Daily articles were accompanied by photos of Mark and Gigliola; of Mark, Gigliola *and* La Mama of Gigliola. A circus of PR preceded the filming of 'the kiss Italy is waiting for.' The media frenzy had all of Italy holding its breath as the "day of the kiss" approached.

Mark: "On the appointed day, as the cameras rolled we were running toward each other in the Naples airport. We ran until we came together in a hug. We looked soulfully into each others' eyes. Our lips grew closer and closer. Then the camera came into a very tight shot of two pair of lips kissing... the lips of our two Italian doubles. When they cut back to a wider shot of us we were hugging as if we had just had the greatest kiss in the world."

Although the kiss was faked Italian newspapers proclaimed GIGLIOLA HA FINALMENTE BACIATO! (GIGLIOLA HAS FINALLY KISSED!).

Chapter 36. 1966. Rome

GIGLIOLA NON E PIU LA RAGAZZA INGENUA! (GIGLIOLA IS NO LONGER INNOCENT!) It was terrific hype. Before the film was finished Mark became a household name in Italy. But because it went over schedule Corbucci decided he'd have to cast another actor as the lead in *Django*.

Mark protested: "This is a script we worked on together. We wrote it for me to play Django."

"I know" lamented Sergio, "but I have no other choice. We have a start date and you're not ready. I'm sorry."

Instead of Mark "they cast a guy with piercing blue eyes, whom they discovered working at a gas station," he recalled with chagrin. His name was Franco Nero.

When it was released *Django* caused a stir. From its opening sequence of a black-clad specter (Nero) dragging a coffin in the mud, later revealed to contain a machine gun, the bloodbath began. There was little plot. But what the film lacked in story it made up for with so much violence that the movie ended up banned in several countries.

Django would ultimately be called one of the most influential Spaghetti Westerns ever made. Corbucci was declared to have defined a new and darker vision of the Spaghetti Western. Although Mark missed starring in it, at least he received a co-writer credit. (Franco Nero, the actor with the piercing blue eyes, would star in Corbucci's Spaghetti Westerns from then on and Corbucci would eventually state that "Franco Nero is to me what Henry Fonda was to John Ford." [Nero went on to co- star in *Camelot* opposite Vanessa Redgrave, who would become his longtime romantic partner.])

After shooting a forgettable rip-off of a James Bond picture in Lebanon, *Agent 777,* Mark got an offer from a director who saw him in *Johnny Oro* and wanted him to play the heavy in a picture he was going to make. The director was Sergio Leone, who had been given $200,000 and a load of leftover film stock and told to make a Western. The film was *A Fistful of Dollars*. But when Mark called his agent, Rossana Pelliccia, to tell her of the offer she was horrified.

"Oh no," she exclaimed, "You can't play a villain at this point in your career. You're a hero."

"But I can't play the hero," Mark tried to explain. "Leone wants a tall, blond actor…"

From Cowboy to Mogul to Monster

"Then you can't be in it!" she repeated passionately. "You absolutely cannot play a heavy in a picture with a third-rate director who's only done one movie, *The Colossus of Rhodes,* that was a disaster!"

On her advice, Mark passed up the role. Meanwhile, he and Sergio Leone had become friends. The director invited him into his cutting room to show how he was writing his script based on the Japanese samurai drama, *Yojimbo.* "Basically, he was copying the Japanese classic scene by scene. He told me that he was going to shoot *A Fistful of Dollars* by letting scenes play out against the music that Ennio Morricone, the Italian composer, had pre-recorded. Instead of writing the music to the action he was going to fit the action to the music." One afternoon, they were having coffee when Leone complained that he couldn't get an important American actor to play the role. Mark sympathized.

"*Aspetta.* You know everyone in Hollywood," Sergio reasoned, in Italian. "Couldn't you get Lee Marvin, Charlie Bronson or someone like that?"

"I don't know."

"Please, Mark. Won't you help me?"

Out of friendship Mark agreed to try. He started by calling some of his contacts in Hollywood, including Meyer Mishkin, the agent for Lee Marvin and Charlie Bronson.

"Come on," Meyers laughed when he heard what Mark wanted, "why would these stars go to Italy to make a Spaghetti Western with somebody named Sergio whatever?"

He struck out with all the other agents he knew in Hollywood. Finally, Mark had to tell Leone that he was not going to get a star to do his western. But when he saw the other man's despair he tried to soften the blow. "Although," he added, "I do know an actor who might be good for the role. He's in a series called *Rawhide.* I can call and see if he might be interested." Leone begged him to call the actor, whose name was Clint Eastwood.

"I called Clint and told him about Sergio and the movie. He said he was interested and I asked my agency in Rome to send Clint a script. Then Sergio went to Hollywood and met with him for three hours at the Polo Lounge in the Beverly Hills Hotel." At the end of their meeting they made a deal on a paper napkin for Clint to get $15,000 dollars as the star of *A Fistful of Dollars.* "And to this day," Mark laughed, "whenever I see Clint he says, 'Mark, it's all your fault.'"

Chapter 36. 1966. Rome

Critics panned *Fistful of Dollars*. Audiences loved it. Eventually, the film would be regarded as a seminal work. As one critic wrote, "Spaghetti Westerns changed forever with obscure director Sergio Leone's *A Fistful of Dollars*. Leone's unique style, artistic camera angles and raw, explosive violence presented a skewed view of the West, making his film different from any Western that had ever come before."

The success of *Fistful* led to more producers making more Spaghetti Westerns. That resulted in more American 'B' stars and character actors coming to Europe to work in them. Some stayed with Mark in his apartment, including Jack ("Jocko") Nicholson, his buddy from Jeff Corey's acting class.

By 1966, Nicholson was thirty-six and had given up on his career as an actor. "At the time there was a saying in Hollywood that if you got to be twenty-four without becoming a major star, you'd never become one." (Nicholson wouldn't become a star until 1969 when he co-starred in *Easy Rider* at the 'advanced age' of almost forty.)

Jack was in Europe to peddle two Westerns he had starred in, directed by Monte Hellman and written by Adrien Joyce (*Five Easy Pieces)*. Although the offbeat *Ride in the Whirlwind* and *The Shooting* would eventually become cult classics, during the three months that Nicholson stayed with Mark, he couldn't sell them to a soul. During that same time Mark was cast as the hero in his next Spaghetti Western, *Johnny Yuma*.

But two weeks before the shoot began he came down with hepatitis from raw mussels he'd eaten in Naples. He was put in a hospital outside of Rome and told he might not be out of there in time for the shoot. A 'sympathetic' Nicholson soon came to commiserate.

"It's a terrible situation," he said, "and I completely understand your plight. So if you want, I'll be happy to take your place in the movie."

"I bet you will," Mark laughed.

He willed himself to recover quickly and had just gotten out of the hospital when he started to shoot *Johnny Yuma*. Nicholson, meanwhile, took off for the Cannes Festival to peddle his movies, carrying the prints in hatboxes and approaching everyone as if they were old buddies. As Bob Evans recalled, "Jack Nicholson was in Cannes trying to sell two pictures that cost $4,000 between them. He starts talking to me, and I don't understand a word he's talking about." But every time Nicholson smiled,

Evans found he couldn't take his eyes off him. He decided to make him an offer, unaware that the actor had never received more than $600 for any picture he'd made.

"Listen, kid, how would you like to play opposite Barbra Streisand in *On a Clear Day You Can See Forever*? I'll pay you $10,000 for four weeks' work."

"I just got a divorce. I have a kid. I have to pay child support." Nicholson replied. "Can you make it $15,000?"

"How about $12,500?"

"I love you," Nicholson said, enveloping Evans in a bear hug. "I'll never forget you as long as I live."

Johnny Yuma took a lively and comic approach to the usual Spaghetti plot. The film included moments of pathos, slick gunplay and plenty of hijinks. It opened with Mark riding in the dusty hot hills of a Western town as the usual hoof-beat rhythms accompanied a theme-song sung by a trio of testosterone-laden male voices: 'Wherever there's a road, he rides, Wherever there's a horse, he rides. Johnny Yuma, don't go, Johnny Yuma, stay here. Let him ride, he will return.'

Mark played the dashing 'Yuma', another cowboy with eyes in the back of his head and a lightning-quick draw. Wearing dark makeup and a buckskin vest, he looked at home in the saddle and on the ground, twirling a gun or shooting bad guys who tormented small boys and innocent women. As the nephew and rightful heir of an elderly rich rancher whose evil wife (sultry Rosalba Neri) murders him to get his money, Johnny arrives to claim his inheritance, which pits him against the mercenary murderess who tries to have him killed, after killing many other men.

To Mark's delight, playing 'Johnny' required range. He was tough - punching the widow in the face after she tries to kill him (which would bring a huge cheer from all the men in the audience when the film was released.) He was tender - rescuing a small boy after he is terrorized by bandits; weeping over his lifeless body when they kill him. He was a spiffy dresser, a babe magnet and a James Bond cowboy with a bag of tricks, including a pocket watch whose intricate lock enables him to open his uncle's secret safe. "The director, Romolo Guerrieri, allowed me to direct myself because I was the American star." He also allowed Mark to cast a

Chapter 36. 1966. Rome

fine Hollywood actor and director, Lawrence Dobkin (who taught Mark about directing when they worked together in television.)

The only rough moments came when he insisted on performing his own stunts "only to be bitten by about ten thousand little bugs when I was doing a scene in a manure pile. I couldn't work for three days and my body was covered in blisters and boils."

The movie was a hit (today, it is regarded as "one of the greatest Spaghetti Westerns of all time.") Mark quickly became "the king of the Johnny's." Roger Corman recalled driving into Rome in a taxi "and seeing Mark's face plastered all over town. It was incredible. There he was, in posters for *Johnny Yuma* and *Johnny Oro* wearing gunfighter outfits and pointing his gun. When I met him for dinner, I said, 'Mark, you're all over Rome!'"

Mark grinned with satisfaction. It was mighty odd, he acknowledged, to have traveled all the way to Italy in order to become a Western star. But he could not have been happier at the way his career was going.

PSO
1985

Chapter Thirty-Seven

August 26, 1985

Century City, California

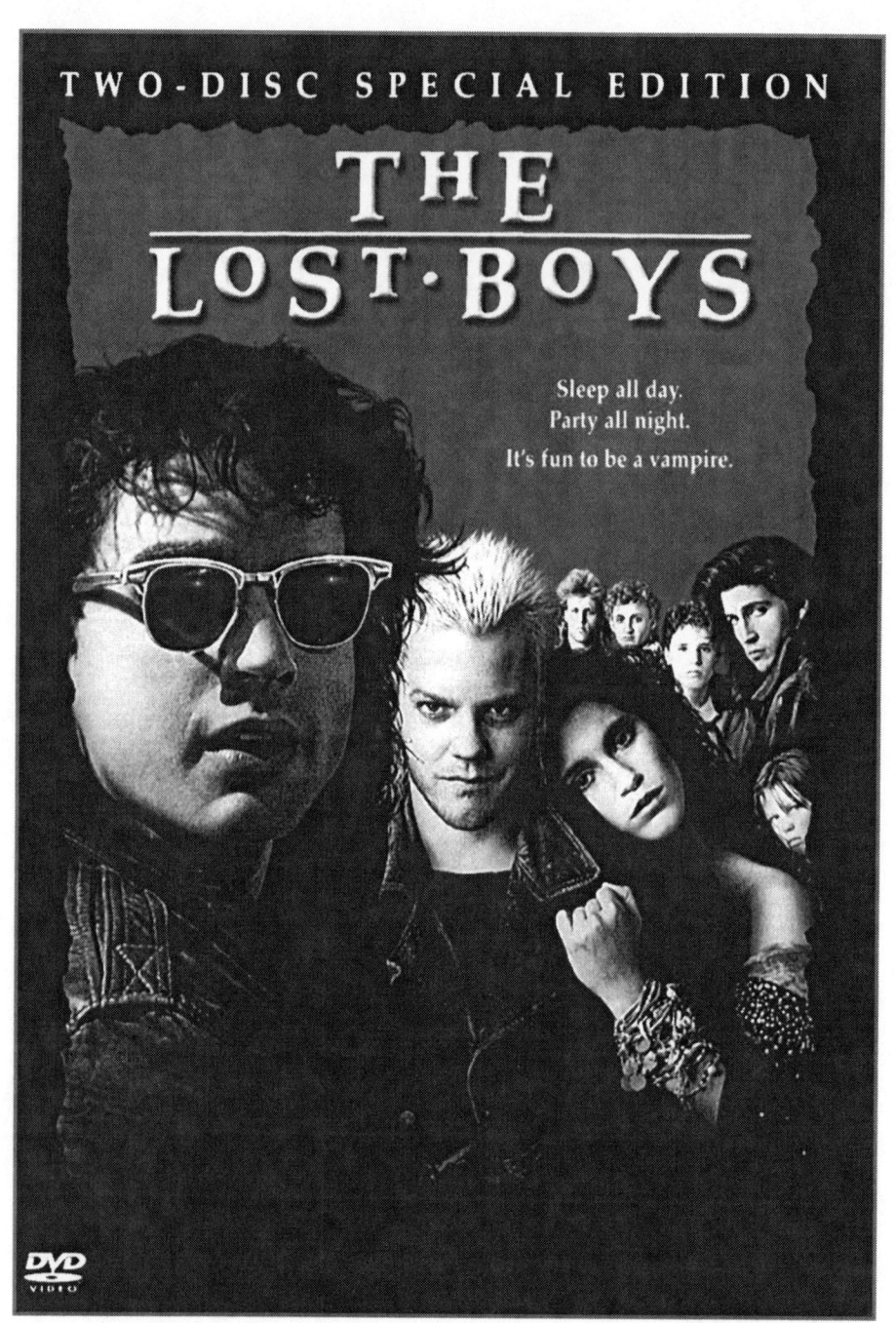

The Lost Boys © *1987,*
Package Design ©*2004 Warner Bros. Entertainment Inc.*

The Damon Family: Mark, Jon, Maggie, Alexis.

OUR BRIGH[T]

NEVER SAY NEVER AGAIN

MISUNDERSTOOD

LA TRAVIATA

BLAME IT
ON RIO

CUJO

THE
OUTSIDERS

A STREETCAR
NAMED DESIRE

BUCKAROO BANZAI

IN LOS ANGELES
10100 Santa Monica Blvd., Los Angeles, CA 90067
Fifteenth Floor   Telephone (213) 552-9977
Telex: 698652   Cable: PSO INC

IN PARIS
18 Rue Troyon
75017 Paris, France
Telex: 650321

PSO at AFM

MARK AND JOHN STOOD SIDE BY side on a hot August afternoon, watching PSO families play Frisbee at the annual picnic. Both men were grinning with satisfaction at the sight. John: "Every summer we measured the company's maturity by the age of its families. All of our employees were single at the first picnic; at the next, some came with their spouse and the first kid." By the summer of '85, many PSOers were there with elementary school-age kids.

It was a visible sign of how things had changed at PSO. And there were other signs of change, too. "By 1985 the company picnics, which used to be fun, got to be pep-talky corporate events," Eddie Kalish recalled. "We went from everyone having a good time with one another to a company picnic where people were sitting in separate groups and didn't interact with one another," said another ex-PSOer.

Korman, their third partner, was setting a new tone at PSO Delphi. He was described in the house newsletter as "a man who hates it when people are late; likes everything in writing and has one of those offices where everything is perfect, spotless, organized, almost antiseptic-looking." He was also quoted as saying that although he liked to eat out three or four times a week and enjoyed Chinese, Japanese, Mexican and Italian food, "I hate the food Mark Damon likes, though – like strange parts of pigs!"

Korman was quietly changing the atmosphere while knifing Mark in the back. But Mark didn't see it. "There's something about Mark that is so trusting of people," explained Maggie. "He let people into his life and didn't have his guard up. He didn't see the dark side. He just thought, 'Those people could never hurt me.'" "Mark trusts people, maybe too much," agreed Lew Horwitz, former head of a prestigious financing group and banker to the stars. "But it's one of the human things about him I really like. There are people who are extremely paranoid and trust nobody and maybe they're enormously successful and have done great things with their lives. I prefer a person like Mark who trusts somebody first and you have to prove that they're bad. You know, innocent until proven guilty."

On the first business day after Labor Day, John got a stunning call from his contact at First National Bank of Boston, Martha Crowninshield: "I'm calling to let you know we are not going forward with Chemical Bank on the $140 million credit line we agreed to fund."

Chapter 37. 1985. Century City

John couldn't believe it. "I don't understand. Negotiations have been going forward for months..."

"I know," she replied coolly.

"What happened?" he asked, stunned.

Crowninshield would only say that Chemical Bank of New York told them a number of things that she didn't agree with and quickly hung up.

John immediately placed a call to their contact at Chemical Bank, with whom he had a long business relationship. Her assistant said Ms. Tulley was unavailable and also ended the call quickly. What was going on?

On the other side of town, Mark was in a screening room in Culver City, reading the latest audience responses to *9 ½ Weeks*. He had worked with editors for months to cut the film to around ninety minutes. "We also added some fun to the piece while restructuring the main thrust of the story." Now, for the first time, audience seemed to embrace the film. Some even went so far as to say that it made them decide to be a little braver and more experimental in their relationships. He was beginning to see the light at the end of a very long tunnel when the phone rang. It was John, relating the calls with their two banks.

In the '80s, there were only two banks that would lend money to independents like PSO: First National Bank of Boston and Chemical Bank of New York. Chemical was the most important of all the New York banks. And the most important man there was Mike Spiegler, head of the Entertainment Industries Group for the past ten years.

Spiegler had an excellent reputation in Hollywood. "Integrity is what we look for first of all when we loan money," he said. "That and a good standing in the movie business." Using those standards he had been doing business with Mark and John for a number of years when he had given them a handshake agreement from Chemical Bank on a $140 million credit line.

Although a handshake deal for hundreds of millions of dollars may not seem likely, that was the way PSO did business. Not just with Spiegler - it was the way they did business, period. "Mark, at the time, was very much of a handshake deal kind of guy," Michael Heuser attested. It was the same with many other independents. After they had Spiegler's handshake on the $140 million PSO had worked with investment bankers, Allen & Co. (Korman's people) to get venture capitalists to invest another $25 million in what was known as a private placement. "That money had already been deposited in the bank in escrow. It was only going to take a few weeks to get the paperwork finished before it would be released to us."

Problem was, the $25 million was based on their having the $140 million line of credit. Now, if both banks were somehow dropping out, Mark and John didn't even want to imagine what would happen next. "Part of our business plan was to put producers under our roof and pay them monies," John explained decades later. "We had started doing that and had already spent $11 million on productions, knowing we could recoup that when the loans closed." Now, if those loans didn't close, they were millions of dollars in the hole.

Mark and John quickly decided that John would fly to New York and meet with Allen & Co. to insure that the $25 million was still in place. Simultaneously, he would work with Korman on negotiating with the banks to secure the $140 million. Mark would stay in L.A., working on their productions. They hung up, believing their game plan was in place. But the house of cards was beginning to tremble.

John remained on the East Coast through the fall of 1985. He tried his best to unravel the mess with the banks while Mark stayed on the West Coast, overseeing the difficult edit of *8 Million Ways to Die;* sales and marketing of *Clan of the Cave Bear* (scheduled for a January '86 release); prepping *Short Circuit* and developing *Flight Of the Navigator* and *The Lost Boys.*

As both men continued to work on their own specialties, PSOers thought it was business as usual. "We often split up," Mark explained. "John would be alone, often in New York, working on the financial end while I would be out here dealing with sales, marketing and production." The only sign of trouble was when Mark and John were forced to downsize the company in October. But most PSOers were so caught up in the momentum of the company's success that they didn't see the handwriting on the wall.

When Adrian Lyne saw the latest responses from the test screenings he accepted the improvement although he hated Mark's constant interference. They were in a mixing studio in Glendale, laying in the final music - a lively soundtrack by Jack Nitzche and hot pop songs chosen by music supervisor Becky Mancuso - when Adrian turned to Mark.

"An important man like you, who's got a whole company to run, how can you come all the way out here to Glendale to work with a composer on a song? Isn't it a waste of your time?"

"I wish I could trust you enough to do it on your own," Mark answered.

Years later Mark mused over that comment: "It's not a waste of time for a producer to tend to every detail, because he or she should make certain that the picture is the best it can possibly be, given the material. In my opinion, if a producer's not around to make sure of that, he doesn't deserve to call himself a producer."

After his difficulties with Lyne on *9 ½ Weeks*, Chapman on *Clan* and Ashby on *8 Million Ways to Die*, Mark was elated when the *Short Circuit* shoot went well. "John (Badham) was wonderful to work with. He had his own ideas, of course, but he was always flexible and willing to work together." Badham: "By that point, all the other producers and I deferred to Mark. If he had an idea, that's what we listened to. He had a good handle on the project and somebody's got to make these decisions. Of course, I would fight for things I believed in but we saw eye to eye pretty nicely."

The biggest problem turned out to Ally Sheedy's hair. "After we had shot three or four days we got into a fight with TriStar over her hairdo," said Badham. "They were fussing about it and making it into a big deal. I remember that with Mark's blessing, I wrote to Jeff Sagansky: 'This hairdo was a personal choice of Ally Sheedy and if you'd like to talk to her about it, please be my guest and pay for re-shooting the first five days. We're happy to do it.' Which just shut them up."

In November, Mark went to MIFED to sell and to schmooze. He talked up their movies with typical hyperbole: *Short Circuit* was "a high-tech science fiction comedy adventure about a peace-loving robot"; *Flight of the Navigator*, "which has qualities of *E.T.* without being derivative, has the potential of absolutely exploding and going through the roof" and *The Lost Boys* was "an absolutely original thriller about vampires, teenage boys and a beautiful girl set in Northern California, loosely based on *Peter Pan*." Mark's enthusiasm sold the pictures worldwide. "Mark is an eternal optimist," said Eddie Kalish. "That's why he's such a good salesman.

From Cowboy to Mogul to Monster

Whether he believes in a movie or not, he certainly convinces himself for the purpose. And he convinces other people."

Next, Mark worked on revisions to the script for *Navigator*. Written by Mark H. Baker and Michael Burton, it had originally been with Jeffrey Katzenberg and Michael Eisner at Disney until the studio took too long to give a green light and the film's producers took it to Mark. "Initially, we were only interested in selling the foreign rights to PSO to cover half of the production costs," recounted one of the producers, Dimitri Villard, "but Mark was so enthusiastic about the movie he made us an offer we couldn't refuse." After PSO stepped in, Michael Eisner, in his first day as Chairman and CEO at Disney, called Mark and made a deal for Disney to distribute it in the US.

Randal Kleiser, the director of *Grease* and *Island of The Blue Dolphins,* humorously recalled script meetings with Mark, "who was always looking to push the movie into an action mode to sell it to the international buyers. While Disney was always pushing it into family." "Let's have the Air Force shoot down the spaceship," Mark would say. "Let's make the little boy cry," Disney would say. "Overall, it was a give and take that made the movie better because of those two ways of being pulled," Kleiser concluded.

By the end of 1985, PSO Delphi's slate of movies was looking good: *Clan of the Cave Bear* was set for a January release; *9 ½ Weeks* was set for February; *Short Circuit* was scheduled for release in May and *Flight of the Navigator* was about to start shooting.

By the end of 1985, John was making no further headway with the banks. He had learned there was a war going on *within* Chemical Bank and a war going on *between* Chemical and First Bank of Boston. He continued to work with the banks, hoping they would honor the credit line they had both promised to fund.

Years later he admitted, "Hard as I tried to maneuver, there was just no way to win."

Italy

1967 – 1973

Chapter Thirty-Eight

July 28, 1967

Naples, Italy

With Robert Mitchum in *The Battle of Anzio* (1968).

Playing his first villain, depraved George Bellow Ferguson in *Requiescant* (1967), co-starring Pier Paolo Pasolini.

Chapter 38. 1967. Naples

"I'LL BE LUCKY TO GET OUT of this alive," Mark thought to himself as he dodged flying beer bottles while dangling from an enormous chandelier high above a huge congressional ballroom in Naples. "Hey, you chickens. Come and get me!" he yelled to the 100 WW2 soldiers below him as he swung wildly from one end of the room to the other, trying to break the record for 'the longest time under fire.' Soon the air was thick with flying bottles in a stunt that was supposed to be funny but looked dangerous. It turned out that it was. "They were supposed to throw fake bottles but a couple of extras decided it would be more fun to throw real bottles of beer." After one of them hit Mark in the neck he kept on swinging across the room from the chandelier, unaware that he had just suffered a fractured vertebra in his neck.

The movie was *The Battle of Anzio,* a WW2 epic in which he played an American soldier alongside Robert Mitchum, Peter Falk, Robert Ryan, Reni Santoni, Giancarlo Giannini (in his movie debut) and Arthur Kennedy. The American/Italian film was a Dino DeLaurentiis production with funding from Columbia Pictures, shot entirely in Italy with Italian technicians and a Hollywood cast and director. Veteran Edward Dmytryk (*The Caine Mutiny, The Young Lions*) was directing the picture and Mark had taken it in hopes that it would keep his name alive in Hollywood. But it was doomed from the start. According to Reni Santoni, "there was no script. There was some idea, which might have been cool, about men making war because they need to. But what it turned into was seven dwarves lost in the woods. In this war movie, seven guys win the war."

Robert Mitchum had probably not read the script (in which he was playing a skeptical war correspondent) before arriving in Rome, fresh from an inspiring visit to Vietnam. When he declared it to be "violently anti-American" a battle began between star and director Dmytryk. Writers were flown in. Changes were made to appease Mitchum. Changes were made to appease Dmytryk. The script was rewritten before they filmed, while they filmed, sometimes they filmed without anything written down at all.

Mitchum called Dmytryk an "old fool." Dmytryk demanded a ticket home. The last straw came when they were shooting a battle scene and the men's rifles were wiggling in the wind. Dmytryk demanded to see them close-up and discovered that the rifles were made of rubber. He stormed into DeLaurentiis' office, rubber rifle in hand. Dmytryk: "And that's when I found out that DeLaurentiis was a deal maker more than a picture maker.

379

I showed him the rubber guns and he shrugged. 'What can I do? The dealer with the good guns cheated me. You'll just have to use them.'

By the time Mark was pelted with the bottles tensions were high. Eager not to add to the troubles he went right into his next scene. He was running up onto the beach in his helmet when Dmytryk called, "Cut." "Mark, get your head up!"

"Okay, Eddie."

He tried another take.

"Cut!" Dmytryk yelled again. "Mark, get your head up! I can't see your face."

"I'm trying," he said, "but this must be a very heavy helmet. I can't keep my head up."

A doctor was called to the set and he discovered the fracture in Mark's neck. He continued to work, neck-braced between takes. He also continued to play poker between takes with Peter Falk, Reni Santoni and Joseph Walsh in what *The Rome Daily American* would later call "the longest poker game on record."

Anzio was still shooting when Mark was cast in his next film, *School Girl Killers*, a comic Italian thriller in the popular 'giallo' (mystery thriller) genre. "Damon Bicycles in Rome" wrote *Hollywood Reporter*, citing that "Damon will work during the day at Cinecitta Studios on *Anzio* and bicycle to the back lot for his role in *School Girl Killers* after dark."

School Girl Killers (*The Young, The Evil and The Savage*) was directed by Anthony Dawson (AKA Antonio Margheriti). Alongside British castmates Michael Rennie (known to Americans as 'Harry Lime' in the TV series "The Third Man" as well as the lead in *The Day the Earth Stood Still*) and Sallie Smith, Mark added humor to his role as a riding teacher in a girl's boarding school where he beds all the women while a killer is on the loose.

Originally developed by Mario Bava, the film had all the ingredients of a typical 'giallo': murders, sex, religion and nightmarish flashbacks. The central idea was that a killer kept continually killing the wrong girl while searching for a specific target. Although it wasn't the first thriller to be set in a girls' school "it might have been the first to fully exploit the psycho-killer and 'Ten Little Indians' possibilities of this creepy setting,"

Chapter 38. 1967. Naples

wrote one critic decades later. "Plus, the morbid joke of the killer keeping the first body around right under the nose of the later victims led to Bava's *Black Sabbath*, which in turn inspired *Halloween* and after that came a host of other imitators."

"In that picture the thing I was most proud of was being able to make a horse rear up in practically a 90 degree angle," Mark remembered. "People said, 'Be careful, it's dangerous, you could fall backwards.' But I was showing off what I had learned in Spaghetti Westerns." When he was cast in *Train for Durango,* a Spaghetti Western with his old flame, Dominique Boschero, Mark began to shoot *three* pictures simultaneously. "I would do *Anzio* the whole day, shooting at Nazi's, then I'd shoot *Train* at night, where I played a gun-toting dandy who appears behind a machine gun wearing a jacket, tie and a beret as he mows down banditos. Then I'd take off two days and jump into *Killers*."

Next he moved on to play his first villain, the infamous George Bellow Ferguson in *Requiescant (Kill and Pray)* a surreal Spaghetti Western directed by genre professional Carlo Lizzani. With its themes of racism and hints of depravity, *Requiescant* was an interesting movie. It opened on a celebration over a newly declared peace between native Mexicans and American settlers in a town on the Mexico/San Antonio border. After the Mexicans throw down their guns, a dark-cloaked man rides in on a white horse and orders their massacre. Once he is satisfied that every unarmed man, woman and child is dead, the man rides off, unaware that a young boy has survived and will grow up to be a bounty hunter vowing revenge on him.

Ferguson was an evil, bizarre, woman-hating Union Army commander and Mark relished playing the decadent dandy in a Dracula-cloak: "I remember a line I made up as he strangles his wife: 'Emma, I've always admired your dignity. Don't disappoint me in dyin'.'"

He managed to get a small part for Barbara Frey and she spent evenings with him and his old friend, writer and director Pier Paolo Pasolini, who played a Mexican priest who guides a band of Mexican freedom fighters while preaching nonviolence. "War murders pity," Pasolini declaimed in the film, an appropriate sentiment from the renowned pacifist who was also one of the most provocative figures in Italian cinema. (With his controversial views on homosexuality, Marxism and atheism, Pasolini would ultimately end up murdered in 1975 in still-mysterious circumstances.)

Before *Requiescant* was finished, Mark was cast in yet another film. Once again, he shot two films simultaneously, alternating between playing

Alan O'Dale, a rogue and an outdoorsman in *Robin Hood (The Scalawag Bunch)* and terrorizing the town in a Southern accent as evil George Bellow Ferguson.

Some reviewers found *Requiescant* "original" and "offbeat." Others described it as "a surreal, bizarre and sadistic Spaghetti Western filled with brutality and druggy overtones." Most praised Mark's performance as Ferguson, "a madman who is eccentrically gay." (Think Johnny Depp in *Pirates of the Caribbean*.) Today, the film is regarded as one of the best Spaghetti Westerns directed by Lizzani.

Mark went on to play Ivanhoe in *La Spada Normanna,* another epic where he scaled castle walls, dueled in spectacular swordfights and even danced a jig. Then he became the first American to co-star with a top Russian actor in *The Forbidden*, a tale of two WWII prisoners who cannot speak each other's language but plan to escape from a Nazi POW camp.

Over the next five years he played the hero in a steady stream of Spaghetti Westerns and a smattering of horror movies and swashbucklers He made twenty-five films in seventeen different countries in Europe, developing fluency in Italian, German, French, Spanish and "a nodding acquaintance with the Slavic tongues and 27 words of Arabic." He drove from location to location in his Alfa Romeo while retaining the apartment in Rome with Barbara Frey. But their relationship steadily deteriorated. "Partly because I was constantly working and she wasn't. Partly because she was an alcoholic, which I only learned late in our relationship." Mark used the failing relationship as an excuse to sleep with any woman he chose while deriving much of his satisfaction from his varied roles.

Some films were more interesting than others. On many he got hurt. "In *I Morti non si contano (Cry for Revenge),* a Spaghetti Western directed by Rafael Romero Marchent, a squib that was supposed to go off *after* I passed went off just as I was passing instead. It hit me in the eye and I was blind for days." He was almost trampled in *The Lions of Saint Petersburg* "after I rode across a vast plain leading the charge of 100 Cossacks. I was on a horse that was very nervous. We took off across the snow, galloping faster and faster until, just as I went past the camera, the horse crumpled and dropped. He had a heart attack and died on me." The horse pinned Mark to the ground while 100 other horses whizzed by inches from his head. "I figured it was the end. Either every bone in my body was already crushed or I was about to get killed by the other horses."

When they finally stopped shooting they pulled the horse off him and Mark got up, happy to be alive. But when he had trouble standing "I felt some liquid in my boot. And when I took it off I found out it was filled with blood." The stirrup, which had stayed attached to his foot when the horse fell, had broken his foot and made a deep gash in his toe, which was bleeding profusely.

They took Mark to a country hospital in Bulgaria where he ended up undergoing surgery without anesthetic. "They just gave me a bottle of vodka and said, 'Keep drinking until you tell us you're ready.'" Regardless, he finished the last scene in the film, a sword fight, in a cast all the way up his leg. "I could only do one thrust or parry before I fell over so they had a guy whose whole job was to catch Mark Damon's fall."

He was recuperating in a little hotel in Sofia when Barbara called to tell him she was leaving him. Mark didn't want to end things long distance and convinced her to come and be with him. But their relationship remained troubled. By then, he and Barbara had lived together for seven years "while Barbara's parents gave her a hard time, saying that I didn't respect her enough to marry her and that she was giving me the best years of her life without anything to show for it."

They finally decided to get married on the ancient Campidoglio in old Rome in 1971. Mark: "Perhaps I married her because I felt that it might save our relationship but of course it didn't. The day we got married I was already on the way to seducing one of her bridesmaids. Barbara was actually a willing participant in my flirtation because she had lesbian inclinations. She wanted both of us to go to bed with her bridesmaid and a couple of months later, we did. That was the beginning of the end."

Barbara was consumed with guilt over the tryst. She began to drink even more heavily. Mark threw himself into one forgettable Spaghetti Western after another, mining his roles for all they were worth. In *Pistol Packing Preacher* he opened the film as a lazy oaf who is dozing in a haystack in a felt hat and suspenders when he shoots an ant off his toe rather than getting up to swat it. Later, he used his comic abilities when a 'miracle' from the preacher supposedly cures him of blindness. In *Death at Owell Rock* he played an outlaw with a bristly moustache who disguises himself as a girl in a long red wig. When 'she' beds down with her 'lover' she pours liquor down his throat to get him to reveal the location of the treasure.

Sometimes he succeeded in enlivening otherwise forgettable Spaghetti Westerns by combining physical comedy, farce and gunfights. Along the way, he became a far better actor and much more famous than he had been in the U.S. But by end of 1972, the Spaghetti Western was showing signs

From Cowboy to Mogul to Monster

of age. Action fans were getting bored with them. Martial arts and other genre movies began to grab their attention. "And when Westerns started to go out of style, so did I," Mark commented.

He was nearing forty when he turned his hand to writing. He produced four screenplays he had penned including *The Great Chihuahua Treasure Hunt,* an entertaining caper film in which he starred as a lovable rogue along with luscious Rosalba Neri, "with whom I started a flirtation but we became just good friends. One of the first times." (They would co-star again one year later in *The Devil's Wedding Night.*)

He tried his hand at directing. He acted in other genres - a few thrillers and some horror movies including *Byleth*, the story of a boy who is possessed by the demon of incest and wants to make love to his sister. (Although today it is credited as the first Italian horror movie with an incestuous theme it was not much of a success at the time.)

He played six different characters in *The Golden Chameleon* including a bald, aging Irish cleric; a thick and pompous Teutonic professor; a young geekish student and a dapper but sleazy casino owner. Although it showcased his comic abilities, the film had very little commercial success.

He was growing desperate when he was cast in an erotica directed by Radley Metzger, *Little Mother,* loosely based on the rise of Eva Peron (played by a sexy Christine Kruger). It focused on a ruthlessly ambitious woman known as 'Little Mother' who sleeps her way to political power in an unnamed South American country. Mark co-starred as political activist Riano and shared an elegantly erotic scene with the beautiful and sexy 'Little Mother' in which she is naked in the shower and he is on the other side of the translucent shower door as they 'communicate' (but don't actually touch). Although one critic later called it 'the most arousing scene ever to rate an R,' *Little Mother* was only a middling success.

By 1973 it was increasingly clear that Mark's acting career in Europe was coming to an end. "Twenty-five pictures later, most of which could be easily forgotten, my career was waning because they stopped making Spaghetti Westerns and directors only saw me as a cowboy star." He saw himself as having wasted too many years because he was intent on being a star.

Barbara left him "for someone she hoped would better serve her needs" and Mark felt relief. He knew she would never be the woman he was looking for. But as he looked at his life he was disappointed with his past and worried about his future. Until he got a call from an old friend.

Chapter 38. 1967. Naples

"I had an idea for a picture called *The Arena*," Roger Corman recalled years later "and I wanted to shoot it in Rome. By then, I had heard that Mark had made the move from actor to producer. So I called him and asked if he wanted to produce the movie."

"Great idea," Mark answered quickly. "What's the story?"

Corman explained that it would be a female version of *Spartacus* with two female gladiators in the roles played by Tony Curtis and Kirk Douglas.

"Who are you casting for the leads?"

"Pam Grier and Julie Ward. One is black and the other white so the women will be forced to overcome their racial differences to fight for their freedom. You put in a little money, I'll get the rest. Are you in?"

"I'm in," Mark proclaimed.

"Great. I'll send over the script, the director and the two leads and you just make the picture."

After Mark hung up he drew a long breath of relief. And just like that, he became a producer on his first American movie.

Over the next month he made arrangements for the production - hiring the Italian crew, overseeing the building of sets and scouting locations. He made hotel arrangements for the actors and director, arranged for the balance of financing with Italian banks, set up the shooting schedule, etc. Roger: "He was completely hands-on and very good at being a producer." Mark: "Although I still had not given up hopes of being a major star (actors rarely do) I felt I was laying the groundwork for a change in my career."

One afternoon Corman called with "great news. Julie Ward can't do the film. She had a scheduling conflict."

"Why is that great news?"

"Because I found a terrific replacement," Roger replied. "Margaret Markov."

"Who is she?"

"A beautiful blonde actress who just co-starred with Pam in a big hit for us in America - *Black Mama, White Mama*. I'm telling you, re-teaming them in *The Arena* is going to make it a success in America."

"But what about Europe?" Mark countered. "No one here has ever heard of this Margaret Markov. Why don't we cast an Italian girl for the second lead? Someone who has a name in Europe."

385

The men argued for awhile with Mark lobbying for an Italian actress and Roger insisting on Ms. Markov. Finally, Roger laid down the law. "Sorry, but we've done several pictures with Margaret and Pam and even in low budget films, people know who they are. We're using her and that's the end of it."

Against his will, Mark grudgingly accepted Markov in the movie.

"One last thing," Corman continued. "Margaret Markov will cost $750 a week instead of $500 like Julie Ward."

"Fine," Mark answered with spirit, "as long as you pick up the other $250 a week."

"No, we'll split it," replied the notoriously cheap Corman.

"We will not," Mark retorted. "Margaret Markov is important for you but she doesn't mean a thing in Italy. You pay the extra $250 a week." They argued back and forth until Roger slammed down the phone. "I thought about it for awhile," Mark later recalled, "and finally decided I wasn't going to blow a twenty-year friendship over $125 a week." He called Roger and said they'd split the difference.

Two days before the start of production the two actresses and the director flew into Rome. That night, Mark drove up to the Hotel Cassia to meet Pam Grier and the inexplicably expensive Margaret Markov.

It was a balmy evening, much like the night he'd arrived in Rome twelve years earlier. Until the moment he walked into the hotel Mark believed he had only gone to Italy to boost his acting career. He was about to discover another, life-changing reason why he was destined to be there.

Chapter Thirty-Nine

April 29, 1973

Rome, Italy

Margaret Markov, age 24, the year she met Mark.

Mark, age 40, the year he met Maggie.

Mark and Maggie in Rome.

Chapter 39. 1973. Rome

WHEN MARK STRODE INTO THE LOBBY he was struck by the sight of a tall and stunning young woman with blonde hair that shimmered to her thighs. She was laughing zestfully as she danced an impromptu "Shuffle Off to Buffalo" with Pam Grier.

"Pam and I were playing around while we waited for the American producer to arrive," Margaret Markov (Maggie) later recalled. "All we knew was that someone named 'Mark Damon' was going to take us out to dinner. So there we were, doing a silly dance when he walked in."

With each step towards her, Mark became more and more aware of her joie de vivre and charisma. Her long-legged grace and the peal of her laughter resounded deep within him. By the time he had crossed the lobby, he was smitten by Margaret Markov, the woman he had tried to take out of *Arena*.

Mark took Maggie and Pam out to dinner where Maggie would always remember that he flirted with Pam throughout the entire meal. Decades later, Mark admitted he did it to get Maggie interested: "She was only twenty-four and I had just turned forty, although I told her I was thirty-nine. I didn't think this young chick would go for me unless I did something to make her interested, like if the other girl was attracted to me."

His plans backfired. Maggie: "He was so flirty that I couldn't tell if he liked me or Pam. He didn't realize that I hated that kind of game-playing." At the end of the evening Maggie went back to the hotel assuming that was her last dinner with Mark Damon. Mark went to his penthouse on Via Del Nuoto, eager to take her out again. As for his game-playing, "I was used to having to do that in Europe. Europeans, at the time, viewed male-female relationships with distrust and game-playing was deemed essential."

He dug out Markov's bio and read that she was a native of Pasadena, California and one of ten children; had studied acting in Hollywood and acted in a handful of movies. Her first role was in Roger Vadim's American debut, *Pretty Maids All in a Row* starring Rock Hudson as a psychopathic sex killer and Angie Dickenson as a substitute teacher who deflowers a teen male virgin. Although Maggie played only one of several nubile students in revealing clothes, her image was the one that was prominently displayed in a three-story poster on the side of Grauman's Chinese Theatre.

Next she was cast in *Hot Box,* a Roger Corman women-in-prison film (co-written by the future director of *Silence of the Lambs*, Jonathan Demme) shot in the steamy jungles of the Philippines. Maggie played one of four nurses who break out of a women's prison and become revolutionaries only to be kidnapped by 'The Peoples' Army' and forced to spend most of their incarceration topless.

Then she was paired with Pam Grier in another Corman women-in-prison film, *Black Mama, White Mama*, directed by Eddie Romero (and ripped off from *The Defiant Ones* starring Tony Curtis and Sidney Poitier.) Maggie played a trouble-making revolutionary and Pam was a former harem girl. As prisoners who detest each other the women are being extradited when they escape. Chained together, they stumble, stab and cat-fight their way across the wilderness while half-naked.

Mark realized with a chuckle that *The Arena* (a rip off of *Spartacus* that everyone on the set would soon call *Spartichetta*, or 'little female *Spartacus*') would be her third role as an enslaved woman who tries to escape while managing to escape her clothing.

He couldn't wait to see her again. She had a sexy, blue eyed innocence that he found utterly captivating. "Maggie was a wholesome American girl. Intelligent, sensitive and totally unsophisticated. Having just broken up with Barbara a few months earlier I was yearning for a simple, open relationship with somebody relatively sane."

At the end of her bio he found a curious sentence: "Maggie is eagerly pursuing spirituality." Must be a passing fancy, he thought dismissively.

Over the next week, Mark attended to a myriad of production details while Pam and Maggie learned complicated swordfight routines. Maggie was playing Viking Princess Bodicia. Pam (clad in a leopard-skin tube dress) was Nubian Princess Mamawi. Both had been kidnapped as slaves, forced to have sex with their captors and to fight as gladiatrixes in the Roman arena. By the time Bodicia and Mamawi are forced into a duel to the death they have revolutionized the other female slaves (played by Italian actresses Lucretia Love and Rosalba Neri – cast by Mark) and mounted a rebellion against their male captors, culminating in a chase through the Catacombs.

Mark was frequently on set where he and Maggie had long talks between takes. "She was a breath of fresh air. She was serious but fun-loving, optimistic, totally without guile, embracing the world and loving it. She was deep but uncomplicated and excited by her first trip to Europe and all the wonderful possibilities life was offering.

Chapter 39. 1973. Rome

I had just turned forty and had no idea where my career was going (except downwards if I remained an actor.) I had little money, little patience emotionally and little time to get my life straight. The last thing I needed was more hopelessly superficial interactions with European women. I found Maggie's optimism contagious and she was very exciting for me to be around."

Despite director Steve Carver's iron-clad caveat that none of the actors go out at night Mark, Maggie and Pam went out to dinner constantly until it became clear that Maggie and Mark were drawn to each other. From then on, Mark took Maggie to his favorite restaurants where he was hailed with a hearty: 'Marco Damone!' He ordered for them off the menu, conversing with waiters and waitresses in rapid Italian. Maggie was impressed with his cosmopolitan élan and told him so. Mark was impressed with her openness and honesty and told her so.

At twenty-four, on her first trip to Europe, Maggie felt protected and comfortable when she was out with Mark. Without him it was another story. Whenever Pam and Maggie walked on the streets of Rome they were pinched, propositioned, and followed all over town. The mere sight of the tall, gorgeous African-American woman and the long-legged blonde with thigh-length hair overwhelmed Italian men. Maggie was overwhelmed by their reaction.

As they got to know each other, Mark told her about his Hollywood days and his career in Europe. He even told her about some of his women. Maggie began to realize how much experience he had. "And there I was, an innocent ingénue. Looking back, I wonder how in the world this man fell for me? He had been with so many women, and some of them were very sophisticated. Then again," she reasoned, "there's no way in the world he would have looked at me twice if he hadn't decided maybe he should settle down. Because I was very immature in the ways of the world. I had a lot of depth but I was quite the kid."

Maggie told Mark about her romantic history. How she had been married briefly to a director who was twenty years older; had a fling with Roger Vadim and recently lived with the caretaker of Jayne Mansfield's empty mansion where Maggie turned Jayne's huge master bedroom into a meditation room. "I was in love with Eric and when he fell in love with another girl my heart was broken," she confessed. Mark listened carefully, taking note of everything Maggie said. "He made me feel special," she recalled. "I liked that he was interested in me and wanted to be with me." "We were very compatible," Mark agreed. "Plus, Maggie made me laugh." "We just fit," they both agreed.

A week later they were having dinner when they started sharing their favorite things.

"I don't remember the name of my favorite movie," said Maggie, "because I saw it when I was about twelve. All I remember is a scene where a man walked out of a burning building. He had black hair, green eyes and wore a white Victorian style shirt. He was so handsome and he was walking out of this cloud of smoke. When it was over I remember telling my mother, 'Someday I'm going to marry that man.'"

Mark was stunned. "That was me!"

"What?!"

"You're talking about *me* in *The Fall of the House of Usher*!"

Mark didn't know what to make of it. Maggie saw it as a sign that they were meant to be together. "It was clearly a past experience that we've been together before," she said. "Even though I was only twelve when I saw you in that movie I was responding to my heart responding."

Mark shook his head, astounded. When he got home he called Roger Corman and told him about the eerie coincidence. Roger promptly declared himself Mark and Maggie's 'godfather.' "After all, I was the producer who made *Usher* and the one who brought Maggie to Rome. Against your wishes, if you recall."

Soon it was a warm Sunday afternoon and Mark and Maggie were in the countryside outside Rome. They had bought a watermelon from a farmer, enjoyed a picnic, talked, kissed and laughed. Mark was walking alongside Maggie in a forest when he looked at her and suddenly came to a halt.

"I was wearing my hair in braids, a scarf tied around my head 'babushka-style.' All of a sudden I saw that Mark had turned white," she later recalled.

"What's the matter?" she asked, alarmed.

For a moment all he could do was stare, speechless. "I swear to you this is not a line," he began slowly. "It's the truth. I dreamed of you when I was a child."

"What?" Maggie exclaimed.

"When I was seven, I dreamed that I was walking in a forest and a young blonde woman appeared beside me with long hair in braids, wearing a scarf. She said 'Don't worry, one day we'll find each other.' I dreamed it a few times and it was so important that I remembered it vividly until now."

Maggie got goose pimples as Mark stared at her.

Chapter 39. 1973. Rome

"It was you," he breathed.

"It's another sign..." she replied. "We were meant to be together."

Mark had never had coincidences like that with anyone, let alone any other woman. Although he thought of himself as a realist he had no explanation. But even if he didn't know what to make of the strange twists of fate, he knew how he felt about Maggie. And he knew he had never felt that way about any another woman.

Yet as their connection deepened he felt that something wasn't right. He had a nagging worry that despite their mutual declarations of love, Maggie was not letting herself be with him completely. Was she was still in love with her last boyfriend? he wondered. If so, what could he do about it? After waiting a lifetime to meet his soul-mate he was not about to lose her. He mulled it over until he came up with a plan.

They were shooting the film's climactic chase scene in the ancient Catacombs at the Baths of Caracalla when he sat Maggie down.

"You're not giving us a chance," he began. "Because you're measuring me by the yardstick you used for your other boyfriend, Eric."

"I am?" she asked.

"I think so. But it's not going to fit me, Maggie. For us to go forward, you've got to break all your yardsticks."

Maggie was struck by Mark's image.

"All my life," she later said, "when I would think about something I wanted to be or have, I would get an image of it in my mind and focus on it. When Mark said I had to break all my yardsticks I got a very strong visual image in my mind."

"If you commit the way I'm about to commit," he continued, "we could have the greatest relationship imaginable. Because I'm going to commit everything to you. I will be faithful. I will be there for you. I will do things I'm not even sure I can do but I'm going to commit to us. And I want you to do the same."

It was a great sales pitch, greater still because he meant every word of it. It affected Maggie deeply. She loved Mark and she trusted him. She knew she had to do what he was asking for.

"Okay," she said.

After the shoot she wandered off and went down into the Catacombs until she found a place where the roof was broken out and the sun was streaming through.

"I was all by myself in this powerful place with all the history behind it," she later recalled. "I sat down in the middle of the dirt floor, and with the sun coming down, visualized the yardstick I was using between my ex-boyfriend and Mark. And I, literally, cracked it in two in my mind. Then I sat for a while, dusted myself off and went out. And it was totally different between us from then on."

Mark felt the difference. The minute the picture was finished, he pounced. "Don't ever leave me," he said, the words of a man whose first love, his father, had done just that. In Maggie, Mark sensed loyalty, stability, constancy. They were qualities he needed in a woman before he would give his heart fully.

Soon afterwards, Maggie said, "Let's make a pact to always tell each other the truth."

Mark looked uncomfortable.

"I lied to you," he admitted.

Maggie tensed.

"I told you I was thirty-nine but I'm really forty."

She started to laugh.

"You lied about your age and you only shaved off one year when you could easily have done five or ten? You'd better not tell me any more lies. You're a really bad liar!"

A few days later he helped her move out of the Hotel Cassia and into his apartment on Via Del Nuoto "which Maggie loved because the elevator opened directly into my penthouse." From then on, they were together. "I don't remember ever saying 'I'm moving in for life.' I just moved in. It was natural," said Maggie.

On June 23, 1973, six weeks after they met, they flew back to L.A. Maggie was going to close her apartment, put all her things in a trunk and send them to Rome. On the plane they married each other. (Although he was still legally married to Barbara Frey, they had both applied for a divorce.) "I did the wedding ceremony. I was the Justice of the Peace and the husband," Mark joked. "And I fell for it," Maggie quipped, adding, "I married the man who would be my man forever and who has been before."

When they committed to each other "it was for life," Maggie added. "I never had the thought, 'I can get out of this.' Neither did Mark. We never allowed ourselves to say, we can always get a divorce. Not ever."

Chapter Forty

May 21, 1974

Rome, Italy

Arena (1974) – Mark's first production -- stars Margaret Markov, soon to become Maggie Damon.

Maggie co-stars with Mark in *There is No 13* (1974).
Although they made up after fighting nonstop on the set,
they decided never to act together again.

T**HEY WERE FIGHTING.**
"Leave me alone, I look good," Maggie said.
"No, you don't," he retorted. "I know what Italian producers are looking for and they are not looking to see this wonderful actress. They want to see some sexy broad. That's the only way you're going to get work in Italy."

Maggie, on her way to an audition, bristled at his attempts to control her. She was serious about acting, having studied and worked hard. But Mark's age and experience won out. She changed her outfit.

The Arena (AKA *Naked Warriors*) had recently opened in the U.S. with lurid posters: "SEE WILD WOMEN FIGHT TO THE DEATH!" and "BLACK SLAVE vs. WHITE SLAVE!" a bid for fans of *Black Mama, White Mama*. Reviewers responded with headlines of their own: "FOR HEAVEN'S SAKES, NERO, THE GLADIATORS ARE GIRLS!" and "SWEATY SWORD-AND-SANDAL SISTERS!" or "SPEARS, SANDALS AND SKIRTS!"

It was only a moderate success in America and not successful at all in Italy. "It was just another 'filler,'" said Mark. But Maggie wanted to capitalize on the movie and started going out on auditions. Which introduced her to a side of Mark she had not seen before and did not appreciate.

"I couldn't go on an interview without him approving what I was going to wear and how my hair should be done."

Secretly, he wished she would give it up. If only he could support them, he thought, she probably would. Their disagreements over her outfits became a running argument. But it was only one of the difficulties that Maggie encountered living in Rome. "Maggie came from California where everybody says, 'Have a nice day.' They're always polite and open with each other," Mark later commented. "People talk in the elevators and everywhere else. In Italy, they don't communicate that way. If an Italian man is going to have a conversation with an attractive young woman it's because he's thinking of seduction, not because he's being nice."

With her long, blond hair and smiles that never stopped, Maggie continued to stand out on the street. Her natural exuberance and openness made her very different from Roman women and gave Roman men the wrong idea. "If I smiled at a man I was followed down the street, I was followed in my car. It was very unpleasant." Plus, she learned that Roman women don't make friends easily because they are jealous and paranoid about who and what you are. "They never made me feel welcome," she recalled,

Chapter 40. 1973. Rome

"and after a while I found I had to repress my natural exuberance because it was taken as flirtation by the men and suspicious to the women."

She tried to learn Italian but found it difficult. "It's hard to learn a language when you're not feeling sure of yourself. And I was always nervous that people didn't like me."

Despite the difficulties, she never regretted her decision to live with Mark in Rome. Not for a second. "I just jumped into my life," she would later say. She made the best of living in Rome, rejoicing that she could go into the Vatican every day if she wanted. And she made friends with some of the people in the ex-pat American colonies.

Mark, meanwhile, was having more and more trouble getting acting roles. He had always worried about supporting a family as an actor: "What a tough game this acting is," he had written as far back as 1957, "particularly for a man who has to support a family. One can't allow himself the privilege of marrying unless he has means to provide for a family." Now, his fears were coming true.

One night, Mark and Maggie were having dinner with their friends, fellow American ex-pats writer/director William (Bill) Sachs and his wife, Margaret. Bill had written a script, *There Is No 13*, centering on the fantasy girlfriend, his 13th, of a quadriplegic war casualty who can't fulfill his fantasies after having had twelve girlfriends. Bill told Mark he wanted him to play the lead.

"I'll do it," Mark finally agreed. "If I can be a producer. And if Maggie plays 'Number 13.'"

"Done," Bill exclaimed.

Maggie and Mark left the dinner, excited to co-star in their first film together. Then shooting began and all hell broke loose. "I think it's very hard for actors to give each other what they need while they're working together," said Mark years later. "Acting is a self-centered craft and when an actor is working he needs to take more than he gives. Being a serious actor, I was constantly focusing on my character in *13*. It was not a good situation for two people newly in love."

On top of that while they were shooting, Maggie had the worst outbreak of acne in her life. As tensions between them grew, one day she railed at Mark to the crew over something he had done. "A star is a star is a star," Maggie fumed. Mark recalled, "it pissed the hell out of me that she would take snipes at me in front of the crew. Plus it was so unlike her." By the time the shoot was finished they both agreed that working with each other was hell.

401

Because *There is No 13* was a quirky piece and not commercial enough for the European market they were unable to find a distributor for it. So Mark and Bill were overjoyed when they submitted it to the Berlin Film Festival and it was chosen as the closing night feature. The foursome went to Berlin with high hopes.

They later learned that closing night features at the Festival were almost always comedies – light-hearted, commercial, mindless pieces. *There Is No 13* was certainly not light-hearted and was essentially a depressing piece. At the end of the movie, when it was revealed that the entire film had taken place in Mark's character's mind, the audience booed the piece off the screen. "By the time Maggie and I went up on stage to take our bows Bill was catatonic, Maggie was shaking like a leaf and I was very upset that in this 'anticipated moment of glory' I was hating the audience, hating our film, hating myself for being up there and having to smile through this pain. I decided right then and there that there must be a better way to make a living."

Years later, Mark would tell *The New York Times:* "In Italy, I began to write screenplays for myself as an actor but the directors would mess them up so I became a director in order to properly direct myself as an actor. Then, as a director, producers never gave me enough money to do the pictures properly so I became a producer. Finally, after I produced a film that wasn't even distributed I decided to become a distributor. And that was so fascinating I left acting."

In reality, it was not quite so easy.

CHAPTER FORTY-ONE

August 14, 1974

Rome, Italy

Mark and Maggie on a *Benji* Tour in Italy.

Chapter 41. 1974. Rome

At forty-one, Mark cut a handsome figure as he walked briskly down the Via Veneto in his suit and tie. Roman women smiled seductively, hoping to catch his eye; Roman men who recognized him as an actor, as usual, paid no attention. But Mark no longer saw himself as an actor. When he entered the offices of PAC, one of the larger distributors of motion pictures in Italy, all he knew was that he needed a job.

He met with Mario and Piero Bregni, the two brothers who ran the company and spoke only Italian. "I told them I wanted to stop acting and they saw me as a Hollywood star and figured I knew everybody there."

"How can I help you?" he asked.

"Help us get top American films," Piero Bregni answered immediately.

In the 1970's the most popular films in Europe were American. But the only American films that were available to independent overseas distributors like PAC were 'B' or 'C' movies. All the 'A' American movies, the biggest money makers, went to distribution wings of major studio chains like Warner Bros., Columbia or Universal, which had their own people in cities around the globe.

Until they met Mark, the Bregni's, who spoke no English and had no ties to Hollywood, were in the same boat as all other European distributors. They promptly hired him to become the Director of Acquisitions of their International Department. Actually, he *became* their International Department.

From then on Mark left the apartment on Via del Nuoto every morning, dressed in a hand-made Italian suit and carrying a briefcase. He looked like a million bucks even if he was only earning a million lira (about $1,600) a month, slightly under $20,000 a year. "The pay wasn't much but it was a 'serious' job. And I knew I had to do something serious in order to keep Maggie in the style to which I knew she wanted to become accustomed," he would later joke. For the first time in his professional life he wasn't involved in the creative side of movies as an actor, writer, director or producer.

He soon learned that his bosses were different as night and day. Piero, the older brother, was 6'2", had a commanding presence, was respected as one of the top distributors in Italy, President of the Italian Distributors

Union and a passionate and knowledgeable man. He was also very impatient with his employees and his younger brother, Mario.

Mario was about 6' but looked like he was 5'7' because he was always bent over. "Mario had tunnel vision, the manner of an old accountant and lacked all of Piero's creative bent," Mark recalled. "He was completely dominated by Piero. When they were in a room together he would bend his head, rarely looking his older brother in the eyes, keeping up a litany of 'Si, Piero. Si, Piero.' Although Mario was very bright and functioned as the financial director of the company, Piero treated him like a lackey."

Because everything in Italy was about family, the Bregni's spent all their spare time together. Out of the blue, Mark and Maggie were expected to have nightly dinners with the two Bregni brothers, their wives, their children and 'La Nonna' (the grandmother.) They were expected to attend every birthday, anniversary and christening and to go on vacations together. They were expected to become extended members of the Bregni clan. Mark became an instant businessman at the age of forty-one. Maggie became an instant corporate wife at the age of twenty-five. It was an enormous change for the new couple. But Mark was determined to make it in his new role and Maggie was willing to support him all the way.

Meanwhile, Mark watched and learned from Piero Bregni, who was a master of distribution. He taught Mark to tell how a picture was going to do from its first opening, its first weekend, even from its very first showing; how to read box office reports and know exactly what they meant. He watched how Piero would fashion his campaigns to appeal to his Italian public; how he would pull audiences in with artwork and trailers; how he always knew what his Italian public wanted. "I admired Piero for his passion and expertise and his (sometimes) little-boy-like innocence, despite the fact that like all good Italian businessmen, he could be very cunning. Mario followed up with me on all the details (Piero was not a detail man) and would wear me down with his insistence upon every detail being properly reported."

Despite Mark's Herculean efforts, several months passed without his being able to do what he was hired for. He simply couldn't get American pictures for PAC. So he took the Bregni's on a 'shopping trip' to New York with the goal of picking up movies. "It was on that trip that we bought *Benji*, the first picture I officially picked up for PAC. It was not exactly an 'A' movie, just a very well-performing 'B' movie."

Chapter 41. 1974. Rome

By then, Mark had learned enough from Piero about marketing to suggest that if *Benji* opened in Italy without some kind of promotion it would die.

"What do you recommend?" Piero asked.

"How about if Benji the dog comes to Italy and goes on a tour? Performing little shows, something like that."

Piero nodded with approval at his protégé. Soon Benji arrived with Frank Inn, his trainer, and Frank's wife, who had raised Benji; director Joe Camp and his wife and a camera operator named Don Reddy (whom Mark would hire again thirty years later). Maggie and Mark picked them all up at the airport and they traveled with Benji and his entourage on trains from one end of Italy to the other. For the next three weeks, Benji did shows day in and day out and it worked to build an audience. When *Benji* opened as *Beniamino* in Rome, enthusiastic audiences lined up around the block.

Under Piero's tutelage Mark began to get involved with posters and artwork. He started making up copy lines after he went to England and bought a couple of Monty Python pictures for PAC to distribute, including *The Holy Grail*. When Mark learned that Italian audiences didn't know who Monty Python was he started thinking about how to draw them in. "Posters were always saying, 'From the producers who brought you *The Godfather*' or 'From the director who brought you *"The Shining."*'" Mark came up with a takeoff for *The Holy Grail*: 'From the producers who saw *The Godfather*' or 'From the director who saw *Apocalypse Now.*' It was his first marketing campaign and it worked. Italian audiences loved the humor. Piero was impressed.

Soon he came to Mark with a harder test. PAC, which also produced Italian movies, was preparing to produce a comedy, *Culastrisce, Nobile Veneziano,* with Marcello Mastroianni.

"Since you know everybody can you get us a star for this picture?" Piero asked.

"Maybe." Mark thought for a minute. "You know, Peter Sellers would be perfect."

"Where is he?"

"In England."

"Do you know him?"

"No."

407

From Cowboy to Mogul to Monster

"*Fa niente*, go get him," said Piero.

Mark flew to England with Maggie. He was able to inveigle Peter Sellers' number from his agent's secretary. After he made contact with a very reticent and suspicious (at least initially) Sellers he spent the next three days trying to convince him to do the film.

Sellers kept flip-flopping but Mark had to show his bosses how valuable he was. He believed his future depended on getting Sellers to do to the movie. Finally, out of desperation he told the actor , "Did you know that you are Mastroianni's hero?

"Really?" Sellers replied, intrigued.

"Really," Mark swore, lying. "He is dying to work with you. All you have to do is come with me to Italy and meet him."

That did it. Sellers agreed to fly to Rome with them the next morning. But when Mark and Maggie got to the airport Sellers was nowhere to be seen. They boarded the plane without him "and when it took off I was devastated. I saw my new career in ruins."

Ten minutes into the flight somebody opened the bathroom door and ran like crazy, ducking into the first seat in the First Class cabin. It was Sellers. He had been the first one on the plane and hid in the bathroom until takeoff so nobody would see him. "He was very weird but he and Mastroianni hit it off famously when they met."

Although Sellers ultimately turned down the role, Mark had showed the Bregni's that he could get a star to come to them. (Ultimately, when the film was produced it starred Marcello Mastroianni and Adriano Celentano in the role meant for Sellers. "Probably a good thing because Celentano was a very popular singer in Italy (and still is) and his name gave the film a commercial boost that Sellers wouldn't have been able to.")

By 1975 Mark had proved to the Bregni's that he could bring them an important U.S. picture *(Benji);* shown that he could get a star to come to them (Sellers) and demonstrated his knack for marketing *(Grail.)* But the job he had been hired for, getting 'A-list' American films for PAC to distribute, was just as hard as ever.

At the same time, the more he learned about independent distributors in Europe the more convinced he became that they were more effective than the major studios. "The majors had a certain power in what they called the key cities, but the independents went all through the provinces as well. 'We know our chickens,' they would say. They got a movie to show everywhere, while the majors never bothered with the provinces, giving up about a third of their potential revenues."

Chapter 41. 1974. Rome

If only he could only get an important American film to PAC and the other independents, they would make a killing. He was sure of it.

Mark was reading the production charts in *Variety* when he came across *One Flew over the Cuckoo's Nest* that was shooting in Seattle. It was produced by Saul Zaentz and starred his old pal, Jack Nicholson.

By then, Nicholson had been nominated four times for an Oscar as Best Actor in a Leading Role (he would win for *Cuckoo's Nest* in 1976.) "To get a picture for PAC starring him would have been a big thing. But I thought, 'Hey, Jack was my buddy. Hell, Luana, Towne and I used to hang out with 'Jocko.' This will be a piece of cake.'"

Excited, he went to the Bregni's. "I think I can get this one for us," he declared, explaining his connection with Nicholson. The Bregni's promptly financed his trip to Seattle to buy the picture for Italy.

Mark had fun hanging out with Jack, who assured him he would put in a good word with the producers.

"As far as I'm concerned you should get this picture," he said.

Mark met with Saul Zaentz and explained what he had learned about independent distribution. He talked up the advantages of selling the movie to PAC.

"Just tell me what you want for Italy," he asked.

"$400,000," said Zaentz.

"Okay. I'll work that out after I get to Rome and PAC will make you an offer."

"If we can work it out, we will," Zaentz promised.

Mark flew back to Italy, certain that the deal was closed. When Piero and Mario agreed to pay $400,000 for the rights to distribute the movie in Italy Mark made the offer. Then he got a call from Zaentz's office: "We just sold Italy, France, Spain and Germany to United Artists."

Stunned, Mark got Saul on the phone.

"Why didn't you sell it to us?"

"Because I thought about it and doubted I'd ever see a dime from a small foreign distributor that I don't know. While if I sell the foreign rights to a major studio at least I'll see my money. Sorry."

Mark hung up in shock. "Here I was, a known Hollywood actor, an ex-roommate and a good friend of the film's star. And I still couldn't get this film for my bosses."

From Cowboy to Mogul to Monster

When he broke the news to the Bregni's they were disappointed but not devastated (until the film came out and they saw what a huge success it was.) Mark was the one who was devastated. He had failed and he hated failure. He had disappointed his bosses and that made him angry. He was determined to do something about it.

He arranged to meet with the foreign distributors from France, Germany and Spain, who had also lost out on *Cuckoo's Nest*. After he explained why they didn't get the movie, he proposed a solution: "If we want to get big Hollywood movies we'll have to be able to report to producers like the studios do."

"How do we do that?" they asked.

"First, we learn how to do it like the studios do. Then we have to do something more."

"What?"

"We have to organize ourselves into a buying force. Be part of one union that makes a bid for a movie. Maybe when we have all that together we can fight the studios to get big films with big stars."

To do that, Mark got hold of reports from some of the major studios. He pored over them, using his head for numbers and his MBA in business to understand what they did and how they did it. Then he began to teach what he had learned to other independent distributors.

For any American film they distributed, he explained, they would need to show the theatrical box office results broken down by city as well as breaking down all the promotional, advertising and print costs into various categories, including costs of dubbing and subtitling. They would have to show what the amount due to the producers would be after deducting their own distribution fees, marketing costs, and after they recouped the minimum guarantee they had advanced. They would have to report on a monthly basis for the first year and a quarterly basis after that. They would send box office reports to the producers on a weekly basis and analyze for the producers how the picture was performing and how it was faring against the competition. Plus, after three or four weeks in release, they would have to project for the producers what the final box office would be. And there was a lot more.

If they did all that, Mark was convinced that independent distributors would get big American movies. It was an enormous task but Mark was committed to making it happen. "What did I know? I was an actor. I didn't understand what the conventional wisdom was. Plus, after living and working overseas for fourteen years I had broadened myself tremendously.

Chapter 41. 1974. Rome

I would never have proposed what I did to Hollywood if I hadn't seen the rest of the world. And had I been with foreign sales from the beginning of my career, I never would have done that either. But I came in with new ideas because this was all new to me."

When he was sure that his network of independent distributors understood how to report properly he told them: "Next time we'll buy in force. We'll make an offer that represents six, seven, eight different countries and I'll assure Hollywood producers that we all know how to report like the studios." Thus he began to amalgamate independent distributors in Europe.

Along the way Mark was also encouraging the Bregni's to produce a big U.S. film and by the spring of 1976, PAC was finally on board. The timing was perfect. Maggie was pregnant and wanted to go home; Mark was eager to return to Hollywood as a financier and producer. He was sent by the Bregni's to scour the town for a project that had some financing and would appeal to an overseas audience.

After living overseas for years, Mark and Maggie rented a small house on Soper Drive with rooms for the Bregni's to stay in. "Then I contacted a highly reputable entertainment law firm in Hollywood (Kaplan, Livingston) and retained Leon Kaplan, one of the most respected names in Hollywood, as our lawyer." Mark knew that he and the Bregni's needed somebody on that level to give them credibility. Leon talked to his partner, Harold Berkowitz and learned that Harold had recently acquired a new client with money, a studio called Lorimar, headed by Merv Adelson. Apparently, they were looking for projects to produce or co-produce.

They sent Mark the script of the successful novel, "The Choirboys" by Joseph Wambaugh. It was a hard-edged, darkly comedic portrayal of LA cops who get into trouble from their debauchery on their time off, referred to jokingly as "Choir Practice." It was written by a distinguished writer; would be directed by Robert Aldrich (*Dirty Dozen*) and the cast would feature Hollywood stars. It was an 'A' movie that Mark thought had all the right pieces. He contacted the Bregni's to come to Hollywood immediately.

Mario came over to stay at the house on Soper Drive. He and Mark (with their lawyer) began to take part in negotiations with Lorimar. They hoped to structure a deal for PAC to co-finance and co-produce *The Choirboys* with Lorimar in exchange for PAC owning international rights. Piero Bregni came over briefly and met with Merv Adelson. They got along famously.

Adelson, who thought of himself as a supreme negotiator, went toe to toe with Mark in negotiations. Impressed, Piero complimented him on his negotiating techniques. Mark: "Actually, I was completely green about putting together a co-production deal and helped very much by our new law firm. But just the fact that an actor knew (or seemed to know) how to negotiate impressed the lawyers as well as the Bregni's." Piero blessed the deal and went back to Italy, leaving Mario to finish up the final negotiations. Mark: "And he focused on the smallest points and was exceedingly picky to the point of embarrassment. We were almost done when it was time for him to go back to Italy."

On July 9, 1976, Mark and a pregnant Maggie saw Mario off at the airport in LA. They had no idea that they would be the last people to see him before Mario was kidnapped in Rome. Or that they would become the Number One suspects in the case.

Chapter Forty-Two

July 11, 1976

Los Angeles, California

A 55 giorni dal sequestro
Bregni libero al prezzo di 250 milioni

IL PRODUTTORE MARIO BREGNI CON LA MOGLIE DOPO LA LIBERAZIONE

Mario Bregni's kidnapping lasted for 55 days and made all the Italian newspapers. Unbeknownst to them at the time, Mark and Maggie were the prime suspects.

Chapter 42. 1976. Los Angeles

In the early 1970's, Italy was marked by many kidnappings of wealthy businessmen and their families. The most notorious was the abduction of John Paul Getty III, grandson of oil billionaire J. Paul Getty. When Grandfather Getty refused to pay a dime of the $17 million ransom, an envelope arrived with a lock of hair and a human ear. Within days a deal was negotiated and young Getty was found alive. His kidnappers were never caught.

As soon as Mark got the call that Mario had been kidnapped, he and Maggie immediately flew to Rome. They were met by the police, who grilled them for several hours. When they left they were advised that they would be under twenty-four hour surveillance. Mark: "Even though the police said they had little reason to suspect us, nevertheless they had to be prudent."

"*Voi capite, no.*"

"Yes, we nodded. We understood. Later on we learned that the Italian police were not just being diligent; we were their number one suspects, having been the last to see Mario. Even though we were not in Italy when he was kidnapped, they believed we were somehow involved."

Maggie was badly shaken; Mark was furious. They were also terribly worried. When they went to see the Bregni's Mark found Piero was distraught. Despite his callous treatment of his brother he loved him to distraction. Mark: "I found him crying at his desk, saying over and over, 'I want my brother back, I want my brother back.'"

A desperate Piero begged Mark to get in touch with Merv Adelson. "Please call and ask him if he knows who took my brother."

"Why would he know?" Mark asked, mystified.

"Because everyone says he's involved with the Mafia."

"That's just a rumor, Piero."

"Maybe it is, maybe it's not. Maybe he can help get my brother back," Piero pleaded. "Please just call him, I beg of you."

So Mark called Adelson and explained that Mario had been kidnapped. Merv was horrified. "Is there anything I can do?"

"Well," Mark replied, mustering his courage, "word is you are with the Mafia…"

Merv chuckled. "Sorry, I'm not. But this is one time that I wish those rumors were true so I could help you."

Weeks passed without any word of Mario. Things went from bad to worse. Piero, who could think of nothing but his brother, ceased doing business. He was holed up in the office with the shades drawn and guns everywhere. Mark, who had worked like crazy to put the *Choirboys* deal together, was watching his hard work go up in smoke. Maggie, who was growing bigger with every week, was frightened to leave the apartment. The police kept a 24-hour tail on Mark and Maggie.

Then Mark received a note from the kidnappers in letters torn out of the newspaper, demanding that he play 'the bagman.'

It instructed him to bring the ransom money, about $1,500,000 and to wear white tennis shorts (a size too small), a white tennis shirt (a size too small) and tennis shoes with no socks. "Everything had to be white and tight so they could see that I had no gun on me. Why I was chosen, I don't know," he later mused. "Maybe they thought it was safer to go through an American than an Italian source."

Maggie was terrified but Mark was ready to do it until there was a leak to all the Rome newspapers. Headlines blared: "American Spaghetti Western Star Designated by Kidnappers to Deliver Ransom Money." When the kidnapers saw that they withdrew their demands that Mark be the courier.

Fifty-six days after Mario was kidnapped, the Bregni's lawyer went to make a handoff of the ransom money. The next day, the police found Mario drugged and tied up in the back seat of a car on a street not far from Mark and Maggie's apartment.

Mario was hospitalized for weeks, during which he told the police that his kidnappers spoke French. The police deduced they were the French Mafia from Marseilles. They were never caught.

Maggie and Mark made plans to return to the U.S. on October 4, 1976. But first they flew to Tonder, Denmark (the Las Vegas of Europe) to get married. (Like anyone who married in Italy, Mark had had to wait five years for his divorce from Barbara to be finalized.) By then, Maggie was five and a half months pregnant and showing. They were happy to be able to pull off the legal ceremony before their child was born.

They went back to the house on Soper Drive, where Mark was set to produce *The Choirboys*, starring Louis Gossett, Jr., Charles Durning and James Woods. But first, since PAC was putting up 60% of the budget in exchange for foreign rights, Mark had to sell the movie all over the world. Soon he was driving down to La Costa to make his first sales pitch to Sam Nanba and his new career followed from there.

Chapter 42. 1976. Los Angeles

On February 16, 1977, Jonathan Damon was born in Los Angeles. Using the Le Boyer method, Mark picked him up and placed him in a vat of water. "I remember watching his legs kick and thinking how quickly he took to water again. He was enormous. 10 pounds, 22 inches long and a face like a Cherokee Indian and I was very, very proud to be his father."

Despite his pride, Mark soon disappeared into the rigors of producing *The Choirboys*. "It felt good to be in my new position, working out of an office at Warner Bros. It also felt good to pass billboards in English instead of Italian." But after living in Italy for fourteen years he had an unexpected problem adjusting to the U.S. "I had spent so many years overseas that I was no longer as fluent in English. My word constructions would often come out very strange because I was translating in my head from Italian, Spanish, or German into English."

In May, Mark went to the Cannes Festival, where he introduced Joseph Wambaugh to the foreign buyers and sold *The Choirboys* worldwide. Then Mark, Maggie and three-month-old Jonathan went to Rome and closed up their apartment on Via Del Nuoto. "After that we went back to the U.S. and never took up foreign residence again."

PSO

1986

CHAPTER FORTY-THREE

January 25, 1986

Century City, California

Anytime you're sure you've made it, get ready to fall – Mark Damon.

Chapter 43. 1986. Century City

As 1986 began Mark and John were desperately trying to glue PSO Delphi together despite growing evidence that it was coming apart. It didn't help that *Clan* was released in January to terrible reviews: "*Clan of the Cave Bear* is a pretentious little opus that manages to meld the worst aspects of *Quest of Fire* seriousness with the Hot Babe aspect of Raquel Welch's *One Million Years B.C.*, seasoned with knee-jerk Hollywood feminism. Darryl Hannah plays Ayla, the Cro-Magnon woman who apparently invented pretty much every mental discipline and physical discovery known to Man. The director is Michael Chapman, making this the most horrifying shooting by a Chapman since John Lennon."

They were barely recovering from *Clan's* critical blast when *9 ½ Weeks* was released in February to great controversy. The smoldering tag lines that were meant to draw in audiences- "Desire. Infatuation. Obsession. They Broke Every Rule!" - caused them to stay away.

"*9 ½ Weeks* arrives in a shroud of mystery and scandal, already notorious as the most explicitly sexual big-budget film since *Last Tango in Paris*," wrote Roger Ebert. "Some of the most graphic sex scenes between two stars in a Hollywood picture," *Variety* penned. Mickey Rourke and Kim Basinger take you on an erotic odyssey to the limits of sexual obsession in a steamy story of a love affair that breaks every taboo," wrote another reviewer. "Emotionally charged soft porn, *9 ½ Weeks* includes sex scenes that haven't been touched on for years," *The Hollywood Reporter* reported.

You would think that so much brouhaha would lead to lines around the block. Not so. Years later, research would show that when people are confronted with something new and different they often hate it, only to change their minds later. "In 1983," Mark explained, "this was too new and Americans were too Puritanical to go into theatres to see *that* kind of movie. *And* they didn't like other people seeing them there."

"If you spell sex in marketing materials in the U.S. it doesn't sell," Peter Guber agreed. "American audiences aren't comfortable being seen in a mass-audience public place like a cinema complex, seeing something that is notorious because of its sex," said producer Bill Hornburg. "They're afraid they might run into their kids, or neighbors or co-workers."

As a result, in the U.S. the movie earned less than $5 million at the box office (although *9 ½ Weeks* became one of the most popular home videos.) Overseas, it became a success, partially due to Mark's dogged salesmanship: "When I showed it to my French distributor, Philippe Hellman of UGC, he said, 'What am I going to do with this? No one will want to see it.' Four and a half years later, the picture was still playing on the Champs Elysees." *9 ½ Weeks* became the longest playing picture in the history of Paris and went on to earn over $100 million in theatrical box office overseas.

In Europe, the film toppled the barriers of repressive sexuality, and set the standards for the new sexuality of the '80's. When Europeans began to say, 'I just went out and had a 9 ½ weeker' to describe an erotic, intense relationship, the phrase actually became part of the vernacular.

9 ½ Weeks paved the way for Adrian Lyne's future success with *Fatal Attraction* and *Unfaithful*. It made Kim Basinger into a worldwide icon, ushered in numerous roles for Mickey Rourke, and heralded a new career for Zalman King. But in the end, none of the principals were satisfied with the film.

"There are bits and pieces of the movie that work, but I never did get a true sense of the novel. It was a failure, really," Lyne lamented. Rourke: "The director wanted to make the film more commercial. I had no say in it... I signed up to do the script one way, and then I had to do it another way." Even Mark attested, "I was never that happy with *9 ½ Weeks*. I think we got moments of high eroticism but it could have been much better."

Today, twenty years after it scandalized America, *9 ½ Weeks* has become part of the zeitgeist. The kitchen sequence alone has been called 'the sexiest scene ever filmed in an American movie.' Today, you find references to the film in such venerable publications as REDBOOK Magazine, which advises readers to "try Mickey Rourke's game from that scene in *9 ½ Weeks* where he has a bath-robed Kim Basinger close her eyes and sit on the floor while he hand-feeds her a delectable smorgasbord."

Ironically, today, in an entirely different climate for sexually explicit movies, *9 ½ Weeks* is sometimes called 'dated.'

In 1986, 9 ½ Weeks was the second PSO movie to open to lukewarm box office. Blame began to be leveled at Mark, holding him responsible for high-budget movies that looked like box-office flops. While he was fighting battles on the production side the walls were crumbling on the banking side.

Lindsay Tulley ousted Mike Spiegler from Chemical Bank and pronounced, "We shouldn't be doing such risky lending." In a series of falling dominoes, Chemical reneged on the handshake agreement from

Spiegler and First National Bank of Boston pulled out of their agreement. When both banks reneged on the $140 million credit line it toppled the $25 million private placement.

"Suddenly, we were orphans," said John. "We had no friends anywhere. And we had invested $11 million in pictures that were not out yet."

"PSO wasn't the only company to expand in the 1980's based upon monies from bankers who had limited experience in the international market. There weren't many of them and it wasn't hard to spook those kinds of bankers," explained David Saunders. "They were not particularly loath to pull the plug and when they said they wanted out they didn't say it prospectively, giving a date a year in advance. They said, 'We're stopping. Right now.' Despite commitments that were made and films that were in production."

As the walls came tumbling down John and Mark tried some fast shuffles. Although PSO was about to put in the full $17 million budgets on *Short Circuit* and *Flight of the Navigator,* they quickly entered into co-productions with Tri-Star and Viking Films of Norway, respectively. Next came cleaning house. "After I found *The Lost Boys* and developed it with Dick Donner we had to turn it over to Warner Bros. to be financed by the studio."

All of those efforts proved to be temporary. By the end of February, despite John's desperate efforts, no bank would renegotiate on a new line of credit for PSO. Then John called Mark from New York with darker tidings.

"Lew suggested you step down and he take over as CEO."

Mark was stunned. "Why will that help?"

"All I can tell you is that Korman said the banks insist he becomes CEO in order for them to do business with PSO."

"Supposedly, I was the one leading the company into rough financial straits because I was a foreign sales man who knew nothing about production," Mark commented decades later.

At the time, he knew that he was the most likely target since the company was known as 'Mark Damon's PSO.' But being asked to step down as CEO of his own company was appalling. And being blamed for bringing the company to its knees seemed blatantly unfair.

"I'll have to think it over," he told John.

Mark paced in his office. "I don't know exactly what Korman said to the banks," he speculated decades later, "but I would later hear that he blamed me for all of PSO's financial problems. He may have said, 'Mark doesn't know how to control production costs and you'll be better off with me.' He probably said 'Damon is the reason that the company's going down - I'll take over as CEO in order to protect the banks.'"

He stopped pacing. "What is there to think about," he realized bitterly. PSO was simply not going to go forward unless they could get financing. And with him at the helm, apparently that wasn't going to happen. He had to make the sacrifice to save the company he'd built. He called John back.

"Korman can have the title of CEO. But I'm still Chairman of PSO."

He hung up, devastated. "I kept that title to maintain some dignity," he said years later. "Although the fact is, I didn't fool the industry. Sharp people know that once the CEO title is taken away from you 'Chairman' means nothing."

"For the next four months I had a title but no power. I was just hanging on. I was no longer the boss, no longer in charge. And I didn't know how to deal with that because I had been in charge my entire life." Mark also felt a growing distance between him and John.

They had always had adjoining offices with doors that were open to each other. Mark would often listen in on John's calls and vice versa. Now Mark found John's door closed when conversations went on between him, Lew and the banks.

But Mark continued to work on PSO's productions while Korman dealt with the banks "because that's what he had been doing all the time." It was a painful time. "Once I had a meeting and felt like I had to please Korman and John. I remember I was in a cold sweat about trying to pick up a couple of pictures. Most people didn't know that I wasn't controlling and guiding and leading PSO as always. And I didn't know how to deal with that. It was an awful, awful feeling."

Many PSOers knew that the company was having financial troubles and that Mark had stepped down to make way for new financing. But they still believed PSO would pull out of it. "It was always us against the big guys," said John. We were always the underdog." Kevin Koloff: "I knew stuff was going badly. After all, the lay-offs had happened, two rounds of them. But I was like a child of the family, and as the child, you want to hold on to your parents' marriage." Meanwhile, Mark's dogged work on PSO's movie slate kept the flame of hope alive.

Chapter 43. 1986. Century City

The first research screenings for *Short Circuit* doused that flame. There were late-night brainstorming meetings between the creative team and the execs until they recognized the problem was the voice of the robot. It was too deep and mature sounding. Mark: "When we figured out that the audience wasn't finding the robot charming we re-voiced it completely and gave him new dialogue to make him sound like he was a lot younger and more playful."

Mark was in Norway overseeing production on *Flight of the Navigator* when he got word that the next screenings for *Short Circuit* were excellent. With renewed energy he focused on *Flight,* the first film to utilize CGI (computer generated images) courtesy of Jeffrey Kleiser, Randal's brother and the film's digital effects supervisor.

Mark and Randal Kleiser got along very well, gamely trudging through the snow to get to the warehouse that was their soundstage. As Randal recalled, "PSO had secured some of the production funds with the promise of shooting in Norway. The spaceship that was built in Burbank had to be torn apart and flown to Oslo, then taken to a warehouse about an hour away and put together again. It was quite a schlep – the thing was three stories high and made of steel."

Miraculously, when the ordinary warehouse was turned into a soundstage, it worked. Spirits on the production remained high, even when the next problem proved harder to solve: the boy who played the lead (Joey Kramer) couldn't work on Saturdays due to SAG rules so they had to use a local boy who was about 25 and didn't speak English. "When we were shooting him we would say 'Lean right' and he would lean left," Kleiser recalled. "It was a disaster trying to talk to this Norwegian who didn't understand English. But we had no choice." Overall, the production, featuring Sarah Jessica Parker and Paul Reubens (better known as Pee Wee Herman) as the voice of the computer controlling the spaceship, was quite an adventure.

In New York, John was having his own adventure. Despite Korman's role as PSO's new CEO, John couldn't interest a single bank in investing in the company. Over the next month things slowly deteriorated until Korman and Allen & Co. decided to bail. When John learned that their vote was to have PSO Delphi close and quietly disappear he knew it was the final nail in the coffin. Without Delphi behind them, no bank would ever do business with PSO.

At the end of March, he flew to L.A. with a heavy heart. He met with Ken Ziffren, PSO's attorney, who reviewed all the facts and informed him there was no way to save the company. "Your only hope is to go through a bankruptcy," he asserted.

Bankruptcy. A ten-letter-word with the impact of a four-letter curse. A word that connoted shame and failure. In 1986, long before it became a common occurrence in Hollywood, the concept of bankruptcy sent shivers up the spine. Even the spine of a hard-nosed businessman like John Hyde. "It'll kill Mark and me," he feared. "Neither of us will ever be able to work again."

That afternoon, he called Mark in Norway and told him to come back right away. Then he stayed up all night, about to have the toughest meeting in his life.

Chapter Forty-four

April 1, 1986

Century City, California

Chapter 44. 1986. Century City

A HEAVY SILENCE FILLED THE ROOM.
"That's it. We have no choice but to declare bankruptcy," John had just said.

Mark was stunned.

"I couldn't quite comprehend it even though I heard what he said. This was so big and important I just couldn't grasp it."

He knew that no banks had stepped in to fund them. And that they were $11 million dollars in the hole. But hadn't he given up his title to Korman to save the company? And what had Korman done? He'd bailed. Mark's head was spinning but he forced himself to focus.

"Are you sure we can't pull out of it? The pictures we're making are bound to be successful," he pleaded. "*Short Circuit* looks to do $50 million at the box office and *Clan* will make its money because of the deal we did with Warner Bros. *Navigator* will be profitable because of that Norwegian tax shelter and the overseas reaction to *9 ½ Weeks* is sensational..." The more he pleaded PSO's case the more desperate he sounded, even to himself. But he couldn't stop. "If we could only buy ourselves more time, we could weather this...."

John shook his head unhappily. "It's too late."

He began to explain what he had learned from the bankruptcy specialist. That the first step was to pull Delphi out so that the only two shareholders left would be him and Mark. John paused. "But we can't do a bankruptcy if PSO has two shareholders. There needs to be only one person making all the decisions."

It sank in.

"So either you take all the shares of PSO. Or I do," John continued.

Mark's mind reeled. He knew that if he took the shares he would have to go through the bankruptcy.

"I'm willing to do it," he said, finally. "But you'll be much better at it than I could ever be."

"I don't know about that..."

"I do. It makes more sense for you to handle this."

And Mark knew it was true. But the idea of it was too awful to bear. He said nothing for a few moments. Then he did what he had to do. In a heartbeat, he gave up the company he had built from a dream.

"You take all the shares. Close down PSO. I only ask one thing." He paused. "Can you do it in a way to protect our clients, our buyers, our producers...?"

"I'll try my hardest."

The strain between them became palpable. It wasn't that John held Mark accountable for the fall of PSO. He knew how hard Mark had always worked for the company. But somewhere, there was a nagging doubt about the extent of the troubles on their troubled pictures. The eighteen months of multiple edits and re-edits of *9 ½ Weeks*. The disaster of Hal Ashby and *8 Million Ways to Die*. John knew that no one could really control these things. That it was the risk you took in making motion pictures. But he was only human and he wanted to blame the fall of PSO on something or someone.

Mark, on the other hand, had always left the financial side of PSO to John. Not that Mark didn't understand business and high finance. He was the one with the MBA in business, after all. But the financial end, the dealings with the banks had always been John's domain. And somewhere, in the back of his mind, there was a nagging doubt about the extent of John's loyalty to Lew Korman, not that Mark could comprehend John turning against him. He knew that John had worked ceaselessly to find funding for PSO. He knew that no one could control these things. He also knew that the banks were focused on making him the scapegoat.

But in the blinding pain he felt, he wanted to blame the fall of PSO on something or someone. He blamed it mostly on Korman, "who came in as 'the white knight,' accomplished nothing and bailed to save his own ass. *After* causing a rift between John and me."

Looking back decades later, neither man blames the other for the end of PSO. "I don't think what we had was personal rancor," said John. "I think it was because both of us were without an anchor. We were floating on very rough waters." "We were both under tremendous stress," agreed Mark. "Neither of us knew if there would be life after PSO."

From then on, they agreed that John would focus on closing down PSO and Mark would focus on finishing the pictures. A few days later, Delphi and Allen & Co.'s shares came back to the company and Mark quietly gave up his shares to John. A few days after that he moved out of his large office and into a smaller one down the hall. It was only a short walk but it felt like a mile. As Eddie Kalish recalled, "when the bad stuff started to happen, Mark got stuck in a little corner office. I would go in to see him and sit and talk. But they were sad times. Difficult times."

Meanwhile, rumors spread through the industry. There were stories in the trades about PSO being in dire financial straits because of Mark, "the founder and guiding spirit of the nine-year-old Hollywood-based foreign sales company, who has been stripped of two out of three titles in order to drastically reduce his authority."

As he was being blamed, comments from Mark were notably absent from the press. Lew Korman, on the other hand, was amply quoted: "Lewis J. Korman indicated that the reason to join forces with PSO wasn't there anymore. 'With PSO pulling out of production and going back to foreign sales,' he said, 'growth opportunities became limited and weren't yielding the kind of big upside for me and Allen & Co. to take a piece.'"

It was painfully clear. To Korman, this was hardnosed business. To Mark, it was a heartbreak. To John, it was the beginning of a long, hard road: "Our futures were wrapped up in the orderly closing of PSO. We had built the company as the equivalent of a studio overseas. Now, if we didn't close it down in a systematic way it would be a disaster."

In the shuffle to keep up appearances, Gregory Cascante became President and COO. "And Gregory turned," Mark recalled. "When I called him he'd come in when he felt like it. Maybe he resented the fact that we let PSO down. I think he also saw this as a chance to get rid of me and go to the top by himself. He had always been in my shadow when I was the head of the company." John agreed. "Gregory became a different person. Until then, Mark and I used to be able to hold him in check and bounce him between us."

In May, when Mark did not go to Cannes for the first time in twelve years, Cascante went in his place and took the opportunity to lash out at Mark to the press. "The new President of PSO, Gregory Cascante," wrote the trades, "met with reporters here on May 9 to make the point that rumors about PSO's recent foray into film production being a costly move for the company were true. Cascante said that 'significant overages' incurred in making several of its original productions -- *9 ½ Weeks, Clan of the Cave Bear, 8 Million Ways To Die* and *Short Circuit* -- precipitating withdrawal from the field entirely."

"There were no overages," Mark retorted decades later. "We didn't do anything wrong in terms of production. All of our pictures, with the exception of one, were profitable. And three even spouted sequels, something that doesn't happen if the original wasn't a hit: *Short Circuit, 9 ½ Weeks, The NeverEnding Story*. Three out of six. Not a bad ratio."

As PSO was closing, *Short Circuit* was opening to glowing reviews and terrific box office. Roger Ebert called it a thoroughly enjoyable fantasy flick: "There is a robot in *Short Circuit* that is really cute, if "cute" can apply to a robot. Its name is No. 5, and it moves and talks and even seems to think like something that is alive even though we can see, clear as day, that it's made of tubes and wires and photoelectric cells."

It was a great review. So were all the others. But not even the rise of *Short Circuit* would prevent the fall of PSO.

Chapter Forty-five

June 17, 1986

Beverly Hills, California

Chapter 45. 1986. Beverly Hills

At 5:30 AM, Mark woke to a song playing on the radio. It was "Who's Johnny," the theme song from *Short Circuit* sung by El DeBarge. He smashed the off button on his clock radio with frustration. "It was hard to get up in the mornings because I kept hearing that song. And every time I heard it I would die. The movie was a hit. The theme song was a hit. And there I was, wallowing in failure."

Short Circuit, *9 ½ Weeks*, *Clan of the Cave Bear* were all out and generating income. *Flight of the Navigator* would be coming out in July. Even the troubled *8 Million Ways to Die* was scheduled for an October release.

All the movies he had produced were finished but Mark no longer had control of any of them. The bank had taken them over. "It was like I had borne these children and just after their birth someone took them away from me." Despite everything he'd done to make PSO successful, his legs were being cut out from under him.

It was a terrible time. "Mark was completely preoccupied with trying to find a way to get through this," Maggie recalled. "But he didn't come to me in those days when it was really rough. Until one night I broke down."

"Mark, I need you," Maggie pleaded. "Why won't you talk to me?"

He turned to her and for the first time, she saw the rawness of his emotions.

"I don't know what to do," he said. "I can't help you, you can't help me. I don't know what to do any more."

"He started to cry," Maggie remembered, "out of so much frustration and anger and shame. I had never seen him like that before."

Meanwhile, much of PSO's business went on as usual and some PSOers still thought the company would survive. "To a large extent, we kept our problems our problems," John explained, "instead of making them the employees' problems. Their morale and well-being was very important to us." Julian Levin concurred: "I was not in the closed-door meetings and didn't know how much of a knock-down, drag-out fight it was." "John and Mark ran the show so we didn't have access to all the information we would have liked," said Michael Heuser. "All I know is that we scrambled at the end. We had all-nighters, day after day, preparing numbers, trying to keep this beautiful yacht afloat." The final blow came in July when *Flight of the Navigator* turned out to be a good movie but not a big movie. Certainly not big enough to pull them off the reef.

By August 1st, it was time to tell the PSOers it was over. Decades later, John recounted his final speech to the staff with much emotion: "Everyone was there. These were people who had been with PSO from the beginning. 'I can't pay most of you past Friday,' I said, tears coming down my face. 'But all of you should realize that with all of your talents, this isn't the end of the book; it's just the end of the chapter.'"

The stunned PSOers filed away quietly. "All of us bought into PSO," said one ex PSOer. "Knowing how fervently we felt about it ending, we could only imagine Mark and John."

On August 20, *The Los Angeles Times* reported the official end of PSO: "Creditors petitioned Friday to force Producers Sales Organization, a major overseas distributor of Hollywood films, into involuntary bankruptcy proceedings."

On Friday, August 22, a steamy hot morning, few people were out on the wide boulevards of Century City. Even fewer were up in PSO's offices on the fifteenth floor. Instead of the noisy camaraderie at the weekly staff meeting there was a deathly hush. Most PSOers had left for Vestron. The few that remained were packing up their offices. Meanwhile, Kate was downtown, signing the papers that officially put PSO into bankruptcy.

"I couldn't sign those papers," said John.

"Neither could I," Mark added.

They made Kate, the secretary of the corporation, go down and sign them. "After I did it," she recalled, "I couldn't come back to the office. I went straight to the ranch."

It was over. After all of the hoopla and hard work, the brilliance and the brainstorms. After the closeness of the PSO family, the carefully nurtured ties with Hollywood producers, the international circle of first-class distributors. After all of the adulation about "Mark Damon's PSO," when the smoke cleared, fingers were pointed at him.

He was blamed in the press for making bad choices: "It is a well-known fact that the company came unstuck in its move into production. Is the lesson to be learned that sales agents like Mark Damon should remain sales agents and not dabble as producers?"

He was censured for PSO taking on too much, too big, too soon: "It is clear that the level of production and size of PSO's projects placed too great a demand on the company's resources. PSO also plunged further into debt due to several costly box-office duds which included *Clan of the Cave Bear*. For all the monies expended, there was very little product that could catch public imagination."

He was called 'overly ambitious': "For Damon, as with other independents, ambitions overreached and cash flow couldn't afford the gambling time. If any principle seems to have emerged it is that small is safe, big is vulnerable."

"I know that Mark was blamed," Kate recalled decades later, "but I think there was enough blame to go around. And there were enough problems that nobody could have fixed. Things come apart," she reflected. "That's the way life seems to work."

The public auction, which took place in PSO's offices, came next. "I couldn't go," said John. "I went," said Mark, "because I wanted my furniture. As people tried to bid on it I said, 'It's useless because I will outbid you. No matter how much you offer, this is my furniture and I'm going to buy it.' People pulled back because they felt sorry for me."

After ten years of working with John, talking every day about every idea that came up, the men headed off into different directions. "When John and I pulled apart, that was the toughest thing. Because we totally played off each other."

Now Mark was alone, working out of the house. He was facing the loss of his reputation, his livelihood, the possibility that he would lose his home and not be able to support his family. Although some wondered why PSO didn't sue the banks for defaulting on the loans Mark and John were in no position to spend the money for lawyers to fight a legal battle that would have continued for years with no certain outcome.

It was a devastating time. "But the most devastating thing for me was that the end of PSO was the death of my dream," Mark said, years later.

CHAPTER FORTY-SIX

April 25, 1987

Hotel Bel Air

Bel Air, California

Chapter 46. 1987. Bel Air

In the Garden Room of the Hotel Bel Air, Mark watched Hollywood veteran Peter Guber speak to distributors from around the world. If you looked carefully you could see that beneath his smile, Mark's eyes were tired, his face etched with new lines, his hair graying at the temples.

He'd been out of work for eight months. Eight months of leaving the house with his attaché case and going to one meeting after another. Eight months of waking in the middle of the night in panic. Fears of poverty haunted him. His mother's mantra, "a man's character is in his bankbook," played over and over in his mind. To the former Alan Herskovitz from Chicago it was a grim reminder of his Depression-era childhood.

Maggie remembers waking up in the middle of the night and smelling cigarette smoke through the air conditioning filter. "I'd go down to the living room and see him thinking, working. Always worrying, trying to figure it out, to make something happen. It was horrible to see him so stressed."

"The PSO experience changed him a lot," said Eddie Kalish, "because it was his first real public failure. Mark was being characterized as the bad guy and the reason for the whole problem. Despite what really happened, the general impression was that PSO got in too deep in production and into financial difficulty because of the picture choices. Mark was the chooser of the pictures so Mark bore the brunt of the problem." "Mark had plenty of company," David Saunders asserted. "A lot of other independents were running into trouble, too." "The problem was, PSO was the first to go bankrupt," said John ruefully, decades later. "We were the first to do a lot of things."

Reading the trades only made things worse. "PSO STIGMA FOLLOWS U.S. INDIES TO MIFED," *Variety* declared in October, 1986, citing the "stigma of failure brought about by the sudden and unexpected belly-up of Producers Sales Organization." The front-page article quoted an irate member of the American Film Marketing Association: "the bankruptcy was handled with arrogance and total disregard for many relationships."

The post-mortems continued through February, 1987: "The fall of Damon's PSO appears to have made indie companies suspect in the eyes of their overseas customers," decried one of the trades. "More than any of the indies, PSO had been the shining light of the new concept. Mark Damon built an organization worldwide and it became, in the view of many, the model of a successful overseas independent sales and marketing organization. If it could fall, what's next?"

From Cowboy to Mogul to Monster

"Everything we do in our business is a gamble," mused Bobby Meyers. "Mark ran a really good business and it's a pity that PSO went under. But even the biggest guys closed. You get five, six-year cycles in this business and very few independents make it." "The movie business works in cycles," agreed Peter Guber. "There's a movie god and he sits on your shoulder for a number of years. And you'd better get as much done in that time as possible because just as surely, that movie god is going to move on and you're going to fail. So the trick is to make every problem an opportunity." Mark was trying to do just that.

John had moved the operation to a small office on Lankershim Blvd where he, Kate and a few PSOers toiled at the thankless job of closing down the company. "Obviously, we couldn't stay in Century City," said Kate. "It was way too much to pay when you are broke. In that little place, we babysat all the pictures and eventually got them turned back to the distributors and producers and collected what monies we still could." Every night, John went home exhausted.

Mark, on the other hand, couldn't sleep. "I would sit with Maggie until 12:00, 1:00, 2:00 AM drinking brandy and talking, talking, talking." That was when he found out that Maggie, too, had been desperate. Not from Mark's fall from grace but from his absence from her life. "I had always hung in," she later said, " but I had gotten so miserable that I finally thought, 'If this is all it is, I don't know.' I had even talked to Bob, Mark's brother, about it. 'Make a contract with him,' Bob had recommended. 'Have him clarify how much time he can spend with you and with the family. And if he can't do it, you may have to leave him.'"

"The bankruptcy allowed me to step back and talk to Maggie like I hadn't talked to her for years," Mark reflected decades later. "I didn't realize what she was going through when I had no time for her." He also didn't understand the toll that PSO had taken on his children.

"He was always preoccupied," said Jon Damon. "It was never like the work was done." "PSO was a very hard time," Alexis agreed. "I hardly ever saw my dad. He'd come home really late and there were many, many times when I wanted to see him and he wasn't there." As Bobby Meyers explained, "you give up a part of your family when you make that kind of commitment. If there was a birthday party or there was a sale in Tokyo, I went to Tokyo." Now, as he was forced home, Mark discovered what he had almost lost. "I learned that you can become so involved in what you're doing, so totally immersed in it, that you don't know what's going on around you."

Chapter 46. 1987. Bel Air

In time, an offer came from the affable Edward Sarlui and his partner, the enigmatic Moshe Diamant to join them in their company Trans World Entertainment, a company specializing in lower budget, direct to video genre films. "Sarlui thought I was the best salesman around and that this would be a good time to buy me cheap since I was out of work and probably desperate." Mark didn't accept. A short time later he got a call from Peter Guber.

"Jon (Peters) and I want to talk about doing something together."

"Great," Mark replied, immediately interested.

One evening, Guber and Peters came to the house on Benedict Canyon to discuss forming a sales company with him. Although Mark was exhilarated he wanted to make sure it would be a production company, too. "After PSO, I knew I wouldn't be happy just selling other people's films without producing our own." Peter warmed to the idea and said he would talk with his lawyers about a deal. Jon, on the other hand, kept stealing glances at the house, distracted. Mark: "Peter, with his great energy was a source of inspiration to me. Jon was hyper, driving, erratic, forceful, mean, charming at times, and completely irresponsible."

Negotiations for the new company went on for the next couple of months until finally, in March they signed an agreement to form Vision pdg (Peters, Damon, and Guber). Peter thought it would be chic to put the initials of their names in lower case. Mark had never seen this done before, but embraced it because if Peter thought it would make the company stand out, Mark would buy off on lower case. Also joining the company as a fourth partner was David Saunders, who had worked with Guber in business affairs at PolyGram Pictures.

Jon Peters was never around and Mark suspected that Peters' major reason for approaching him was to get his house. "He probably figured he could get it cheap since I was on the ropes. But I couldn't sell that house. Not that I could afford it either. But I felt that if I gave it up I would be throwing in the towel and that would have been devastating to me psychologically."

In April it was a happy occasion at the Bel Air Hotel when Peter and Mark announced the formation of Vision, Mark: "It was like a new lease on life to be in partnership with Peter Guber, one of the smartest and most admired guys in our business." The announcement was also very emotional for Mark. "There they were, some of the top distributors in the world, people I had worked with for years. And this was the first time after PSO's fall that I came out in public and talked about what had happened."

David Saunders was in the room that day: "The fact that the place was packed was a tribute to Mark's relationships. All of those people were his friends and they were delighted that he was back in business in a real way." That morning, *Variety* had proclaimed: *'Damon, like Phoenix, rises from the ashes.'* But as he faced his old friends Mark felt more like a Mourning Dove than a Phoenix. Despite his enthusiasm over this new company, there was a lump in his throat that wouldn't go away.

When it was his turn to speak he began by letting the distributors know that he was going on and would try to do much of what PSO did. "But I'm not trying to duplicate PSO," he added. "This company may be bigger and it may be better but it will never be the same. Because there can never be another PSO..." He started to choke up, stopped for a minute, finished his speech and warmed to the good will from his old friends. Then Mark set about creating Vision with Guber and Saunders.

It was not an easy arrangement. Peter had little time to devote to the company yet he controlled the purse strings. "Even though I was supposedly a partner," Mark recalled, "I felt like an employee, sharing a relatively small office in Guber-Peters' space on the Warner Bros. lot." They began by handling foreign sales on *Bat*21*, starring Gene Hackman. "It was not a bad film but certainly not on the level of the pictures that we had been handling during the last years of PSO. Even with a powerful partner like Peter Guber," Mark said, "I began to realize that the road back up would be long and treacherous."

After about a year, Guber became more and more nervous about running a company with a high monthly overhead and no way of knowing when the money would come in. Re-enter Edward Sarlui and Moshe Diamant, who came to Guber and said they would buy into Vision with Mark at the helm and take over the responsibility of the overhead, leaving Guber with a little piece of the company. Peter accepted the offer, taking a back seat in Vision as Sarlui and Diamant became the major shareholders.

Mark: "From then on I tried to put my heart into selling million-dollar cheap video pictures like *Shoot Fighter* and *Inner Sanctum, Shoot Fighter 2* and *Inner Sanctum 2, Almost Pregnant* and *Night Eyes 3* but it was a tough pill for me to swallow. I felt that I'd fallen so far."

Things began to change on the day Sarlui introduced Mark to his friend and fellow Dutchman, Frans Afman, head of entertainment banking for the venerable Credit Lyonnais, the world's leading lender to Hollywood. The tall, portly Dutchman was genteel, charming and intelligent. Through his years at the bank he had built up Credit Lyonnais's entertainment banking clientele to include Hemdale Films *(Platoon, Terminator)*; Carolco Pictures *(Rambo);* Gladden Entertainment *(The Fabulous Baker Boys)* and others. "Afman was the savior of the business for a while," said Mark. "He was the king. People would line up to get his blessing. One yes from him meant your picture was a 'go.'" On Oscar night 1987, the producers of *Platoon* even thanked Afman publicly for having the money in the Philippine jungle when they really needed it.

Frans and Mark liked each other immediately. "Mark is a sweet guy," said Afman years later, "and a brilliant businessman." "He knew my reputation," Mark recalled, "and figured, 'Damon can probably do it again.'"

When they talked about getting a line of credit for Vision to produce pictures it was a giant step on Mark's long road back.

Chapter Forty-Seven

May 7, 1987

Cannes, France

Mark and Maggie in high spirits with Japanese distributor
Harumasa Shirasu of Toho Towa, who would
distribute *High Spirits* (1988) in Japan.

With Zalman King and Jacopo Capanna in front of
Wild Orchid (1990) marquee in Rome

Chapter 47. 1987. Cannes

Not for the first time in his life, Mark stared at a telegram in disbelief. Unlike the one he'd received from Visconti decades earlier, this was bad news: REREAD *HIGH SPIRITS* SCRIPT. DECIDED NOT TO DO IT. SEAN CONNERY.

"We had been amazed and fortunate to get Sean Connery to star in writer-director Neil Jordan's *High Spirits*," recalled David Saunders, "after Jordan had just scored a hit with *Mona Lisa*. It was a coup for a new company like us." By the time casting was done, they had a great lineup: Connery, Liam Neeson (in his film debut), Darryl Hannah and Steve Guttenberg.

In order to finance the picture Mark had "sold the hell out of it at MIFED and the other festivals," he recalled, with his key selling point that Connery was the star. "Then I arrived in Cannes and was handed that telegram."

It was a disaster. "If you know anything about foreign distributors you know that once they've signed on for one actor and you try to change him, they'll have a problem. I don't care if you had 'Pinco Pallino' (Italian for 'an unknown no name') and now you're putting Tom Cruise in his place. They'll say, 'What?! You're replacing 'Pinco Pallino' with Tom Cruise? No, no, Cruise's last picture didn't do well or he's got dark hair' or whatever."

Within the same day, Peter O'Toole quickly signed on to replace Connery. But Mark knew he had a problem on his hands. He needed to sell the movie to Japan in a meeting the next day. "And if I didn't make that sale I wouldn't be able to do that picture or any of the other pictures I'd announced and the company would go into the toilet."

Mark canceled his other meetings, stayed in his suite at the Carlton and prepared for hours, reading and re-reading the script of *High Spirits*. He took a couple of scenes and memorized them. "I staged the whole thing, even decided where each of my old friends from Toho Towa were going to sit when I acted out the scenes."

From his years of selling to the Japanese Mark knew that this was a type of comedy they did not understand. "If you go to a theater in Tokyo you can see the most raucous American comedies and all you hear is, 'titter, titter, titter.' I knew that the Japanese didn't laugh at our comedies. But I also knew that they'll laugh if you're laughing, because they're very polite."

He carefully set the stage for his meeting. "I didn't even get up to usher in Harumasa Shirasu and 'Tomi' Tomioka. I had my assistant walk them in to find me sitting at my desk, reading the script and laughing. I got up and shook hands but I couldn't stop laughing. This was all carefully acted, of course."

"Why are you laughing so much?" they asked.

"Because I just reread this script and it's so funny. Listen to this scene."

"I took them through three or four scenes where I acted out all the roles of all the actors -- Peter O'Toole, Darryl Hannah, Beverly D'Angelo, Steve Guttenberg, Liam Neeson. I kept on laughing and by the end, I had them laughing too. I also convinced them that the picture would not do well with Sean Connery because people wanted to see him in action films as James Bond. And by God, I turned the whole thing around! By the time I was done they thought Sean Connery was a terrible idea and embraced Peter O'Toole.

Unfortunately, the picture was pretty much of a flop in Japan. But I made it up to them, selling them other movies that were hits."

Production of *High Spirits* did not go smoothly. "On the set Mark clashed constantly with the director," David Saunders recalled. "Neil Jordan was pretty sure that he knew exactly the right way to do things, which was not necessarily true in all cases. But the way Mark articulated his point of view created problems as opposed to solving them. He can be extremely blunt and oftentimes says just what he needs without softening it. Especially in the creative world, that often pisses people off."

Mark: "The problem was that Jordan has a very, very dry sense of humor and didn't really know how to direct comedy. He was heavy, slow and a thinker. He had to mull everything over, which made him absolutely the wrong person to do a comedy. Plus, he thought that burlesque high-jinks was the way to make the film funnier.

I felt that in comedies, shorter is better. So I was trying very hard to get him to pick up the pace. But Neil had just come off *Mona Lisa*, a big success, and felt he knew everything. While here was this 'Hollywood-producer-foreign-sales-person' who was trying to tell him how to do his movies. He was very unhappy with me."

To make matters worse, every evening, after arguing all day with Mark, Jordan would go off with his longtime British producers, Nik Powell and Steve Woolley, to a certain restaurant in London. Mark: "They would talk about the days' brewings and probably about his unhappiness

Chapter 47. 1987. Cannes

with me and how I was interfering with his work." But they always sat at the same table where, whenever he looked up, Jordan found Mark's eyes staring back at him!

For some reason, a poster of *Son of Cleopatra* was hanging on the wall directly opposite Jordan's table. Years later Mark laughed, remembering how the director said he could never escape him. "Finally, he bought the damn poster from them and gave it to me."

High Spirits was skewered by the critics. *The Washington Post:* "High Spirits" is one those things that go bump at the box office – especially if you have money in it… As ghastly as it is ghostly, this slow, low comedy stars O'Toole, a graduate of the Hormel school of acting, who gives a preposterous performance. The supporting actors look stunned, as if they had been smacked in the forehead with loose masonry from the parapets or seen something truly frightening. Maybe it was the rushes. Writer-director Neil Jordan shows no knack for comedy… but he does make good use of the wind machine. It must have been a dark and stormy night when this idea came to mind."

Nevertheless, Mark recalled, the film had great moments and two of his favorite lines. "One was spoken by Darryl Hannah, who, caught in a timeless loop, continues to be murdered by her husband and utters in frustration to Steve Guttenberg, "If he murders me one more time, I'll scream!" The audience roared at that one. The other line is when Steve Guttenberg bemoans to Darryl Hannah the impossibility of their relationship, "You're a ghost. I'm an American. It'll never work out."

Mark was at Cannes, 1989 when he and Zalman King came up with an idea for a new movie. "Based on the success of *9 ½ Weeks* we talked about doing another sexy picture with Mickey Rourke, much as I hated the idea of ever working with him again."

They searched for a title that would sound passionate and wild. Something exotic. They came up with the name of a flower that would fit - an orchid. "Let's call it *Wild Orchid*," they decided. In one night, King wrote up a three-page synopsis about an innocent young female lawyer who is sent to Brazil on her first assignment where she is shocked and intrigued by the erotic demands and sexual behavior of a mysterious millionaire.

From Cowboy to Mogul to Monster

The next day, Mark got hold of Mickey Rourke and got him to commit to playing Wheeler, the millionaire who seduces the young innocent. By the next morning, he'd had a poster drawn up with a copy line for the movie: "Wild Orchid – passion in full bloom." "And with that, the three page synopsis and Mickey Rourke, I sold the picture at Cannes. It had been spawned over a 48-hour period."

With those contracts in hand Mark got the money to finance the picture for Vision. "But Rourke had approval of the actors and he decided that the female lead should be a model named Carrie Otis, whom Mickey went out and bedded right after a screen test. She was pretty awful but gorgeous." They quickly cast solid actors Jacqueline Bisset and Bruce Greenwood in supporting roles. "But when we shot it in Brazil it turned into another disastrous shoot with Mickey Rourke."

Mark recalled that Mickey was "belligerent, drugged on set and a total narcissist. He insisted on doing scenes where he swam and swam in the ocean and had the cameraman shoot close-ups scanning his body from head to toe, panning off his muscular pecs onto his tight abdomen and long legs. They were all totally narcissistic and totally unusable in the film. But we had to pander to Mickey or he would walk off set."

During the shoot Rourke's behavior went from bad to worse. Mark: "Because we desperately needed some good photographic layouts, Zalman and his wife, Patricia asked their friend, the great photographer Annie Liebowitz to fly down to Rio to do a layout of Carré. Mickey was asked if it was okay (we had to pass everything about Carré by Mickey) and he said 'yeah, sure.'

But the day Annie Liebowitz appeared on the set, Mickey took one look at her and said, 'Get that fucking kike off the set or I close it down immediately.' He was screaming, 'I want her out of my sight!' So the entire cost of getting one of the greatest photographers in the world to Brazil had to be eaten by the production because Mickey suddenly decided he didn't like that 'Jew photographer.'"

Carré was completely under his thumb, both mesmerized and traumatized by Mickey. He was her Svengali and he hung around the set whenever she was shooting. Mark: "He was constantly giving her signs for what she should and should not do and totally destroyed the performance that Zalman was trying to get out of her." Bad as that was, Rourke's most egregious behavior occurred when they shot a love scene at the end of the film.

Chapter 47. 1987. Cannes

According to an article that later appeared in "Playboy": "as the clock ticked toward the main event, Mickey refused to come out of his trailer. All of a sudden, he didn't like his wardrobe, he detested the dialog, he hated the make-up. The producers called it 'Mickeyitis.' They had even budgeted for it. Shooting was scheduled for the following day. But half the day went by: no Mickey. Lights and camera were ready, the set dressed. The producers paced the halls; King sat in a corner rewriting something. Still no Mickey. And since Carré was always with Mickey, no Carré either.

At last, word arrived: Mickey had overslept, and so had Carré. Fifteen minutes later, dressed in identical terry cloth robes, the stars arrived. Only those crew members essential to the filming were allowed to stay on the set. The doors were locked, guards posted. Mickey and Carré took their places on the floor at the foot of the bed. A camera pointed down from the ceiling. Another was on the left, one on the right -- they were everywhere because who knew how many times King could actually get them to do this? The cameras ran out of film; the actors didn't seem to notice. The cameras were reloaded and rolled again; they still didn't seem to notice."

Mark: "At a certain point Mickey entered Carré and decided that for the sake of realism, they should really fuck. Carré was too overwhelmed by Mickey to object. So she let herself be made love to in full sight of the entire crew, and eventually worldwide audiences.

Even though we cut out the most explicit parts in the final print, word circulated that the two had actually made love. When shots of the love scene were smuggled by someone on our crew to "Playboy," for an obviously big payoff, the magazine made a 'lot of hay' out of our two leads 'doing it' on screen. It certainly didn't hurt the launch of the film. But what Mickey did to Carré was revolting."

The night before *Wild Orchid (Orchidea Selvaggia)* premiered in Rome at Christmas-time, they held a screening for Italy's top critics, directors and actors. The audience started to giggle about 2/3 of the way through the film. "Zalman had a tendency to write very stultified scenes and unfortunately, Mickey had a monologue which was pretty pretentious. By the end of the movie, people were roaring hysterically."

Mark was dying in his seat. On one side of him sat Zalman King, who was catatonic; on the other side was the Italian distributor Jacopo Capanna, an old friend to whom Mark had sold the movie.

"How are you?" Mark asked him.

"Fine. We'll be OK, we'll be OK," he answered, sweating bullets.

Surprisingly they were. The next day there were lines around the block as Italians flocked to the **Adriano** theatre in Rome for the premiere. Mark and Jacopo quizzed the movie goers when they came out from the theater. The biggest demographic was young Italian girls who thought the movie was so romantic, touching, and wonderful. Jacopo looked at Mark and said, "Tel'ho detto, tel'ho detto!" meaning "I told you so, I told you so!" But Mark knew Jacopo was as surprised as he was at the enthusiasm of the movie goers.

Orchidea Selvaggia went on to be a huge hit in Italy, and made a lot of money for Jacopo's company, Artisti Associati. To this day, Mark and Jacopo remain good friends. Wild Orchid became a big success in every country in the world, even spawning a popular line of lingerie and clothing shops throughout the world. When it opened in the U.S., however, critics excoriated Rourke.

Janet Maslin wrote in the *NY Times:* "Mickey Rourke does little besides casting smugly appreciative glances at Carré Otis's every move and in general behaving like a spider who has eaten too many flies. Early in his career, Mr. Rourke managed to do this sort of thing very seductively with a charming nonchalance. This time he seems puffy, sleazy and sadly ineffectual…"

Rourke's career would soon go into the toilet and his self-destructive behavior would continue for the next decade. By the time he decided to leave acting to become a boxer many others in Hollywood agreed with Mark: "There are very few people I detest in this world but Mickey Rourke certainly heads that list. Whenever other producers ask what it was like to work with him I am brutally honest. A person like Rourke doesn't deserve to have success in our business," he concluded, "no matter how talented an actor he may be."

PART THREE

2001 – 2006

No great thing is created suddenly, any more than a bunch of grapes or a fig. Let it first blossom, then bear fruit, then ripen.
- Euripides

If you have the three 'C's, you stay young: Cuore (heart), Cervello (brains) and Coglioni (balls).
- Dino De Laurentiis

Chapter Forty-eight

February 23, 2001
Loews Hotel on the Beach
Santa Monica, California

Chapter 48. 2001. Santa Monica

It's easy to see why the game of pachinko is beloved in Japan. The game face is a wild mandala of neon pink and green on a background of red and chrome yellow feathers. As you turn the knobs, steel balls are propelled into a maze of spinning wheels. If the balls trigger a jackpot, colored lights flash and music plays.

Most Japanese play the game at pachinko parlors. But one of the highest stakes pachinko games ever played was done by two elegant men in the penthouse suite of MDP Worldwide at the American Film Market 2001.

For eight days that February, the annual AFM was the epicenter for more than 300 motion picture companies and 7,000 film buyers and sellers from all over the world. They flooded the four story atrium-style lobby of the Loews Hotel, conversing in every language.

Upstairs, entire floors of small hotel rooms were set up as offices with open doors where single distributors sat at desks, eyeing passing buyers with hungry interest. Posters lined the hallways, offering lurid titles: *Parts of the Family*, 'the first intelligent film about cannibalism'; *Citizen Toxie: A Tale of Two Toxies!!* Eager buyers squeezed into elevators alongside oddities like a seven-foot condom or a purple-haired young woman in hot pants leading a costumed gorilla around on a chain. It was a zoo out there.

But if a buyer took the elevator to the penthouse, walked down a long hallway and opened the double doors of the Penthouse Suite of MDP he found himself in a different world. The skylit foyer, which held a six-foot tall light-box that beamed the company logo, opened into a spacious living room with white leather couches, million-dollar ocean views and lavish wraparound balconies.

Behind the reception desk sat Tamara Stuparich De La Barra, a lovely young Swede with an open smile who greeted distributors in seven different languages. At one end of the room platinum-blonde Tatyana Joffe, MDP's Russian-born Vice President of Administrative Affairs sat at the walnut conference table, painstakingly taking notes on the finer points of a UK sale-leaseback which MDP could use to help finance their films. At the other end, Eurasian Reiko Bradley, Executive Vice President of Distribution, and the only salesperson at the Market who spoke fluent Japanese, was deep in conversation with several Italian distributors. A cluster of German buyers watched an action packed trailer of *The Body* on a 60" plasma TV showing Antonio Banderas as a concerned young Jesuit Priest. A knot of French distributors huddled on a leather couch, going over contracts.

From Cowboy to Mogul to Monster

Down the hall from this international beehive of activity lay a private office where Mark sat behind a gilt desk, illuminated by the soft glow of a Chinese Tang horse lamp. A lazy bamboo ceiling fan re-circulated his constant cigarette smoke. Across the desk from him sat his old friend, Hiro Furukawa from Nippon Herald, the venerable Japanese distributors.

It was their third meeting to discuss *The I Inside,* a complicated thriller that Mark was selling.

"Let's see, what are we going to get for *The I Inside?*" said Mark.

Silence from Hiro.

"You know what we're asking, yes?"

"Yes."

"What would you offer?"

Hiro smiled. "Lucky 7."

Mark laughed.

"You know pachinko in Japan?" Hiro asked.

"Yes."

"Well, 7 is the lucky number in pachinko."

It was Mark's turn to smile. "But 777 is even luckier, right? That's a *big* hit."

"777 is very lucky, yes."

"Is that what you're offering me?" asked Mark, 'innocently.' "$777,000?"

"No," said Hiro. "I only offered you $700,000."

Mark, energized, grabbed a yellow pad and came out from behind the desk to sit next to Hiro. He wrote down a number and showed it to him.

"Actually, Hiro," he began, "I need $800,000 from Japan for *The I Inside* .Not $700,000. But 777 is three times luckier than $700,000 so look at it this way - I lose $23,000 but you gain a three times lucky hit film."

He stuck out his hand.

"You like to have 777, right?" said Hiro, his hand in his lap.

"Yes!" Mark declared with enthusiasm, his hand outstretched, a smile on his face.

"777. Don't you think it's too high?"

"No, it's lucky!"

After a moment, Hiro stuck out his own hand.

"Okay," he grinned.

They shook on it. And two of the most venerable men in the independent film business started grinning like schoolboys over a nickel bet on a frog.

460

Chapter 48. 2001. Santa Monica

Suddenly, the room flooded with three young, hotshot acquisitions executives from Nippon Herald. They questioned Hiro in rapid Japanese and looked worried when they heard what he'd agreed to. They knew he was a soft touch when it came to Mark's sales pitches and always tried to be present in their meetings to protect their boss from him.

"You came too late," Mark crowed, "the deal's done."

It was another moment of triumph for the business-man who remained an eternal optimist despite all of his ups and downs.

By 2001, the taint of PSO's bankruptcy had stayed with Mark for a long time. During the late 1980's, even as he produced movies with Vision, he felt the loss. But by the time the '80s gave way to the '90s PSO was in good company. Almost every other independent film company had also gone bankrupt: Mario Kassar and Andy Vajna, who formed Carolco, closed; Hemdale was ultimately forced by Credit Lyonnais to sell its library to pay off its loans; Golan and Globus shut down Cannon Film Group; even De Laurentiis was swept aside in the recession that wiped out the independent film business in the late '80s. By the early '90's there were virtually no independents left. Those that remained got snapped up by conglomerates.

"The biggest people in the independent business were the ones who fell the hardest," Mark attested, "including Frans Afman. He was forced to resign from the entertainment loan business he had built for Credit Lyonnais and was never able to come up to that level again. He always says that one day he'll write a book titled 'FAMOUS PEOPLE WHO USED TO KNOW ME.'"

By the early 1990's Vision was also running into problems with Credit Lyonnais after Afman had been replaced by his successor, Bastin, "who was just interested in parading around as Hollywood's new shining knight while forcing Vision and other companies to their knees."

David Saunders saw the handwriting on the wall and left to head up Triumph for Sony. Mark also left Vision in 1993 to form a new company. He called it MDP, "which was supposed to stand for 'Marketing Distribution Production'. But I didn't fool anybody. Everyone knew it meant 'Mark Damon Productions.' Starting with $10,000 of my own money, over the next five years (1993-1998) we built to a net worth of $12 million, while maneuvering the treacherous waters of the independent film business." MDP acquired films for foreign distribution and produced movies including the Pate brothers' *Deceiver*. .

Mark's acting career was briefly revived when the directors convinced him to play Tim Roth's father in the film, which only reinforced the wisdom of his decision to leave acting. Still, years later, when asked how it felt to see himself as an actor on-screen, Mark noted: "I feel that somehow I knew that young man and liked him. He had a purity and an enthusiasm that I still recognize in myself today."

Over time, MDP became 'Alliance', then 'Behaviour' when the company was bought out by a Canadian company and became a publicly traded company on the Toronto Stock exchange. "Then the Canadians breached the contract, never paid me my full purchase price or gave me the lines of credit they promised. My recourse was that I got the majority of the company back and in 1999, Behaviour became MDP. Again." Bobby Meyers remembered being at a cocktail party Mark threw at an AFM: "He stood up on a table and said, 'I want to welcome everybody to the third 'second-annual MDP party.' I thought that was really funny."

"The history of the independent film business involves the constant reinvention of individuals and the folding of one company and the creation of another, which turns out to be the same company with another name," Eddie Kalish explained. "Let's face it – PSO, Vision, MDP, Behaviour – they're all Mark. Maybe with different partners or alliances. But a rose by any other name..." "We're in the business of turning problems into opportunities," Peter Guber concurred "and Mark has done that quite well. He has a unique enthusiasm for life that seems to keep him forever young."

Despite his enthusiasm, Mark worried constantly. He worried about how the next picture was going to come out, whether he'd get the right director and actor, whether he'd get the money for it. He lost sleep over the problems he had with different distributors and different films. About who was not paying him, and why. "The picture business is constant anxiety," he admitted in 2001. "And the independent picture business has gotten more and more and more difficult. Today it's almost impossible. I continue to ask myself how much longer we can go on and just hope for one hit that carries us through for a year. And if we don't get that, what are we going to do? Do I have to wind up the business? It's constant anxiety."

"Still, Mark has always been able to turn around, regroup and find a new way," David Saunders added. "And that comes, I'd say, from a couple

Chapter 48. 2001. Santa Monica

of things. Probably the most important thing in the business is longevity and Mark has been doing it a long, long time." Many in Hollywood, like independent film exec Kathy Morgan believe Mark's longevity comes from acting with integrity. From not burning his suppliers or his distributors so that he continues to do business with contacts he forged thirty years ago.

Mark has his own theories. "When people ask me, 'What's the secret of your longevity?', I say it's making films that you think people want to see. Or films that I would want to see anyway, because at the end of the day, it's your own gut instinct that counts. Going with your gut, that's one of the most important parts of being in this business. You can listen to everybody. But at the end of the day, you have to do what YOU feel is right.

For example, one day my old young friend, Fran Kazui, brought me a script written and to be directed by two unknowns, Trey Parker and Matt Stone. It was called *Orgazmo*.

I loved the idea right away and I trusted the instincts and ultimate cool of Fran, a young Jewish director from Brooklyn who married a Japanese distributor, Kaz Kazui, and directed a film for Kaz called *Tokyo Pop* before going on to direct the feature of *Buffy the Vampire Slayer*. Fran's passion for *Orgazmo* won me over, and I said, "Good, let's produce it together."

"We can't sell a movie called *Orgazmo*!" exclaimed Rob Aft, MDP's first employee.

"We cannot do a dollar in presales on this,"

"I know you can't," Mark retorted. "I know that people are gonna look at you if you even say the name and think, 'what the hell are these guys up to?' That's why we'll wait until it's finished to sell it."

When it was done, *Orgazmo* was irreverent but hilarious. It was a little easier to sell and even got domestic distribution. "He took a chance of those guys but Mark really believed in it," said Rob, "and it turned out to have been the right decision. Creatively it was one of the riskier things he did but it was so well received that today it's a cult classic."

Regardless of the company name he went by, Mark continued to take chances on interesting young writers and directors. He followed his gut and hired talented first-timers whom everyone else in Hollywood turned down. Sometimes, it didn't pan out. Other times it paid off big-time. In a few years, one of Mark's biggest gambles - on a first-time writer-director and a difficult script - would garner its lead actress countless awards, including an Oscar.

At the end of the AFM 2001, as he did every evening, Mark drove home to Maggie, up the long, winding driveway to the house off Benedict Canyon. And he thought, as he had many times before, "I'm not positive I believe in destiny and soul-mates but if we're not soul-mates then we're what soul-mates should be. Despite how long we've been together, there is nobody I would rather spend time with than Maggie. She has boundless enthusiasm and despite the maturity and sophistication she has gained over the years, she continues to retain a delicious little-girl quality which I find so endearing."

"I love my husband," Maggie added. "I love what he does, I love when he loves me and when he has time to really focus on me. I love that I know him from other lifetimes and that it's not just this lifetime that we've loved each other. I am a greater person for having been with Mark. He helped me to grow up and learn to be in the world. He gave me the reins in the marriage to follow my heart's desire of a spiritual path. I think we give totally, 100% to each other, in our own way."

Mark parked in the brick driveway and walked past the Balinese garden with its giant bamboo plants, bird's-nest ferns and potted pink azaleas. He passed the large, wraparound deck shaded by colorful umbrellas and furnished with Indonesian teak. It was a place where he often entertained clients, having found that doing business in the serene atmosphere often yielded success. He glanced up at the traditional Japanese-style bamboo teahouse that framed the view of surrounding hillsides. Hand-built by master carpenters and flown in from Japan, the structure was composed of Japanese cedar and sesame bamboo with tatami-mat flooring. "In the evening, the sun lights up the deck and the tea-house and gives the whole area a magical, almost mystical aura, not gold so much as luminescent," Mark said. "It's as if I'm in my own magic, secret garden that lets me rise above the stress and put things into perspective."

He entered the two-story foyer with a life-sized statue of Quan Yin, the Buddhist goddess of mercy, on the landing of the stairs. The aroma of fresh basil and garlic beckoned him into the kitchen. Maggie was cooking Spaghetti alla Putanesca tonight. His favorite.

He went in and greeted her with a kiss. It was the perfect way to end the day.

CHAPTER FORTY-NINE

February 29, 2004

Kodak Theatre

Hollywood, California

©Newmarket Films; courtesy of Newmarket Films.

Matthew Photographic Services

With Raju Patel, Liz Taylor, and Michael Jackson at party in Mark's house celebrating the Jackson / Damon / Patel film-production partnership.

From Cowboy to Mogul to Monster

If you saw Mark Damon at the 76th Annual Academy Awards you probably wouldn't picture him in a ten gallon hat. If he flashed his dazzling smile at Maggie your first thought wouldn't be 'Ooh, vampire fangs.' And if you gazed at his handsome face it would be hard to guess that he was about to turn seventy-one.

As an actor he'd played rebels, heroes, a king and a fool in over fifty teenflicks, Spaghetti Westerns and swashbucklers. Over the past fifty years he'd been a singer, teen idol, writer, producer and astute businessman.

Tonight, Charlize Theron, star of his latest production, *Monster,* was up for an Oscar for Best Performance by an Actress in a Leading Role. But if you saw Mark Damon at the 2004 Academy Awards you must have been dreaming. Because he was sitting at home, watching it on TV with Maggie and the kids. After all his accomplishments he no longer needed to go to the Oscars to nab another bit of glory.

The last three years (2001-2004) had seen the usual ups and downs of Mark's career. There had been his party for international distributors at the 23rd AFM to kick off MDP's *Beyond the Sea*, the story of Bobby Darin. Held in a ballroom converted into the Copacabana nightclub circa 1960, Mark, ever the showman, greeted his guests from a small wooden stage: "Welcome to the first annual MDP Nightclub Luncheon, which is why I'm dressed like a nightclub singer. But don't worry, I'm not about to sing," he laughed.

Suddenly, music came up, the back doors opened and Bobby Darin burst into the room singing "Hidey Ho." He snapped his fingers and danced up a storm on his way to the wooden stage. Actually, it was Kevin Spacey playing Darin, as he would in the film *Beyond the Sea*, and doing a damn good job of it. Although Mark and MDP didn't end up doing the movie he would look back on the event with fond memories.

There was the brief but highly publicized production partnership with Michael Jackson's Neverland Entertainment, announced at a launch party for 300 foreign distributors at the house on Benedict Canyon. Maggie had transformed a tent over the pool into an Indian-themed Nirvana where everyone feasted on curries and papadams while they waited for Jackson to arrive.

One hour after he was due, Mark took the stage. For the next fifteen minutes, he killed time, lamenting that although Jackson was late he

Chapter 49. 2004. Hollywood

would be there soon. Most of the guests began to doubt that Jackson had ever intended to show up but they humored Mark, laughing at his jokes. Meanwhile, Jackson was sitting in Mark's office with Liz Taylor, who was showing Maggie her enormous diamond ring.

Enjoying himself immensely, Mark continued to build up the tension until he finally nodded to Maggie to bring them in. When his guests cheered at the sight of Jackson entering with Liz Taylor on his arm, Mark silently congratulated himself. He'd gotten all the mileage he could out of the pop star's appearance.

When the Neverland deal fell apart soon afterwards, Mark was neither surprised nor disappointed. The appearances of Jackson and Taylor at his lavish party were reward enough, he decided. After fifty years in the business he was intimately acquainted with its vicissitudes.

He took the changes in stride when, over the next few years, his company name morphed from MDP to Media 8 then to Foresight, Unlimited. He also took the constants in stride.

He still traveled six months of the year, running men half his age to the ground; he was still a workaholic, determined to produce, sell and distribute unique independent movies worldwide. He was still having fun, still committed to discovering promising young writer and directors. And he was always looking for the next hit.

🎥 🎬

On a cloudy Sunday afternoon, he finished reading a script by a first-time female writer/director about a female serial killer. It had been sent to him by the manager of the young writer, Brad Wyman and his producing partner, Donald Kushner. Mark: "I said this isn't bad. It's a challenging script but it's based on a true-life story, which means a film would be taken seriously if it was well done. Plus, it's a serial killer movie and they usually do well. *And* there's a good love story. I thought, 'if I can get two great looking actresses to make love in a serial killer film that's well-reviewed, that should make a couple million dollars.' Worst-case scenario, I figured, even if the film didn't come out well there would still be some DVD and video value in it." Mark was inclined to do it. And so, the third part of the title of this book was born.

And so the third part of our title was born. The script was called *Monster*.

From Cowboy to Mogul to Monster

When Mark met with the writer, twenty-nine-year old Patty Jenkins, a lively, dark-haired dynamo who was a graduate of the director's program at the American Film Institute they talked for three hours about her script and her relationship with Aileen Wuornos, the woman the FBI labeled America's first female serial killer.

He praised Patty's decision to focus on a year in the life of the prostitute who became a killer after being brutally raped and beaten by a 'john.' He agreed with Patty's move to portray Aileen's emotional conflict over her love for her girlfriend, which makes her determined to get control of her life even as her killing spree escalates.

"How do you know so much about this woman?" Mark asked Patty.

"I've been writing to Aileen ever since I saw Nick Broomfield's documentaries about her" Jenkins replied. "She fascinated me and I told her I wanted to do a movie on her."

Eventually, Wuornos, who had been on Death Row for twelve years and was scheduled for execution in a few months, had given Patty the rights to twelve years of her correspondence from Death Row with a childhood friend. "I started reading the letters and tried to immerse myself in her psyche. I read through trial transcripts, police records, watched her filmed interviews. I really wanted to get to know this woman that society called a 'monster.'"

Mark was deeply impressed by her conviction to the project. "Patty Jenkins is one of the most compelling, seductive human beings I've ever met. She had such compassion, caring and such knowledge of her material that by the time the meeting was done I said, 'I gotta go with this.'" First, though, he wanted to see one of her movies.

"But I don't think my shorts will convince him to let me do a serious dramatic movie," Patty told Brad Wyman.

"What else have you got?"

"Well, I have this video with shots of my dog hanging from a rope on a tree for an hour, whirling herself around..."

"Send that," Brad laughed. "Knowing Mark, he'll appreciate the joke."

Mark: "So this video starts with a dog hanging onto a rope from a tree. And I'm thinking, this has gotta go somewhere. For the next 58 minutes I watch that dog bouncing around. I had people coming in but I couldn't walk away. I was *sure* that something was going to happen. And it didn't!"

Chapter 49. 2004. Hollywood

He called Patty. "I thought the story structure was fine, but I felt the dog's performance was flat." Patty laughed hysterically.

"That sealed the deal for me," she said. It's really surprising to have a producer and financier get that joke. He could have been insulted. Instead he thought it was funny. That's the enjoyable balance of Mark - he's a really strong businessman but he has a great sense of humor."

If his reaction surprised Patty and her partners, so did his offer. By then, *Monster* had been shopped to other indie companies who offered to make it for a million dollars. Mark knew you couldn't make a serious dramatic movie for that money. He offered to put up $2.5 million in exchange for the rights. He knew it was a gamble. But he loved the project.

Over the next few months, Charlize Theron was cast as Aileen and Christina Ricci agreed to play Selby, her female lover. Mark worked with Patty on the script before production began. Their goal was to give audiences a glimpse into Wuornos' psyche in order to empathize but not sympathize with her.

Mark: "We knew it couldn't seem like we were supporting what she did." But it was a fine line to walk, one that led to many heated discussions between director and producer. "Mark had real passion for the story and the art of telling it," Patty later said. "We had many battles but neither of us ever crossed the line. If he said something and I challenged him back, he would surprise me by how flexible he was. Sometimes he would laugh and say, 'I guess you're right.' In retrospect, the best you can ask for is a producer like Mark, someone who is fighting for the good of the film and the artistic vision of it."

As a result of their meetings the script changed in significant ways. Patty: "I had written lines about Aileen and Selby talking about a ferris wheel. It was Mark's idea to have them actually be <u>on</u> the ferris wheel and that scene ended up being many peoples' favorite."

When production began in Florida, Mark was on the set for the first day. He was initially shocked by Charlize's transformation into Aileen. The statuesque beauty had gained 30 pounds, acquired a beer belly and jowls, shaved off her eyebrows and colored her hair until it looked like straw. She was fitted with two pairs of crooked, big teeth with which she had to learn to speak. Makeup artist Tony G applied layers of makeup to create her splotchy skin and put gelatin on her eyelids to make them sag. As one critic later put it, her face looked like it was rearranged by a blowtorch.

Patty assured him that Charlize's physical changes were necessary for her to be able to climb inside the skin of the serial murderess. "I was

471

committed to playing the ugliness, pain, desperation and humanity of the woman because I wanted to be able to live with myself afterwards," Charlize told the press.

Mark accepted that and returned to LA. Over the next month, he viewed dailies and talked with Patty frequently. She reassured him that Charlize's performance was incredible. He, in turn, had to reassure the people at Media 8 who were convinced that nobody would go to a movie to see Charlize Theron looking like that.

After viewing some dailies, however, Mark began to get worried. "It seemed to me that Charlize wasn't getting sufficiently inside the character. I knew that she would view videos of Aileen in her dressing room before going on set to shoot and I was concerned that at times she was imitating what she was seeing on the video. I began to worry that it was becoming almost too much of a caricature and that she wasn't capturing the essence of the woman."

He picked up the phone and called Charlize. If he had thought about it carefully he would have called Patty, told her his concerns and if she agreed with him, she might have found a way to talk to Charlize about it. Mark: "But I didn't think it through. I just called Charlize and got her at the worst possible time. She had just had a *great* all-night shoot and she was exhausted, emotionally drained. I mentioned my problem to her as gently as I could but she started crying and said, 'I can't take this anymore, I just can't take this.' And she hung up on me."

"Charlize ended up really angry with Mark," Patty confirmed. "Maybe because she wasn't in a place of more open communication. They clashed and both of them were left with a bad taste in their mouth." Mark quickly backed off. "I will just trust what's happening and go with it," he told Patty. "And from then on, he was completely supportive," she reflected. Although the conflict between him and Charlize continued to cast a shadow over their relationship Patty appreciated Mark's bluntness. "It's rare to find someone in the business with Mark's reputation and power who is still honest and upfront with you."

When the movie was shot, "Mark, unlike a lot of executives who just give notes, sat with us in the editing room and saw things and tried things," said Patty. Mark: "Every time we went a little too sympathetic towards Aileen we had to bring her back. Every time we became a little too objective and distant, we had to bring *us* back. It was a critical balance." Patty: "He made an enormous contribution to the film and I realized he is a bit of a closet artist. He's had to be about the money and the business

Chapter 49. 2004. Hollywood

but he's one of those producers who you can see gets genuinely frustrated with his own artistic interest in the project."

By the time he saw the final cut Mark felt they had done the best they could with the material although he had no idea how the film was going to do. In August, 2003, he started taking *Monster* to the studios in search of distribution.

"Charlize's performance is incredible," one studio said, "but the movie's too tough."

"Audiences will never want to see this," another studio pronounced.

"Give the picture some time," advised a third. "Go the Festival route, build a buzz about it and maybe we'll consider putting it out in a year."

"The picture has a buzz already," Mark countered. "People have heard about Charlize's performance and they're talking about it on the internet. It's not going to sustain that interest for a year. The picture has to go out now."

Every studio said no. They all told Mark he was crazy. It looked like *Monster* was another indie that would slip between the cracks with no distribution. Mark refused to give up. He was certain that the film had to go out in 2003 and convinced that he could convince somebody of his logic. "So the battle began with agents of our actors and our director, with lawyers and managers. Everyone was telling me it had to go out in 2004. I said, 'Charlize, they're wrong;' 'JJ, they're wrong;' 'Abby, they're wrong;' 'Fran, they're wrong.' 'We don't know what the competition's going to be in a year and by then the picture's gonna be old news.'"

Finally, Bob Berney, President of New Market Films, an independent distribution company, agreed with Mark. Berney, having marketed and distributed *The Passion of the Christ*, *My Big Fat Greek Wedding*, *Y Tu Mamá También* and *Memento*, was clearly the best man for the job. He took on *Monster* because he loved it, even though he knew it would be difficult to gear up in time to release it in 2003.

Soon *Monster* was slated to open in four theatres in December, the latest a movie could open and still qualify for the Academy Awards. Media 8 invested two and a half million dollars in an advertising campaign. "Although we knew that if the picture didn't open strong enough we would have lost the gamble," Mark recalled. The company wanted to put up even more money for marketing but they couldn't afford it. Then he learned that Blockbuster had heard about *Monster* and wanted it for their stores. "They said they would put up $9 million for prints and advertising

From Cowboy to Mogul to Monster

and cross-promote the picture in all their stores across the country. So I sold my soul to Blockbuster." He licensed all the domestic rights on the film, except theatrical, to them. "But what seemed a good deal for us at the time turned out to be a very bad deal in retrospect because the movie did extremely well, especially on DVD."

When *Monster* opened in four theatres in New York and L.A. at Christmastime, 2003 some critics lauded Theron's physical and emotional transformation into Aileen Wuornos: "Not since De Niro has any actor become so unrecognizable as Charlize Theron who goes low-life in a brave performance as serial killer Aileen Wuornos." Others dubbed Theron 'Beauty as the Beast" and found the film "unremittingly grim."

Not one critic thought *Monster* would make any money.

Then Roger Ebert and Richard Roeper reviewed *Monster* on their nationally syndicated television show: "I have nothing but praise for the breakthrough performance by Charlize Theron who portrays real-life serial killer Aileen Wuornos," said Roeper.

"Never once did I think I was seeing Theron acting," Ebert added. "She BECAME Wuornos and I was mesmerized by what was happening on that screen..."

"It is one of the best performances in the history of the cinema," Roeper agreed.

"If this movie doesn't win the Oscar then they might as well retire the award because this is the performance of the year," concluded Ebert.

The next day, calls started coming in to Media 8 from theatres that wanted the movie nationwide. In January, at the Sundance Festival Mark had the satisfaction of being congratulated by all the studios that turned him down. "Mark, you were right," they said, words that were music to his ears. He still loved to hear that he was right despite all of his success. Like everyone, inside of Mark Damon was the kid he'd been - dorky Alan Harris - with the same insecurities he had once had.

Over the next few months Charlize Theron won the Screen Actors Guild Award, the Silver Bear Award at the Berlin Film Festival and the Golden Globe Award for Best Actress in a Drama. She garnered a dozen more honors from the Broadcast Film Critics Association, the National Board of Review, the San Francisco Film Critics Circle, the CNN Radio Movie Awards, an IFP Spirit Award and others. *Monster* and Patty Jenkins also won an IFP Spirit Award for Best First Feature. On February 29, 2004 Charlize Theron won the Academy Award for Best Performance by an Actress in a Leading Role.

Chapter 49. 2004. Hollywood

Patty, Charlize and Mark had captured lightning in a bottle. "*Monster* was a movie that looked like such a bad idea," Patty mused two years later. "But some people, like Mark and Charlize, said 'Maybe it is, but for some reason I'm going to try.' We all took a chance on it against all odds. And we all got riches in return."

Monster catapulted Patty Jenkins into the spotlight. It gave new thrust to Charlize Theron's career and established her as a great cinematic actress. "It has been one of the biggest successes of my own career," Mark told the press. "And it's very nice that it happened in my 50th year in the business."

Epilogue

October, 2005

Hollywood, California

With Kevin Costner on the set of *The Upside of Anger* (2005).

EPILOGUE. 2005. Beverly Hills

"I'M GOING TO TELL YOU A little story..."

Wearing an impish grin, Mark strode across the stage to a large pad of paper on an easel as 100 film professionals watched carefully, having woken early to hear him speak at an 8:00 AM Women in Film breakfast.

"About 150,000 years ago," he began, "in India there was a Swami named Ram Titi. One day he was watching his students jostle for position, putting each other down to get ahead, each trying to be the top of the class. He said to them, 'Students, I have a math puzzle here.' And he drew a line..." Mark drew a long black line on the easel. "Then the Swami asked them, 'How can you make this line shorter?'" The audience pondered until Mark called on a woman.

"You erase it?"

"Ah, but how can you make the line shorter *without* erasing?" No answers. "It's simple..." He drew a longer line above the first. Everyone nodded, understanding.

"But how does this little puzzle apply to us in Hollywood? To this dog-eat-dog business where people often get ahead by climbing over the dead bodies of those that came before them?"

Mark leaned forward earnestly. "You don't make others smaller. You make yourself bigger. That's the secret. Instead of attempting to diminish each other, we made ourselves greater. And by making ourselves greater, we open ourselves up to a myriad of possibilities and ideas, a myriad of new ways of telling a story. For all the stories have already been told; it's the way you tell them that makes your film unique. See, I've been in this business for fifty years. And I've seen a lot of ups and plenty of downs. Plenty. Yet I still think Hollywood is a great town. A terrific town. Especially when people learn to embrace and support each other, the way so many of you do. And I honestly believe that if more people will make themselves greater, Hollywood will become even greater and I will be even prouder to be a part of it."

At the age of seventy-two, Mark looked youthful and vigorous. He was a frequent speaker at Hollywood events, explaining "the industry's been good to me and I like giving back." Despite the fact that independent movies were now highly lauded, gleaning Oscars and critical acclaim, they had also become more and more difficult to finance. Mark frequently found himself cheerleading young and anxious independent producers, to whom he was introduced as "the man who has defied gravity and one of the world's leading authorities on international distribution."

From Cowboy to Mogul to Monster

Decades after he first preached the concept of 'one world' to deaf ears in Hollywood, it had become an accepted reality. Many years after studio heads thought he was crazy when he insisted there was a fortune to be made in overseas money for American movies, a *Variety* headline recently proclaimed: "Mission Impossible III bowed to $48 million in the U.S. while earning $70 million overseas." Today, Mark was known as "the Man who sold Hollywood to Europe" or "the Man who sold Europe to Hollywood." His hard-fought arguments had long since become standard practice. His persistence had opened doors for countless others. As Mark put it, "that MBA I got before I became an actor really came in handy."

On his 50th anniversary in show business *The Hollywood Reporter* published a sumptuous spread on him, proclaiming that "the sum total of what Mark Damon has accomplished in his prolific five decades in show business is staggering..." "Damon is a master of reinvention," wrote *Variety*. "He's seen it all," agreed Cassian Elwes, head of William Morris Independent. "He's done everything. He is a Titan in the business." "When he speaks, everybody listens," attested Lewis Horwitz, who served on the Board of Directors of IFTA (the Independent Film and Television Alliance) with Mark. "He's a leader who has wonderful ideas and people want to carry them out. Plus," he added with a laugh, "the guy never tires of working. He's worse than I am. Always doing something, getting something done, always networking, with *everybody*. He's on the phone, calling somebody saying 'let's have lunch, dinner, breakfast, eat somewhere, he's always doing business."

"He works Saturdays, Sundays, mornings, noon and night," Maggie agreed. "He's addicted to work. It's a sincere addiction but after thirty-four years of marriage I've accepted it. After all, I'd rather have my husband addicted to work than to drink." She laughed as she recalled a recent phone call from a foreign salesman working for Mark, who is half his age. "The guy said, 'Help! Mark's running me to the ground. I can't keep up with him!'"

"Sometimes my wife talks about me retiring," Mark joked when he spoke to a recent audience, "but it's not gonna happen!" "He's the original Energizer Bunny," said Michael Heuser, who also used to work for Mark. Peter Guber claimed, "The guy is forever young." "My life just keeps getting better and better," Mark agreed.

On the lecture circuit, some young filmmakers, after hearing all the ups and downs throughout his long career, wondered where he found the inner strength to keep on going when things were down. When he was scared. When it didn't look like it was going to work out. Mark explained: "I think any time that something hits you that is overwhelming, you have to say, 'This is an opportunity.' And you have to find out how to turn it around to make it work to your advantage. There can't be anything that lays you so low that you can't find a way to deal with it. It can be as desperate a blow as you can take, but there'll be something in there, something you can use to turn it to your advantage. Honestly, I've come across a lot of failures... but the way I've saved myself is by saying, "I'm going to make this somehow work for me... I'm going to make this somehow work for me." Inevitably, his years of experience and disarming honesty reassured and affected young filmmakers in his audiences.

One young filmmaker, twenty-three year-old Greg Marcks, had written a dark comedy that juggled time from multiple and overlapping viewpoints. *11:14* told a seemingly random yet vitally connected story involving five characters in a set of incidents including murder and deceit that converge one evening at 11:14 PM. "This movie is more of a 'when-dunnit' than a 'who-dunnit'," Greg explained to Mark when they met in his company offices. To Greg's astonishment, Mark pored over the grid he'd made with the names of the five characters at the top and their varied stories and overlapping plot points beneath it in columns. The young filmmaker had no idea that it tweaked Mark's early fascinations with puzzles.

Greg: "I was sort-of shocked. You've got to remember - I was 23 years old at the time and probably looked 18. I already felt I was at a disadvantage just based on my appearance. But he just sat there during our meeting with my producers and his people, good poker face, said "Alright, well...." And he left. The next day, Mark called to say he had read the script and decided to put up all the money for the film. Just like that. He took a huge chance on me. He thought I was a sound investment although he had no real basis to make that decision on."

When the successful 70-something producer worked with the 23-year old writer-director on his first film, Greg's experience mirrored that of Patty Jenkins: "In any relationship you're going to have some butting of heads," he observed, "but the nice thing about Mark is that I never felt like it was a matter of *ego* for him. If he had an idea that he felt very strongly about he would argue strongly, I would counter argue and he would *listen*. That was the important thing. That he didn't just wait for me to shut up

From Cowboy to Mogul to Monster

and then say, 'this is the way we're going to do it.' That's not to say I didn't lose a lot of the arguments..."

Patti Jenkins concurred: "What I remember most about Mark is that his bark is worse than his bite in a really entertaining way. He kind-of carries himself as the power that be when you first meet him. But if you challenge him back in the same way, he'll just laugh and say "I guess you're right."

PSOers would have empathized with Greg Marcks when he recalled going with Mark to the Deauville Film Festival, where the film was nominated for the Grand Special Prize. Greg: "One night, Mark took me, my girlfriend and Maggie out to a French restaurant where, since he speaks the language, he ordered for everyone."

"I have the perfect delicacy for you," Mark told Greg. He ordered what he described as 'peasant sausage, the staple of the diet here. "You're gonna love it," he enthused.

Greg: "So we get this sausage thing and it looks terrible and smells worse."

"Go on, try it!" Mark urged.

Greg tasted it. It was *awful*. "Oh yeah, it's great!" he said, trying to be polite. His girlfriend took a bite and spit it out.

"Ugh, it's disgusting!"

Greg: "I was mortified. But Mark started cracking up. And I realized, 'Oh, he got me, he totally got me.'"

Hijinks aside, by the time *11:14* was finished Greg had experienced an intense collaboration with Mark. "He was very, very involved in editing. To the *frame*. And in the sound design. That was when I realized that Mark is not just a producer who wants to do the deal and then step away. He really is a filmmaker."

After its release *11:14* was lauded by critics as "a breakthrough feature debut by a brilliant young writer/director that gains a foothold in territory that is Tarantino." To date, the inventive film has developed a cult following worldwide.

When Mark read *The Upside of Anger,* a script written by Mike Binder, "I was touched and intrigued by the plight of a woman raising four daughters after her husband had just left her. She had to deal with her own pain and her anger, so she resorted to drink. Vodka. Grey Goose. The best. She felt sorry for herself, she was angry and in her anger, she ignored the pain of her daughters. But the script I read was so filled with humor and human touches that even though we, the audience, were angry with her we also empathized with her. Not necessarily sympathized, but empathized. Because all of us at one time or another have been there. I thought audiences might respond to this quirky, off-beat comedy-drama and the fact that we had Kevin Costner and Joan Allen committed to doing it."

Mark's gut instinct told him the film was going to work. But first he had to find a way to get it made. "In the old days, I could have told the buyers we had Kevin Costner, went to the markets, sold the shit out of the picture and had all the financing I needed to make it. But these aren't the old days anymore. And Kevin Costner, as great an actor as he had been, wasn't enough to pre-sell a picture."

So Mark went to Germany and got 20 percent of the budget; then to the UK and got about 15 percent there. That, combined with some bank gap, some loan money and a couple of presales made the picture workable." But along with this patchwork quilt of financing came one problem.

"We have to shoot the film in London," he told Mike Binder.

"What do you mean, London? This picture is set in the suburbs of Detroit."

"We have to shoot in London."

"But London doesn't look like the suburbs of Detroit!"

"Make the *suburbs* of London look like the suburbs of Detroit!"

"What are you trying to say?!"

"I'm saying, London or the film doesn't get made."

"London it is!" proclaimed Binder. And so London became Detroit and Binder provided insightful direction of his script. When it was released, Joan Allen's strong work in *Upside of Anger* was dubbed Oscar-worthy. Kevin Costner's performance was heralded "a whopper surprise from an actor who is back at the top of his game after years of coasting." The film was a success with audiences and critics who proclaimed it "a fiercely funny human comedy with jokes that sting and leave marks."

Once again, Mark had produced a hit movie. Once again, his role in bringing it to life was largely overlooked in Hollywood. "I've been an actor, writer, director, producer, foreign salesman and what do they call me? 'The great survivor!'" Mark laughed at the irony. "There is a perception of me being the best film salesman in the business but it tends to overshadow other aspects of my ability or talent. For instance, I think I'm a very good

From Cowboy to Mogul to Monster

producer. I really produced many films. I didn't just finance them and put together the package. I worked with writers, I sat in editing rooms. I worked hard on many pictures and some of that was my most satisfying work." It was so satisfying that it contributed to Mark's decision to change his role from financier to full-fledged producer at age 72.

"I believe it was Omar Khayyam who once said, 'the moving finger writes, and having written moves on.' That thought came forcefully back to me on my 50th Anniversary in the world of entertainment. It told me it was time to move on." So read the announcement for Foresight Unlimited, yet another new company for Mark, founded in 2005.

"Moving on means finding new challenges, new worlds to conquer, new ways of doing and thinking about things. But to me, more importantly, it means doing the things that I enjoy most. And while working on *Monster*, I was reminded that what I enjoy most is producing films. So I have put together a slate of feature films which I will be producing with overseas partners. New worlds to conquer, new films to make, new relationships to forge; a world of infinite possibilities and a new name.

When I was just starting out as an actor, the great Lew Wasserman told me, *"To survive in the film business, you must have unlimited foresight."* So, since I am often referred to as the "ultimate survivor", FORESIGHT UNLIMITED seemed like the perfect new name. More importantly, my wife, Maggie, did the numbers and from a numerology standpoint, she said the numbers were great, so that did it!"

Soon after Foresight Unlimited opened its doors, the company partnered with a Siberian coal mining tycoon to bankroll the first Russian-American co-production of a feature film. Mark took off for three months in Moscow where he produced *Captivity*, directed by Roland Joffe and shot at MosFilms studio. When he added *Oh, Jerusalem*, shot on location in Greece, to Foresight's production slate, Mark's 2005 travels took him to Germany, France, Italy, Russia, Greece, the UK and Canada. He was on the road for a good six months of the year, producing, selling, wheeling and dealing. Despite all that activity, Mark continued to make his family a priority: "The only thing of importance that came out of the demise of PSO was the resurrection of my relationship with Maggie. I was never able to bring another company to the level of PSO again. But I also never took my relationship with my family for granted again."

In 2007 Maggie and Mark celebrated their 34th anniversary, marking the date they 'married' each other on the plane to the U.S. In the same year, Mark flew 1000's of miles to deliver the keynote address at Alexis' college graduation and proudly saw Jon enroll in his alma mater, UCLA.

Today, Mark can accept the fact that he is on top again "because I will never again ignore how important Maggie and my kids are in my life." Today, happiness, which was never his goal, is closer than ever. Today, he looks at the business with new eyes: "I remember flying back from Europe and seeing the sky at sunset. It was beautiful. Purple hues everywhere. And suddenly I had this epiphany: 'Who says I have to do this forever? I could do anything else. I do not have to suffer this if I don't want to." Today, Mark continues to works 24/7. Not because he is haunted by fears of poverty but because he loves it. Because to Mark, "work," as Noel Coward quipped, "is more fun than fun."

When he was nine, Alan Harris promised himself that he would become someone important, the best at what he did. He spent most of his life aspiring to that goal and achieved it again and again. Then he went beyond the best. Beyond the mind to the heart. His is a never ending story.

Addendum 1: Buyers, Sellers, and Remembrances of Things Past

By: Mark Damon

Film buyers are illogical, emotional, stubborn, opinionated, unrealistic, rude, fabricators, slow payers, anger prone, and mean.

Film buyers say the exact same thing about film sellers.

Rarely have I gone through a film market where there hasn't been one nasty argument with a disillusioned buyer who didn't get the film he wanted at the price he wanted to pay. The cases are endless, but a few have stuck out in my mind over the years. And sometimes the buyer is right. Rarely!! But I do remember a few occasions.

One was with my favorite Russian buyer, Tigran Dokhalov. Tigran is a very savvy distributor, very knowledgeable, very well educated, whose command of the English language is probably even better than mine. Tigran's company is called West Video, and he had been our exclusive Russian distributor for years. Tigran was proud of his relationship with MDP, and later with Media 8. And in cases where one deals primarily with one distributor in a territory, the sales company and the distributor find that exclusivity often pays off, both in trust and in manageable business relationships. There's a give and take because you know that a buyer is going to be there when you need him and he knows that the seller will not try to take undue advantage of him. If that exclusive buyer gets hurt on one picture you try to make it up to him on another one. You want to keep him profitable and in business so he can continue to be "your guy" in that territory.

In sales companies, certain sales people handle certain territories. At MIFED one year, I had an aggressive new sales person, who had been assigned Russia. Frankly, because Russia was a small market at that time, at least in terms of the minimum guarantees they would put up, I did not pay close attention to this situation. As we did our sales tally at the end of the market, I noticed that we didn't close our pictures with Tigran. Another buyer, who we had never done business with, had offered $20,000 more on title and she closed with the other buyer. Tigran was shocked that I would allow such a thing to have happened, and he was more than angry, he was deeply hurt. I only found this out at a subsequent market when his Los Angeles based representative, Gloria Feldman, told me that we had lost Tigran forever because of how shabbily he felt he had been treated and especially because there had been no recognition of his loyalty over the years. I asked Gloria if she would set up a meeting with Tigran, which she did. I apologized to him and told him it would never happen again, and told him that from this point onward, only I would deal with him. And since then, he has taken every picture of ours and Tigran and his wife Asnif, have become close personal friends as well as business associates.

It doesn't always work out this way. Some distributors are just hard pressed to forgive. And what's amazing, though probably normal, is how buyers and sellers have completely different takes on what happened during a negotiation, especially if it was an unsuccessful one. Their individual recollections of the facts are almost "Rashomon-esque". A perfect case in point was with Nigel Green of Entertainment Film Distributors in the UK, perhaps the most important independent distributor in all of Europe. Way early in the business, I used to deal with his father, Michael Green, when Nigel and his brother, Trevor, were just pups in the business. I got along very well with Michael and took an immediate liking to Nigel. Nigel was extremely bright, sardonic with a very sharp wit, and a very droll sense of humor. What I particularly loved about Nigel was how he could be sold by a salesman. Not only could be, but *wanted* to be. If a film salesman, during his pitch, could show Nigel a way to market the film, or give him an insight into the film's commercial possibilities, that would often turn him from negative, or neutral, to very positive. Nigel was an adept negotiator, and I've always enjoyed thoroughly our business tussles. At any rate, I dealt with Nigel and Trevor exclusively for a number of years.

Then came that fatal incident in Cannes of 1992. I came to the market selling *Rudyard Kipling's The Jungle Book*, in which I was partnered with young Raju Patel, who had developed the script. We made a deal for the

US distribution of the film with Disney just before arriving in Cannes, and the Disney people told me that they wanted to acquire a number of foreign territories as well. As *The Jungle Book* was a very hot project, I wanted to give it to as many of our distributors as possible before having to close a deal with Disney for the balance of the foreign territories. Talk about "a man with a mission". I was frantic to favor as many of our distributors as possible before Disney snapped up all the open territories. I met with Nigel, quoted him my price for the United Kingdom, and he told me that he was interested, but he didn't make an offer. I hounded him and haunted him telling him that Disney would take the territory if he didn't make an offer. He'd heard these kinds of threats many times from salesman, and he didn't budge. I told him it was not a tactic and begged him to give me an answer. He wouldn't. Then towards the end of the market, I was forced to sit down with the Disney people and they insisted on taking the UK as well as a number of other territories, *and* they insisted on closing right there at the market.

When Nigel found out sometime later that *The Jungle Book* had gone to Disney, he was unforgiving. For many years afterwards, he would not talk to me, nor visit our office at the markets. I had lost one of our best distributors, and a good friend. And the worst part of it was, it was his FAULT! Yet, Nigel would never talk about it. He simply shunned me like the plague.

I called Nigel early one morning in August of 2003, and told him that Kevin Spacey wanted to make the Bobby Darin story, and wanted to sing for Nigel. Could I set this up? Nigel was very gracious and agreed to see me and Kevin. Kevin did a performance of Bobby Darin songs in Nigel's office that would have knocked your socks off. Nigel was blown away and agreed to acquire the British rights for the film. I finally had broken down the barriers with EFD, thanks to Kevin's performance. Even though *Beyond the Sea* went on to be a commercial disaster, at least it had helped to reestablish relations with Britain's most important distribution house.

In January of 2008, Nigel and I, once again on friendly terms, closed a deal for *Beyond A Reasonable Doubt*, starring Michael Douglas, and being produced by myself and Moshe Diamant. While we were chatting, the unmentionable *Jungle Book* incident came up. Nigel was quite surprised to hear my version of the story. He shrugged his shoulders and said, "But Mark, that is not what happened. I told you I didn't want to close the deal until I knew who the director of the film was." I had absolutely no recollection of this as a condition, and Nigel had no recollection of my version of the story. And, the fact is, we will never know what the *real* version was. It's all in the mind of the beholder.

There's one more distributor who, to this day, has still not forgiven, Sammy Hadida. Sammy, who heads up Metropolitan Film Export in France, is one of the best distributors in the world. Sammy is very dynamic, very likeable, a very smart producer, a superb distributor, erudite, intelligent, very, very charismatic, a tough negotiator, and totally unforgiving.

Sammy, his brother Victor, and I had done many deals together, until that fatal MIFED of the year 2000. We were selling *The Musketeer*, directed by Peter Hyams, again produced by old friend Moshe Diamant. Sammy wanted the film badly as he had a hole in his summer release schedule for 2001. But I didn't know how badly he wanted the film until our negotiations had broken down.

As in so many cases, I was not the final arbiter, but the lending bank was. The agreement with our lender, a Cologne based bank new to the film business, was that every deal for a major territory would be passed by them for approval. I told this to Sammy, but he didn't believe me. He made a low ball offer with very difficult distribution terms, and impossibly long payment terms. I shook my head in dismay and tried to negotiate better terms. Sammy was unmovable. I finally asked, "Is any of this negotiable?" Sammy said, "Those are my terms, and I will not move from them." "Are you sure?" I asked. "Absolutely" he said.

My next meeting was with SND, another top French distributor, headed by the affable and quite brilliant, Thierry DesMichelle. His offer was very precise. He offered a higher minimum guarantee, very acceptable distribution terms, and quick payment terms. I then called the bank and went through both offers with them. It was not even close, the conclusion was obvious. The SND offer was accepted. I told Thierry, and he was very happy.

Sammy's Los Angeles representative, again Gloria Feldman, visited me the next morning and asked me about Musketeer. I told her that I had sold the film to SND. Gloria quickly reported this to Sammy and 10 minutes later I had a fuming Mr. Hadida barge into my office, furious. He asked me how I could have sold it without coming back to him. I told him exactly what happened and reminded him that he had stated his terms were not negotiable and that it was his final offer. That I had reported it all to the bank, and they made the decision very easily. Sammy looked at me incredulously, and said, "I will match all of SND's terms."

I answered, "Too late, it's done." Sammy started to swear at me, and I quickly jabbed back. "Why did you tell me that there was no negotiation in your offer, if you were actually prepared to negotiate? If you wanted the film so badly, why were you so tough and absolutely unmoving?" "You have to give me the film!" yelled Sammy. "I'm sorry Sammy, the deal is done." He stormed out of the office, and has never dealt with me since. When we see each other, he's pleasantly charming, but he will not do business with me. He even told someone, who tried to intervene and bring us together again, to just "stay out of it".

It's unlikely we'll ever do business again, but I really wonder what his side of the story is. I'm sure his recollection is so different from mine. I will probably never know, but I bring these stories up to demonstrate there is no true black and white in these situations. And even though memories blur, and the colors mute over the years, you can be sure that there is never going be a *true* version to any of these incidents that both parties would later recognize.

I guess that's what quantum physics is all about. There is never one reality. We all see things differently and can never know exactly how another person views things. And if one creates his own reality, he can control his own destiny, but these are ramblings for another book at another time. It doesn't change the fact that all film buyers are illogical, stubborn, opinionated, etc., etc., but I do love them. And to this day, I still get excited by a great sale of a great film to a great distributor.

Addendum 2: Damon's Epilogue to his Epilogue

By: Mark Damon

My biography deals mostly with my life through the end of PSO, and touches briefly on some of the highlights in the 20 some odd years that followed PSO. Those years have gone by so quickly, and so much of it has become a blur, you can almost call it "Daze in the Life of Mark Damon". But there have been too many important people in my life since PSO who deserve being singled out, not to be lost in the daze and the blur.

I spoke briefly about Vision pdg, which then became Vision international. And while Vision had its problems with Credit Lyonnais, and was relatively short lived, there still were noteworthy accomplishments and noteworthy relationships were spawned. Unfortunately, my relationship with Edward Sarlui withered, but I have remained a close friend and production partner with Moshe Diamant, one of the smartest guys in the business, and one of the most able producers I've worked with. As of this writing, we are co-producing a film together called *Beyond A Reasonable Doubt*, directed by Peter Hyams, starring Michael Douglas. Moshe, his beautiful wife Ilana and his wonderful children, Limor, Sigal, Sagiv, Michael, and Elli, remain very close friends to this day.

And during the Vision times, I learned about US domestic distribution when Vision set up its own distribution theatrically through Triumph (a division of Sony) which was headed up by my former partner at Vision, David Saunders. Overseeing theatrical marketing and booking of the theaters was Elliott Slutsky, a charmer full of passion for distribution, who has now entered the ranks of Miramax, as one of its heads of theatrical booking. Also Jeff Fink oversaw our video, and David Garber, still a good friend through the years, was in charge of all television and ancillary markets. It was a brief but exciting period, in which the most successful of our US releases was *Wild Orchid*, which, as I had mentioned earlier, even spawned a chain of successful lingerie stores in Europe, and especially in Russia, where this chain is aptly called Wild Orchid. I guess it's the Russian version of Victoria's Secrets.

Another of the Vision/Triumph releases was the Dolph Lundgren starrer *I Come In Peace*, which was not memorable except for the last line of the movie (which I penned). As Dolph Lundgren, a robot, staggers forward he repeats, plaintively, to the good guy, "I come in peace," at which point the good guy aims his double barrel shot gun at Dolph, blows him away, and then adds, "and you go in pieces." A big laugh in the theater greeted Dolph's body parts floating all over the landscape.

Vision later morphed into MDP Worldwide. Although I continued to protest that MDP was short for Marketing, Distribution, and Production, the know-it-alls of the business were sure it stood for Mark Damon Productions (while Maggie thought it stood for Maggie Damon Productions!). I didn't seriously protest that allegation.

While PSO spawned a number of top level players in the business, Vision and MDP certainly contributed their share. Some of the best entertainment attorneys in the business, started at MDP. Two of today's top female entertainment lawyers, Jenna Sanz-Agero, (formerly Piccolo) and Caroline Blackwood (a top executive at New Line) started at MDP under the tutelage of Steve Monas, who now heads up the very successful Business Affairs legal firm. Ortwin Freyermuth and Kevin Koloff, who both started at PSO, came back to MDP and restarted their independent legal careers under my urging. Kevin had been a music attorney at Paramount for many years before coming back to MDP, and then later going off to head his own music entertainment law firm. Ortwin became one of the top European tax shelter attorneys. Though headquartered in California, he spends most of his time traveling in Europe. When I catch him in LA, we work out together, talking incessantly about diets and women.

MDP also hosted some of the top foreign sales people in the business. Among them are Mark Horowitz, Rob Aft, Reiko Bradley, Tamara Stuparich De La Barra, Eric Christensen, and Brian O'Shea. I'm happy to say that both Tamara and Reiko are still working with me at Foresight.

The one notion that I have based my entire outlook on is to avoid the conventional, and to avoid "conventional wisdom". True wisdom is anything but conventional. I guess in today's lingo, it would be considered "thinking outside the box". I remember very distinctly the first time I had put that into practice. It was one night in Rome with my good friend Avv. Gianni Massaro, the dean of Italian entertainment lawyers, and a true "outside the box" thinker. We were concluding a deal with RAI television for a package of films and we were trying to overcome a glitch in the deal. At about 3 in the morning, as we were puzzling over our strategies, Gianni said to me, "Enough. We are hemming ourselves in by the parameters that this negotiation has been setting. Let's forget them, and start all over by setting new parameters, parameters that work for us instead of restrict us. I think the words he used were "pensare fuori la materia", which would roughly translate to "think outside the box". And with a brand new approach, we went into RAI the next morning and got every point we wanted. It had been the biggest picture package RAI had ever done to that date, and it was accomplished only because we overcame our mental shackles. I remained close friends with Avvocato Massaro (avvocato means lawyer in Italian) throughout the years, and will always remember fondly the night we broke through with our thinking.

Through the years I continue to be drawn to people who constantly avoid thinking conventionally. Among them, Datty Ruth, the venerable godfather of the home video business in Germany, Tim Levy, a British financial wizard with whom I've done many tax shelter deals and whose inventiveness constantly amazes me, my old friend Werner Koenig, the wizard behind Helkon in Germany, whose brilliant career was cut short by a tragic skiing accident, Mike Mendelsohn, and Lew Horwitz, pioneers in independent banking and film financing, who helped shape independent film financing as we know it today, Robert Lantos, as innovative corporately as he is creatively, Aurelio de Laurentiis, the Italian producer/distributor, who just recently acquired the Naples soccer team after making more money than he knew what to do with in the film business, and Courtney Solomon, the 35 year old producer/director/screenwriter/film distributor, who continues to find ways to outdo himself. Then Leonid Minkovski and Serge Konov, two Russian producers who were determined to bring Western style production and important major studio level films to shoot in Russia. Together we made the first Russian American co-production. I came to know and admire their creativity, and I'm sure we'll be working together again. And the list goes on and on.

As a matter of fact, almost all of the distributors I've worked with through the years fall into this category of innovative thinkers. You cannot be among the top distributors in the world without invention, creativity, and workaholic passion. Film distribution is continuing to find new ways of attracting audiences to view films and you only succeed with continuous fresh invention. So I salute these free thinkers, and good friends of mine whom I've stayed close with throughout these many years. I know I've mentioned a number of them previously in the book, but if I've failed to mention them earlier, I want to be certain to include the Three Amigos from TRIPICS in Spain, Jose Hueva, Luis and Felipe Ortiz. They forever work hard, play hard, and laugh even harder. No matter how bad things may go when a picture doesn't work, these guys will always find something to laugh about. What a joy they've been to be with. Then there's Fulvio and Federica Lucisano, heads of Italian International Film. My relationship with Fulvio goes all the way back to the days when he distributed *The Fall of the House of Usher* in Italy. Fulvio, one of the true gentlemen of the business, has been a friend now for almost 50 years, and Federica, his daughter, is now carrying on the business just as avidly and with just as much grace and charm. Pierre Kalfon, who must have distributed about 20 of our films in France, ever handsome, ever debonair, and ever a good friend of Maggie's and myself. I mentioned Kaz and Fran Kuzui previously with whom I produced *Orgazmo*. Their Kuzui Enterprises was the gem of independent Japanese distribution. What an energizing and unique relationship is theirs. When Kaz first met Fran, an oh-so-bright, oh-so-cute, aspiring Jewish film director from the Bronx, he could speak almost no English. The two of them fell madly in love and today spend their time between Tokyo, India, Los Angeles, and everywhere else in the world.

The list goes on and on: Horacio Altamirano, the dean of Latin American cinema and a gentleman in every sense, Frank Agrama, the head of Harmony Gold and still vital in his 80s. My friendship goes back to the time he tried to hire me as an actor for the first film he wanted to direct. Thankfully for both of us, that never happened, but we still remain close to this day. Al Munteanu, the head of the distribution company SquareOne in Germany, who was a radio talk show host and comedian in his early days, the late Alex Sessa, whose work is carried on by his son Sergio, now the king of Latin American television. Bernard Brawerman, head of Les Films d'Elysee in the Benelux. I will remember Bernard best for his incorrigible negotiating technique. There's not a word I could say that he would not counter somehow. Everything we did was a negotiation. I remember one time I had asked him what the current time difference was between Los Angeles and Brussels, he said "10 hours". "Oh?" I responded. "I thought the time difference today was only 8 hours". "Let's compromise at 9" said Bernard, always negotiating. "Done" said I. Such great laughs!

Then there's Jaime Comas, who also like me, has been in the business forever. Jamie was once a co-producer on one of the spaghetti westerns I shot in Spain and we remained close friends ever since, together with his wife MariCruz, and his three great kids, Eva, Patricia, and Jaime Jr. While they're trying to take over Jaime's business, he still fights to keep his place at the head of the clan. I'd be remiss not to mention another icon in our business who continues to reinvent himself, Per Samuelsson. In his latest incarnation, he is living in Sweden while his former employee, Jorgen Kristiansen, continues to reinvent himself out of Denmark. And the most handsome, most charming of them, and the most astute buyer in Italy is Faruk Alatan, who cut his teeth with Vittorio Cecchi Gori and Tarak Ben Ammar, and now heads up acquisitions for the Silvio Berlusconi founded Medusa. Yet, when we get together, we rarely talk business, we just philosophize for hours.

The lawyers in my life; too numerous to mention, but two of them stand above the madding crowd of lawyers; Patty Glaser, the most feared entertainment litigator in the business, and Peter Dekom, my counselor and good friend over the years. I would be remiss not to mention my longtime association with the members of IFTA – Independent Film and Television Alliance (formerly AFMA). I currently serve as Vice Chairman to this worldwide association of film sellers and distributors, working alongside the likes of the wonderfully warm, wonderfully smart, very straight shooting Avi Lerner, the very affable Paul Hertzberg, the intense, but very humorous Pierre David, the multi-talented icon Steven Paul, the passionate veteran of foreign sales Peter Elson, the past chairmen of IFTA, the beautiful and always well spoken Kathy Morgan, the very capable and very amusing Michael Ryan, and the very efficient and intelligent Jonathan Wolf and Jean Prewitt, who keep IFTA running in the most well organized of manners.

And a last salute to all the people who make it worthwhile, friends of long standing like my high school and college buddy, John Gabriel and his wife Sandy, Gary and Karen Mehlman, and their daughters Romy and Alexandra, Peter Hoffman, a longtime counselor and friend, and Adriana Chiesa, the regal queen of foreign sales, who I've known and admired more years than she cares to remember, my some time producing partner Rudy Cohen and his wife Smadar.

And let me pay a personal tribute to my wife Maggie, married 35 years now and more in love with her than ever. She raised Jonathan and Alexis when I had little time to help her, and she has always been the mainstay and the delight of my life. And she's never been as beautiful as she is today, but somewhat less beautiful than she will be tomorrow and tomorrow and tomorrow.

I love you Maggie, forever and a day. You make it all worthwhile.

TODAY

Mark Damon is the CEO and Chairman of Foresight Unlimited. He continues to reinvent himself with every year.

Maggie Damon holds a seat on the Board of Directors of the Siddha Meditation Center of Los Angeles. She still connects with distributors and their wives world-wide and supports Mark in all his endeavors. She continues to create a rich life, revolving around spirituality and her love for family and friends.

Jon Damon is a drummer, singer, and composer. He is studying American Literature and English at UCLA.

Alexis Damon is pursuing a Masters Degree in Spiritual Psychology at the University of Santa Monica.

John Hyde became an industry bankruptcy expert after PSO. Ironically, as he handled one entertainment bankruptcy after another, what he later learned could have prevented PSO from going under. John went on to become CEO and Executive Producer of Animation at Film Roman. Recently, he added the title of President/CEO of the newly formed Starz Media. He still comes to work in jeans and cowboy boots and drives up to Fairlea Ranch every Friday.

Kate Morris married John in Las Vegas in 2000 after they had lived together for 22 years. She runs the extensive operations of Fairlea Ranch, which has grown to over 1500 acres and is one of the largest breeders in the country of American Quarter Horses.

PSOERS

Although *the PSO* family was scattered to the four winds of Hollywood, "anyone and everyone who ever worked for PSO left there knowing the business and their job backwards and forwards and inside out. And almost everyone went on to a big job," stated independent producer Gloria Feldman.

<u>Gary Barber</u> subsequently formed Spyglass, whose first picture was *The Sixth Sense*. He is the only PSO alumna who has had a horse run in the Kentucky Derby.

<u>Gregory Cascante</u> is currently President and Chief Executive Officer of CEO Films and August Entertainment.

<u>Kathy Cass</u> retired from the business and lives down the road from Kate and John Hyde in Visalia, California. She proudly attends every workshop held at Home Depot U.

<u>Arianna Cipes</u> is an actress who has painstakingly tracked down her father's (Edgar Ulmer) films and worked with various archives to preserve his cinematic legacy.

<u>Paul Guay</u> went on to a successful career as a screenwriter. He conceived and co-wrote *Liar, Liar,* co-wrote *The Little Rascals* and *Heartbreakers* and writes, acts and produces for film, television and theatre.

<u>Michael Heuser</u> is the CEO of Storm Entertainment and producer of dozens of films including *Hurlyburly, Modern Vampires* and A *Brooklyn State of Mind*.

Eddie Kalish runs Ambergate Associates and KDM Inc, a full-service entertainment marketing agency in Santa Monica, CA.

Kevin Koloff, until recently was head of business affairs and legal for music at Paramount. He has since opened his own firm, and is collaborating once again with Mark.

Julian Levin is Executive Vice President of International Sales & Distribution for Twentieth Century Fox.

Diane Slattery lives in Paris, and continues to work in public relations. Recently she did unit publicity for Mark on *Monster, The Upside of Anger, Oh Jerusalem,* and *Captivity.*

Twenty years later, ex-PSOers speak of the rise of PSO with great enthusiasm and of its fall with great sorrow. They talk about the company the way people speak of a young person who died suddenly, in the prime of his life.

They have remained in touch over the past two decades. They are very loyal where Mark and John are concerned. They still have reunions.

Mark Damon Filmography

Actor

1. *Deceiver* (1997) .... Wayland's Father
   ... aka Liar (UK)
2. *There Is No 13* (1974) .... George Thomas
3. *Es knallt - und die Engel singen* (1974) .... Fairbanks
   ... aka Bang, and the Angels Sing (International: English title)
   ... aka Do I Kill You or Do You Kill Me?
   ... aka Les Humphries: Es knallt - und die Engel singen (West Germany)
   ... aka Lo matas tú o lo mato yo (Spain)
   ... aka Mena forte più forte... che mi piace! (Italy)
4. "*The Protectors*"
   - Decoy (1973) TV Episode .... Nick Archer
5. *Tumba de la isla maldita, La* (1973) .... Peter
   ... aka Crypt of the Living Dead (International: English title)
   ... aka Vampire Woman (UK)
   ... aka Vampire Women (USA)
   ... aka Young Hannah: Queen of the Vampires (USA: reissue title)
6. *Plenilunio delle vergini, Il* (1973) .... Karl Schiller
   ... aka Full Moon of the Virgins (International: English title: literal title)
   ... aka The Devil's Wedding Night (USA)
7. *Little Mother* (1973) .... Riano
   ... aka Blood Queen
   ... aka Immoral Mistress

503

... aka Sie nannten ihn kleine Mutter (West Germany)
... aka Woman of the Year (USA)

8. *Byleth - il demone dell'incesto* (1972) .... Duke Lionello Shandwell

9. *Spada normanna, La* (1972) .... Ivanhoe
   ... aka Espada normanda, La (Spain)
   ... aka Retour d'Ivanhoe, Le (France)
   ... aka The Norman Swordsman

10. *Lo chiamavano Verità* (1972) .... Veritas
    ... aka They Call Him Veritas (USA)

11. *Monta in sella, figlio di...!* (1972) .... Felipe
    ... aka Great Treasure Hunt (USA)
    ... aka Repóker de bribones (Spain)

12. *Confessioni segrete di un convento di clausura* (1972) .... Domenico

13. *Questa libertà di avere... le ali bagnate* (1971)

14. *Posate le pistole, reverendo* (1971)
    ... aka Pistol Packin' Preacher (USA)

15. *Leoni di Petersburgo* (1971)
    ... aka Lions of St. Petersburg (USA: TV title)

16. *Arciere di Sherwood, L'* (1970) .... Allen
    ... aka Arciere di fuoco, L' (Italy: alternative title)
    ... aka Arquero de Sherwood, El (Spain)
    ... aka Grande chevauchée de Robin des bois, La (France)
    ... aka Long Live Robin Hood
    ... aka The Scalawag Bunch

17. *Anzio* (1968) .... Wally Richardson
    ... aka Batalla de Anzio, La (Spain)
    ... aka Sbarco di Anzio, Lo
    ... aka The Battle for Anzio (UK)

18. *Tutto per tutto* (1968) .... Johnny
    ... aka All Out (USA)
    ... aka Copperface (USA)
    ... aka Go for Broke
    ... aka Hora del coraje, La (Spain)
    ... aka One for All (UK)

19. *Nude... si muore* (1968) .... Richard Barrett
    ... aka School Girl Killer
    ... aka Sette vergini per il diavolo
    ... aka The Young, the Evil & the Savage

20. *¿Quién grita venganza?* (1968)
    ... aka Cry for Revenge (USA)
    ... aka Dead Men Don't Count! (International: English title)
    ... aka Morti non si contano, I (Italy)

21. *Kiedy milosc byla zbrodnia* (1968) .... American Prisoner
    ... aka Rassenschande: When Love Was a Crime

22. *Temptation* (1968)

23. *Colpo doppio del camaleonte d'oro* (1967) .... Vittorio

24. *Morte non conta i dollari, La* (1967) .... Lawrence
    ... aka Death Does Not Count the Dollars
    ... aka Death at Owell Rock (USA)
    ... aka No Killing Without Dollars (USA)

25. *Johnny Yuma* (1967) .... Johnny Yuma

26. *Requiescant* (1967) .... Ferguson
    ... aka Kill and Pray
    ... aka Kill and Say Your Prayers
    ... aka Let Them Rest
    ... aka Mögen sie in Frieden ruhen (West Germany)

27. *Treno per Durango, Un* (1967) .... Brown
    ... aka Train for Durango
    ... aka Tren para Durango, Un (Spain)

28. *Dio, come ti amo!* (1966) .... Luis
    ... aka ¡Cómo te amo! (Spain)
    ... aka How Do I Love You? (International: English title)

29. *Johnny Oro* (1966) .... Johnny Oro/Ringo
    ... aka Ringo and His Golden Pistol

30. *Agente segreto 777 - Operazione Mistero* (1965) .... Dr. Bardin
    ... aka Secret Agent 777 (International: English title)

31. *Cento cavalieri, I* (1965) .... Fernando Herrero
    ... aka 100 Horsemen
    ... aka Cien caballeros, Los (Spain)

... aka Hundert Ritter, Die (West Germany)
... aka Hundred Horsemen
... aka Son of El Cid

32. *Figlio di Cleopatra, Il* (1964) .... El Kebir
... aka Son of Cleopatra

33. *Sfida al re di Castiglia* (1964) .... Pietro I - Re di Castiglia
... aka Pedro el Cruel (Spain)
... aka Rey cruel, El (Spain)
... aka The Tyrant of Castile (USA)

34. *Tre volti della paura, I* (1963) .... Vladimire d'Urfe (segment "The Wurdalak")
... aka Black Christmas
... aka Black Sabbath (USA)
... aka The Three Faces of Fear
... aka The Three Faces of Terror
... aka Trois visages de la peur, Les (France)

35. *The Young Racers* (1963) .... Stephen Children

36. *The Reluctant Saint* (1962) .... Aldo
... aka Cronache di un convento (Italy)
... aka Joseph Desa (UK)

37. *Ho Ucciso Mio Marito* (1962)
...aka I Killed My Husband

38. *The Longest Day* (1962) (uncredited) .... Pvt. Harris

39. *Beauty and the Beast* (1962) .... Eduardo

40. *Peccati d'estate* (1962)
... aka Island Affair (USA: TV title)

41. *Giorno più corto, Il* (1962)
... aka Giorno più corto commedia umoristica, Il
... aka The Shortest Day (USA)

42. *The McGonigle* (1961) (TV) .... Artie Dale

43. "Hawaiian Eye"
- *Caves of Pele* (1961) TV Episode .... Carl Wakila

44. "Disneyland"
... aka Disney's Wonderful World (USA: new title)
... aka The Disney Sunday Movie (USA: new title)

... aka The Magical World of Disney (USA: new title)
... aka The Wonderful World of Disney (USA: new title)
... aka Walt Disney (USA: new title)
... aka Walt Disney Presents (USA: new title)
... aka Walt Disney's Wonderful World of Color (USA: new title)
- *Zorro: The Postponed Wedding* (1961) TV Episode .... Miguel Serrano

45. "*Zorro*"
    - *The Postponed Wedding* (1961) TV Episode .... Miguel Serrano
    - *The Iron Box* (1959) TV Episode .... Eugenio

46. "*National Velvet*"
    - *The Big Shot* (1960) TV Episode .... Victor Winters

47. "*The DuPont Show with June Allyson*"
    ... aka The June Allyson Show
    - *The Lie* (1960) TV Episode .... Cliff White

48. *House of Usher* (1960) .... Philip Winthrop
    ... aka The Fall of the House of Usher (UK) (USA)

49. *This Rebel Breed* (1960) .... Frank
    ... aka The Black Rebels (USA)
    ... aka Three Shades of Love (USA: reissue title)

50. "*Lock Up*"
    - *The Case of Corporal Newman* (1960) TV Episode

51. "*Tales of Wells Fargo*"
    - *A Matter of Honor* (1958) TV Episode .... Running Horse

52. *The Party Crashers* (1958) .... Twig Webster

53. *Life Begins at 17* (1958) .... Russ Lippincott

54. "*Panic!*"
    ... aka No Warning (USA: second season title)
    - *Patrol* (1958) TV Episode .... Dave

55. *Young and Dangerous* (1957) .... Tommy Price

56. *Between Heaven and Hell* (1956) .... Pvt. Terry Co.G

57. "*The 20th Century-Fox Hour*"
    ... aka Fox Hour of Stars (USA: rerun title)
    - *The Hefferan Family* (1956) TV Episode .... Harold
    - *In Times Like These* (1956) TV Episode .... Rusty Age 17

58. *Screaming Eagles* (1956) .... Pvt. Lambert
59. *"Alfred Hitchcock Presents"*
    - *Place of Shadows* (1956) TV Episode .... Ray Clements
60. *"Cavalcade of America"*
    ... aka DuPont Presents the Cavalcade Theatre (USA: fourth season title)
    ... aka DuPont Theater (USA: fifth season title)
    - *Star and Shield* (1956) TV Episode
    - *The Prison Within* (1956) TV Episode .... Bill
61. *Inside Detroit* (1956) .... Gregg Linden

Producer

1. *Beyond a Reasonable Doubt* (2009) *(in production)* (producer)
2. *It's Alive* (2008) (executive producer)
3. *Captivity* (2006) (producer)
4. *O Jerusalem* (2006) (producer)
5. *The Upside of Anger* (2005) (executive producer)
6. *Beyond the Sea* (2004) (executive producer)
7. *Monster* (2003) (producer)
8. *11:14* (2003) (executive producer)
9. *The United States of Leland* (2003) (executive producer)
10. *The I Inside* (2003) (producer)
11. *Extreme Ops* (2002) (executive producer)
    ... aka Extremist (Philippines: English title)
12. *FeardotCom* (2002) (executive producer)
    ... aka Fear Dot Com (Germany) (USA: promotional title)
13. *The Musketeer* (2001) (executive producer)
14. *The Body* (2001) (executive producer)
    ... aka Geheimnisvolle Grab, Das (Germany)
15. *Love & Sex* (2000) (executive producer)
16. *Eye of the Beholder* (1999) (executive producer)
17. *Grizzly Falls* (1999) (executive producer)
    ... aka Grizzly Falls (Canada: French title)
18. *A Dog of Flanders* (1999) (executive producer)
19. *Orgazmo* (1997) (executive producer)
20. *Deceiver* (1997) (executive producer)
    ... aka Liar (UK)
21. *The Blackout* (1997) (executive producer)
    ... aka The Blackout (France)
22. *The Second Jungle Book: Mowgli & Baloo* (1997) (executive producer)
    ... aka Jungle Book 2: Mowgli and Baloo
    ... aka Rudyard Kipling's The Second Jungle Book: Mowgli and Baloo

23. *Loved* (1997) (executive producer)
24. *The Winner* (1996) (executive producer)
25. *The Jungle Book* (1994) (executive producer)
    ... aka Libro de la selva, El (USA: Spanish title)
    ... aka Rudyard Kipling's The Jungle Book (USA: complete title)
26. *Stalingrad* (1993) (executive producer)
27. *Red Shoe Diaries* (1992) (TV) (executive producer)
    ... aka Red Shoe Diaries the Movie (USA: video box title)
    ... aka Wild Orchid III: Red Shoe Diaries
28. *Wild Orchid II: Two Shades of Blue* (1992) (executive producer)
    ... aka Wild Orchid 2: Blue Movie Blue
29. *Diary of a Hitman* (1991) (executive producer)
30. *Inner Sanctum* (1991) (executive producer)
31. *Beastmaster 2: Through the Portal of Time* (1991) (executive producer)
32. *Dark Angel* (1990) (executive producer)
    ... aka I Come in Peace (USA: new title)
33. *Wild Orchid* (1990) (producer)
34. *Vietnam, Texas* (1990) (executive producer)
35. *High Spirits* (1988) (executive producer)
36. *Bat*21* (1988) (co-producer)
37. *Mac and Me* (1988) (executive producer)
38. *The Lost Boys* (1987) (co-executive producer)
39. *Flight of the Navigator* (1986) (executive producer)
    ... aka The Navigator (Norway)
40. *Short Circuit* (1986) (executive producer)
41. *8 Million Ways to Die* (1986) (executive pbroducer)
42. *Nine 1/2 Weeks* (1986) (producer)
43. *The Clan of the Cave Bear* (1986) (executive producer)
44. *Unendliche Geschichte, Die* (1984) (executive producer)
    ... aka The NeverEnding Story (UK) (USA)
45. *Boot, Das* (1981) (executive producer) (director's cut)
    ... aka The Boat (USA: dubbed version)

46. *The Choirboys* (1977) (executive producer)
47. *The Arena* (1974) (producer)
    ... aka Naked Warriors (USA: reissue title)
    ... aka Rivolta delle gladiatrici, La (Italy)

Index

Symbols

11:14 xv, 481, 482, 509
1220 Kedzie 15
20th Century Fox 161, 164, 241
20th Century Fox Hour, The 161, 164, 241
8 Million Ways to Die 328, 431
Black Mama, White Mama 385, 392, 400
Passion of Mind 15, 212, 406, 452, 463, 471, 473, 493, 495

A

ABC Motion Pictures 123, 323
Actor's Studio, The 164
Adams, Christy 86
Adelson, Merv 26, 411, 415
Adriano Theater 454
Adventures of Buckaroo Banzai in the 8th Dimension 153
Adventures of Robin Hood, The 31
AFMA 497
Afman, Frans 445, 461
Aft, Rob 463, 494
Agent 777 359, 505
Agrama, Frank 299, 496
Aida 34
Aiken, Elaine 164, 181
Alatan, Faruk 497
Aldrich, Robert 26, 411
Allen, Joan 483
Allen, Karen 58
Allen & Co. 316, 317, 371, 372, 425, 430, 431
Allen & Company 316, 317, 371, 372, 425, 430, 431
All the Fine Young Cannibals 227
Almost Pregnant 445
Altariba, Beatrice 343
Altimirano, Horacio 496
American Bandstand 198, 230
American Film Market (AFM) 459
Anders, Luana 224, 228, 239, 344
Andropov, Yuri 141
Anne, HRH Princess 92
Anzio 378, 379, 380, 381, 504
Apocalypse Now 407
Arena, The 385, 392, 400, 511
Arena, The 511
Arkoff, Sam 247
Arnow, Max 226
Arquette, Rosanna 327, 329, 332, 334
Artisti Associati 454
Ashby, Hal 327, 328, 332, 334, 430
Aspen Films 55
Astaire, Fred 253
Atlantis 135
Attenborough, Sir Richard 5, 21
Auel, Jean 260
Author's Playhouse 106
Awake and Sing 85
A Fistful of Dollars 154, 359, 360, 361
A Quiet Place 32, 34, 39, 231, 241

B

Badham, John 48, 320
Baker, Diane 85, 231, 239
Baker, Josephine 309
Baker, Mark H. 374
Ball, Lucille 253
Banderas, Antonio 459
Bankhead, Talullah 161
Bankruptcy 426, 429, 436, 441, 442, 461, 499
Barber, Gary 92, 501
Bare, Richard 242
Barney's Beanery 230
Bart, Peter 333
Basinger, Kim 133, 211, 212, 213, 421, 422

513

*Bat*21* 444, 510
Battle of Anzio, The 378, 379
Bauman, Doreen 35
Bavaria Studios, Munich 119
Beauty And The Beast 136, 254, 506
Begelman, Davd 121, 153
Behavior Worldwide xv, 69, 163, 229, 328, 451, 452, 454, 459, 494
Being There 328
Belmondo, Jean-Paul 309
Bel Geddes, Barbara 181
Ben-Hur 272
Benedict Canyon Drive xvi, 322, 443, 464, 468
Benji (Beniamino) 404, 406, 407, 408
Ben Ammar, Taraq 133
Berg, Jeff 329, 332, 333
Berg, Jeffrey 318
Berkowitz, Harold 411
Berlin Film Festival 402, 474
Berlusconi Silvio 497
Berney, Bob 473
Between Heaven and Hell 158, 162, 507
Beulah 106
Beverly Amusement Park 42
Beverly Hills 37, 39, 75, 77, 95, 117, 147, 161, 164, 165, 169, 325, 360, 433, 477
Beverly Hills Hotel 164, 165, 360
Beyond a Reasonable Doubt 489, 493
Beyond The Sea 468, 489, 509
Bianchi, Giorgio 307
Binder, Mike 482, 483
Bisset, Jacqueline 452
Bizet, Georges 33, 34
Biziou, Peter 211
Blackwood, Caroline 494
Black Mama, White Mama 385, 392, 400
Black Sabbath 311, 339, 344, 345, 381, 506
Blake, Robert 161, 231
Block, Lawrence 322, 329, 330
Blockbuster 473, 474

Bloomgarten, Kermit 165
Boccaccio '70 273, 274, 275
Body, The 459, 509
Body Heat 212
Bond, James 133, 278, 359, 362, 450
Borodin, Aleksandr 33, 34
Boschero, Dominique 275, 283, 304, 305, 346, 381
Bradley, Reiko 112, 333, 459, 494
Brandauer, Klaus Maria 133
Brando, Marlon 160, 163
Brandt, Willy 64
Brawerman, Bernard 496
Bregni, Mario 26, 414
Bregni, Piero 405, 406, 411
Bridges, Jeff 327, 329, 332
Broccoli, Albert 'Cubby' 53, 133
Broccoli, Cubby 133
Brokaw, Norman 104
Bronson, Charles 181, 330, 360, 416
Broomfield, Nick 470
Bucholz, Horst 346
Buckaroo Banzai. 153
Burke, Graham 55, 132
Burnett, Carol 84, 86
Burton, Michael 374
Burton, Richard 309
Burton, Tim 345
Buttons, Red 435
Byleth 384, 504
Byrnes, Edd 225, 228, 230, 238

C

CAA 216
Cabot, Susan 227, 232, 239
Caldwell, William 76, 77, 78
California magazine 317
Callas, Maria 274
Camp, Joe 407
Campbell, Bob 343, 344
Cannes Film Festival xv, 4, 90, 123, 258
Cannon Films 128, 342
Cannon Film Group 461

Canon 39
Canter's Deli 34
Canton, Mark 318
Capanna, Jacopo 132, 448, 453
Captivity xv, xvi, 484, 502, 509
Cardinale, Claudia 141
Cardinale, Claudine 141
Carey, MacDonald 161
Carlton Hotel 62, 129, 258
Carmen 34
Carolco Pictures 445
Carpenter, John 345
Carrera, Barbara 133
Carrey, Jim 92
Carson, Johnny 3
Carson Drive 39, 78
Carver, Steve 393
Carver, Tina 160
Cascante, Gregory 110, 111, 112, 113, 115, 126, 131, 135, 431, 501
Cass, Kathy 92, 113, 115, 121, 133, 135, 317, 501
Castro 140
Cat On A Hot Tin Roof 181
CBS/Fox Video 316
CBS Authors Playhouse 106
Celentano, Adriano 408
Chandler, Karen 188
Change of Seasons 56
Chapman, Michael 262, 264, 421
Chemical Bank of New York 371
Chicago 6, 9, 10, 13, 14, 15, 16, 31, 32, 35, 40, 190, 227, 243, 261, 351, 441
Chicago Cubs 15
Chiesa, Adriana 497
Choirboys, The 25, 26, 27, 47, 61, 411, 416, 417, 511
Christensen, Eric 494
Christy, George 228
Cinamatheque Francais 347
Cincinnati Kid 11, 12, 14, 16, 33, 34, 40, 42, 78, 104, 130, 161, 171, 185, 228, 243, 341, 362, 370, 393, 474

Cinecitta Studios 380
Cinema Group 47, 58, 69, 123, 183, 211, 358, 371, 461
Cinquetti, Gigliola 353, 356, 358
Cipes, Arianne Ulmer 58, 110
Cipes, Jay 58
Clan Of The Cave Bear 260
Clark, Dick 121, 198, 230
Classical music 33, 34, 36
Claxton, Bill 225
Clift, Montgomery 163
Cocker, Joe 217
Cock 'N Bull 230
Coconut Grove, The 253
Cohen, Rudy 497
Cohen, Smadar 497
Colossus of Rhodes, The 360
Columbia Studios 5
Comas, Eva 497
Comas, Jaime 132, 497
Comas, Jaime Jr. 497
Comas, Mari Cruz 497
Comas, Patricia 452, 497
Comencini, Luigi 133
Coming Home 328, 331, 332, 333
Compulsion 241
Connery, Sean 123, 133, 152, 309, 450
Contest Books 77, 78, 185
Continental Management 310
Convy, Bert 231
Corbucci, Sergio 309, 311, 351
Corey, Jeff 86, 231, 239, 240, 361
Corman, Roger 202, 227, 232, 247, 250, 332, 341, 363, 385, 391, 394
Costner, Kevin 478, 483
Cottafavi, Vittorio 311, 345, 347
Cotten, Joseph 272
Count of Monte Cristo, The 15
Coward, Noel 485
Crawford, Broderick 158, 162, 272
Credit Lyonnais 445, 461, 493
Crowninshield, Martha 370
Cruise, Tom 121, 449

515

Crystal Theater 15
Culastrisce, Nobile Veneziano 407
Cumas, Jaime and Maricruz 497
Curtis, Tony 253, 385, 392
Cusumano, Joey 174
Cyrano's 230

D

D'Angelo, Beverly 450
Daily Variety 333
Dalton, Abby 231
Damman, Janet 112
Damon, Alexis 114, 499
Damon, Jon 442, 499
Damon, Maggie (see Markov) 2, 398, 494, 499
Damon, Mark iii, v, xv, 3, 10, 14, 46, 99, 106, 107, 111, 113, 123, 130, 145, 149, 156, 164, 177, 186, 190, 204, 225, 226, 227, 228, , 230, 231, 260, 274, 283, 286, 292, 309, 310, 312, 320, 353, 358, 370, 383, 391, 420, 423, 436, 441, 461, 468, 474, 480, 487, 493, 494, 499, 503, 253
Damone, Marco 308, 311, 393
Damon and Pythias, story of 106
Dante, Joe 345, 347
Darin, Bobby 230, 468, 489
Dark at The Top of the Stairs, The 185
Das Boot xii, 3, 4, 5, 70, 71, 93, 97, 143, 154, 259
David, Pierre 497
DAV (Disabled American Veterans) 76, 79, 80
Dawson, Anthony 380
Day After, The 121, 123, 124
Dead and Buried 248
Dean, James 165, 240
Dean, Jimmy 225
Death at Orwell Rock 383, 505
Death at Orwell Rock 383
Deauville Film Festival 482

DeBarge, El 435
Deceiver 462, 503, 509
Defiant Ones, The 392
Dekom, Peter 57, 497
Delon, Alain 271
Delphi Film Associates 120
Delphi III 120, 262, 265, 266, 316, 317, 318, 322, 323, 370, 374, 421, 425, 429, 430
Dementia 13 344
Demme, Jonathan 341, 391
DeNiro, Robert 155
Derek, Bo 56
DesMichelle, Thierry 490
Devil's Wedding Night, The 384, 503
De Fait Jean-Luc 142
De Laurentiis, Aurelio 132, 495
De Laurentiis, Dino 57, 106, 455
De Niro, Robert 129, 130, 142
Diamant, Elli 493
Diamant, Ilana 493
Diamant, Limor 493
Diamant, Michael 493
Diamant, Moshe 443, 444, 489, 490, 493
Diamant, Sagiv 493
Diamant, Sigal 493
Diamond, Neil 48
Diary of Anne Frank 165, 186
Diary of Ann Frank, The 165, 186
Diller, Barry 323
Dillon, Matt 97, 121
Dio, Como Te Amo (God How I Love You) 353
Disney, Walt Studios 3, 26, 47, 48, 49, 53, 65, 92, 111, 112, 122, 149, 150, 151, 211, 316, 317, 318, 408, 410, 411, 473, 474, 507
Distribution xiv, 3, 26, 50, 63, 111, 112, 113, 151, 316, 318, 405, 406, 409, 410, 462, 463, 473, 479, 489, 490, 493, 495, 496
Di Sica, Vittorio 271
Django 353, 359
Dmytryk, Eddie 307, 379, 380

Dmytryk, Edward 307, 379
Dobkin, Lawrence 363
Dokhalov, Tigran 487
Doldinger, Klaus 259
Domingo, Placido 5
Donner, Laura Shuler 121, 126
Donner, Richard 322, 323
Doolittle, John 261
Dorothy Chandler Pavilion 1, 3, 19, 21, 97
Douglas, Kirk 61, 65, 385
Douglas, Michael 489, 493
Doumani, Fred and Ed 174
Dowling, Doris 229
Downey's 181, 182, 185
Do I Kill You or Do You Kill Me? 503
Driscoll, Bobby 228, 229
Durning, Charles 416

E

E.T. 5, 373
Eastwood, Clint 154, 286, 360
Easy Rider 361
Ebert, Roger 421, 431, 474
Ebsen, Buddy 162
Eichinger, Berndt 64, 123, 132, 154, 259
Eisner, Michael 374
Ekberg, Anita 272
Elfman, Blossom 32
Elfman, Danny 34
Elfman, Louis 12, 32
Elfman, Milt 32
Elfman, Richard 34
Elfman, Rose 31
Elfman-Harris, Lillian 12
Eliasberg, Michael 121
Elson, Peter 497
Elwes, Cassian 131, 132, 135, 328, 480
Ende, Michael 119, 154
Endless Love 149, 151
Entertainment Industries Group 371
Estevez, Emilio 121
Eurovision Song Contest 358

Evans, Bob 120, 121, 126, 128, 171, 172, 176, 361

F

Fabulous Baker Boys, The 445
Fairfax High School 40, 192
Fairlea Ranch 266, 499
Falk, Peter 253, 379, 380
Fall xiii, 16, 166, 228, 229, 242, 312, 321, 329, 372, 381, 383, 420, 430, 432, 441, 442, 444, 495, 502
Fall of the House of Usher, The 202, 246, 247, 248, 250, 252, 253, 394, 496, 507
Farmer, Frances 228, 229
Feinberg, Mal 40, 78, 79, 80
Feldman, Gloria 488, 490, 501
Fellini, Federico 272
Ferguson, George Bellow 378, 381, 382
Ferguson, Helen 104, 106, 161, 163, 225, 226
Festival di Sanremo Music Competition 358
Festival of Two Worlds in Spoleto 276
Films d'Elysee 496
Filmways 495
Film Finance group xii, xv, 4, 47, 48, 50, 58, 65, 69, 90, 93, 97, 115, 120, 122, 123, 128, 138, 171, 173, 175, 176, 211, 258, 318, 341, 347, 402, 411, 430, 441, 449, 452, 459, 461, 470, 474, 479, 480, 482, 484, 487, 488, 490, 495, 496, 497, 499
Film Roman xii, 499
Final Countdown, The 58, 61, 62, 63, 64, 65
Fink, Jeff 493
Finn Air 139, 145
First Artists 26
First National Bank of Boston 370, 371, 423

517

Flashdance 212, 216, 259
Fleischer, Richard 162
Fleming, Janet 58, 110, 113
Flight of the Navigator xiii, 113, 373, 374, 423, 425, 435, 510
Flynn, Errol 15
Flynn, Joe 105
Foa, Arnoldo 345
Fonda, Henry 308, 359
Fonda, Jane 3, 5, 21
Forbes Magazine 11, 105, 145, 163, 317, 422, 453
Forbidden, The 382
Forbidden, The (Rassenschande) 382
Ford, John 359
Ford Coppola, Francis 121, 153, 173, 341, 342
Foreign distributors 48, 53, 65, 69, 91, 92, 124, 129, 130, 133, 153, 154, 171, 266, 410, 449, 468
Foreign film sales business 3
Foreign sales market 27, 49, 50, 57, 145, 153, 318, 411, 423, 430, 431, 444, 494, 497
Formosa's Café 230
Formula 1 Lotus 3, 35
Formula One Lotus 343
Forsey, K. 259
Fort Apache, the Bronx 496
Foster, David 320
Foster, Gary 320
Franciosa, Tony 186
Frankenheimer, John 182
Frank Mancuso, President of Paramount 151
Frantic Pictures 342
French Mafia 416
Frey, Barbara 56, 57, 64, 292, 346, 347, 381, 382, 396
Freyermuth, Ortwin 494
Friday the 13th 145
Friedman, Irv 11, 12, 15, 39
From Here to Eternity 229
Frostee Freeze 78
Furukawa, Hiro 132, 460

G

Gabriel, John 497
Gabriel, Sandy 497
Gallico, Paul 53
Gallin, Sandy 322
Gandhi 5, 21
Garber, David 493
Garcia, Andy 329, 332, 334
Garland, Beverly 239
Garner, James 253
Gassman, Vittorio 272, 309
Gazzara, Ben 186, 272
Geffen, David 323
Geissler, Dieter 260
Gentle, Lili 161, 225
Gentry, Race 85, 106
Germans 4, 5, 56, 70, 71, 93, 130, 151
German Bundestag 64
German war film 5
Gersh, Phil 255, 271
Getty, J. Paul 415
Getty, John Paul III 415
Gianinni, Giancarlo 379
Gilbert, Ben 39
Girard, Bernie 229
Girardot, Annie 141
Gladden Entertainment 445
Glaser, Patty 497
Globus, Yoran 128
Godfather, The 53, 55, 128, 173, 407
Golan, Menachem 128, 342
Golan and Globus 461
Golden Chameleon, The 285, 384
Golden Globe xiii, 227, 239, 252, 253, 474
Golden Globe Awards, The 253
Goldzband, Marlene 16
Gorbachev, Mikhail 141
Gori, Vittorio Cecchi 132, 497
Gossett, Louis Jr. 416
Gould, Elliot 52
Grade, Lew 57
Graham, Sheila 310
Grant, Cary 242
Grease 374

Great Chihuahua Treasure Hunt, The 384
Green, Michael 488
Green, Nigel 63, 488
Green, Trevor 132
Greenfield, Bob 12, 16, 63, 78, 81, 120, 121, 126, 128, 129, 130, 132, 171, 172, 173, 174, 176, 185, 242, 254, 255, 329, 342, 343, 344, 347, 348, 361, 442, 473, 488
Greenwood, Bruce 452
Green Acres 322, 499
Gregg, Christina 343
Grey, Nadia 310
Grier, Pam 385, 386, 391, 392
Griffith, Chuck 341, 342, 343
Group Theater, The 183
Grove, Martin 266
Guay, Paul 92, 112, 114, 119, 501
Guber, Peter 149, 150, 260, 421, 441, 442, 443, 444, 462, 480
Guerrieri, Romolo 362
Guinness, Arthur 47
Guinness, Arthur Sons and Co. Ltd 47, 49
Guinness, Peter 71, 91
Guinness Beer 47
Guinness Book of Records 47
Guinness Film Group 47, 58
Gunga Din 31
Gung Ho 15
Gussin, Zave 14, 15
Guttenberg, Steve 321, 449, 450, 451

H

Haberman, Stan 79
Hackett 165
Hackman, Gene 444
Hadida, Sammy 490
Hadida, Victor 490
Hallmark Playhouse 106, 163, 166, 180, 181, 183, 231
Halloween 145, 381
Halsey, Brett 253, 278

Halsey, Christian Solomon 308
Hamilton, George 225, 227, 253
Handprint Entertainment xiii, 57, 135, 148, 316, 366, 371, 411, 443, 445, 461, 468, 484, 488, 494, 495, 497, 499, 501, 502
Hannah, Darryl 260, 261, 262, 421, 449, 450, 451
Harman, Estelle 85, 87, 105, 161
Harman's, Estelle Actors Workshop 85
Harmony Gold 496
Harold and Maude 328
Harris, Al 34, 40, 41, 73, 80, 84, 99, 104, 107, 193
Harris, Alan 6, 7, 10, 11, 14, 28, 34, 76, 85, 102, 104, 106, 190, 474, 485
Harris, Irv 39
Hart, Dolores 231, 239
Helkon 495
Hellman, Jerome 332
Hellman, Monte 361
Hellman, Phillippe 132
Hemdale Films 445
Hendler, Gary 211
Herr Dreyer 152
Herskovitz, Alan 441
Herskovitz, Irving 11
Hertzberg, Paul 497
Heuser, Michael 113, 114, 115, 116, 130, 265, 317, 371, 435, 480, 501
Hickman, Dwayne 237
High Spirits 448, 449, 450, 451, 510
Hill, Graham 343
Hines, Gregory 173
Hodgkin's Disease 254
Hoffman, Dustin 172
Hoffman, Peter 497
Holliday, Judy 186
Hollywood Foreign Press Association 253
Hollywood Reporter 34, 47, 104, 153, 226, 266, 302, 318, 380, 421, 480

519

Holy Grail, The 407
Hope, Bob 242
Hopkins, Anthony 56
Hopper, Dennis 235, 238
Hormel school of acting 451
Hornburg, Bill 421
Horowitz, Mark 494
Horwitz, Lew 298, 495
Hotel Cassia 386, 396
Hotel Hassler 272
Hot Box 391
House of Usher, The 202, 246, 247, 248, 249, 250, 252, 253, 394, 496, 507
Howard, Sandy 47, 48, 49, 58
Howell, C.Thomas 121
Hudson, Rock 104, 106, 253, 274, 391
Hueva, Jose 298, 496
Humboldt Park 14, 15
Hunter, Jeff 85
Hunter, Tab 106, 238
Hunt Brothers 153
Huston, Anjelica 323
Huston, John 297, 323
Huth, Hanno 132
Hyams, Peter 490, 493
Hyde, John xii, xiii, 2, 3, 46, 47, 49, 56, 57, 69, 113, 115, 155, 172, 260, 320, 426, 499, 501
Hyde, Kate 334

I

IFTA 480, 497
Imitation of Life 227
Inn, Frank 407
Inner Sanctum 445, 510
Inner Sanctum 2 445
Inside Detroit 158, 160, 161, 508
Inside Moves 104, 105, 215, 265, 327, 431, 471, 472, 474, 484, 501
International Creative Management, ICM 318, 329
International distribution xiv, 479

International Star of Tomorrow 4, 61, 62, 308, 331, 498
In provinces 408
In the Heat of the Night 328
Ireland, John 238, 272
Island of The Blue Dolphins 374
Italian palazzo 341
Italia Film of Lebanon 311, 359
Italy xiii, xv, 4, 5, 25, 26, 27, 35, 48, 50, 58, 97, 132, 141, 150, 267, 269, 271, 272, 274, 276, 277, 303, 307, 308, 310, 311, 335, 337, 341, 343, 346, 348, 349, 351, 353, 355, 358, 359, 360, 363, 375, 377, 379, 386, 387, 397, 400, 402, 403, 404, 405, 406, 407, 408, 409, 412, 415, 416, 417, 453, 454, 484, 496, 497, 503, 504, 505, 506, 511
Itzkowitz Delicatessen 14
Ivanhoe 293, 382, 504
Iwo Jima 15
I Come In Peace 494
I Inside, The 460, 509
I Killed My Husband 283, 305, 506
I Morti non si contano (Cry for Revenge) 382

J

Jackson, Michael 298, 300, 467, 468
Jagger, Mick 328
Jaguar Lives 48
Janssen, David 253
Japan xv, 4, 61, 62, 63, 97, 121, 132, 149, 448, 449, 450, 459, 460, 464
Jenkins, Patty 470, 474, 475, 481
Jewish Fairfax District 32
Jewison, Norman 328
Joffe, Roland 484
Joffe, Tatyana 459
Johnny Oro (Ringo and His Golden Pistols) 351
Johnny Yuma 361, 362, 363, 505

Johnson, Dorothy 228
Johnson, President Lyndon 122
John Burroughs Junior High 34
Jonesfilm Productions 211
Jones Apparel Group 211
Jordan, Neil 449, 450, 451
Joyce, Adrien 361
Jugend Films 63, 64
Jungle Book, The 488, 489, 510

K

Kalfon, Pierre 110, 132, 496
Kalish, Eddie 50, 112, 121, 126, 130, 131, 264, 317, 318, 370, 373, 430, 441, 462, 502
Kangaroo 52
Kaplan, Leon 411
Kaplan, Livingston 411
Kaplan, Livingston et. al. 411
Kapoor, Raj 141
Karate Kid 48
Karloff, Boris 339, 344, 345
Kassar, Mario 128, 461
Katzenberg, Jeffrey 374
Katzman, Sam 160
Kaufman, Victor, CEO of Tri-Star 211, 275, 490, 507
Kaufman-Lerner 275
Kaye, Danny 237
Kelly, Grace 163
Kennedy, Arthur 379
Kennedy, President John F. / Jack 122
Kennedy, William 173
Kenosha, Wisconsin 12
Kernochan, Sarah 212
KGB 141, 143, 144
Khayyam, Omar 484
Kidnapping 414
Kimmel, Sidney 211
King, Zalman 212, 422, 448, 451, 453
King Kong 31
King of Cannes, The 123
King of Comedy, The 129
Klein's Drugstore 14

Kleiser, Jeffrey 425
Kleiser, Randal 113, 374, 425
Knight, Shirley 231
Knop, Patricia Louisianna 212
Koenig, Werner 495
Kohner, Paul 121
Kohner, Susan 201, 227, 253
Koloff, Kevin 58, 116, 132, 316, 424, 494, 502
Konov, Sergei 495
Korman, Lewis J 120, 431
Kramer, Deborah 263
Kramer, Joey 425
Kristiansen, Jorgen 497
Kruger, Christine 384
Kubotani, Moto 61, 62, 63, 132
Kushner, Donald 469
Kuzui, Fran 463, 496
Kuzui, Kaz 463

L

L'Observatore Romano 346
L'Osservatore Romano 346
Ladd, Alan Jr. 155
Lancaster, Burt 253
Lane, Diane 122, 173
Lansing, Sherry 323
Lantos, Robert 495
Last Detail, The 263, 328, 329, 330
Last Train Stop Love 346
Laughton, Charles 181
La Cienega Park 39, 42, 104
La Dolce Vita 272, 278
La Spada Normana 293, 382
La Traviata 5, 34, 97
Leone, Sergio 123, 153, 154, 351, 359, 360, 361
Lerner, Avi 497
Levin, Julian 92, 112, 126, 435, 502
Levin, Meyer 241
Levy, Tim 495
Lewis, Jerry 129, 130
Liar, Liar 92, 501
Liebowitz, Annie 452

Life Begins at 17 224, 228, 507
Light's Diamond Jubilee 105
Limentani, Annalena 275, 310
Lipman, Carol Sue 122
Little Lord Fauntleroy 92
Little Mother 384, 503
Lizzani, Carlo 311, 381
Loews Hotel 457, 459
London xii, 65, 70, 71, 91, 92, 93, 105, 450, 483
Longest Day, The 308, 309, 506
Loren, Sophia 253
Lorimar 26, 333, 411
Lost Boys, The 322, 366, 372, 373, 423, 510
Los Angeles Times, The 145, 248, 436
Love, Lucretia 392
Love Story 212, 469
Love Thy Coach 84, 86
Lowe, Rob 121
Lowell Elementary School, Chicago, Illinois 14
Lualdi, Antonella 284, 346
Lucisano, Federica 496
Lucisano, Fulvio 132
Lumet, Sidney 5
Lundgren, Dolph 494
Lyne, Adrian 211, 212, 213, 319, 372, 422

M

"Method", The 163
Macchio, Ralph 121
MacLaine, Shirley 56
Mac and Me 510
Maddock, Brent 320
Madison, Guy 272
Magnani, Anna 273
Majestic Hotel, The 123
Malden, Karl 163
Mancuso, Becky 373
Mancuso, Frank 151
Manfredi, Nino 141
Manley, Ned 41

Mansfield, Jayne 393
Man in Rio, The 452
Marchent, Rafael Romero 382
Marcks, Greg 481, 482
Margheriti, Antonio 380
Markov, Margaret / Maggie Damon 2, 250, 294, 385, 386, 391, 398, 494, 499
Mark Damon Fan Clubs 227, 230
Mark takes over 213
Marpa xi, xiv
Marvin, Lee 360
Marx, Groucho 42, 104
Marx, Gummo 42
Marxism 381
Maslansky, Paul 48
Maslin, Janet 454
Massaro, Avv. Gianni 495
Mastroianni, Marcello 272, 407, 408
Matilda 52, 53, 55, 56
Maugham, W. Somerset 267
Mayer, Louis B. 113
MCA/Universal 5, 48, 149, 151, 320, 328, 405
McCadden Place 34, 35
McClory, Kevin 133
McLaren, Bruce 343
McNall, Bruce 153
McNeill, Elizabeth 212
McNichol, Kristy 97
McQueen, Steve 163
MDP Worldwide xv, 459, 494
Mead, Syd 321
Medavoy, Mike 48
Media 8 Entertainment xv, 469, 472, 473, 474, 487
Medusa 497
Mehlman, Alexandra 497
Mehlman, Gary 497
Mehlman, Karen 497
Mehlman, Romy 497
Meisner, Sanford 163, 166, 180, 181, 225
Meisner Technique 225
Member of the Wedding, The 106

Memento 473
Mendelsohn, Mike 495
Mercouri, Melina 141
Meredith, Burgess 181
Merlin, Jan 161
Meteor 48
Method, The 181
Metropolis 259
Metropolitan Film Export 490
Metzger, Radley 384
Meyers, Bobby 25, 26, 57, 93, 131, 134, 442, 462
MGM Studios 50, 135
MIFED xv, 27, 53, 55, 119, 151, 152, 153, 154, 265, 266, 373, 441, 449, 488, 490
Milan xii, xv, 53
Milarepa xi, xiv
Milchan, Arnon 129
Milian, Tomas 277
Million Dollar Baby 56
Milner, Martin 161
Minkovski, Leonid 495
Miramax Films 493
Mishkin, Meyer 360
Misunderstood 133, 134
Mitchell, Les 86
Mitchum, Robert 53, 309, 378, 379
Modugno, Domenico 358
Monas, Steve 494
Monicelli, Mario 273
Monroe, Marilyn 163, 187
Monster 119, 247, 248, 249, 250, 470
Montenaro, Toni 263
Monty Python 407
Moore, Alvy 161
Moore, Roger 153
Moore, Terry 162
Moreno, Rita 203, 231, 242
Morgan, Gary 56
Morgan, Kathy 463, 497
Moroder, Giorgio 212, 259
Morricone, Ennio 360
Morris, Kate 2, 48, 58, 70, 499

Moscow xiv, xvi, 122, 137, 138, 140, 141, 142, 484
Moscow Film Festival 122, 138
MosFilms Studio 484
Motion Picture Association MPAA 122
Mr. Mom 153
Mulvehill, Charles 330
Munteanu, Al 496
My Big Fat Greek Wedding 473

N

Nanba, Sam 21, 25, 61, 62, 63, 416
National General Pictures 26
Needles, California 29
Neeson, Liam 449, 450
Neighborhood Playhouse School of Theater 163
Neo-Realism 271
Neri, Rosalba 362, 384, 392
Nero, Franco 359
Neue Constantin 154
NeverEnding Story, The xiii, 110, 118, 119, 123, 154, 259, 260, 318, 431, 510
Neverland Entertainment 468
Never Say Never Again 123, 132, 133, 152, 153
NewsLife 104
New Girl In Town 239
New York Times, The 123, 143, 145, 402
Nicholson, Bill 15
Nicholson, Jack 104, 174, 231, 232, 323, 330, 341, 361, 409
Nicita, Rick 216
Night Eyes 3 445
Nippon Herald 25, 62, 460, 461
Nitzche, Jack 373
Non ho l'eta' ('I'm not old enough to love you') 358
North Street Theater 31
Notarianni, Pietro 277
Novak, Kim 105

523

O

O'Brien, Pat 160
O'Keefe, Dennis 158, 160
O'Shea, Brian 494
O'Toole, Peter 449, 450
Octopussy 153
Odets, Clifford 85
Ogarlov, Russian Minister Marshal 145
Oh, Jerusalem xvi, 484
Oingo Boingo 34
Oliver, Susan 227
Once Upon a Time in America 123, 153, 154, 155
One Flew Over the Cuckoo's Nest 409
One From the Heart 79, 114, 276, 341, 485
One Million Years, B.C. 421
On a Clear Day You Can See Forever 362
Oooh, What You Do To Me 230
Orgarlov, Marshal 145
Orgazmo 463, 496, 509
Orion Pictures 171
Oritz, Felipe 298, 496
Ortiz, Luis 298
Oscar 21, 53, 56, 97, 242, 261, 328, 329, 409, 445, 463, 468, 474, 483
Oscars 111, 468, 479
Otis, Carrie 452
Outsiders, The 110, 121, 123, 153

P

PAC 26, 50, 405, 406, 407, 408, 409, 411, 416
Page, Geraldine 163
Pal, George 135
Palais du Cinema 123
Paluzzi, Luciana 254, 277, 278, 306, 307
Paoli, Gino 308
Paramount Classics 50, 112, 113, 128, 151, 172, 173, 494, 502
Paramount Pictures 50, 112, 113, 128, 151, 172, 173, 494, 502
Paris 91, 271, 272, 421, 422, 502
Parker, Sarah Jessica 425
Parker, Trey 463
Parsons, Louella 228, 240
Parton, Dolly 322
Party, The 228, 229, 507
Pasolini, Pier Paolo 381
Passion of the Christ 473
Pastner, Sid 230
Patel, Raju 299, 300, 467, 488
Pate brothers 462
Paul, Steven 497
Peccati d'Estate 506
Peck, Gregory 163, 184
Pelliccia, Rossana 310
Perkins, Tony 238
Peron, Eva 384
Peters, Jon 260, 443
Petersen, Wolfgang 3, 4, 5, 21, 71, 97, 119, 259
Peter Pan 373
Peter the Cruel 3, 339, 345
Peyton Place 239, 240, 278
Photoplay 226
Photoplay Magazine 226
Piazza Margana 265, 307, 309, 341, 347
Pickup Girl 105
Picnic 186
Pidgeon, Walter 309
Pistol Packing Preacher 383
Platoon 445
Playboy 47, 58, 453
Players Ring 104
Players Ring Theater 104
Pleshette, Suzanne 239
Poitier, Sidney 392
Police Academy 48
Pollack, Sydney 5
Polo Lounge 164, 360
Polygram 149, 443
Pope of Greenwich Village 212
Poverty 36, 39, 79, 441, 485

Powell, Eleanor 113, 126
Powell, Nik 450
Power, Tyrone 11
Pretty Maids All In A Row 391
Prewitt, Jean 497
Price, Vincent 246, 247, 248, 249, 250
Princess Bride, The 92, 120, 121, 392
Princess Restaurant, The 120, 121
Prizzi's Honor 323
Prochnow, Juergen 71
Producers Sales Organization, PSO as as Trailblazer 47, 266, 436, 441
Producers Sales Organization, PSO as Camelot 47, 266, 359, 436, 441
Producers Sales Organization, PSO as different than US 47, 49, 140, 266, 342, 374, 436, 441, 489, 493, 494
Producers Sales Organization, PSO as Independent Major 47, 266, 316, 436, 441
Producers Sales Organization, PSO as Tiffany of AFM xv, 47, 266, 369, 436, 441, 459, 462, 464, 468
Prokofiev 33
Promotion 149, 230, 407
PR Publicity 92, 104, 122, 164, 242, 278, 308, 309, 310, 358
PSOers xiii, 112, 113, 114, 115, 116, 121, 131, 133, 134, 135, 261, 332, 370, 372, 424, 435, 436, 442, 482, 501, 502
PSOnly company newsletter xii, xiii, xv, xviii, 2, 3, 4, 5, 17, 21, 44, 46, 47, 48, 49, 50, 52, 53, 54, 56, 57, 58, 60, 61, 62, 65, 68, 69, 71, 72, 77, 88, 91, 92, 93, 97, 108, 110, 111, 112, 115, 116, 118, 119, 120, 122, 123, 126, 128, 130, 132, 133, 134, 135, 138, 139, 142, 143, 146, 149, 150, 151, 152, 153, 154, 155, 167, 170, 171, 175, 176, 211, 212, 218, 256, 258, 260, 262, 264, 265, 266, 297, 312, 316, 317, 318, 319, 322, 323, 329, 332, 333, 334, 364, 369, 370, 371, 374, 418, 420, 421, 422, 423, 424, 425, 429, 430, 431, 432, 435, 436, 437, 441, 442, 443, 444, 461, 462, 484, 493, 494, 499, 501, 502
Psycho 380
Puffy 454
Puzo, Mario 128
Puzzles 31, 41, 42, 50, 76, 77, 228, 481
Puzzle contest 42, 43, 77

Q

Quan Yin 464
Quest, The 119
Quest of Fire 421
Quiz Kids 12
Quo Vadis 272

R

Radin, Roy 175
Raft, George 11, 13
Raging Bull 263
RAI television 495
Rambling Reporter Column 104
Rambo 128, 445
Ram Titi 479
Ransohoff, Martin 56
Rassam, Paul 132
Rawhide 360
Ray, Nick 164
Reagan, President Ronald 145
Rebel Without a Cause 164, 165
Rebentrost, Kilian and Dagmar 132
Rebus puzzle 31, 42
Reddy, Don 407
Redgrave, Vanessa 359
Red Square 140, 142
Reed, Pamela 261
Reluctant Saint, The 306, 307, 506

Rennie, Michael 380
Renoir, Jean 271
Reporting 318
Requiescant 311, 378, 381, 382, 505
Requiescant (Kill and Pray) 381
Reubens, Paul 425
Rex Theater 15
Rhue, Madlyn 201, 239
Ricci, Christina 471
Ride in the Whirlwind 361
Rilke, Rainer Maria 239
Rise xiii, 48, 57, 111, 153, 227, 384, 432, 464, 502
Robards, Jason 181
Robertson, Cliff 153, 186
Robin Hood (The Scalawag Bunch) 382
Robsahm, Margarete 343
Rocca, Daniela 279
Rocco and His Brothers 271
Roeper, Richard 474
Rogers, Kenny 322
Rohrbach, Gunther 4
ROME 91, 255, 265, 269, 270, 271, 272, 273, 275, 276, 278, 279, 292, 303, 307, 308, 309, 310, 322, 337, 341, 347, 349, 353, 355, 360, 361, 363, 379, 380, 382, 383, 385, 386, 387, 390, 393, 394, 396, 397, 400, 401, 403, 407, 408, 409, 412, 415, 416, 417, 448, 453, 454, 495
Romero, Eddie 392
Rome Daily American, The 380
Roosevelt High School 16
Rossellini, Franco 274, 351
Rossellini, Roberto 271
Rossia Hotel 140
Rostov, Nikolai 102
Roth, Tim 462
Rourke, Mickey 211, 212, 215, 319, 421, 422, 451, 452, 454
Royal Academy of Dramatic Arts (RADA) 105
Ruddy, Al 53
Rumble Fish 153, 212

Rush, Barbara 85
Ruth, Datty 495
Ryan, Michael 497
Ryan, Robert 379

S

Sachs, Margaret 401
Sachs, William 401
SAG 106, 216, 425
Sagansky, Jeff 373
Salke, Alan 121
Samuelsson, Per 497
Santoni, Reni 379, 380
Sanz-Agero, Jenna 494
Sarlui, Edward 443, 444, 493
Saturday Night Fever 320
Saunders, David 93, 423, 441, 443, 444, 449, 450, 461, 462, 493
Saxon, John 342
Sayles, John 260
Scandia 164, 230
Scarface 11, 259
Schatzberg, Jerry 133, 134
Schell, Maximilian 307
Schildkraut, Joseph 165
Schildkraut, Pepi 184
Schildkraut, Rudolph 165
Schippers, Thomas 276
Schneider, Romy 275
School Girl Killers 380
Schultz, Max 237
Schwab's 230
Schwartz, Al 14, 15, 16
Schwartzman, Jack 133
Scorsese, Martin 130, 345
Scott, Pippa 104, 105, 106
Screaming Eagles 161, 231, 508
Screen Actors Guild 106, 474
Screen Gems 163, 225
Screen Life 164
Sellers, Peter 407, 408
Selznick, David O. 105
Semel, Terry 121, 260, 323
Senator International 56

Senior, Enrique 316
Sessa, Alex 496
Sessa, Sergio 496
Shampoo 328, 329
Sharpe, Karen 85
Shatner, William 344
Shaw, George Bernard 181
Sheedy, Ally 321, 373
Sheen, Martin 61
Sheena, Queen of the Jungle 174
Sherwood Productions 153
Shining, The 407
Shirasu, Harumasa 61, 62, 132, 134, 448, 449
Shochiku 61, 62
Shooting, The 361
Shoot Fighter 445
Shoot Fighter 2 445
Shortest Day, The 309
Short Circuit xii, 265, 318, 320, 372, 373, 374, 423, 425, 429, 431, 432, 435, 510
Short Circuit 2 xii, 265, 318, 320, 372, 373, 374, 423, 425, 429, 431, 432, 435, 510
Short Circuit 3 xii, 265, 318, 320, 372, 373, 374, 423, 425, 429, 431, 432, 435, 510
Siddha Yoga Meditation Center 499
Signoret, Simone 309
Silent Flute 48
Silkwood 110
Silver Bear 474
Simpson, George P. 78
Sinatra, Frank 238
Sirk, Douglas 227
Sixteen-point test for the name 107
Sixth Sense, The 92, 501
Slattery, Diane 111, 114, 502
Slattery, Mary Jo 211
Slutsky, Elliot 493
Smith, Sally 380
Smokehouse Restaurant 160
SND 490
Solomon, Courtney 495

Sontag, Susan 276
Son of Cleopatra, The 348
Son of El Cid, The (The Hundred Horseman) 311, 345
Spacey, Kevin 468, 489
Spaghetti Westerns 3, 5, 272, 311, 351, 359, 361, 363, 381, 382, 383, 384, 468
Spain xii, xv, 5, 132, 150, 311, 345, 346, 351, 409, 410, 496, 497, 503, 504, 505, 506
Spartacus 385, 392
Spartichetta 392
Speaking to Hannah 106
Spiegler, Mike 371, 422
Spielberg, Steven 5
Spyglass Entertainment 92, 501
SquareOne 496
St. Johns, Richard 47, 53, 61, 69
Stallone, Sylvester 128
Stan's Drive-In 225
Stanislavsky 163
Stanislavsky, Constantin 163
Stanley, Kim 186
Stanwyck, Barbara 253
Stapleton, Maureen 186
Steiger, Rod 163
Stevens, Connie 197, 223, 225, 229, 230, 239
Stoddard, Brandon 123, 323
Stone, Oliver 322, 327, 329, 330
Strasberg, Lee 163, 185
Strasberg, Paula 186
Strasberg, Susan 181, 186, 227, 309
Strassman, Marcia 48
Stravinsky 33
Streisand, Barbara 362
Stroyberg, Annette 272, 278
Stuparich De La Barra, Tamara 459, 494
Sundance Film Festival 474
Sun Looks Down, The 13, 31, 32, 321, 395, 396, 464
Swayze, Patrick 121
Swift, Jonathan 227

T

Tanen, Ned 48, 149, 150
Tarses, Jay 320
Taylor, Elizabeth 253, 467, 469
Taylor, Joyce 136, 254
Taylor, Liz 253, 467, 469
Teenflicks 3, 225, 468
Teen idol 468
Terminator 445
Terminator 3 445
Terminator 3 445
Tessari, Duccio 352
There Is No 13 399, 402
Theron, Charlize 468, 471, 472, 474, 475
The Member of the Wedding 106
The Shooting 361
This Rebel Breed 200, 203, 242, 243, 252, 253, 507
Thompson, J. Walter 145
Thriller 322, 344, 373, 380, 460
Thunderball 132, 133, 278
Toho Towa 61, 62, 134, 448, 449
Toho Towa bested PSO 61, 62, 134, 448, 449
Tokyo Pop 463
Tolstoy 227, 344
Tomas Milian 277
Tomioka, Tomi 449
Tony G 471
Tootsie 5
Toronto xii, xv, 462
Tor Margana 270, 307
Towers, Cliff 106
Towne, Robert 231, 237, 327, 329, 330, 341
To an Actor 165
To Hell and Back 54, 55, 62, 65, 85, 87, 91, 128, 143, 155, 158, 162, 172, 212, 228, 237, 327, 401, 409, 449, 463, 507
Trans World Entertainment 443
Tri-Star 211, 212, 316, 423

Tripics 496
Triumph 5, 21, 65, 93, 141, 266, 271, 461
Triumph Releasing 5, 97, 461, 493, 494
Tryon, Tom 161
Tulley, Lindsay 422
Turman, Larry 320
TV Star Parade 13, 56, 57, 105, 106, 121, 123, 142, 145, 154, 160, 161, 172, 183, 212, 231, 237, 278, 380, 459, 468, 503, 504, 506, 507, 508, 510
TV World 13, 56, 57, 105, 106, 121, 123, 142, 145, 154, 160, 161, 172, 183, 212, 231, 237, 278, 380, 459, 468, 503, 504, 506, 507, 508, 510

U

U.S.S. Nimitz 65
UCLA 43, 50, 78, 83, 84, 85, 86, 87, 105, 161, 342, 485, 499
UCLA Daily Bruin 87
UCSF Dental School 255
Ulmer, Edgar 58, 501
United Artists 65, 92, 133, 409
United States of Leland, The 509
Universal Studios 320
Upside of Anger, The 478, 482, 502, 509
Utah xii, xv

V

Vadim, Roger 278, 391, 393
Vajna, Andy 461
Valenti, Jack 122, 138
Variety 104, 153, 226, 230, 260, 316, 333, 344, 409, 421, 441, 444, 480
Varsi, Diane 231, 239, 241, 242
Vaughn Williams, Ralph 33
Verdict, The 5
Verdon, Gwen 182

Versini, Marie 343
Vestron Inc. 436
Via Veneto 272, 405
Vidal, Gore 274, 275
Vidor, King 105, 106
Viking Films 423
Village Road Show 55
Village Voice, The 55, 181, 212
Villard, Dimitri 374
Vincenti, Joseph 132
Visalia xiii, 265, 501
Visconti, Luchino 255, 271, 273
Vision International 493
Vision pdg (Peters-Damon-Guber) 443
Vitti, Monica 141
Von Sydow, Max 133

W

Wagner, Robert 158, 162
Wahl, Ken 58
Waites, Thomas G. 261
Wald, Jerry 240
Wallach, Eli 163, 181
Wall Street Journal, The 128, 153, 266, 317
Walsh, Joseph 380
Wambaugh, Joseph 411, 417
Wanderers, The 58
Ward, Julie 385, 386
Warner Brothers 48, 54, 148, 155, 260, 318, 366, 405, 417, 423, 429, 444
War and Peace 102, 105, 106, 227
War Games 3, 11, 32, 63, 102, 105, 106, 153, 227, 271, 309, 358, 381
War of the Kisses, The (La Guerra Dei Baci Di Mark e Gigiola) 358
Wasp Woman, The 227
Wasserman, Lew 484
Waters, Ethel 106
Waynberg, Sammy 64, 132
Wayne, John 309

Weigel, Herman 119
Weitz, John 228
Welch, Raquel 421
Weld, Tuesday 185, 232, 234, 235, 237
West Avenue 36, 39
West Video 487
Wexler, Haskell 331
We of the Never Never 123, 132, 133, 152, 153
Whitehead, Martin 78
White House 122
William Morris Agency 104
William Morris Independent 132, 480
Wilson, S.S. 320
Winters, Shelley 163, 186
Wohlrabe, Juergen 63, 64, 65
Wolf, Jonathan 497
Wood, Natalie 159, 164, 165, 186
Woods, James 416
Woodward, Joanne 163
Woolley, Steve 450
Wray, Fay 161
Wright, Theresa 185
Wrigley Field 15
Wuornos, Aileen 470, 474
Wurdalak, The 344, 345, 506
Wurlitzer, Rudy 331
Wyman, Brad 469, 470

Y

Yojimbo 360
Young, Loretta 253
Young and Dangerous 196, 222, 225, 226, 507
Young Racers, The 341

Z

Zaentz, Saul 409
Zanuck, Darryl 85, 162
Zanuck, Richard 162, 225
Zanuck, Suzy 85
ZBT boys 79, 80
ZBT Fraternity 79

Zeffirelli, Franco 5, 274
Ziffren, Ken 135, 425
Zimmerman, Pattie 110, 126
Zorro 15, 507
Zoub's Drugstore 14

Printed in the United Kingdom
by Lightning Source UK Ltd.
129446UK00003B/28-348/P